About Your Family Tree Maker Software and

Trademarks

TABLE OF CONTENTS

INTRODUCTION

They start younger and younger these days, but the two-year-old
Steve Madwin pictured here went on to become an invaluable member
of the Family Tree Maker Quality Assurance team.

INTRODUCTION

Congratulations on selecting Family Tree Maker to preserve and protect your family's heritage. Use it to store any kind of family information, from names and birth dates to priceless family stories, pictures, and videos.

Family Tree Maker is quick and easy to use, but also robust enough for the most serious genealogist. You enter basic family information into a Family Page, just as if you were filling out a form. Optional screens let you enter more extensive information and store pictures, sounds, and OLE (Object Linking and Embedding) objects like video and audio clips. From the information you enter, Family Tree Maker can automatically create trees, calendars, timelines, maps, and much more. You enter information only once — Family Tree Maker does the rest of the work for you.

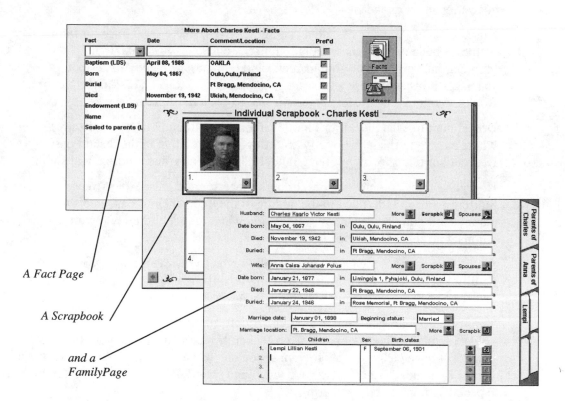

A Fact Page

A Scrapbook

and a FamilyPage

Figure I-1. A few of the places where you can enter information

DISPLAYING YOUR INFORMATION

You may wonder how Family Tree Maker can create several different documents from information that you only have to enter once. Family Tree Maker creates all of these different items by using **views**. Views are different ways of looking at the information that you enter.

For example, if you want to print an Ancestor tree, Family Tree Maker shows you an Ancestor Tree view of your information. Or, if you want a calendar filled with family birthdays and anniversaries, Family Tree Maker shows you a Calendar view of your information.

PRINT SEVERAL KINDS OF TREES

When you are ready to print family trees, Family Tree Maker will create them for you. You can choose from many styles of Ancestor and Descendant trees, as well as Hourglass and All-in-One trees (see Figure I-2) that display both ancestors and descendants.

Ancestor trees (sometimes called "pedigree" trees) make great gifts for family members because they show an individual's roots. Two parents, four grandparents, eight great-grandparents, and more are printed with perfect spacing. You can choose a Fit to Page Ancestor tree to get a one-page tree, or a Book Layout tree or Custom Ancestor tree to get a multiple-page tree.

Descendant trees are ideal for family gatherings and reunions because they show where everyone fits in the family. Starting with a relative in the distant past, a Descendant tree shows children, grandchildren, great-grandchildren, and so on.

Hourglass trees combine the best of both Ancestor and Descendant trees. Starting from an individual in the middle of the tree, an Hourglass tree shows parents and grandparents above and children and grandchildren below in a compact arrangement of boxes.

All-in-One trees, as the name implies, allow you to see everyone in your entire Family File without building it from a single, or primary, individual. This has been one of the most requested Family Tree Maker features.

Your printed trees can contain any type of information that Family Tree Maker holds, including photos. Family Tree Maker prints them right in your tree. If you don't have electronic photographs, you can leave space in the boxes to attach photos by hand. You can also have video and sound in your trees. This can be especially fun at family gatherings!

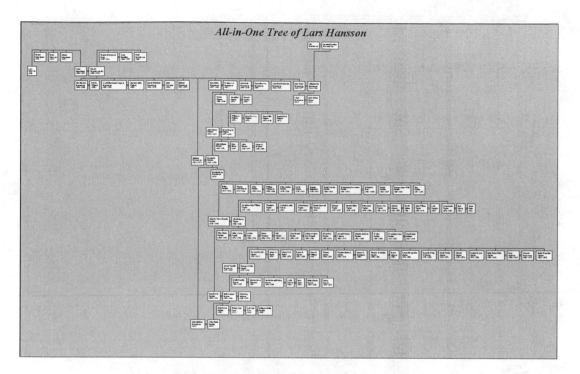

Figure I-2. The All-in-One tree view

ENTER ANY TYPE OF INFORMATION

Beyond the basic names and dates, you can extend your family research to include military service, occupations, and even characteristics like height, weight, and personality. You can track an individual's medical history or write several pages of stories, habits, jokes, and favorite recipes — the extra information that really makes an individual come to life.

In addition, Family Tree Maker's **Scrapbook** feature lets you add multimedia elements to your collection of family information. Scrapbooks can store almost any type of information, including Kodak Photo CD pictures; sound, video, text files; and other picture formats, such as bitmaps, TIFF files, JPEGs and more. Each individual and each marriage has a Scrapbook, so you can use your creativity to put together a wonderfully complete collection of family information to pass from generation to generation.

Figure I-3. The FamilyFinder Center

RESEARCH YOUR FAMILY HISTORY AT HOME

Family Tree Maker's specialty has always been organizing family information
and creating family trees. Now, with Family Tree Maker's **FamilyFinder
Center**, you have a convenient starting point for researching and expanding your
family history. Combining powerful search tools, concise, accurate reports, and
links to genealogy-related Internet Web sites, the FamilyFinder Center brings the
world of genealogy research to the comfort of your home. You can expand your
research even more with the Web-based **FamilyFinder Search** and powerful
Internet search tools from **Family Tree Maker Online**. The resulting
FamilyFinder Report, in combination with the **Research Journal** and its built-
in "**To Do**" list, provide an easy-to-use, yet serious system for tracking your
family history.

FamilyFinder Report

This shows CDs and genealogy-related Internet sites that may have information on people in your file.
Stars indicate confidence in each match: ★★★★★ Highest   ★ Lowest
Click on folders to open or close: 📁 New Matches   📁 Previous Matches
Last updated January 29, 1999. Source: CD. To update the report, Click here

---

5-STAR MATCHES
5-star ranking indicates source that is virtually certain (95% chance or better) to hold information about your family members.

DONE	QUALITY	MATCH	SOURCE	
☐	★★★★★	📁 Perkins, Alice Paula and 6 others	CD 708: World Family Tree: Vol. 8	Tree 1726

WORLD FAMILY TREE MATCHES
Each World Family Tree entry is an entire family file contributed by a family researcher like yourself. Most include 100 or more individuals.
(Click here for information on contributing to the World Family Tree.)

📁 Top 10 World Family Tree Matches

DONE	QUALITY	MATCH	SOURCE	
☐	★★★	📁 Perkins, Alice Paula and 2 others	CD 701: World Family Tree: Vol. 1	Tree 4145
☐	★★★	📁 Hansdotter, Anna	CD 709: World Family Tree: Vol. 9	Tree 2453
☐	★★★	📁 Perkins, Charles De La Grande	CD 706: World Family Tree: Vol. 6	Tree 3282
☐	★★★	📁 Perkins, Charles De La Grande	CD 723: World Family Tree: Vol. 23	Tree 2102
☐	★★	📁 Mason, Josiah Terville, Jr.	CD 722: World Family Tree: Vol. 22	Tree 1438
☐	★★	📁 Mason, Josiah Terville, Jr.	CD 727: World Family Tree: Vol. 27	Tree 1957
☐	★★	📁 Perkins, Alice Paula	CD 701: World Family Tree: Vol. 1	Tree 2886
☐	★★	📁 Perkins, Alice Paula	CD 702: World Family Tree: Vol. 2	Tree 877
☐	★★	📁 Perkins, Alice Paula	CD 702: World Family Tree: Vol. 2	Tree 2670
☐	★★	📁 Perkins, Alice Paula	CD 702: World Family Tree: Vol. 2	Tree 4422

📁 More World Family Tree Matches (73 total)

OTHER FAMILY ARCHIVE CD MATCHES
Family Archive CDs are huge repositories of genealogical source information. Click on any category for details.

Census Records	|	Family Histories	|	Land Records	|	Marriage Records
Military Records	|	Passenger Lists	|	Pedigrees	|	Vital Records

📁 Top 10 Family Archive CD Matches

DONE	QUALITY	MATCH	SOURCE
☐	★★★	📁 Mason, Josiah Terville, Jr.	CD 5: Marriage Index: AR, MO, MS, TX
☐	★★★	📁 Mason, Josiah Terville, Jr.	CD 191: Family History: Southern Genealogies #1
☐	★★★	📁 Perkins, Alice Paula	CD 403: Selected U.S./International Marriage Records
☐	★★★	📁 Perkins, Alice Paula	CD 18: Family Queries: Everton's "Roots" Cellar
☐	★★★	📁 Perkins, Alice Paula	CD 210: National Genealogical Society Quarterly, Vols. 1-8
☐	★★★	📁 Hansdotter, Anna	CD 354: Passenger and Immigration Lists Index

Figure I-4. The FamilyFinder Report

The **FamilyFinder Report** shows your search results. Some matches are on Family Archive CDs, and some are on the Internet. Family Archives are a growing collection of CDs containing information from a variety of records, such as census and marriage records, Social Security death benefits records, and linked pedigrees. You can print the information you want from the Family Archives, or copy it directly into your Family File.

Family Tree Maker also contains the **Genealogy "How-To" Guide**. This step-by-step guide tells you what questions to ask, where to go, and how to find important facts about your ancestors, using sources both in the United States and abroad. With this interactive guide, you can go straight to the information regarding your heritage, and bypass information that isn't useful to you.

FAMILY TREE MAKER ONLINE

Family Tree Maker Online is a Web site on the Internet where you can find valuable genealogical resources to speed your research. Visit us soon for expert answers to your Family Tree Maker and genealogy questions. Share tips, tricks, and success stories with other users, while your research experiences and successes help us develop future versions of Family Tree Maker. It's a great way to stay informed about Family Tree Maker as well as other interesting and useful products. In addition, as a Family Tree Maker user, you are exclusively entitled to post free classified ads, access the Family Tree Maker Online message boards, create a home page with information from your Family File, and more. These exclusive online features are free through December 31, 2000.

You can access the Family Tree Maker Online Web site by clicking a button in your Family Tree Maker software. You will need a modem and one of the following:

- An America Online® account and software (version 3.0 or later)

- Microsoft® Internet Explorer software (version 3.0 or later) and Internet access

- Netscape Navigator™ software (version 3.0 or later) and Internet access

Note: Beta versions, or browsers bundled with other software are not always compatible with Family Tree Maker.

If you have a different Web browser and Internet access, you can still go to the Family Tree Maker Online Web site and take advantage of the public features offered there.

Our Internet address is: **www.familytreemaker.com**

Visit the Family Tree Maker Online Web site often! We are constantly adding new features and services to make your family research easier and more enjoyable. You'll want to come back again and again to take advantage of all that Family Tree Maker Online has to offer.

SYSTEM REQUIREMENTS

Family Tree Maker requires an IBM PC or compatible that meets the requirements listed below. Please realize that these are the *minimum* requirements. As with all programs, a faster processor, more RAM, and more free disk space will enhance performance.

Also keep in mind that the more family information you enter, the more free hard disk space and available RAM you will need. If you plan to include many pictures, sounds, or videos in your Family Tree Maker Scrapbooks, you will need a substantial amount of hard disk space.

If your system does not meet these minimum requirements, *we cannot guarantee that the program will function correctly.* You will need to upgrade your system to meet these requirements if you wish to use Family Tree Maker.

Component	Minimum Requirement
CPU	P90 or faster (P120 recommended)
Operating System	Microsoft® Windows® 95 or higher
RAM	16MB RAM (32MB recommended)
	Note: As with all Windows programs, more RAM and a faster CPU will improve performance
Free Disk Space	50MB (after installation)
CD-ROM Drive	This drive must be part of your system — as opposed to a drive that you access via a network
Monitor	640x480 display, 256 colors (or higher)
Printer	Most popular Windows printers are supported
Mouse	Microsoft compatible

Figure I-5. System Requirements

Optional Devices

You can take advantage of Family Tree Maker's optional features with the following optional devices:

- Modem (to connect to Family Tree Maker Online)
- Scanner (to digitize graphic images)
- Kodak Photo CD-compatible CD-ROM drive (to use Kodak Photo CDs)
- Video capture card (to use video clips)
- Sound card (to use audio clips)

CUSTOMER REGISTRATION

We offer registered users the following special benefits: free technical services over the telephone with Family Tree Maker, special discounts on future versions of Family Tree Maker, and information about Family Tree Maker accessory programs and services. Please fill out and return the registration card so that you can start taking advantage of these extras.

Note: When you use Family Tree Maker Online, you will need to provide additional registration information.

ORDERING PRODUCTS

When you would like more information about a product you are interested in purchasing or when you want to place an order, contact The Learning Company Customer Service, Parsons Division. You can speak directly to a customer service representative Monday through Friday, 6:00 AM to 5:00 PM, Pacific Standard Time. You can also write to the address below or send a fax (please include your address and phone number so that we can contact you).

The Learning Co.
1700 Progress Drive
P.O. Box 100
Hiawatha, IA 52233-0100

Customer Service:
(Phone/Fax)
319-395-0115 Phone
319-395-7449 Fax

Note: If you need **technical assistance** with Family Tree Maker see Appendix B, "Troubleshooting," at the end of this User Guide.

If you prefer to use one of our international numbers, you can speak directly to an international customer service representative Monday through Friday from 8:00 AM to 5:00 PM Greenwich Mean Time.

Country	Phone	Fax
UK	+44-870-741-6821	+44-870-741-6822
France		+44-142-952-1005
Germany		+44-142-952-1005

FAMILY TREE MAKER PRODUCT UPGRADE PLAN

We periodically make new versions of our software available to registered users at substantial discounts. Be sure to return your registration card so that we can notify you as soon as upgrades become available.

Note: We value *all* of our customers, however, the high cost of postage prevents us from mailing update information to our international customers. We encourage you to contact our American or European Customer Support department periodically to find out about the latest version of Family Tree Maker.

We strive daily to make Family Tree Maker the best product possible. Please drop in often and visit us at our Web site: **www.familytreemaker.com**

Chapter 1

PROGRAM SETUP

Laura Howard made more than this masterpiece on her first day of
kindergarten at Fay Lane Grammar School in Garden Grove, California.
That day, Laura, Assistant Product Manager for Family Tree Maker, made
friends with a girl who is still one of her best pals.

PROGRAM SETUP

This chapter tells you how to install Family Tree Maker on your computer, how to start your first new **Family File** with the Startup Wizard, and gives you a quick introduction to the on-screen Help system.

Whenever you have to type something into your computer, the letters are shown in **bold like this**. If you have any difficulties when installing Family Tree Maker, please see Appendix B, "Troubleshooting," for answers to the most common questions.

INSTALLING FAMILY TREE MAKER

To use Family Tree Maker, it must be installed on your hard disk. You cannot run it directly from the original CD-ROMs. If you already have a version of Family Tree Maker installed on your hard drive, just install the new version over the old version. Don't worry, this will not harm your Family Files.

Family Tree Maker utilizes an automated installation system — built into the CD-ROM —making setup fast and easy, whether you are a first time user, or upgrading a previous version.

Using the Automated Setup Installer

To install Family Tree Maker using the new automated Setup Installer, simply insert the Family Tree Maker Installation Program CD into your CD-ROM drive and follow the directions.

1. **Welcome** — The Setup Installer begins running automatically, displaying a series of screens welcoming you to the program and asking you to read and approve the license agreement.

2. **Choosing a Destination Directory** — The normal destination directory for Family Tree Maker is a folder called "FTW" located on your hard drive. In most instances, this will be your "C" drive. If you already have Family Tree Maker installed in another location, the Setup Installer will detect it and use the same location to install the new version. Don't worry, this will not harm your Family Files.

3. **Select Optional Components** — During installation, you will see a dialog box titled "Select Optional Components." These items are not required to run Family Tree Maker and are made available as options in case you want to minimize the size of the installation. If you wish to use any of these

components at a later time, you will be able to access or install them directly from the installation CD.

> **Note:** You do not need to install any of the remaining CD-ROMs in this package.

4. **Select Program Group or Folder** — The default group or folder is "Family Tree Maker," but you may create/choose another folder if you wish.

5. **Install Files** — You will see messages and progress meters as the appropriate files are installed on your hard drive.

6. **Select Browser** — The Setup Installer will detect any previously installed copies of Netscape, Internet Explorer, or America Online and display them in a drop-down list, allowing you to select the browser of your choice.

> **Note:** If your browser was not listed, you can still set it up manually. You'll find step-by-step setup instructions for all compatible Web browsers on Family Tree Maker's Technical Support Web site at: **http://www.familytreemaker.com/support.html**

7. **Customer Registration** — We offer registered users the following special benefits: free technical services over the telephone with Family Tree Maker, special discounts on future versions of Family Tree Maker, and information about Family Tree Maker accessory programs and services. Please fill out and return the registration card now, or register online.

   When you use Family Tree Maker Online — you will need to provide additional registration information in order to obtain your unique user number. **Important**: this unique number ensures that you are the only one who can create and modify your home page and post messages to the message board in your name.

> **Note:** If you purchased your upgrade directly from The Learning Company, you were already registered at the time of purchase.

8. **Setup Complete** — After completing the installation process, click **Finish**.

   Family Tree Maker will automatically start "World of Genealogy," a brief movie that provides an overview and introduction to the program.

> **Note:** From the **Help** menu, select **View Tutorial** if you would like to replay the "World of Genealogy" movie at a later date.

Special Note about the Read Me File

The Read Me file now appears in Online Help rather than as part of the installation process. To read the file, from the **Help** menu, select **Read Me**.

Please be sure to read this information before beginning to use Family Tree Maker. It will contain news regarding additions or changes to the program that were made after this manual was printed.

Manual Installation of Family Tree Maker

If, for some reason, Family Tree Maker does not launch automatically with the automatic Setup Installer, please follow the instructions below.

Note: Family Tree Maker automatically suggests the best choices, so if you come to a screen that you are unsure about, choose **OK**.

1.   Click the Windows® **Start** button and then select **Run**.

Windows displays the Run dialog box.

2.   In the **Open** field, type `D:SETUP`

Note: The "D" in "D:SETUP" stands for drive D. If you are installing from a CD-ROM drive other than drive D, type that letter instead. For example, to install from drive E, type `E:SETUP`

3.   Click **OK** and follow the instructions on the screen to complete the installation.

During the installation, you will see a dialog box titled "Select Optional Components." These items are *not required* to run Family Tree Maker and are made available as options, in case you wish to minimize the size of the installation.

Note: You don't need to install any of the remaining CD-ROMs. If you wish to use any of these components at a later time, you will be able to access/install them directly from the installation CD.

For more information about the Internet and Family Tree Maker Online, see "Using Family Tree Maker Online" in Chapter 7.

Special Note about Web Browsers and Internet Service Providers

Family Tree Maker is fully integrated with Family Tree Maker Online — the premiere genealogy Web site on the Internet. Before going to Family Tree Maker Online from within Family Tree Maker, you must first set up the Web browser that you want Family Tree Maker to use. If no browser is present, or the wrong browser starts when you attempt to go online, you can use the following steps to set up the browser of your choice (Netscape, Internet Explorer, or America Online).

To set up your Web browser for use with Family Tree Maker:

1. From the **Internet** menu, select **Browser Setup**.

2. Click **Continue** to search your computer for compatible Web browsers.

   Family Tree Maker displays a list of available Web browsers.

3. If your browser is not highlighted in the window, click the button next to the name shown to display a list of available browsers.

4. Highlight your browser, and then click **Continue**.

   Family Tree Maker will display a confirmation message saying that your browser has been successfully installed.

5. Click **OK** to return to Family Tree Maker.

Note: If this is your first time using Family Tree Maker, you will see a welcome screen requesting that you establish an online account. If you have already used, and been online with Family Tree Maker, click **Existing Online Account.**

Internet Service Provider (ISP) — ISPs are local, regional, or national services that provide access to the Internet. There are thousands of ISPs around the world. Subscribers usually pay either a monthly or hourly usage fee. In addition to an account with an ISP, you need a browser software program such as one of those listed above. These programs are available from most software retailers and are generally available for download from the Web at no cost to you.

STARTING FAMILY TREE MAKER

After you finish installing Family Tree Maker, the fun begins! Just start Family Tree Maker, and create a new file with the Startup Wizard or, if you are upgrading from a previous version of Family Tree Maker, open an existing file. You'll be ready to start entering your family information in no time.

Note: You do not need any of the Family Tree Maker CDs in the CD-ROM drive to start the program. The only time you need to insert these CDs is when you want to use the FamilyFinder Index (see Chapter 7).

To start Family Tree Maker after you have installed it on your hard disk:

1. Click the Windows **Start** button.

2. From the **Start** menu, select **Programs**, then **Family Tree Maker**, and then from the submenu, select **Family Tree Maker**.

    Family Tree Maker displays the title screen and then either:

    - Opens your Family File from a previous version of Family Tree Maker for Windows and you can begin working immediately, or...

    - Displays the Open Family File dialog box shown in Figure 1-1. Continue with Figure 1-2, "Creating Your First Family File."

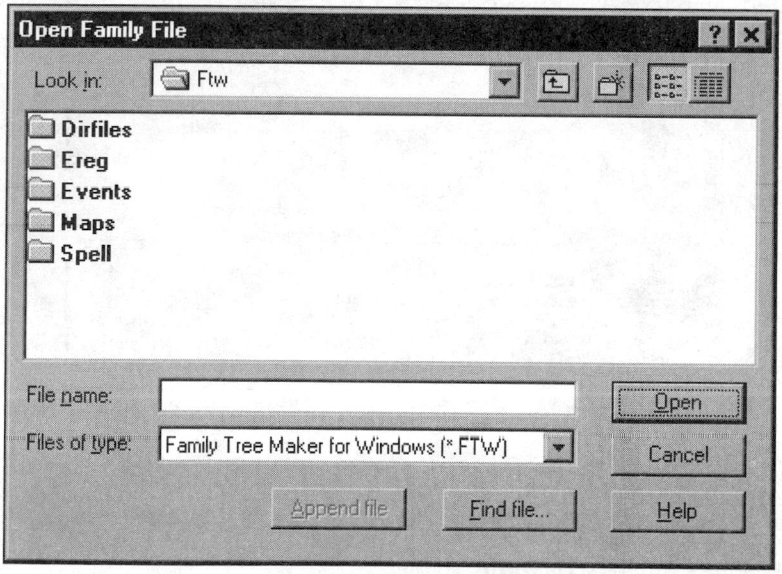

Figure 1-1. The Open Family File dialog box

CREATING YOUR FIRST FAMILY FILE

After you start Family Tree Maker, you're ready to create your Family File. If you've never used Family Tree Maker before, follow the steps below for the **FamilyFinder Startup Wizard** (see Figure 1-3).

Note   If you want to open a PAF file, a file from another genealogy software program that supports GEDCOM, or a file from a previous version of Family Tree Maker that did not open when you started Family Tree Maker, see "Opening Existing Files" in Chapter 13.

The FamilyFinder Startup Wizard

To start a Family File and begin working with Family Tree Maker, follow the instructions below:

1. From the **Open Family File** dialog box (Figure 1-1), click **New**.

   Family Tree Maker displays the New Family File dialog box.

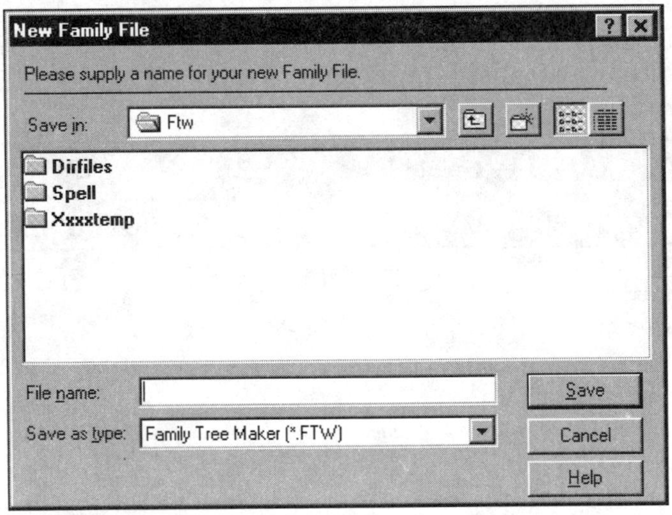

Figure 1-2. The New Family File dialog box

2. Type a name in the **File name** field.

   Your file name can be as long as you want. Family Tree Maker will automatically add the "FTW" extension to the name you type.

3. After you enter a name for your new Family File, click **Save**.

Family Tree Maker displays the opening page of the Startup Wizard.

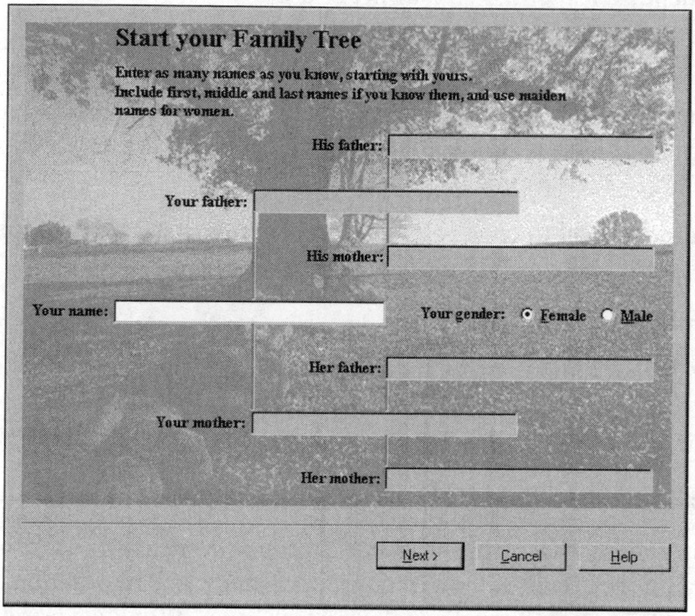

Figure 1-3. The Startup Wizard opening dialog box

4. Follow the on-screen instructions (remember to use maiden names for females) and when completed, click **Next**.

Family Tree Maker closes the entry screen and displays the **Births** dialog box.

5. Again, follow the on-screen instructions to fill out the Birth and Location information for the individuals you entered above, then click **Next**.

Family Tree Maker closes the Births dialog box and displays the **Deaths** dialog box.

6. Follow the instructions and complete the dialog box, then click **Next**.

Family Tree Maker closes the Deaths dialog box and displays the **FamlyFinder Search** dialog box.

7. The FamilyFinder Search is a great way to quickly provide you with a list of potential matches to the names you've entered so far in your Family File. To use the FamilyFinder Search to create a FamilyFinder Report, which we recommend, select either an **Online**, or a **CD**-based-search.

   Family Tree Maker automatically opens your Browser and conducts a search based on the names you've provided. The result is a FamilyFinder Report that you can use to begin researching and verifying the potential matches shown for the individuals in your Family File (see Chapter 7, "Researching Your Family From Home").

8. If you do not want to create a FamilyFinder Report at this time, select the **Click here if you don't want to search** check box.

9. Click **Finish**.

   Family Tree Maker displays a reminder message, then takes you to your Family Page.

WHERE TO GO FROM HERE

After you install and start Family Tree Maker, you're ready to begin entering your family information. If the Windows environment is new to you, look through your Windows manual and the next section, "Windows Basics and Family Tree Maker," before you continue. Then, proceed with the rest of this chapter, followed by Chapter 2, "Tutorial."

If you're already familiar with using Microsoft Windows, skip to "Getting Help," in this chapter, for information about using Help and customizing Family Tree Maker. Then, go through Chapter 2, "Tutorial," to learn how to use the main features of the program.

WINDOWS BASICS AND FAMILY TREE MAKER

To use Family Tree Maker, you should be familiar with basic Windows concepts such as using a mouse to click, double-click, drag, and navigate between menus.

A mouse generally has two buttons, a **primary button** and a **secondary button**. Usually, the primary button is the left mouse button and the secondary button is the right mouse button. Some left-handed individuals switch these positions.

The primary and secondary mouse buttons serve different functions in Family Tree Maker. The primary button is the button you use to select items and menu commands, and the secondary button opens the **secondary mouse button menu**. The secondary mouse button menu is a floating menu that Family Tree Maker displays when you click an item with the secondary mouse button. To select a command on the secondary mouse button menu, place the mouse pointer on the command and click with the primary mouse button. When you click outside of the secondary mouse button menu, the menu disappears.

The secondary mouse button menu is available everywhere except in the FamilyFinder Center view. The secondary menu contains the most commonly-used commands for the current view, although the menu commands vary according to what you click within a particular view. You can also access all of the commands on the secondary mouse button menus using the menu bar (see Figure I-4, "Basic Windows elements").

For a list of frequently asked questions (FAQs) about Family Tree Maker and Windows see Appendix B, "Troubleshooting."

The rest of this section points out some of the important features on several Family Tree Maker screens.

Title bar:
Look here to see the name of the
current Family File

Menu bar:
Click here to use the drop-down
menus

Toolbar:
Click these
buttons to
change views

Field:
Click any
field to enter
information

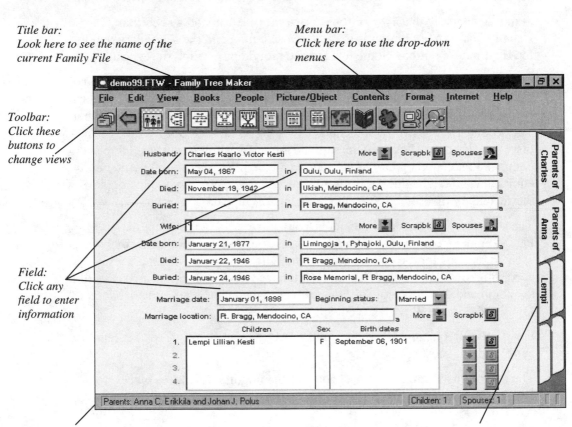

Status bar: Look here for useful information

Tab: Click here to see Lempi's Family Page

Figure 1-4. Basic Windows elements on the Family Page

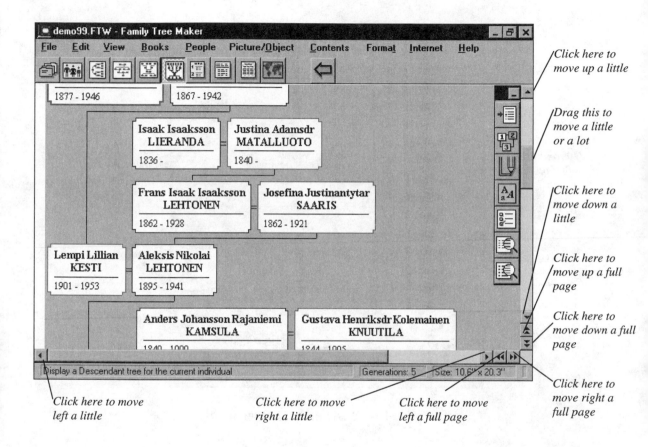

Figure 1-5. Scroll bars

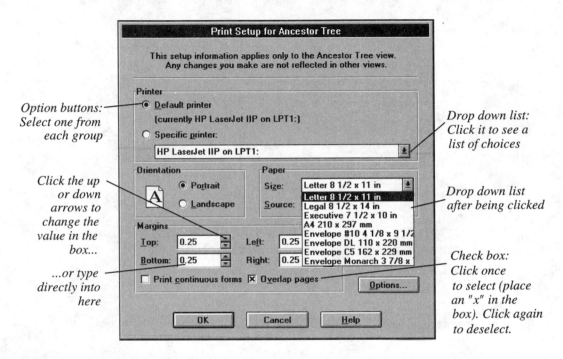

Option buttons:
Select one from
each group

Click the up
or down
arrows to
change the
value in the
box...

...or type
directly into
here

Drop down list:
Click it to see a
list of choices

Drop down list
after being clicked

Check box:
Click once
to select (place
an "x" in the
box). Click again
to deselect.

Figure 1-6. Basic dialog box elements

GETTING HELP

Like most other Windows products, Family Tree Maker has an on-screen Help system. An on-screen Help system is just like your paper manual, except it is an interactive part of the program. It can tell you how things work and help you navigate through the many different areas of Family Tree Maker. Help is also where you can enter information that identifies you as the person who prepared the Family File in the User Information dialog box.

Opening the Help system is simple: from the **Help** menu, select **Contents**. Or, you can press ⌷. To get help about a particular menu command, first click the menu, next use the arrow keys to highlight the command, and then press ⌷. To get help in a dialog box, click the **Help** button in the dialog box. The Help system displays information specifically tailored to that dialog box. For a complete description of how to use this Help system, from the **Help** menu, select **How to use Help**.

Family Tree Maker has three other types of help: **Cue Cards**, **Bubble Help,** and **Tooltips** (see "Selecting Help System Preferences" in this chapter).

Cue Cards appear automatically when you enter a view. They give you tips about what you can do in that view. Click **OK** to close a Cue Card after you finish reading it.

Bubble Help pops up when you hold your mouse pointer over things like buttons and fields for more than two seconds. It gives you instructions related to the item under your mouse pointer. When you move your mouse pointer away from a Bubble Help window, it closes.

You can prevent Cue Cards or Bubble Help windows from appearing in Family Tree Maker by deselecting the check box for either Bubble Help or Cue Cards in the Help Tools dialog box (see "Selecting Help System Preferences").

Tooltips behave similarly to Bubble Help. Use it to find out what's what in the toolbars. As your mouse pauses over a button, a small pop-up window displays the name of that feature.

Note: Once a Tooltip for any button has been displayed, the Tooltips for adjacent buttons will display immediately as you move the mouse pointer across the toolbar.

The "How-To" Guide

Family Tree Maker also contains a Genealogy "How-To" Guide to help you trace your family tree. This step-by-step guide tells you what questions to ask, where to go, and how to find important facts about your ancestors from sources both in the United States and abroad.

The "How-To" Guide has several different sections. It contains everything from information about basic research techniques to a directory of hundreds of addresses and phone numbers that can help with your genealogical research. And, unlike genealogy books, this guide is interactive. You can go straight to the information regarding your heritage and bypass any information that isn't useful to you. It even contains census abstracts and form letters in five different languages that you can print.

To open the Genealogy "How-To" Guide:

1. From the **Help** menu, select **Genealogy "How-To" Guide**.

   Family Tree Maker displays the Contents screen shown in Figure 1-7.

2. Select the first topic **All about using the Genealogy "How-To" Guide**.

   Family Tree Maker displays instructions on using the Genealogy "How-To" Guide.

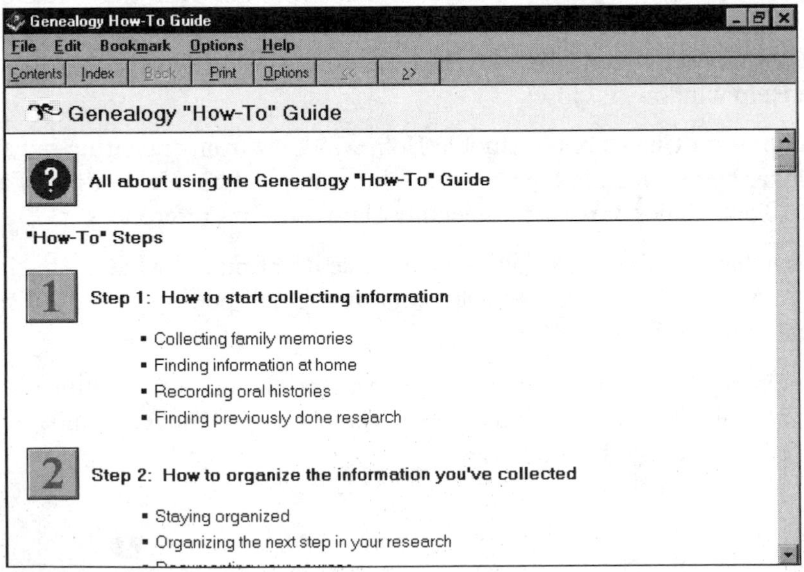

Figure 1-7. Genealogy "How-To" Guide Contents page

Entering User Information

Family Tree Maker provides a form in which you can enter information that identifies you as the person who created the Family File. This information is then automatically added to your World Family Tree contributions.

To enter user information:

1. From the **Help** menu, select **User Information**.

    Family Tree Maker displays the User Information dialog box.

2. After you enter your information, click **OK**.

    Family Tree Maker closes the dialog box and saves your changes.

CUSTOMIZING FAMILY TREE MAKER

Using the **Preferences** feature, you can customize different parts of Family Tree Maker. For example, you can customize the Toolbar, choose default date formats, change field labels, and select when Bubble Help and Cue Cards appear.

The following sections show you how to set Startup, Reference Number, Spell Check, Help System and other preferences, as well as how to enter your name, address, and other personal information to the file.

Selecting Startup Preferences

To set your Startup preferences:

1. From the **File** menu, select **Preferences**. From the submenu, select **Startup**.

   Family Tree Maker displays the Startup dialog box. Each of your options is described in this section.

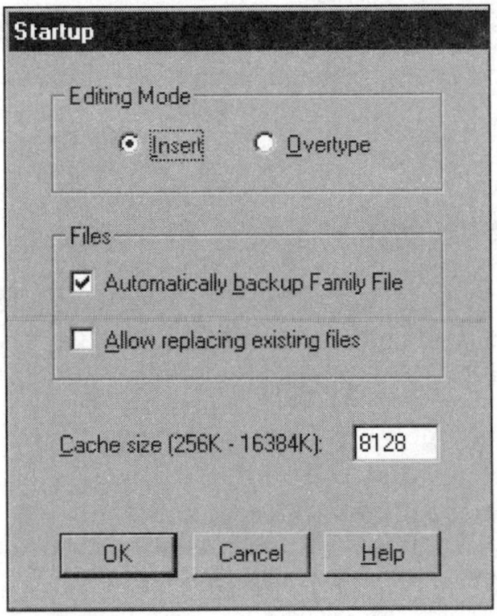

Figure 1-8. The Startup dialog box

Editing Mode — Selecting **Overtype** lets you type over old text. The old text is lost forever, and the new text is put in its place. Selecting **Insert** mode places new text in front of the old text.

Automatically backup Family File — Normally, Family Tree Maker saves a copy of your Family File when you exit the program or open a new Family File. The backup file has the same name as the original file, but with the extension **.FBK**. You can use this backup file if your original file is ever lost or damaged. However, since the backup file takes up space on your computer's hard drive, you may want to deselect this option if your computer's hard drive space is limited.

To help save space on your hard drive, you can also make your own compressed backup files to store on diskettes or in other directories. The backup copies that you create manually have the extension **.FBC**. See "Backing Up Your Family File" in Chapter 13. Making regular backup copies of your Family File can help ensure that you won't lose all of your genealogical information if something ever happens to the Family File that you work with regularly.

Allow replacing existing files — Normally, Family Tree Maker does not allow you to replace an old Family File with a new file of the same name. If you select this option, Family Tree Maker only gives you a warning message before it writes over an existing Family File. Any files that you choose to overwrite will be lost permanently.

To protect your Family Files as much as possible, make sure that "Automatically backup Family File" is selected and "Allow replacing existing files" is *not* selected.

Note: The "Allow replacing existing files" setting does not have any effect on *backup* files. Family Tree Maker will *not* allow you to overwrite a backup file.

Cache size — The cache is the memory where Family Tree Maker stores recently used information. The program runs most efficiently if you make the optimum amount of cache available to Family Tree Maker. If you have large Family Files, you should have a larger cache, but if you have small Family Files, you should have a smaller cache. With larger Family Files, a good rule of thumb for the cache size is about one-fourth of your computer's available memory. The maximum cache size is sixteen megabytes.

2. After you make your selections, click **OK**.

    Some Startup preferences do not take effect until you exit Family Tree Maker and then restart the program.

Selecting Automatic Reference Number Preferences

Family Tree Maker can assign reference numbers to individuals and marriages in your Family File automatically. You can review and override the numbers if you wish. Family Tree Maker will not change any of the existing reference numbers in your file.

To set your reference number preferences:

1. From the **File** menu, select **Preferences**. From the submenu, select **Reference Numbers**.

    Family Tree Maker displays the Reference Numbers dialog box.

2. Select any of the following options:

    Individuals — Activates the assignment of automatic reference numbers to individuals in your Family File. You can also choose the type of numbering scheme you want to use: **Numbers only**, **Prefix plus numbers** (a number preceded by up to four letters or numbers), or **Numbers plus suffix** (a number followed by up to four letters or numbers).

    Marriages — Activates the assignment of automatic reference numbers to marriages in your Family File. You can also choose the type of numbering scheme you want to use: **Numbers only**, **Prefix plus numbers** (a number preceded by up to four letters or numbers), or **Numbers plus suffix** (a number followed by up to four letters or numbers).

3. After you make your selections, click **OK**.

    Family Tree Maker assigns reference numbers to all of the individuals and marriages in your Family File that did not already have reference numbers. The automatic reference numbers appear in blue and your existing numbers appear in black. You can review and override the automatic numbers in the More About Lineage and More About Marriage dialog boxes (see Chapter 5, "Entering Detailed Information") by simply editing the automatically generated numbers. Any numbers you change will appear in black.

Selecting Spell Check Preferences

You can use the Spell Check Preference dialog box to control which words Family Tree Maker includes when checking your Family File.

To select spell check preferences:

1. From the **File** menu, select **Preferences**. From the submenu, select **Spell Check**.

   Family Tree Maker displays the Spell Check dialog box.

2. Select any of the following options:

   Ignore known names — By default, Family Tree Maker recognizes most of the names in your Family File as words that are spelled correctly. If you want to disable this option, turn off this check box.

   Ignore capitalized words — When this option is on, Family Tree Maker does not attempt to correct words that consist only of upper case letters, such as abbreviations for state names and acronyms. When it is off, it flags these words as misspelled.

   Ignore words with numbers — This option controls whether Family Tree Maker treats words that include numbers as misspellings. If you often use alpha-numeric reference numbers in your notes, you can select this option to avoid having to constantly approve them in your text.

3. After you make your selections, click **OK**.

Selecting Help System Preferences

Cue Cards and Bubble Help windows contain helpful hints and tips to keep you on track while you work with Family Tree Maker.

To turn Cue Cards and Bubble Help windows on or off:

1. From the **File** menu, select **Preferences**. From the submenu, select **Help Tools**.

   Family Tree Maker displays the Help Tools dialog box.

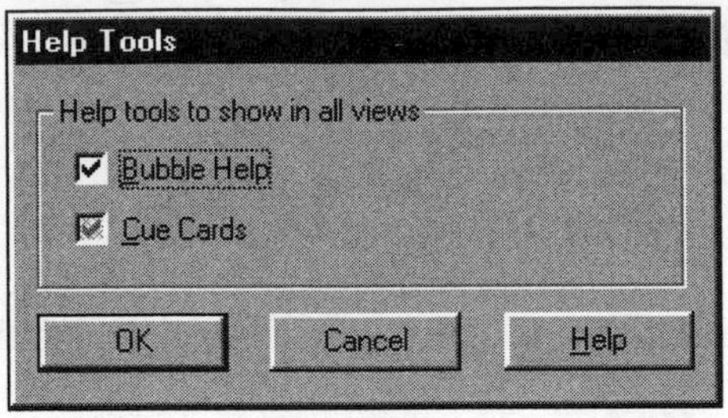

Figure 1-9. The Help Tools dialog box

2. Select your Help Tools preferences as described below.

    Bubble Help — Select this check box if you want Bubble Help to appear while you are working. If you don't want the Bubble Help to appear, deselect this check box.

    Cue Cards — Select this check box if you want Cue Cards to appear while you are working. If you don't want the Cue Cards to appear, deselect this check box.

    Note: If you notice that the Cue Cards check mark is gray, it means that you've turned off some, but not all, of the Cue Cards. You can turn off only some of the Cue Cards by selecting the Cue Cards check box in the Help Tools dialog box, and then selecting the "Click here if you don't want to see this window again" check box on the Cue Cards you do not want to see.

3. After you make your selections, click **OK**.

    Family Tree Maker closes the dialog box and saves your changes.

Customizing the Toolbar

Family Tree Maker makes it easy for you to customize the main toolbar. Now you can display the buttons you want for the features you use most often. Just select your choices from a list of available buttons to add them to your custom toolbar list.

To add or remove toolbar buttons:

1. From the **File** menu, select **Preferences**. From the submenu, select **Toolbar**.

    Family Tree Maker displays the **Customize Toolbar** dialog box. It contains two lists: the list on the right shows the buttons currently selected for the toolbar, and the list on the left shows the buttons you can add to the toolbar.

To add a button to the toolbar, select that icon in the list on the left and then click [>] (Include). To remove a button from your toolbar, select that icon in the list on the right and then click [<] (Remove). When you add an icon, it moves to the list on the right. When you remove an icon, it moves to the list on the left.

2. If you want to change the order in which the buttons appear in the list of available buttons (and on your toolbar), select the icon you want to move in the right-hand list.

   You can choose from the following options:

   Move up — moves the selected icon up one position in the list on the right, and one position to the left on the toolbar.

   Move down — moves the selected icon down one position in the list on the right, and one position to the right on the toolbar.

   Use defaults — deletes any changes you have made and returns the toolbar to its original settings.

3. After you make your selections, click **OK**.

   Family Tree Maker makes your changes and displays your customized toolbar.

   Note: Depending on your computer monitor's resolution, you may not be able to add every available button to the toolbar.

The Side Toolbar

Family Tree Maker contains many features and options that are not always visible in every view. In order to make it easier to access the options available to you in various views, Family Tree Maker incorporates a special side toolbar. This toolbar automatically appears along the right margin in each of the tree and report views. Take a moment to review this convenient addition — we're sure you'll find it helpful and easy to use.

Using the Side Toolbar

Family Tree Maker automatically changes the buttons that are displayed in the side toolbar depending on the view you have chosen. Side toolbars contain a title bar (with no text), and buttons that are the same size as the main toolbar. Simply click any of the buttons to see the most frequently used features or option dialog boxes available for the current view.

The side toolbar can also be minimized, or made smaller, by clicking the small icon located in the upper right corner of the title bar. When the toolbar is minimized, it appears only as a small title bar.

Figure 1-10. The Side Toolbar (Report view)

To restore the toolbar to its full size, click the maximize icon in the upper right corner of the title bar.

Note: Remember: you can take advantage of the new "Tooltips" feature to identify the buttons that appear on any toolbar (see "Getting Help" in this chapter).

Chapter 2

TUTORIAL

1920 — Helping to shield his younger brother from the Massachusetts winter, Edgar A. Spencer procrastinates on the long journey to school. Liz Lieber, his granddaughter, is a Marketing Specialist for the Family Archive Unit of Banner Blue.

TUTORIAL

This tutorial shows you how easy it is to use Family Tree Maker by leading you step-by-step through the main features of the program. It uses as its example the ancestry of Abraham Lincoln, the 16th president of the United States.

First, you will enter information about Abraham Lincoln's family, back through his parents and grandparents. Then, you'll enter a brief story about Abraham. Finally, you'll print a Custom Ancestor tree, just one type of tree you can create with Family Tree Maker. All together, this should take about an hour, but don't feel that you have to do it all at once.

In the process, you will learn about many of Family Tree Maker's most useful commands and options, but don't put the manual away once you've done this tutorial! Read the other chapters as you work with Family Tree Maker — you'll find out about even more features and become a Family Tree Maker expert.

BEFORE YOU START

This chapter assumes a few things:

- You know how to use a typewriter or computer keyboard. (Hunt-and-peck typing is fine!)

- You've already read Chapter 1, "Program Setup."

- Family Tree Maker is installed and set up on your computer.

- Your printer driver is correctly installed and configured under Windows.

If you haven't done these things, go back and follow the instructions in Chapter 1. Consult your Windows manual if your printer driver is not properly configured. After you complete the items listed above, you're ready to begin this tutorial.

STARTING FAMILY TREE MAKER

After you start Family Tree Maker, you can begin the tutorial.

To start Family Tree Maker:

1. Turn on your computer.

2. Click the Windows **Start** button.

3. From the **Start** menu, select **Programs**, then **Family Tree Maker,** and then **Family Tree Maker** once again from the submenu.

    Family Tree Maker appears in a few moments and displays the Open Family File dialog box. (If the Open Family File dialog box doesn't appear, from the **File** menu, select **New Family File** and skip to step 5.)

4. Click **New**.

    Family Tree Maker displays the New Family File dialog box

5. Type a name for the new Family File in the **File name** field.

    All the information that you enter about all of your relatives is stored in a Family File. Family Tree Maker uses the information in this file to create special documents for you, such as family trees and calendars.

    Since you're going to enter information about Abraham Lincoln's family in this tutorial, type `LINCOLN` in the **File name** field. Family Tree Maker will automatically add the file extension "FTW".

    Note: To store your Family File in a different drive or folder than the one shown, make that selection in this dialog box. You cannot select a floppy diskette drive (or other removable media) because your Family File **must** be on your hard disk while you're working on it. You can, however, keep a backup copy on a floppy diskette.

6. Click **Save**.

    Family Tree Maker displays the opening page of the Startup Wizard (see "The FamilyFinder Startup Wizard" in Chapter 1).

    Since you have already worked with the Startup Wizard, click **Cancel**, and then click **Yes** to quit the tree entry and go to the Family Page.

    You are now ready to start entering information about the Lincoln family.

PART I: ENTERING FAMILY INFORMATION

In this section you'll enter information about several generations of the Lincoln family. Follow all the steps exactly, and within an hour or so you will be printing your first family tree!

The **Family Page** is where you enter information about the individuals in your family. It is made up of a series of **labels** and **fields**. A field is a place for you to type information. A label tells the purpose of a field.

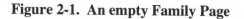

Figure 2-1. An empty Family Page

The row of words across the top of the screen is called the **menu bar**. When you click one of the words on the menu bar, such as "Edit," a list of commands appears below it. This list is called a **pull-down menu**. You choose items from the menu bar and pull-down menus to do things such as edit your information and print family trees. The tabs along the right side of the Family Page take you to other Family Pages. (These tabs are blank now, since you haven't entered any names yet.) The buttons placed throughout the Family Page take you to other parts of the program. You'll learn more about these buttons and tabs later.

Filling Out the Family Page

On this Family Page you'll enter some facts about Abraham Lincoln's immediate family, starting with Abraham Lincoln himself.

Figure 2-2 shows what the completed Family Page will look like. The steps that follow tell you how to get your computer screen to look like the figure.

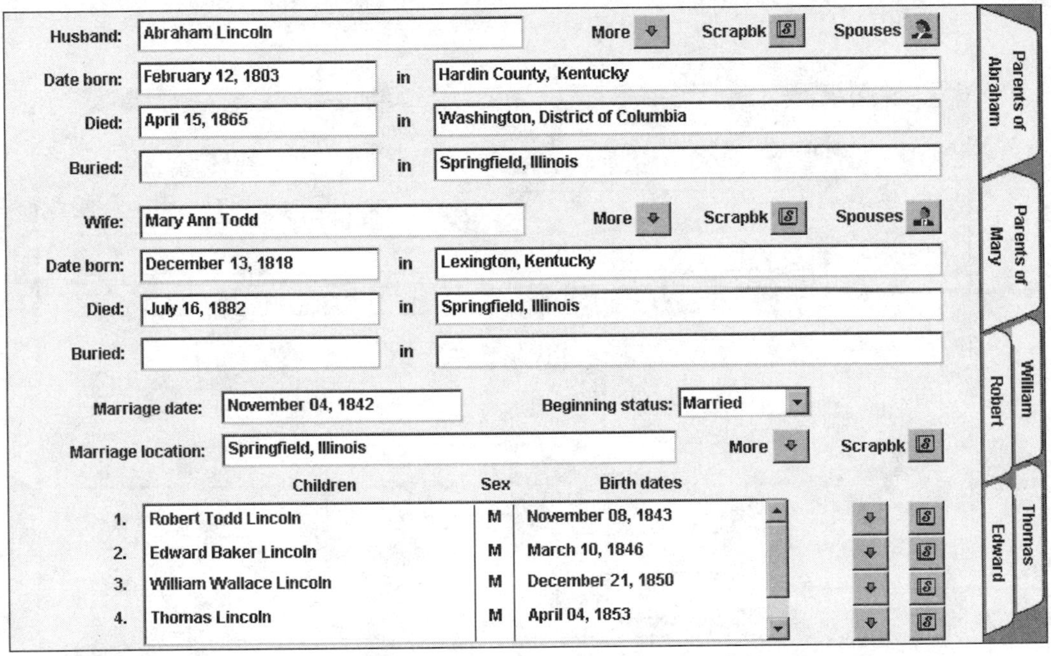

Figure 2-2. Abraham Lincoln's Family Page, completely filled out

The cursor is already in the "Husband" field. (The cursor is the blinking vertical line. It marks where the next character you type will appear.) In this tutorial, any letters that you should type are shown in **bold letters like this**.

1. Type **Abraham Lincoln** in the **Husband** field.

   If you make a mistake, use ⬅ to move the cursor back to the left, and use Backspace ⬅BkSp to delete the incorrect characters. The Backspace ⬅BkSp key deletes characters as it moves the cursor to the left. If you need to move the cursor back to the right, press ➡.

The ⬅ and ➡ arrow keys are usually on the right side of the keyboard; sometimes they're part of the numeric keypad (the rectangular arrangement of number keys — not the ones across the top of your keyboard). If you press the arrow keys but you get numbers on the screen, press Num Lock ▦ to put the numeric keypad into cursor-moving mode.

You can also fix mistakes by simply typing over them with the correct information. To do so, press Insert ▦ to turn on overwrite mode. (Because Family Tree Maker starts in insert mode, pressing insert now turns insert mode off and overwrite mode on.) You know when you're in overwrite mode, because the **status bar** at the very bottom of your screen displays the letters "OVR." Pressing Insert ▦ a second time turns overwrite mode off.

2. Click the **Date born** field and watch the tabs on the right side of the screen.

   As soon as you have provided the husband's name, Family Tree Maker creates a Family Page for Abraham's parents. The tab on the right side of the page labeled "Parents of Abraham" can take you to their Family Page. You will enter information on that page later in this tutorial.

   You can also move between fields by using Tab ▦ or ▦.

   If you notice a mistake in the "Husband" field after you move the cursor out of it, click in the field with your mouse pointer, and then use ⬅ or ➡ to move to your mistake. Use Backspace ▦ to delete the incorrect characters, then type in the correct ones.

3. Type **Feb 12 1809** in the **Date born** field.

4. Click the **in** field and watch what happens.

   When you leave a date field, Family Tree Maker automatically converts what you've typed to a standard date format. You can type the date almost any way that you would like; Family Tree Maker can usually figure out what you mean. If Family Tree Maker cannot understand your date, it asks you for clarification. Simply retype the date in a more standard format (as shown in step #3).

5. Type the name of Lincoln's birthplace — **Hardin County, Kentucky** — in the **in** field.

6. Fill out the next two fields with the following information: `15 Apr 1865` for the date of his death, and `Washington, District of Columbia` for the location.

   Don't be afraid of making mistakes. This is just a tutorial, nobody's keeping score, and typographical errors won't hurt the computer.

7. Type the following information for Lincoln's wife into the proper fields (refer to Figure 2-2 if you need help):

   `Mary Ann Todd`

born	`Dec 13, 1818`	in	`Lexington, Kentucky`
died	`July 16, 1882`	in	`Springfield, Illinois`

   You fill in the information for a wife the same way you do for a husband, being especially careful to use the wife's maiden name (her last name before she was married). This is important to avoid confusion and make it easier to trace her side of the family.

   Remember to click in the next field after you fill in the information for a particular field — don't try to type all that information into the same field! Refer to Figure 2-2 if you're unsure into which field to type your information.

   As with Abraham, Family Tree Maker automatically creates a Family Page for Mary's parents and reformats dates as you exit the date fields.

8. The Lincolns were wed on `November 4, 1842`, so type that into the **Marriage date** field.

9. Click the **Beginning status** field after you type the marriage date.

   Family Tree Maker displays a drop-down list of relationship codes when you click this field. The **default** for the "Beginning status" field is "Married," so you don't need to change anything in this field. A default is what's already in a field when you come to it. Family Tree Maker uses defaults in several places to make your work quicker and easier.

   If they had never been married, you'd be able to select a different relationship code, such as "Unknown." Since the Lincolns don't fall into this category, move on to the next step.

10. Click the **Marriage location** field and type `Springfield, Illinois`

You're now finished entering basic information about Abraham Lincoln and his wife, Mary, so you can move on to their children.

11. Click the first row in the **Children** list.

This list is where you record the names, sexes, and birth dates of a couple's children. Be sure to always record the full name, including the last name.

12. In the field where the cursor now lies (the first row in the **Children** list), type `Robert Todd Lincoln` and press [Enter←].

Notice that Family Tree Maker automatically fills in the name "Lincoln" for you. Again, this is Fastfields at work.

13. As soon as the cursor moves to the **Sex** field, an "F" appears. Type **M** over the "F" and then press [Enter←] to go on to the **Birth dates** field.

"F" for "Female" is the default value for the "Sex" field.

14. Type `11/8/43` into the **Birth dates** field and press [Enter←].

Family Tree Maker converts the date you type into a standard date format.

15. Type the following information into the appropriate fields for the Lincolns' other four sons:

`William Wallace Lincoln`, sex **M**, born `Dec 21, 1850`
`Edward Baker Lincoln`, sex **M**, born `March 10, 1846`
`Thomas Lincoln`, sex **M**, born `April 4, 1853`
`Tad Lincoln`, sex **M**, born `UNKNOWN`

Be sure to enter their full names. As you can see, the information for the children isn't as extensive as the information for the parents — at least not on this page. Later in this tutorial, you'll see that each child has his or her own Family Page where he or she appears as a (potential) husband or wife.

Even though the Family Page only displays four children at a time, you can enter up to ninety-nine children for each marriage. Use the scroll bar on the right side of the "Children" list to display the other children.

Fastfields

You may have noticed that as you began to type the name "Lincoln," Family Tree Maker automatically filled it in for you. This is because name and location fields, in addition to a few other fields, are Fastfields.

Location Fastfields remember the names of the last 50 locations that you've entered into any location field. This means that when you move the cursor into a location field and start typing the name of a town that you've previously entered into Family Tree Maker, Fastfields automatically tries to fill it in for you. You don't need to do anything special, just keep typing the name of the town until Family Tree Maker gets it right or runs out of guesses. You may save time this way, but if Fastfields doesn't have the correct location name, you certainly won't lose any time. Other Fastfields work in the same way. For more information, see "Fastfields" in Chapter 3.

Sorting Children

If you entered the children in the order that we listed them, they're not in birth order. It's generally a good idea to have the children in birth order, so Family Tree Maker has a special command that sorts the children for you.

To sort the children on a Family Page:

1. From the **People** menu, select **Sort children**.

    Family Tree Maker displays a message asking you to confirm that you want to sort the children.

2. Click **OK**.

3. Look at the list of children.

    If the children weren't in birth order before, notice that they are now.

Congratulations! You've just finished filling out your first Family Page. To make sure all of the information is correct, compare your Family Page to Figure 2-2.

If any of the information is different, go back and change it. Just click the fields whose information you need to change and use ⬅ and ➡ to move around within a field. See Figures 3-3 and 3-4 in Chapter 3 for a complete list of cursor-moving keys and a list of editing keys.

Filling Out Other Family Pages

Look at the right side of the screen — the tabs now say "Parents of Mary," and "Parents of Abraham." There are also tabs for each child, labeled "Robert," "Edward," "William," and "Thomas." You can click these tabs to go to other Family Pages in your Family File.

Note: The fifth child, Tad, is still on this page. You can see him by using the scroll bar on the right side of the "Children" list.

Each Family Page holds two generations — parents and their children. As you work on your own Family File, you fill out many Family Pages, moving both forward and backwards in time. Your Family File is like an album filled with pages of information about your family.

For the purposes of this tutorial, you'll only go backwards in time and fill out the Family Pages for Abraham Lincoln's parents and grandparents. To go forward in time, you would fill out Family Pages for his children, grandchildren, great-grandchildren, and so on. In your personal Family File you'll do both.

On the next page, you begin going backwards in time by filling out the Family Page for Abraham's parents.

Lincoln's Parents' Family Page

Fill out the Family Page for Lincoln's parents:

1. Click the **Parents of Abraham** tab to go to Lincoln's parents' Family Page.

    Family Tree Maker displays Lincoln's parents' Family Page.

    This Family Page is already partially filled out — one of the lines in the "Children" list contains Abraham Lincoln's information. This is because Family Tree Maker copied the information from Lincoln's Family Page to his parents' Family Page.

2. Enter the following information for Lincoln's father, Thomas Lincoln, his mother, Nancy Hanks, and their marriage:

    `Thomas Lincoln`
    born `Jan 6 1778` in `Rockingham County, Virginia`

    `Nancy Hanks`
    born `Feb 5 1784` in `Campbell County, Virginia`
    died `Oct 5 1818` in `Spencer County, Indiana`

    Married `12 June 1806`

You don't have the information for the death of Thomas Lincoln, nor for the location of Thomas and Nancy's wedding, so you could either leave those fields blank or enter a question mark (?) in them. For now, just leave them blank. They were married, so you do not need to change the "Beginning status" field. For this tutorial, you don't need to enter any more information about their children. Check what you've typed against Figure 2-3.

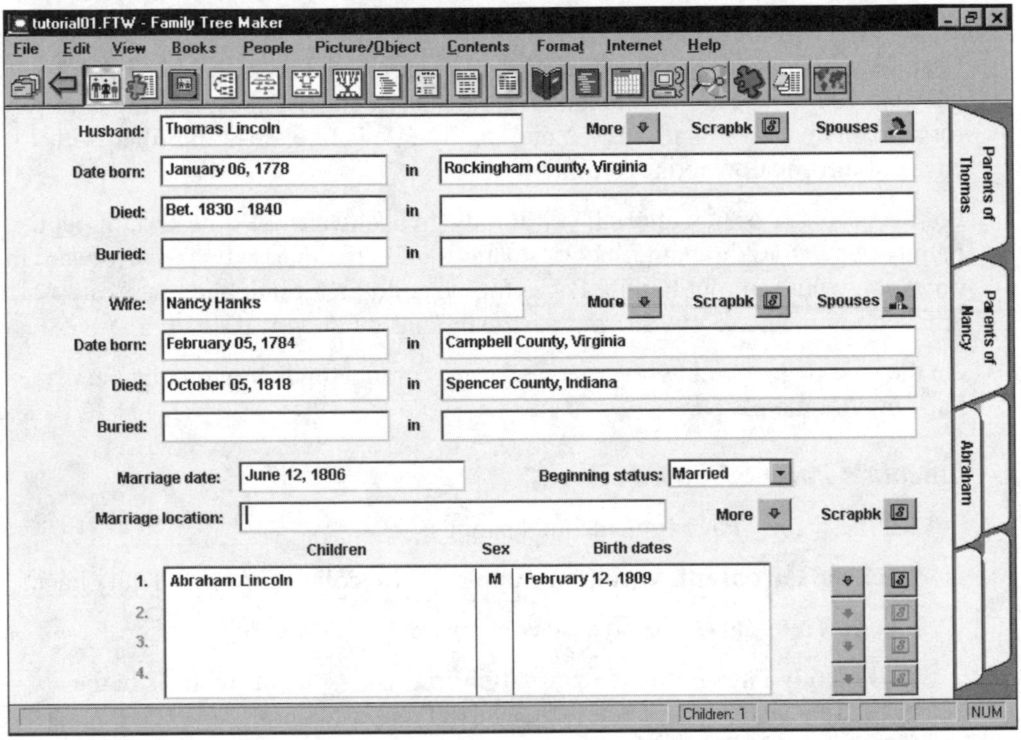

Figure 2-3. Completed Family Page for Thomas and Nancy

You now need to go back one more generation to fill out two more Family Pages — one for Abraham Lincoln's paternal grandparents (the parents of his father, Thomas), and one for his maternal grandparents (the parents of his mother, Nancy).

Don't skip this part of the tutorial. You won't have to enter a lot of information, and you will need this information to create beautiful trees in Part IV of the tutorial.

Lincoln's Paternal Grandparents' Family Page

In this section you'll learn how to add information if either the husband or wife has been married more than once.

1. On the Family Page that shows Thomas and Nancy as husband and wife, click the **Parents of Thomas** tab.

   Family Tree Maker displays the Family Page of Thomas' parents.

2. Enter the following information about Lincoln's grandparents.

   Lincoln's paternal grandfather was also named **Abraham Lincoln**, and was also born in **Kentucky**. His paternal grandmother was **Bathsheba Herring**. That's all of the available information.

   Check what you've typed against Figure 2-4 to make sure it's accurate. If necessary, go back and make changes.

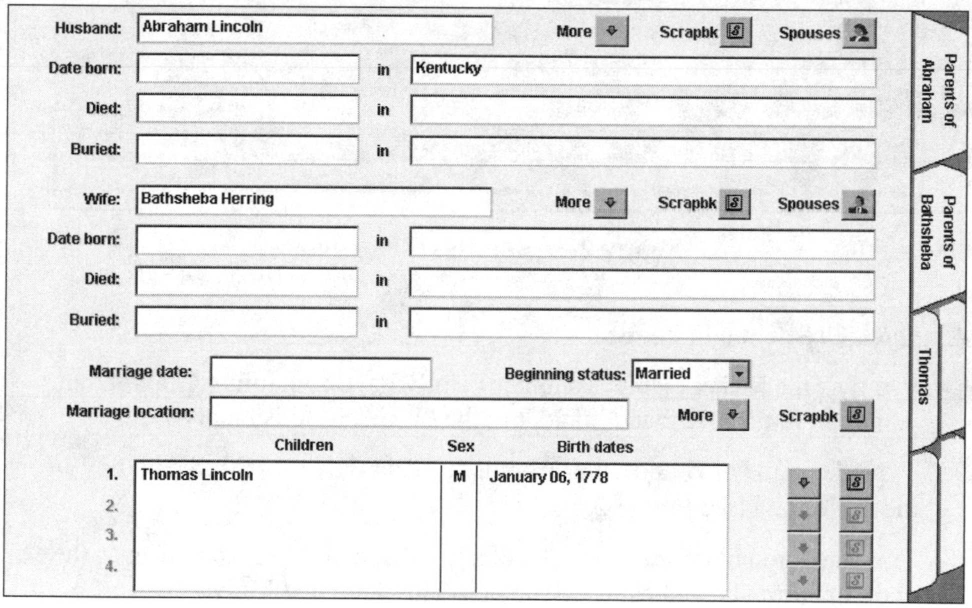

Figure 2-4. Completed Family Page for Abraham and Bathsheba

Note: Ordinarily, when you don't know the date of an individual's death, enter a question mark (?) in the date of death field. For the purposes of this tutorial, however, you can leave these fields blank.

3. It turns out that Grandfather Abraham was married to another woman before
    he married Bathsheba Herring. To the right of Grandfather Abraham's name,
    there is a button labeled "Spouses." Click this button to add information
    about Grandfather Abraham's other wife.

    Family Tree Maker displays the Spouses dialog box in Figure 2-5. You have
    the choice of going to an existing spouse or creating a new spouse. Each
    individual in Family Tree Maker can have up to 99 spouses.

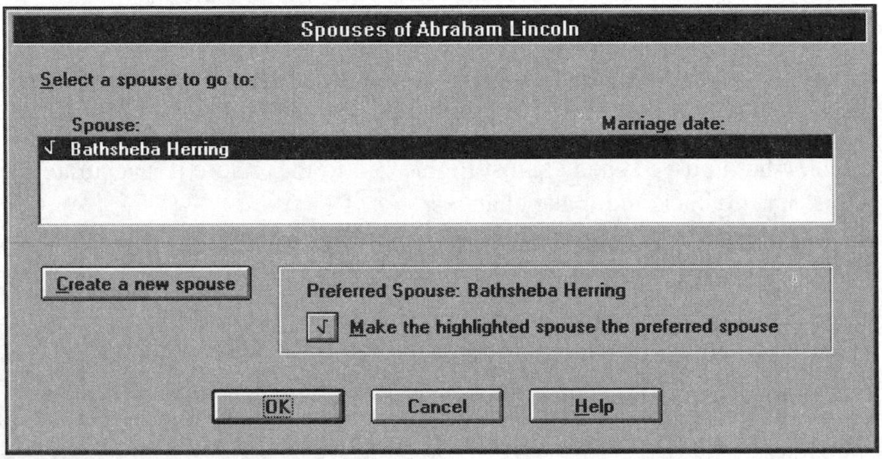

Figure 2-5. Spouses dialog box

4. Click **Create a new spouse**.

    Family Tree Maker displays another Family Page containing Grandfather
    Abraham in the "Husband" field, but the "Wife" field is empty.

5. Type the name of Grandfather Abraham's first wife, `Mary Shipley` in
    the **Wife** field (see Figure 2-6).

    There are no children to list on this Family Page because Thomas was the
    child of Abraham and Bathsheba, not of Abraham and Mary.

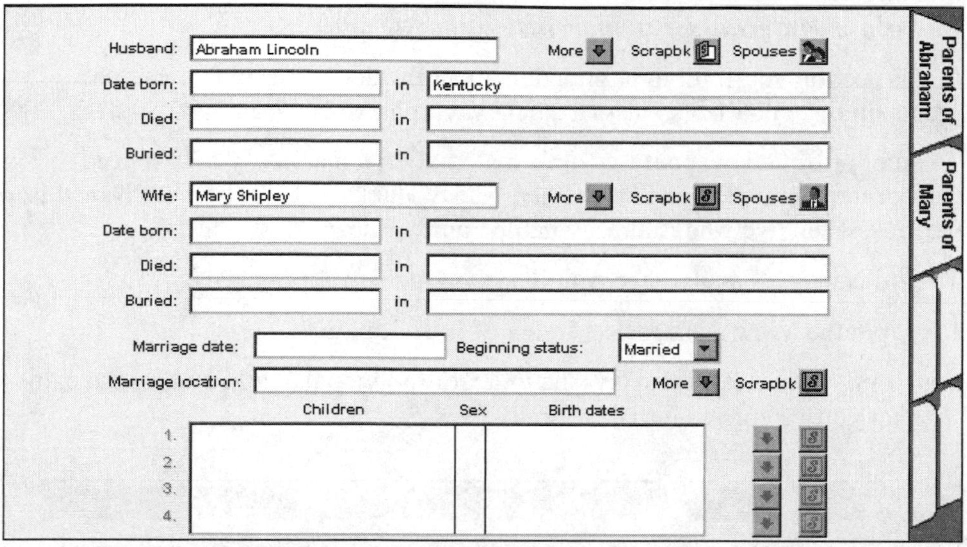

Figure 2-6. Completed Family Page with Abraham and Mary

6. Click Grandfather Abraham's **Spouses** button again.

   Family Tree Maker displays the Spouses dialog box, which now shows both of Grandfather Abraham's wives.

   Note: There is a check mark next to Bathsheba's name. This indicates that she is the preferred spouse of Abraham. This tells Family Tree Maker that you want Bathsheba to be shown when you display Abraham's Family Page, not Mary.

7. In the list of names, click **Bathsheba Herring**.

8. Click **OK**.

   Family Tree Maker returns you to Abraham's and Bathsheba's Family Page.

Lincoln's Maternal Grandparents' Family Page

In this section you'll fill in information about President Lincoln's maternal grandparents. You'll also learn a quick way to move between Family Pages.

To enter information about Lincoln's maternal grandparents, you first need to display the Family Page of his mother, Nancy Hanks. This is because Nancy is the closest relative who is already in the Family File.

To find Nancy's Family Page, you'll use the Index of Individuals:

1. From the **View** menu, select **Index of Individuals**.

    Family Tree Maker displays the Index of Individuals. It lists all of the names that you've entered into this Family File.

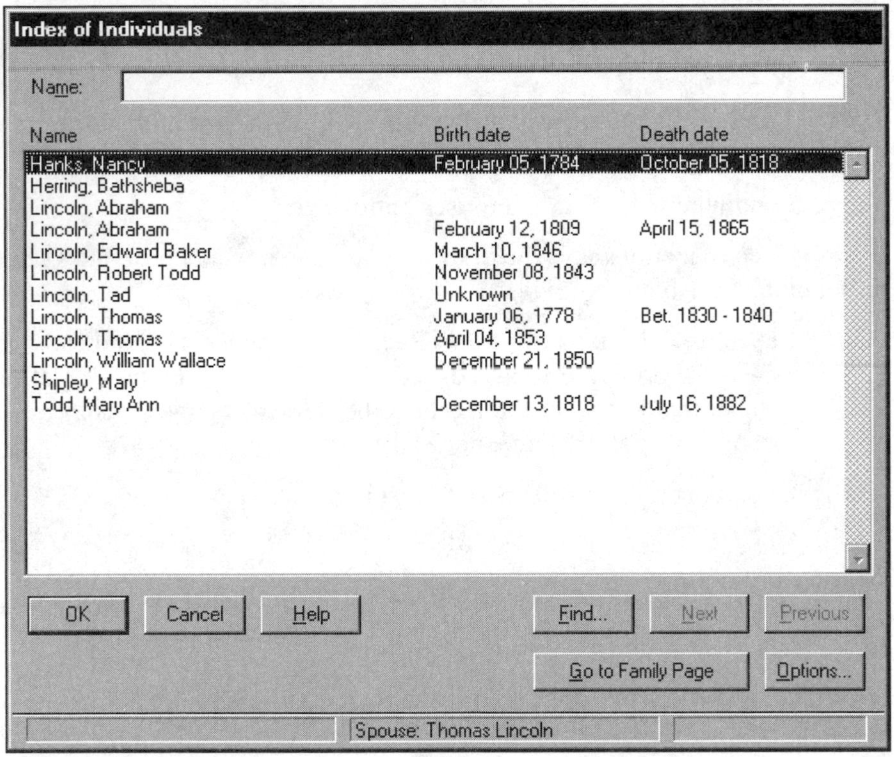

Figure 2-7. The Index of Individuals

2. Click **Hanks, Nancy** so that it is highlighted.

3. Click **Go to Family Page**.

   Family Tree Maker displays Thomas's and Nancy's Family Page (see Figure 2-3).

Now you're ready to fill in information about the President's maternal grandparents. The only information you have is the name of his maternal grandfather — Joseph Hanks.

1. Click the **Parents of Nancy** tab on the right side of Thomas and Nancy's Family Page.

   Family Tree Maker displays the Family Page of Nancy's parents.

2. Type `Joseph Hanks` in the **Husband** field.

That's all there is to enter for Nancy's parents. Now you are ready to return to President Lincoln's Family Page. This time you'll use a different feature in the Index of Individuals to do this.

1. From the **View** menu, select **Index of Individuals**.

   Family Tree Maker displays the Index of Individuals. You can see that Abraham Lincoln is listed twice in the Index of Individuals. President Lincoln is the one who was born in 1809. However, this is a good chance to practice using the Find command.

2. Click **Find** at the bottom of the Index of Individuals.

   Family Tree Maker displays the Find Name dialog box.

3. Type `Abraham` in the **Name** field.

4. Click **OK**.

   Family Tree Maker closes the Find Name dialog box and highlights the first "Abraham Lincoln" listed in the Index of Individuals. That's President Lincoln's grandfather, so it's not the individual that you want.

5. Click **Next**.

   Family Tree Maker highlights the second "Abraham Lincoln" in the list. That's President Lincoln. You want to go to his Family Page.

6. Click **Go to Family Page**.

   Family Tree Maker displays President Lincoln's Family Page.

Removing an Individual from Your File

It's always good practice to check your information from time to time. Sometimes you'll find that you have made a mistake. But don't worry — Family Tree Maker has commands that can help you find some types of errors automatically. See "Checking Your File for Errors" in Chapter 6. In this case, a closer look at the records shows that Tad Lincoln was not a separate child, but in fact, "Tad" is Thomas's nickname. To correct this mistake, you'll delete Tad.

To remove Tad from the file:

1. Click the down arrow at the bottom of the scroll bar on the **Children** list so that Tad becomes visible.

2. Click Tad's name.

3. From the **People** menu, select **Delete Individual**.

   Family Tree Maker displays a dialog box asking you to confirm that you want to delete Tad.

4. Click **Yes**.

   Tad is now gone from your file. Family Tree Maker returns you to Tad's parents' Family Page.

Note: It's important to remember to use the Delete Individual command whenever you want to remove someone permanently from your file. Using the backspace or delete keys to remove someone only removes their name — it doesn't remove any of their other information or any of their relationships with other individuals.

PART II: THE MORE ABOUT DIALOG BOXES

Family Tree Maker provides five other dialog boxes for each individual in your Family File. These dialog boxes are collectively called More About dialog boxes because they let you enter more information about an individual.

Entering Brief Facts

Next, add a bit more information about President Abraham Lincoln — specifically, that he was a rail splitter in his youth.

1. Click **More** to the right of Lincoln's name.

    Family Tree Maker displays the Facts dialog box. It contains fields where you can enter short comments and facts about an individual, such as their occupation or date of immigration (see Figure 2-8).

    Note: Family Tree Maker remembers which More About dialog box you were using last. If the dialog box you see now is not the Facts dialog box, don't worry. It simply means you were exploring Family Tree Maker before doing this tutorial. To open the Facts dialog box, click the **Facts** button at the top right of the currently open More About dialog box.

2. Click the Fact Name drop-down list and select "Occupation" from the list. In this case, an appropriate fact name exists for the information we want to enter. If the fact name we wanted to use was not in the list, we could simply add it by typing it into a blank fact name field. Family Tree Maker would then add it to the list of facts for use in the future.

3. Click the **Comment/Location** field, and then type `Rail splitter (in youth)`. Since this isn't something that happened on a specific date, leave the **Date** field blank.

    You could continue adding more facts in this dialog box, but for now, leave it at this one fact.

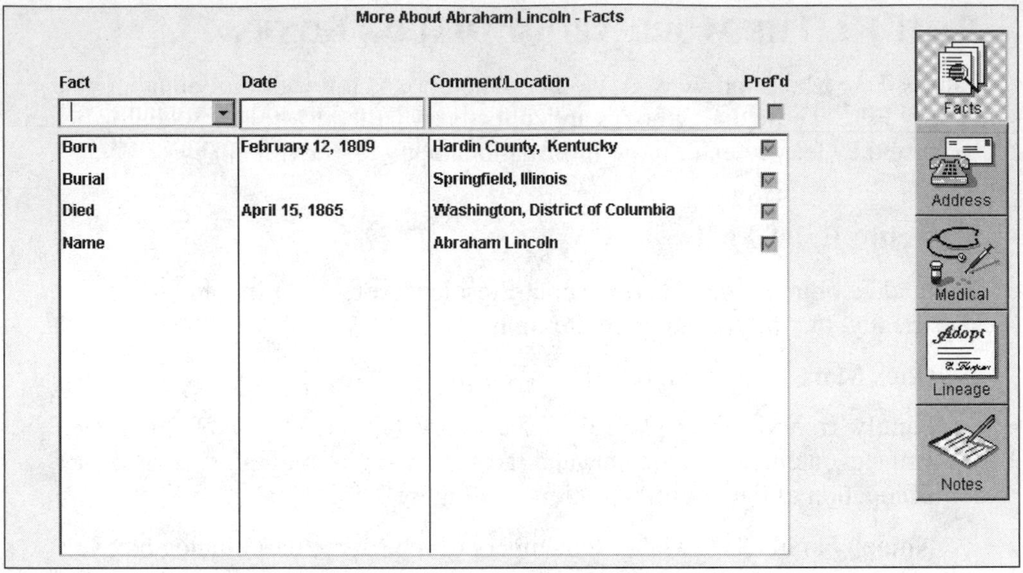

Fact	Date	Comment/Location	Pref'd
			☐
Born	February 12, 1809	Hardin County, Kentucky	☑
Burial		Springfield, Illinois	☑
Died	April 15, 1865	Washington, District of Columbia	☑
Name		Abraham Lincoln	☑

Figure 2-8. Facts dialog box

The Other More About Dialog Boxes

You'll notice that on the right side of the More About dialog boxes there are five buttons labeled "Facts," "Address," "Medical," "Lineage," and "Notes." You can click these buttons to take you to these More About dialog boxes. You won't enter information in all of these More About dialog boxes now, but here's a short description of each one.

In the Medical dialog box you can enter an individual's physical and medical information, such as height, weight, and cause of death. The Address dialog box is for entering an individual's address and phone number. This information would be handy if you wanted to print an address list for your family. In the Lineage dialog box you can record an individual's nickname and any special title that they use. You can also record special information about that individual's relationship with their parents, for example, you can indicate that they were adopted as a child. Finally, there is the Notes dialog box, which you can use to record several pages of stories and notes about an individual. You'll enter some information in the Lineage and Notes dialog boxes in the next few sections.

Entering Nicknames into the Lineage Dialog Box

People frequently have nicknames that they prefer to use. For example, earlier, you learned that Tad Lincoln was Thomas Lincoln's nickname. Abraham Lincoln was also known as "Honest Abe." You can record nicknames in the Lineage dialog box. This is also a good place to record name changes.

To enter a nickname for Abraham Lincoln:

1. Click **Lineage** on the right side of the Facts dialog box.

   Family Tree Maker displays the Lineage dialog box.

2. Click the **This person is also known as (aka)** field.

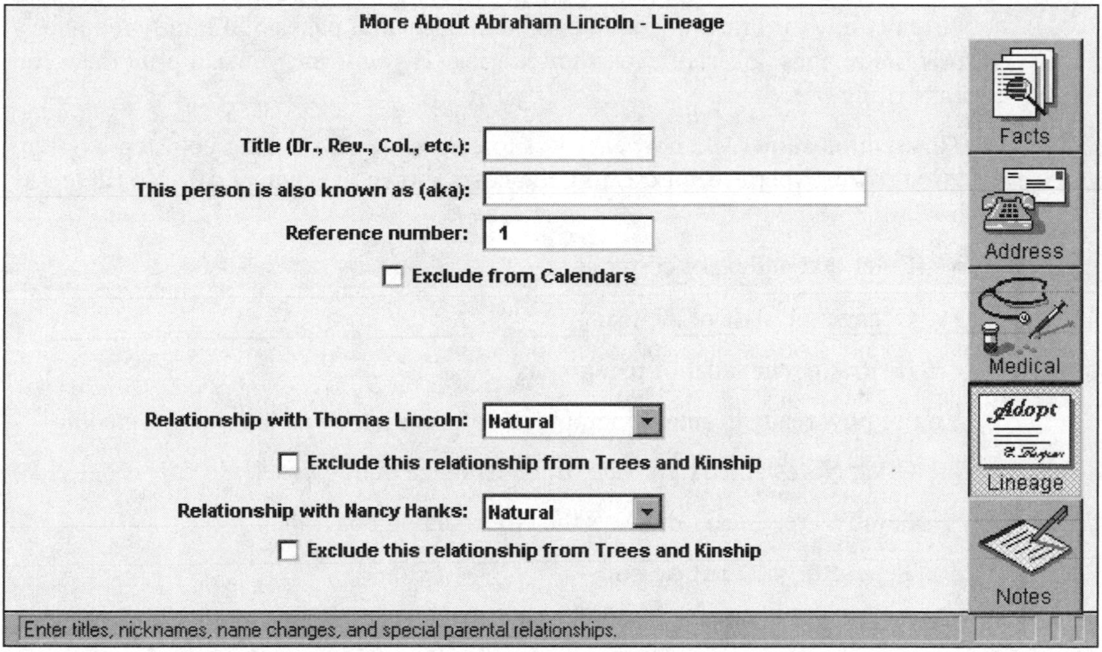

Figure 2-9. Lineage dialog box

3. Type **Honest Abe**

Notice that you entered just the nickname. This is because Family Tree Maker gives you the option of printing nicknames as part of the full name or instead of the given name. In this case, you'll get to choose either "Abraham Lincoln," "Honest Abe," or "Abraham Honest Abe Lincoln" when you print.

For information on how to use automatic reference numbers to minimize errors in data entry, see "Selecting Automatic Reference Number Preferences," in Chapter 1.

Entering Lengthy Information into the Notes Dialog Box

The Notes dialog box is a mini word processor. In it you can record and organize virtually any information you like, including several pages of a family member's favorite recipes, jokes, or even short stories. If you want, you can print them for easy filing.

This section shows you how easy it is to enter notes by leading you step-by-step through the experience of creating the notes shown in Figure 2-10. You'll learn how to:

* Enter text and make corrections

* Change the style of the text

* Rearrange the order of paragraphs

You're now ready to enter biographical information about Abraham Lincoln.

1. Click **Notes** at the right side of the **Lineage** dialog box.

Family Tree Maker displays the Notes dialog box.

2. Type **He volunteered**

If you make a mistake, use ⬅ to move the cursor back to the left and use Backspace ⬅BkSp to delete the incorrect characters. The Backspace ⬅BkSp key deletes characters as it moves the cursor to the left. If you need to move the cursor back to the right, press →.

3. Continue typing on the same line: **and became a Captain in the Black Hawk War of 1832**.

4. Press the space bar twice.

Do *not* press Enter⬅. If you do, press Backspace ⬅BkSp to move the cursor back to the end of the sentence you typed in step 2.

5. Type **He commented afterwards that he saw no live, fighting Indians, but had a good many bloody struggles with the mosquitoes**.

    As you can see, if a word doesn't fit at the end of a line, Family Tree Maker automatically moves it to the beginning of the next line. You should only press ⌜Enter◄┘⌟ when you reach the end of a paragraph.

6. Press ⌜Enter◄┘⌟ to end the paragraph.

7. Press ⌜Enter◄┘⌟ to create a blank line.

8. Type the second paragraph:

    Abe Lincoln had a passion for learning. He only had one year of formal schooling, but he would walk for miles to borrow books to teach himself math, science, and law.

Your screen should now look like the one shown in Figure 2-10. Different monitors can fit different amounts of text on each line, so don't worry if your screen doesn't look exactly like the figure.

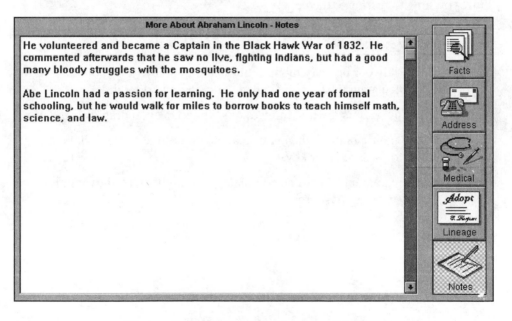

Figure 2-10. Notes for Abraham Lincoln

Changing Text

You may want to change your notes after entering them. In the following steps, you'll make a simple textual change and find that Family Tree Maker automatically reformats your notes for you.

1. Move the mouse pointer in front the of the "l" in "learning" and then click the primary (left) mouse button so that the flashing cursor appears in front of the word "learning."

   The word "learning" is in the first line of the second paragraph.

2. Type **knowledge**

3. Press ⌷delete⌷ until all of "learning" is deleted.

   Family Tree Maker reformats each paragraph for you automatically as you insert or delete words.

Moving Paragraphs

The paragraphs in our example are really in the wrong order. The next few steps show you how to rearrange them.

1. Move the mouse pointer to the beginning of the second paragraph, in front of the "A" in "Abe."

2. Press and hold your primary mouse button and then drag the mouse down to the end of the paragraph. This is called "clicking and dragging."

   Notice that characters are highlighted, or **selected**, as you drag over them.

3. Release the mouse button when you're at the end of the paragraph, being careful not to press another key.

   The second paragraph should be completely highlighted, as shown in Figure 2-11. If it isn't, start over from step 1.

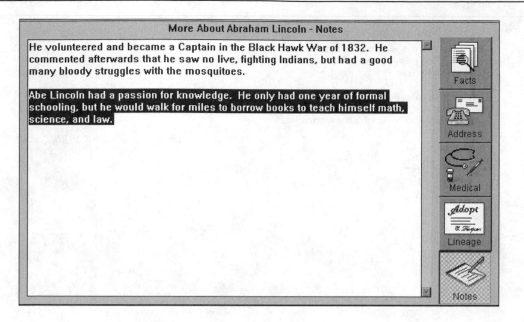

Figure 2-11. A highlighted, or *selected*, paragraph

4. From the **Edit** menu, select **Cut**.

   The paragraph disappears from the screen, but it's not gone. It's in a temporary storage place in memory called the **Clipboard**. Using **Paste**, you can insert the paragraph back into your notes wherever you like.

5. Move the cursor to the beginning of the first paragraph by clicking in front of the "H" in "He."

6. Press ⌜Enter⌐⌐⌍ twice to make space for the paragraph you're about to paste in.

7. Press ⌜↑⌍ twice to move the cursor to the top of the screen.

8. From the **Edit** menu, select **Paste**.

   Family Tree Maker now pastes the paragraph from the Clipboard into your notes as shown in Figure 2-12. In a few simple steps, you moved an entire paragraph from the end of your notes to the beginning.

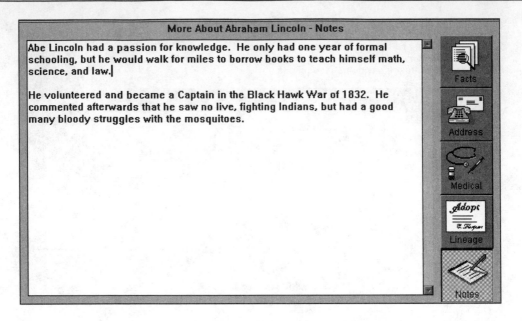

Figure 2-12. Abraham's newly arranged Notes dialog box

Printing Your Notes

Before you begin this set of steps, make sure that the Notes dialog box with
Abraham Lincoln's notes is still on your screen.

1. Adjust the paper so that the print head is at the top of the page.

    Ignore this step if you have a paper tray (as most laser printers do), sheet
    feeder, or plotter.

2. Turn on your printer.

3. From the **File** menu, select **Print Notes**.

    Family Tree Maker displays the Print dialog box.

4. Click **OK** to begin printing your notes.

    The printer starts printing; in a few moments you'll have a printed copy of
    your notes about Abraham Lincoln. You're now done entering lengthy text
    for Abraham, so you can return to his Family Page.

5. From the **View** menu, select **Family Page**.

    Family Tree Maker returns you to the Family Page.

PART III: SCRAPBOOKS

Each individual and each marriage in your Family File has a **Scrapbook**. You can store any type of electronic information, such as scanned pictures or other scanned memorabilia; sound clips, video clips, and OLE objects such as word processor documents; and even Kodak Photo CD pictures in these Scrapbooks. Each item that you place into a Scrapbook is called a **Picture/Object**. With Scrapbooks, you can create a wonderful collection of memories about each of your family members!

In this section you'll learn how to insert a picture into a Scrapbook. You'll also find out how to tell Family Tree Maker to print Pictures/objects in trees and other Family Tree Maker documents.

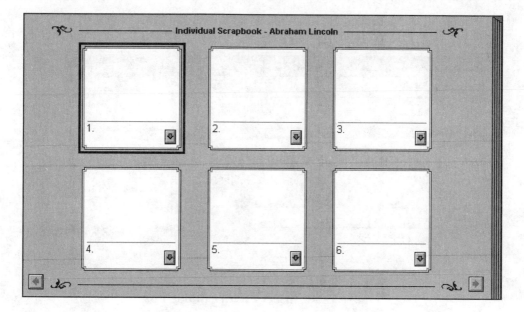

Figure 2-13. An empty Scrapbook page

Placing an Item in a Scrapbook

There are five different ways to place items into a Scrapbook. Each of these methods is described later in the manual, but for now, you'll just use the Insert Picture command to insert a picture of Abraham Lincoln that we have provided. You'll begin by opening Abraham Lincoln's Scrapbook. Make sure that you are on Abraham Lincoln's Family Page and that the cursor is on his name.

1. From the **View** menu, select **Scrapbook**.

   Family Tree Maker displays Abraham Lincoln's Scrapbook. Since there are no items in Abraham Lincoln's Scrapbook, the Scrapbook opens to the first page with the first empty Picture/Object area selected.

2. From the **Picture/Object** menu, select **Insert Picture from File**.

   Family Tree Maker displays the Insert Picture dialog box.

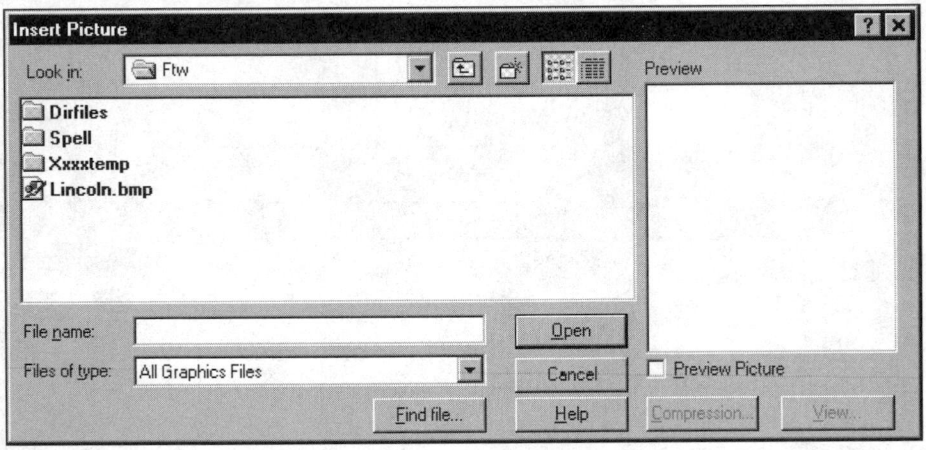

Figure 2-14. Insert Picture dialog box

3. Click the **Look in** drop-down list and select **C:** as the drive.

    If you installed Family Tree Maker on a drive other than drive C, then select that drive.

    In the box below the "Look in" field, Family Tree Maker displays a list of all the files and folders on the selected drive.

4. Double-click the **FTW** folder.

    If you installed Family Tree Maker in a folder other than "FTW," select that folder instead.

    Family Tree Maker displays a list of all the graphic files in the selected folder.

5. In the box below the "Look in" field, click **lincoln** to select it.

6. Click **Open**.

    Family Tree Maker displays the Edit Picture dialog box (see Figure 2-16). In this dialog box you can rotate, flip, or crop your picture before you place it into the Scrapbook (see "Editing a Picture" in this chapter).

    Note: If you want to edit a picture, this is the best time to do it. This is because Family Tree Maker compresses images for storage.

Editing a Picture

You can rotate, flip, and crop pictures. Rotating a picture lets you turn it in the right direction when it's facing the wrong way. Flipping allows you to turn your picture around if it's backwards. Cropping lets you select a portion of a picture to place in your Scrapbook. Now you'll crop the picture that you just brought into Family Tree Maker.

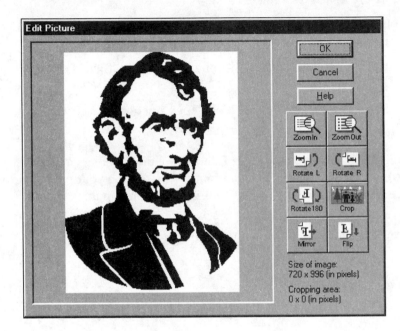

Figure 2-15. The Edit Picture dialog box

1. Position the cross-hair (large plus sign) over the exact spot where you want the top left corner of the cropped picture to be.

2. Press and hold the primary mouse button while you drag diagonally to the exact spot where you want the lower right corner of the cropped picture to be, then release the mouse button.

    The area of the picture that remains after the picture is cropped has a box around it. If you do not like the position of the box, simply repeat steps 2 and 3 to create a new box.

3. When you have a box around the area of the picture that you want to keep, click Crop.

Family Tree Maker deletes the part of the picture that you chose to crop off, and shows you a sample of the cropped picture. If you want to remove even more of the original picture, repeat steps 2, 3, and 4.

4. Click **OK**.

   Family Tree Maker permanently crops the picture and places the new cropped version in the Scrapbook.

As you can see, when you place a picture in a Scrapbook, Family Tree Maker displays a miniature (thumbnail) version of it. However, you can always display the picture at full size by double-clicking it. You can also print pictures in trees, Family Group Sheets, on labels and cards, and more. "The More About Picture/Object Dialog Box" section below, explains more about printing pictures.

The More About Picture/Object Dialog Box

After you insert an item into the Scrapbook, you should use the More About Picture/Object dialog box to create a caption for it and to tell Family Tree Maker in which documents you want the picture to print. (An item that has been inserted into the Scrapbook is called a **Picture/Object**.)

1. Select the Picture/Object by clicking it once.

2. From the **Picture/Object** menu, select **More About**. You can also open the More About Picture/Object dialog box by pressing [Ctrl] + [M].

   Family Tree Maker displays the More About Picture/Object dialog box.

3. Click the **Caption** field and type `Abraham Lincoln`

   This caption appears on the Scrapbook page beneath the Picture/Object after you click **OK**. (But don't click **OK** yet.)

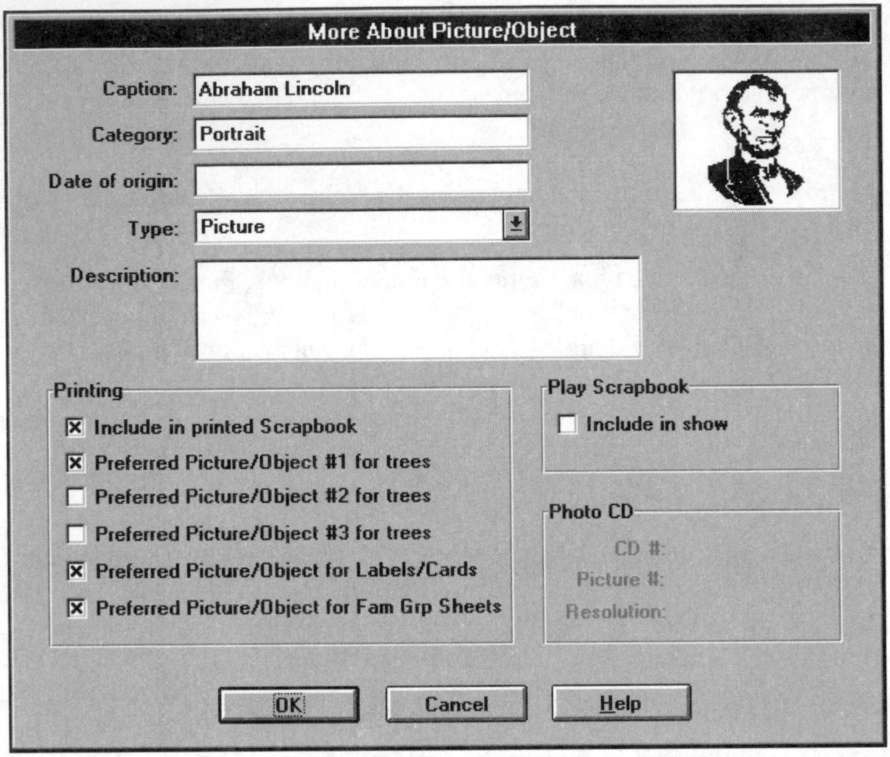

Figure 2-16. The More About Picture/Object dialog box

4. Click in the **Category** field and type `Portrait`

   Make sure to fill in this field for each item that you place in the Scrapbook. You can create as many different categories as you like, but it is important to place similar photos in the same category. Categories are useful when it's time to print or search for a Picture/Object. For example, if you wanted to look at all of the Pictures/Objects related to birthdays and you had given all of the family birthday Pictures/Objects the category "Birthday," you'd be able to locate the birthday pictures easily.

   When photos are in the same category, it's also easy to include them as a group in a document. For example, if you wanted to print a tree that contained each individual's picture and each individual had a picture in the "Portrait" category, you could easily print a tree that had a portrait in each individual's box.

5. In the **Type** field Family Tree Maker has already selected **Picture**.

   This field is used to identify what the Picture/Object is. For example, it could be a picture or sound clip. Family Tree Maker automatically identifies the items that it recognizes. Otherwise, it enters "Unknown" into the field and allows you to choose from the drop-down list.

   Make sure to complete this field for each item that you place in a Scrapbook. You need this information when you print or search for a Picture/Object.

6. Click the **Description** field and type the following: `Portrait of Abraham Lincoln`.

   You can use this field to describe your Pictures/Objects more thoroughly than you can in the "Caption" field.

7. Notice that Family Tree Maker has already selected the **Include in Printed Scrapbook** check box.

   When you select this check box, Family Tree Maker includes this Picture/Object in printed Scrapbooks. If you don't want a particular Picture/Object to appear in printed Scrapbooks, make sure this check box is not selected in its More About Picture/Object dialog box.

8. Select the **Include in Show** check box.

   Family Tree Maker can display the items in a Scrapbook on the screen sequentially, similar to a slide show. When you select this check box, Family Tree Maker includes this Picture/Object when you play the Scrapbook. See "Playing a Scrapbook" in Chapter 5.

9. Make sure that the **Preferred Picture/Object #1 for trees** check box is already selected.

   The "Preferred Pictures/Objects for trees" check boxes make it easier for you to select Pictures/Objects when you print trees. You use these check boxes to select the three Pictures/Objects that you are most likely to print for an individual.

   For example, if you pick each individual's birthday photo as the "Preferred Picture/Object #1 for trees" and tell Family Tree Maker to include "Preferred Picture/Object #1 for trees" when you print a tree, the tree would contain each individual's birthday photo.

Please note that for each Scrapbook, you can only designate one Picture/Object as the "Preferred Picture/Object #1 for trees." The same holds for "Preferred Picture/Object #2 for trees" and so on.

If you want to include more than three Pictures/Objects in a tree, you can use Categories, described in step four, when it is time to print.

10. Select both the **Preferred Picture/Object for Labels/Cards** check box and the **Preferred Picture/Object for Fam Grp Sheets** check box.

The same rules apply to "Preferred Picture/Object for Labels/Cards" and "Preferred Picture/Object for Fam Grp Sheets" as for "Preferred Picture/Object for trees," described in the previous step. However, you can designate only one Picture/Object for each of them.

11. Click **OK**.

Family Tree Maker returns you to the Scrapbook view.

12. From the **View** menu, select **Family Page** to go to Lincoln's Family Page.

If you plan to use Scrapbooks, look at the second half of Chapter 5 (starting with "Scrapbooks: The Basics") for more information about how to edit, play, and insert items into Scrapbooks. Displaying Scrapbook pages is described in Chapter 8.

PART IV: PRINTING A FAMILY TREE

You've entered information about several of Abraham Lincoln's family members, so now you can display and print his family tree. If this were your own family tree, you'd probably want to add more information.

You may remember from the introduction to this manual that Family Tree Maker can create several types of trees: Ancestor trees, Descendant trees, Hourglass trees, and All-in-One trees. Family Tree Maker creates these trees using **views**. You enter your family information once, and Family Tree Maker uses views to display your information in different ways. For example, when you want an Ancestor tree, Family Tree Maker displays your information in the Ancestor tree view. Or, when you want a Descendant tree, Family Tree Maker displays your information in the Descendant tree view. All of the tree views are listed on the View menu.

Changing Views

In this section, you'll first look at a Descendant tree to give you more practice changing views. Then, you'll look at an Ancestor tree and print it.

Right now your Family Page should show Abraham Lincoln in the "Husband" field. If you are not on Abraham Lincoln's Family Page, go to the Index of Individuals, find Abraham Lincoln (the one who was born in 1809), and then go to his Family Page (if you aren't sure how to do this, see "Lincoln's Maternal Grandparents' Family Page" and Figure 2-7, in this chapter).

Make sure that the cursor is on Lincoln's name. By placing the cursor on Lincoln's name, you are making him the **primary individual**. The primary individual in a family tree is the main person in the tree. For example, if you are creating a Descendant tree, the primary individual is at the very top of the tree, and the tree shows the primary individual's descendants.

To display Abraham's Descendant tree:

1. From the **View** menu, select **Descendant Tree**. From the submenu, select **Standard**.

   Family Tree Maker displays a standard Descendant tree on your screen. At the top of the tree there are boxes containing information about Abraham Lincoln and his wife, Mary. Beneath them are boxes containing information about each of their four children. You could also have chosen to see this same information displayed in a fan style. We'll do that next.

2. From the **View** menu, select **Descendant Tree**. From the submenu, select **Fan**.

   Family Tree Maker displays the "same" tree, only now the boxes are arranged in a fan style instead of the standard vertical style. Ancestor, descendant, and hourglass trees all have the fan option.

3. From the **View** menu, select **Zoom**, and then select the **Actual Size** option button from the dialog box that Family Tree Maker displays.

   Family Tree Maker shows Abraham's Descendant tree at Actual Size. Using the Zoom command does *not* change the size of your tree when you print.

   You can use the scroll bars that are along the bottom and right side of your tree to move around and look at different parts of the tree. When you're through looking at the tree, move on to the next step.

4. Now, to see someone else's Descendant tree, choose a different primary individual. From the **View** menu, select **Index of Individuals**.

Family Tree Maker displays the Index of Individuals.

5. Click **Nancy Hanks**, and then click **OK**.

Family Tree Maker displays a Descendant tree showing the descendants of Nancy Hanks and Thomas Lincoln. If you want to print the tree, you would do it from here, but instead, you'll print an Ancestor tree.

Displaying an Ancestor Tree

To display an Ancestor tree for President Lincoln, you need to make him the primary individual again and then switch to the Ancestor Tree view. You could find President Lincoln just by going to the Index of Individuals and clicking on his name, but this is a good opportunity to try out Quick Search.

To find someone with a Quick Search:

1. From the **View** menu, select **Index of Individuals**.

Family Tree Maker displays the Index of Individuals. Notice that there is a flashing cursor in the "Name" field at the top of the screen. Use this field to do your search.

2. Type **Lincoln, Abraham**

Notice that you type his last name first. With each character you type, Family Tree Maker moves the highlight closer to the name you want to find. It stops on the first Abraham Lincoln, the President's grandfather (see Figure 2-17).

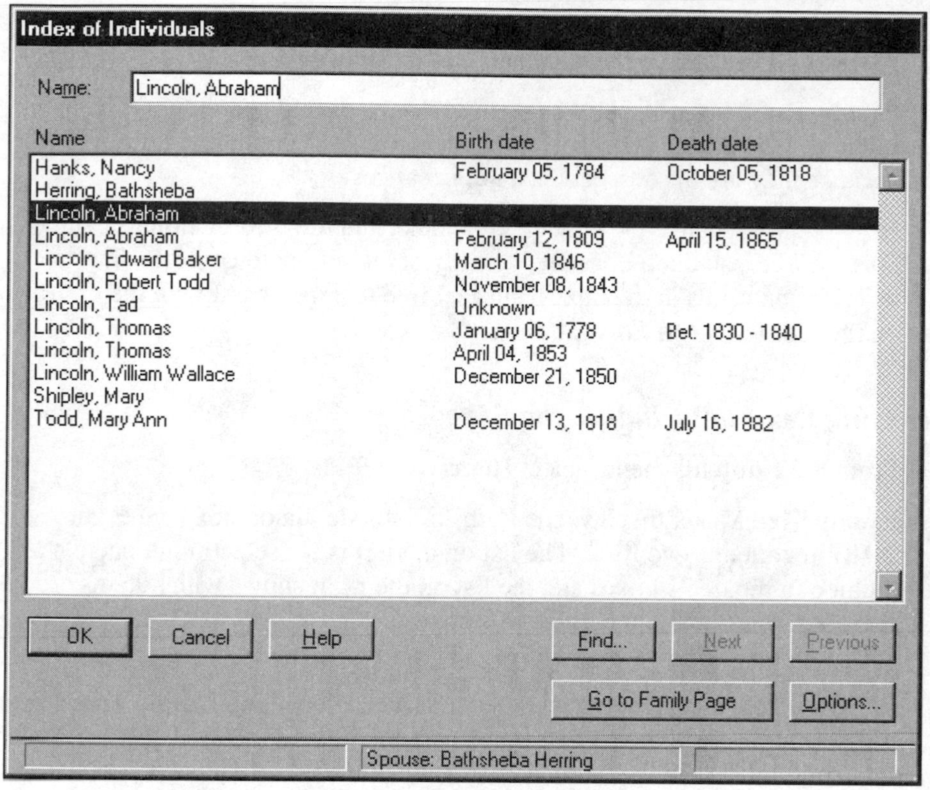

Index of Individuals

Name: Lincoln, Abraham

Name	Birth date	Death date
Hanks, Nancy	February 05, 1784	October 05, 1818
Herring, Bathsheba		
Lincoln, Abraham		
Lincoln, Abraham	February 12, 1809	April 15, 1865
Lincoln, Edward Baker	March 10, 1846	
Lincoln, Robert Todd	November 08, 1843	
Lincoln, Tad	Unknown	
Lincoln, Thomas	January 06, 1778	Bet. 1830 - 1840
Lincoln, Thomas	April 04, 1853	
Lincoln, William Wallace	December 21, 1850	
Shipley, Mary		
Todd, Mary Ann	December 13, 1818	July 16, 1882

OK   Cancel   Help   Find...   Next   Previous

Go to Family Page   Options...

Spouse: Bathsheba Herring

Figure 2-17. Quick Search in the Index of Individuals

3. Press ⬇ once to highlight the President.

4. Click **OK**.

Family Tree Maker displays a Descendant tree with Abraham Lincoln as the primary individual. Why does it display a Descendant tree? Because the Descendant Tree view is the view that you were in before you changed to the Index of Individuals view. When you're in the Index of Individuals, clicking OK returns you to the view that you were in before you opened the Index of Individuals. The name you highlight in the Index of Individuals is the name you see when you return to the previous view.

5. Now you want to see an Ancestor tree, so from the **View** menu, select **Ancestor Tree**. From the submenu, select **Standard**.

Family Tree Maker displays a standard Ancestor tree containing Abraham Lincoln, his parents, and his grandparents. His children are not in this tree because they are his descendants, not his ancestors.

Now you can change the way the tree looks and the information it includes to create a tree you like. For now, you'll just learn how to control what information prints in the boxes, but feel free to experiment with the options on the **Contents** and **Format** menus!

Selecting Items to Include in the Boxes

1. From the **Contents** menu, select **Items to Include**.

Family Tree Maker displays the Items to Include dialog box (see Figure 2-18); it contains two lists. The list on the left is for selecting items to include in the tree's boxes and the list on the right shows which items are currently selected to be in the tree's boxes.

The items that are currently selected are Name, Birth date and location, Marriage date and location, and Death date and location. Family Tree Maker uses examples to give you an idea of how the items will print. For example, the item that says "First Middle Last" tells you that individuals' complete names will print. If it just said "First Last," you would know that middle names wouldn't print. Family Tree Maker does the same thing with dates.

Just for practice, you'll remove some items from Abraham's tree.

2. Click the death date item in the list on the right. Unless you previously chose a different format, it says **d: Date in Location**.

```
┌─────────────────────────────────────────────────────────────────┐
│ Items to Include in Ancestor Tree                                 │
│  Available items:                    The boxes in your tree contain these items: │
│ ┌──────────────────────────┐ ┌───┐  ┌──────────────────────────┐ │
│ │Name                    ▲│ │ > │  │First Middle Last (aka)   │ │
│ │aka                      │ └───┘  │b: Date in Location       │ │
│ │Birth date/location      │ ┌───┐  │m: Date in Location       │ │
│ │Marriage date/location   │ │ < │  │d: Date in Location       │ │
│ │Death date/location      │ └───┘  │                          │ │
│ │Picture/Object           │ ┌───┐  │                          │ │
│ │Adoption                 │ │ << │  │                          │ │
│ │Age at birth of first child│ └───┘  │                          │ │
│ │Age at birth of last child│        │                          │ │
│ │Age at death             │        │                          │ │
│ │Age at first marriage    │ ┌───────┐│                          │ │
│ │Baptism                  │ │ Font... ││                          │ │
│ │Bar Mitzvah              │ └───────┘│                          │ │
│ │Bas Mitzvah              │ ┌───────┐│                          │ │
│ │Blessing                 │ │Options...││                         │ │
│ │Burial                   │ └───────┘│                          │ │
│ │Caste                    │ ┌───────┐│                          │ │
│ │Cause of death         ▼│ │Move up ││                          │ │
│ └──────────────────────────┘ └───────┘│                          │ │
│                              ┌────────┐│                          │ │
│                              │Move down││                         │ │
│                              └────────┘└──────────────────────────┘ │
│      ┌──────┐      ┌────────┐      ┌──────┐                       │
│      │  OK  │      │ Cancel │      │ Help │                       │
│      └──────┘      └────────┘      └──────┘                       │
└─────────────────────────────────────────────────────────────────┘
```

Figure 2-18. The Items to Include dialog box

3.   Click ☐ (Remove).

   This removes that item from *all* the boxes in the Ancestor tree. Now, select a new item to include: each individual's age at death.

4.   In the list on the left, click **Age at death**.

5.   Click ☐ (Include).

   Family Tree Maker displays the Options: Age at Death dialog box.

6.   Make some formatting selections and then click **OK**.

   Family Tree Maker moves "Age at death" into the list on the right.

Now you're going to change the format of one of the items that you already included in the boxes of Abraham's tree: each individual's name.

1.   Click **First Middle Last (aka)** in the list on the right.

   Family Tree Maker highlights the item.

2.   Click **Options**.

   Family Tree Maker displays the Options: Name dialog box shown in Figure 2-19.

3. Click the **Format** drop-down list and select **First Last**.

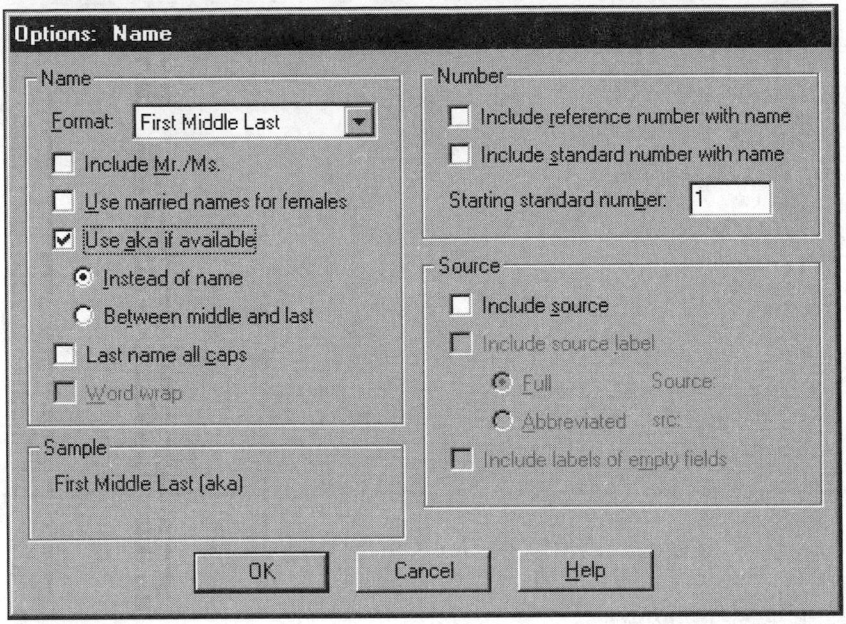

Figure 2-19. The Options: Name dialog box

As you can see, there are other format options you can choose to format the Name item. For now, you'll change just this one.

4. Click **OK**.

Family Tree Maker displays the Items to Include dialog box with the newly-selected name format displayed in the list on the right.

5. You can include many more items in a tree, but for now, click **OK**.

Family Tree Maker returns you to the Ancestor Tree view with the items you just selected shown in your tree.

Printing a Tree

Now, to print Abraham's tree:

1. Adjust the paper so that the print head is at the top of the page.

    Ignore this step if you have a paper tray (as most laser printers do), sheet feeder, or plotter.

2. Turn on your printer.

3. From the **File** menu, select **Print Ancestor Tree**.

    Family Tree Maker displays the Print Ancestor Tree dialog box.

4. Click **OK** to begin printing your tree.

Saving Information in Family Tree Maker

You may think that it's about time to save your information, but with Family Tree Maker, you don't have to. Family Tree Maker is a database program, so it automatically saves your information while you are working. You won't even notice that it's happening. Family Tree Maker also saves your information right before you quit.

While Family Tree Maker doesn't have a Save command, it does have a Backup command. This command makes a copy of your Family File to store in a safe place. You can also make a second copy of your Family File on your hard disk, so it's easy to go back to this copy if something goes wrong. You'll want to use this command frequently — perhaps each time you use the program (see "Backing Up Your Family File" in Chapter 13).

Quitting Family Tree Maker

When you finish using Family Tree Maker, you need to quit the program. Never shut off your computer before quitting Family Tree Maker.

To quit Family Tree Maker:

1. From the **File** menu, select **Exit**.

    Family Tree Maker saves your information and then closes the program.

2. If you're done using your computer, click the Windows **Start** button, select **Shut Down**, select the **Shut down the computer** option button, and wait for the message that tells you it is safe to turn off the computer.

What to Do Next

To learn more about Family Tree Maker, skim through the rest of this manual. We encourage you to go through all the menus again, particularly the Format and Contents menus from within a tree view. There are many more options to choose from when creating and printing a tree.

Chapter 3

ENTERING BASIC INFORMATION

Ninfa Corona de Garcia on her wedding day in El Chante (Municipio de Autlan), Jalisco, Mexico. Today her niece, Claudia Miyar, is the Lead Quality Assurance Engineer for Family Tree Maker.

ENTERING BASIC INFORMATION

The first step in creating trees and reports is to enter information about your family as described in this chapter. (Chapters 8, 9, and 10 describe how to display, customize, and print the information you've entered.)

A QUICK OVERVIEW

To enter basic family information, such as names and birth dates, you fill out an electronic "page," called a Family Page (see Figure 3-1 on the next page). It is the first screen that you see after you open a Family File. Each nuclear family (two parents and their children) has its own Family Page.

You can add more details about each family member by filling out a series of **More About** dialog boxes. You can also store pictures, video clips, sound clips, and other OLE objects in each individual's Scrapbook. These are described in Chapter 5.

From time to time as you're entering information, Family Tree Maker will automatically save the information in your Family File. Your Family File is where all of the family information that you enter into Family Tree Maker is stored. You should not create a new Family File for every Family Page that you fill out.

Since Family Tree Maker saves your information automatically, you don't have to. However, as you add to your Family Files, you will want to regularly make a backup copy on a new floppy diskette (or other removable media) that you store in a safe place. If your Family Files are accidentally deleted or damaged, you can then use your backup copy and you won't have to rebuild your files from scratch. To learn how to back up your Family Files, see "Backing Up Your Family File" in Chapter 13.

While you're learning to use Family Tree Maker, don't be afraid to experiment. If you get lost, you can press F1 at any time to get on-screen Help.

THE FAMILY PAGE

The Family Page is a view that shows all the members of a nuclear family: two parents and their children. This is the main **view** for entering information about your family. In Family Tree Maker, a "view" is a way of looking at information. For example, when you look at information on a Family Page, you are looking at the Family Page view. If you choose to display that same information as a Descendant tree, we say that you are looking at the Descendant Tree view. We'll talk about moving between views later in the manual. In this chapter, we'll just describe how to enter information in the Family Page.

Family Tree Maker shows only one Family Page on the screen at a time, but your Family File can hold many Family Pages, just like a photo album can have many pages. In Chapter 4, "Moving Around," we'll show you how to move between different Family Pages.

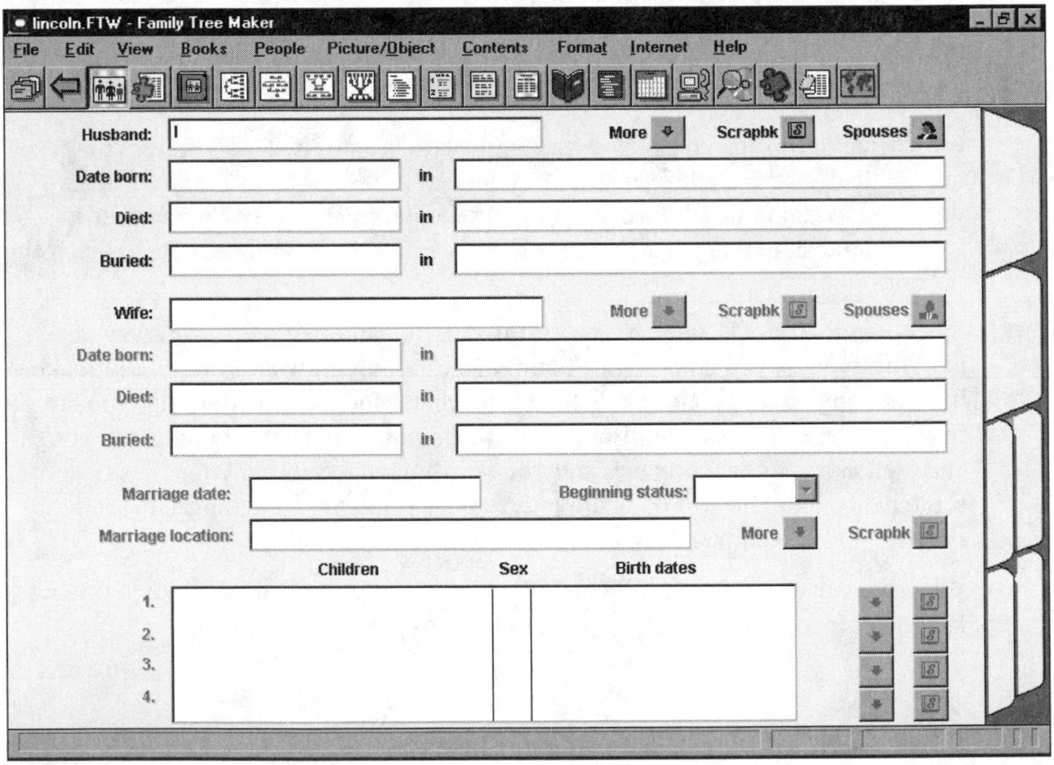

Figure 3-1. An empty Family Page

The row of words across the top of the screen is the set of menus that you'll be using. This is called the **menu bar**. When you click one of the words on the menu bar, such as "Edit," a list of commands appears below it. This list is called a **pull-down menu**. You will choose items from the menu bar and pull-down menus to do things such as edit your information and print family trees.

Below the menu bar is the **toolbar**. It contains buttons that you can click to display different views or to open dialog boxes, depending on which buttons are available.

Entering Family Information

When you start a new Family File, the Family Page appears blank as it does in Figure 3-1. It is ready for you to begin entering family information.

A Family Page is just like a paper form. It consists of labeled blanks to fill with information. The blanks are called fields and the labels that describe the blanks are called field labels. Right now, the fields have conventional labels, such as "Husband," "Wife," and "Children." You can change some of these labels if you want to. See "Preferences for Labels," on the next page.

You type information into the fields and then move from field to field using Tab 🔄, Enter 🄴, the cursor keys 🔽 and 🔼, or by clicking fields with your mouse pointer. To save typing time, you can also copy and paste information from one field to another. See "Cutting, Copying, and Pasting" in this chapter for more information.

Some fields only allow you to enter certain kinds of information. For example, sex fields only allow you to enter an "M," "F," or a question mark. You can try to enter something else, but Family Tree Maker will catch it and ask you to fill in the field appropriately. Family Tree Maker can also catch conflicting information that you enter. For example, if you enter a child's birth date that is prior to the mother's birth date, Family Tree Maker will catch this conflict. To turn this type of error checking on and off, see "Data Entry Checking Preferences" in this chapter.

Some fields are "Fastfields." Fastfields help you enter your information into Family Tree Maker more quickly by remembering the words that you type most often. We'll describe Fastfields in "Fastfields" later in this chapter.

Preferences for Labels

Changing field labels is useful if you want your Family Tree Maker records to match other genealogical records that you have. You can change a variety of labels on the Family Page and in the Facts and Marriage dialog boxes (see "Entering Facts" in Chapter 5). You can also change the abbreviations for estimated dates (see "Preferences for Dates and Measures," in this chapter).

To change field labels:

1. From the **File** menu, select **Preferences**. From the submenu, select **Labels**.

   Family Tree Maker displays the Labels dialog box (see Figure 3-2).

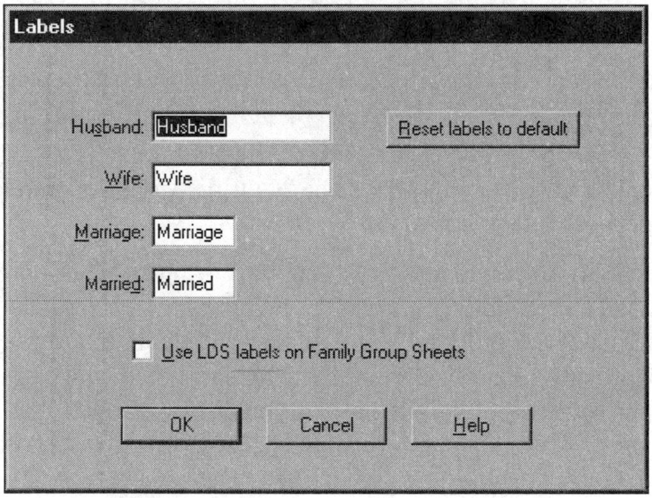

Figure 3-2. The Labels dialog box

2. Type over the old labels with your new, preferred labels.

3. If you want your Family Group Sheets to conform to LDS standards, select **Use LDS labels on Family Group Sheets**. For details, see "LDS Ordinance Information" in the on-screen Help.

4. After you make your changes, click **OK**.

If you later decide that you want to restore the field labels to their default values, select **Reset labels to default**.

Preferences for Sorting the Facts Page

Family Tree Maker allows you to sort the facts displayed in your More About Facts page by either the fact name or date.

To choose the sorting options for the Facts page:

1. From the **File** menu, select **Preferences**. Then, from the submenu, select **Facts**.

   Family Tree Maker displays the Facts Page preferences dialog box.

2. Make your selection to sort either by **Fact name**, or by **Date**.

3. After you make your selection, click **OK**.

   Family Tree Maker closes the dialog box.

Data Entry Checking Preferences

Family Tree Maker can help you minimize mistakes in your Family File by examining information as you enter it in Family Pages. For example, Family Tree Maker will compare a child's birth date with his mother's death date to make sure that the child was born before the mother died. If Family Tree Maker finds questionable information, it will display a dialog box that gives you the option to correct the information. For a complete list of the errors that Family Tree Maker can identify, see "Data Errors Report" in Chapter 6.

Family Tree Maker can also examine the information that's already in your Family File. See "Checking Your File for Errors" in Chapter 6 for more information about other methods of checking for errors.

To turn on the error checking options:

1. From the **File** menu, select **Preferences**. From the submenu, select **Error Checking**.

    Family Tree Maker displays the Error Checking dialog box.

2. Select the check boxes for the types of errors that you want Family Tree Maker to look for.

3. After you make your selections, click **OK**.

    Family Tree Maker closes the dialog box.

Moving the Cursor

The fastest way to move around the Family Page is to move the mouse pointer to the fields where you want to type and then click the primary mouse button. You can also use your computer keyboard to move the cursor around the Family Page. Figure 3-3 shows which keys work as navigational keys.

Press this key...	To do this...
[↑]	Move the cursor to the field above the current field
[↓]	Move the cursor to the field below the current field
[←]	Move the cursor one character to the left
[→]	Move the cursor one character to the right
[⇄] (tab)	Move the cursor to the next field
[⇧ Shift] + [⇄]	Move the cursor to the previous field
[home]	Move the cursor to the beginning of the current field
[end]	Move the cursor to the end of the current field
[Enter ↵]	Move the cursor to the next field
[Ctrl] + [←]	Move the cursor to the previous word
[Ctrl] + [→]	Move the cursor to the next word
[Ctrl] + [home]	Move the cursor to the husband, or if in the "Children" list, move to the first child
[Ctrl] + [end]	Move to the first empty row in the "Children" list
[PgUp]	Move up through the list of children
[PgDn]	Move down through the list of children

Figure 3-3. Keys for moving the cursor on the Family Page

Editing Information

Family Tree Maker has the same basic editing commands that most other Windows programs have: Cut, Copy, Paste, and Undo. You can cut, copy, and paste any text in Family Tree Maker, including dates, locations, causes of death, notes, and telephone numbers. These commands make it easy to move information around and can help you avoid manual deleting and retyping.

When you cut text, you remove it from its original location. You can then place the text in another location with the Paste command. When you copy text, you leave the text in its original location, and then you place a copy of it in another location with the Paste command.

Note: You should NOT cut and paste an individual's name. Cutting an individual's name DOES NOT delete that individual. To delete someone, use the Delete Individual command (see "Removing an Individual from Your Family File" in chapter 6). Cutting and pasting an individual's name DOES NOT move that individual to another location. To move an individual and all of the information associated with that individual, use the Detach and Attach commands, described in "Changing Relationships in Your Family File" in Chapter 6.

Cutting, Copying, and Pasting

To cut and paste or copy and paste text in Family Tree Maker:

1. Highlight the text that you want to cut or copy.

   To highlight text with a mouse, place the mouse pointer in front of the first character you want to select. Press and hold the primary mouse button while you drag the mouse until the last character you want to select is highlighted. Then, release the mouse button.

2. From the **Edit** menu, select either **Cut Text** or **Copy Text**.

   The text (or a copy of it if you are copying the text) is placed in a temporary storage place called the **Clipboard**. You can use the Paste command to insert the contents of the Clipboard wherever you like.

3. Place the cursor where you want to paste the information. If you want to *replace* a section of existing text with the information that you've just copied or cut, highlight the text that you want to replace.

4. From the **Edit** menu, select **Paste**.

   Family Tree Maker inserts the text or pastes it over the selected text. Since the Clipboard is not erased until you use the Copy or Cut command again, you can paste the same text as many times as you like.

Reversing a Command

Using Undo, you can reverse the very last editing command that you performed. For example, if you cut some text, selecting Undo right away will restore it.

Note: To reverse an editing command, you must select Undo as the very next command. Otherwise, it will not reverse the command that you want to reverse.

When you select the Edit menu, you may notice that the Undo command says different things at different times. For example, it may say "Undo Paste," or "Undo Copy," to indicate which command it will reverse.

To reverse an editing command:

1. Don't type any new text or perform any other editing commands. If you do, you won't be able to use Undo on the command that you want to reverse.

2. From the **Edit** menu, select **Undo**.

   It doesn't matter where your cursor is — Family Tree Maker will remember what it was that you did last and reverse it.

3. If you want to restore the editing command that you've just reversed, select **Redo** immediately.

   Note: If you accidentally deleted text using the **Cut** command, there is another way to restore it. Simply position your cursor where you wish to replace the text. Then, from the **Edit** menu, select **Paste**.

From time to time you may make a minor mistake when entering information about your family. For example, you may make a spelling error. The following table shows you which keys you can use to edit the information in a field.

Press this key...	To do this...
[←BkSp] (backspace)	Back up and erase the previous character
[ins]	Switch between insert and overwrite modes
[delete]	Delete characters to the right, one by one
[alt] + [←BkSp]	Reverse your last editing command
[Ctrl] + [X]	Cut highlighted text and place it on the Clipboard
[Ctrl] + [C]	Copy highlighted text and place it on the Clipboard
[Ctrl] + [V]	Paste text from the Clipboard to your Family Page
[Ctrl] + [Z]	Undo/Redo the last editing command
[⇥] (tab)	Move the cursor to the next next tab stop or field.
[Enter←]	End a paragraph and move the cursor to the beginning of the next line

Figure 3-4. Editing keys

Entering Names

The "Husband," "Wife," and "Children" fields on the Family Page are where you enter names. The "Husband" and "Wife" fields work as Fastfields (see "Fastfields" in this chapter) for last names. In the "Children" list, Family Tree Maker also automatically inserts the husband's last name after the children's first and middle names. You can type over the name that Family Tree Maker inserts if the children have different last names.

It's always best to enter an individual's full given name, including the middle name (don't use initials). Also, be sure to enter first names first. Nicknames should be entered in the Lineage dialog box (see "Entering Nicknames, Titles, and Parental Relationship Information" in Chapter 5). In addition, when entering a woman's name, always use her maiden name (her name before she was married). "Name" fields can hold up to 48 characters.

Note: You can *print* names differently from the way you enter them. For example, you can print last names first or split names onto two lines. You also have the option of printing women with married names instead of maiden names or printing everyone's nicknames instead of given names. However, to print names in different ways, you must enter them completely (first, middle, and last name), with nicknames in the Lineage dialog box, and then let Family Tree Maker do the hard work for you.

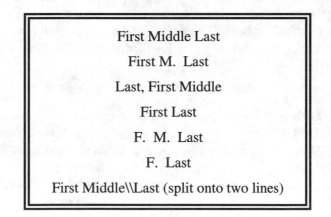

First Middle Last

First M. Last

Last, First Middle

First Last

F. M. Last

F. Last

First Middle\\Last (split onto two lines)

Figure 3-5. Some of the name formats Family Tree Maker can create

Nicknames — It's quite acceptable to include nicknames in your Family File. To enter them, use the Lineage dialog box (see "Entering Nicknames, Titles, and Parental Relationship Information" in Chapter 5).

> **Note:** For individuals who have a two-name first name, such as Betty Jo, or Bobby Lee, type "**Betty**⌨️**0160Jo**" or "**Bobby**⌨️**0160Lee**" in the name field. This is a special code number that allows Family Tree Maker to recognize that these two names behave as one.
>
> While holding down the "**Alt**" key, the number sequence **0160** must be entered on the *numeric keypad* — not with the numbers on the normal keyboard. You will not see these characters display as you type them, but you will see the space appear automatically when you release the "**Alt**" key.

Name changes — Any name changes should also be entered in the Lineage dialog box (see "Entering Nicknames, Titles, and Parental Relationship Information" in Chapter 5). For example, if "Johann Smythe" changed his name to "John Smith," you could enter "Johann Smythe" as his name on the Family Page and record the fact that he was also known as "John Smith" in the Lineage dialog box.

Unusual last names — Family Tree Maker can usually tell the last name from other parts of an individual's name. However, if at some point you notice that it has incorrectly identified someone's last name, place the entire last name between backslash characters. The backslash characters will not appear in any printed documents. In the example below, Family Tree Maker interprets the last name as "Irish Hess."

```
Constance \Irish Hess\
```

Last names with suffixes — If a suffix is attached to the last name (for example, "Jr." or, "Ph.D.") be sure to separate it from the last name with a comma (John Smith, Jr.). The comma lets Family Tree Maker know that the suffix is not the last name. This way, the name will appear under the correct letter of the alphabet in the Index of Individuals and other alphabetized lists. You don't need to use commas with Roman numerals, unless the number is greater than eight.

Missing last names — In some cultures, last names aren't used. To show that an individual has no last name, place two backslash characters together without a space between them at the end of the name. The backslash characters will not appear in any printed documents. In this example, the individual "Running Bear" has no last name.

```
Running Bear\\
```

Titles — Do not enter titles such as "Mr.," "Mrs.," or "Dr." on the Family Page. You can use the Titles dialog box described below, to select titles such as "Mr." or "Mrs." for most of the individuals in your Family File. For anyone with a special title, such as "Dr." or "Reverend," see the description of the Lineage dialog box (see "Entering Nicknames, Titles, and Parental Relationship Information" in Chapter 5).

Preferences for Titles

When you display or print Family Tree Maker trees, reports, and other views, you can choose to include titles, such as "Mr." and "Mrs.," in front of people's names. You can select default titles for most of the people in your Family File in the Titles dialog box, described below. If anyone in your Family File uses another title, such as "Dr." or "Reverend," enter that title in the Lineage dialog box (see "Entering Nicknames, Titles, and Parental Relationship Information" in Chapter 5).

To change title preferences:

1. From the **File** menu, select **Preferences**. From the submenu, select **Titles**.

   Family Tree Maker displays the Titles dialog box.

2. Make your changes in the Titles dialog box. Each of your options is described below.

   Married Males/Married Females — The title that you type here applies for all men and women who are currently married or have ever been married. The defaults are "Mr." and "Mrs."

   Not married Males/Not married Females — The title that you type here applies for all men and women who have never been married. The defaults are "Mr." and "Ms."

Children Males/Children Females — Any title that you type applies for all children. The default is to have no title.

Children are individuals younger than X years old — All individuals under the age that you type in this field have the "Children" title. All individuals this age and over have either the "Married" or "Not married" title. The default age is 13.

Use defaults — Use this button to reset the titles and the cutoff age to their default values.

3. After you make your changes, click **OK**.

   Family Tree Maker saves your changes.

Entering Dates

The "Date" fields in Family Tree Maker are very smart and flexible and can handle any date after 1/1/100 A.D. You can enter a date almost any way you want, but when you move the cursor out of the field, Family Tree Maker automatically puts the date in a standard format. The first time you use Family Tree Maker, the standard format will be the same as the default format that's selected in your Windows Control Panel. You can change the standard format and even use European formats. See "Preferences for Dates and Measures" in this chapter. "Date" fields can contain up to 49 characters.

There may be events for which you don't know an exact date. Or, you may be certain of the year, but not certain of the day and month. Figure 3-6, on the next page, shows how you can record estimated and partial dates.

You type this…	You get this…
1776	1776
Jul 1776	July 1776
4 Jul	July 4
Est 7/4/1776	Abt. July 4, 1776
Abt 7/4/1776	Abt. July 4, 1776
About 7/4/1776	Abt. July 4, 1776
Circa 7/4/1776	Abt. July 4, 1776
Cir 7/4/1776	Abt. July 4, 1776
Bef 7/4/1776	Bef. July 4, 1776
Before 7/4/1776	Bef. July 4, 1776
Aft 7/4/1776	Aft. July 4, 1776
After 7/4/1776	Aft. July 4, 1776
?	Unknown

Figure 3-6. How to enter estimated dates

Notice that in Figure 3-6, "About" and "Abt." are used to indicate approximate dates. If you like, you can change these words. See "Preferences for Labels" in this chapter to change these labels.

Leaving a date field blank means the event hasn't happened. For example, if someone is not dead, leave the date field for that event blank. If they died, but you don't know the date of death, type a question mark. Entering a question mark means that you know the event happened, but aren't sure when. You can also type "Dead," "Deceased," and "Unknown" in death date fields.

If you merged information from the World Family Tree (see "The World Family Tree Project" in Chapter 12), some date fields may contain the word "Private." This is to protect the privacy of individuals who are still living.

Family Tree Maker also understands date codes used by the Church of Jesus Christ of Latter–day Saints. See the topic "LDS Ordinance Information," in the on-screen Help for details.

Note: If your research uncovers multiple dates or names for the same event, Family Tree Maker allows you to enter the conflicting information (see "Adding Alternate Facts or Names," in Chapter 5).

Double Dates — Family Tree Maker can display double dates to account for the crossover between the Julian and Gregorian calendars. If you enter a date that falls *between* December 31 and March 25 for any year before 1753, a double date will appear.

You can specify a double date by typing both of the years in the field. For example, you can type either Jan 1, 1493/4 or Jan 1, 1493/1494; both display as January 1, 1493/94. If you don't type in both of the years, Family Tree Maker assumes that the year you typed is the second year. For example, if you type January 1, 1494, it's displayed as January 1, 1493/94. See "Double Dates" in the Genealogy "How-To" Guide for more information. If you would like to change the double date cutoff year to something other than 1751, see "Preferences for Dates and Measures" on the next page.

Entering Date Ranges

Sometimes your research will only allow you to narrow down an event or milestone to a probable period of time, rather than a specific date. Family Tree Maker allows you to enter this kind of information, whether it is over a range of days, months, or even years.

Refer to the next section, "Preferences for Dates and Measures" for more about how to successfully enter date ranges.

You type this . . .	You get this . . .
September 3 – 6, 1932	Bet. September 3 – 6, 1932
Bet. Sep 24, 1718 and Oct 1, 1718	Bet. Sep.24 – Oct. 1, 1718
September 1943 to September 1945	Bet. Sep. 1943 – Sep. 1945
Bet. 2/2/1908 and 10/1/1909	Bet. February 2, 1908 – October 1, 1909

Figure 3-7. How to enter date ranges

Preferences for Dates and Measures

In the Dates & Measures dialog box, you can change the double date cutoff year and the standard date format for your date fields. You can also choose between the English and Metric measurement systems.

Figure 3-8, on the next page, lists possible date formats. Use the date format that's most comfortable for you, because it's important not to make mistakes with dates in your family information.

To choose a date format and to select a measurement system:

1. From the **File** menu, select **Preferences**. From the submenu, select **Dates and Measures**.

    Family Tree Maker displays the Dates & Measures dialog box.

2. Select the date format that you want.

   If you don't want to use double dates, type 0 (zero) in the **Double date cutoff year** field.

```
July 4, 1776
Jul 4, 1776
4 July 1776
4 Jul 1776
07.04.1776
04.07.1776
07-4-1776
07/04/1776
```

Figure 3-8. Possible date formats

3. Choose between using the English (inches and feet) or Metric (centimeters and meters) measuring system.

4. Choose the **Prefix** and **Separator** styles you want to use to display date ranges.

5. Choose the **Date Labels** you want.

6. After you make your selections, click **OK**.

   Family Tree Maker saves your changes.

Entering Locations

"Location" fields are for entering an individual's place of birth, death, or marriage (these fields are usually preceded by the field label "in"). Normally, you enter the city and state. You might want to enter the county if it's important.

To conserve space, enter the country name only if it's unusual. For example, if most family members were born in the United States, you would only enter the country for the few relatives who were born outside of the United States.

Note: Your trees will look better if you enter information in a consistent way. For example, either abbreviate states or spell them out. Don't abbreviate in some cases and spell them out in other cases.

Sometimes when Family Tree Maker prints single-page trees, it has limited space for the location fields. If Family Tree Maker needs to abbreviate a location, it will always try to keep the last word in the location field. This means that if you enter a state and a country in each location field, it may print the country, but drop the state. "Location" fields can contain up to 256 characters.

Be sure to put commas between the city, county, state, and country names. Correct punctuation allows Family Tree Maker to abbreviate correctly when it is necessary.

Special Note about Comments/Locations to Display in Maps

When displaying maps, Family Tree Maker looks for comment/location information in the More About Facts and Marriage pages (see "Entering Facts" in Chapter 5). Note that these fields are different from those mentioned above in "Entering Locations."

Fastfields

To help you save time when entering family information, Family Tree Maker has a special feature called Fastfields. Most of the Fastfields in Family Tree Maker are location fields, such as birth location, death location, and marriage location fields, so we'll use locations to explain how Fastfields work.

The Fastfields feature remembers the names of the last 50 locations that you've entered into any location field. This means that when you start typing the name of a town that you've previously typed in a location field, Fastfields automatically fills in the rest of the letters for you.

For example, say that you have typed the following two birth locations into Family Tree Maker: "Abilene, Louisiana" and "Arlington, Virginia." Then, you go to another birth location field and type the letter "A." Fastfields immediately looks for a location, beginning with "A," that you've typed previously. Since "Abilene, Louisiana" is alphabetically the first location beginning with an "A," Fastfields automatically places "Abilene, Louisiana" into the field. If you then type an "r" after the "A," Fastfields replaces "Abilene, Louisiana" with "Arlington, Virginia." If "Arlington, Virginia" isn't the name that you want in that birth location field, you just continue typing the name that you want, such as "Argyle, New York." In short, Fastfields refines its suggestions as you type and quits making suggestions when it no longer has any logical choices to offer.

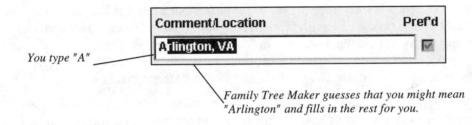

You type "A"

Family Tree Maker guesses that you might mean "Arlington" and fills in the rest for you.

Figure 3-9. Fastfields help you fill some types of fields by guessing at what you are typing. When the guess is wrong, just keep typing.

In addition to location fields, Fastfields work with last names in the "Husband" and "Wife" fields. Also, the first time you type a name in a "Children" list on a Family Page, Family Tree Maker automatically inserts the husband's last name after the child's first name. If the child has a different last name, simply replace the name that Family Tree Maker inserted with the correct name. Any additional children will automatically get the same last name as the first child, although you can change those too, if necessary.

The other fields that work as Fastfields are "Cause of death," "Picture/Object category," "Comment/Location," and "Sources." You'll also find that Fastfields work in the Find Individual feature (see "Locating Individuals in Your Family File" in chapter 4).

If you are not comfortable using Fastfields, you can turn them off. See the next section, "Preferences for Fastfields." You can also delete individual words from a Fastfield word list. You may want to do this if Family Tree Maker suggests a word that is misspelled. See "Deleting Words from a Fastfields Word List," on the next page.

Preferences for Fastfields

In the Fastfields dialog box, you can choose which fields work as Fastfields. This way, if you are not comfortable using Fastfields, you can turn them off.

To change Fastfields preferences:

1. From the **File** menu, select **Preferences**. From the submenu, select **Fastfields**.

    Family Tree Maker displays the Fastfields dialog box.

2. Select the check boxes for the fields you want to act as Fastfields or de-select the fields you don't want to act as Fastfields. Click **All** to select all of the check boxes. Click **None** to deselect all of the check boxes.

3. After you make your selections, click **OK**.

    Family Tree Maker closes the dialog box and saves your changes.

Deleting Words from a Fastfields Word List

You may want to delete a word from a Fastfield word list if it is misspelled or if you don't use it very often.

To delete a word from a Fastfield word list:

1. Go to a Fastfield for the type of word that you want to delete. For example, if you want to delete a location, go to a location field.

2. Start typing the word.

3. When the word appears, click the trash can button that appears on the right side of the Fastfield.

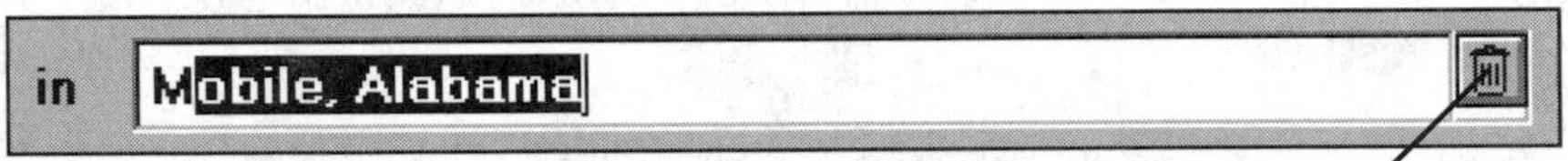

Click here to delete "Mobile, Alabama"
from the Fastfield word list.

Figure 3-10. The trash can button

Family Tree Maker deletes the word from the Fastfield word list. The word remains deleted until you type it in a Fastfield again.

4. If necessary, type the correct information in the field where you just deleted the Fastfield word.

Entering Information About
Marriages, Partnerships, and Friendships

The "Marriage" fields record the date and location of a couple's marriage. You can also record the status of their relationship in the relationship status fields. For example, if a couple were married, you would select "Married" from the "Beginning status" drop-down list on the Family Page. Or, if it isn't certain that a couple were ever married, you would select "Unknown."

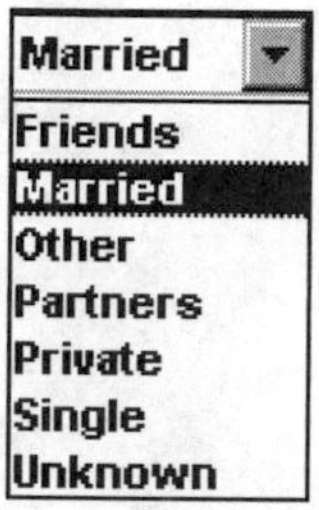

Figure 3-11. The Beginning status field drop-down list

When both a husband and a wife are present, the default for the "Beginning status" field is "Married," but you can select any of the following terms from the drop-down list: Friends, Married, Other, Partners, Single, and Unknown. When you choose "Partner" or "Friend" in the "Beginning status" drop-down list, Family Tree Maker automatically substitutes "Meeting date" for "Marriage date" in the records you're keeping about those two individuals. You can also have Family Tree Maker assign automatic reference numbers to individuals and marriages. Automatic reference numbers streamline the process of assigning numbers and can help you reduce data entry errors and duplications that occur during manual entry (see "Using Automatic Reference Numbers" in Chapter 5).

If you merged information from a World Family Tree (see "The World Family Tree Project" in Chapter 12), some marriage fields may contain the word "Private." This is to protect the privacy of individuals who are still living.

Each marriage has its own set of More About dialog boxes for recording additional information about a marriage, including special marital events. For more information about the More About dialog boxes for a marriage, see "Entering Brief Marriage Facts" in Chapter 5.

Entering Information About Children

The "Children" list at the bottom of the Family Page is for recording the names, sexes, and birth dates of the children of the parents on that Family Page. The date field in the "Children" list works just as it does for the husband and wife. The "Name" field is a Fastfield (see "Fastfields" in this chapter) for last names. Family Tree Maker automatically inserts the husband's last name after children's first and middle names. You can type over the name that Family Tree Maker inserts if the children have different last names.

Children	Sex	Birth dates
1 Robert Todd Lincoln	M	November 8, 1843
2 Edward Baker Lincoln	M	March 10, 1846
3 William Wallace Lincoln	M	December 21, 1850
4 Thomas Lincoln	M	April 4, 1853

Figure 3-12. The Children list

The "Sex" field accepts the letters "M" and "F" for "male" and "female," as well as "?" for cases where the sex is unknown. The default is female. Because the sex of a child determines where he or she appears in the construction of family trees, it's important that you fill in the sex correctly.

Note: You can change a child's sex at any time by typing over the current sex. If the child is married, the spouse's sex will not change automatically.

There are different ways that you can enter the names of children who were not born to their parents, such as stepchildren, foster children, or adopted children. Some people prefer only to record bloodline relationships in their family trees, while others just want to show who makes up the family.

If you are interested in tracing your family's bloodline, only enter the names of children born to the parents listed on a particular Family Page. In this case, you should enter stepchildren only as children of their birth parents. In addition, if you want to trace the family bloodline, you probably don't want to enter adopted and foster children.

If you want to record *everyone* who makes up the family, enter all children as you wish. You can enter adopted, foster, and stepchildren as children of their foster, adoptive, or stepparents and leave it at that, or you can use the Lineage dialog box to indicate the special nature of the relationship (see "Entering Nicknames, Titles, and Parental Relationship Information" in chapter 5). If children have more than two parents due to divorce and remarriage or other circumstances, you can enter those children on multiple Family Pages.

You can add up to 99 children on each Family Page. The Family Page appears to allow only 4, but when you press ⌈Enter←⌋ after the fourth child, the list scrolls up, revealing space to add more children.

When you enter children on a Family Page, it's a good practice to list them in the order in which they were born. The oldest child goes first. If you are unsure of the exact birth date of a child, but know that the child was born before or after one of his siblings, give the child an approximate birth date using "Before," "After," "About," "Circa," or "Estimated." This way, the child will sort in the correct birth order. See "Entering Dates" in this chapter.

Sometimes you'll uncover new children that need to be inserted between two children that are already listed. You may also find errors in children's birth dates so that you need to reorder them. Family Tree Maker provides commands such as Move Child, Insert Child, and Sort Children that let you rearrange children (see "Rearranging Children" in this section for details).

Caution: Never attempt to rearrange children by typing over names that are already there. Use the Sort Children command instead (see "Sorting Children by Birth Order" in this section).

If you type over a name, all information associated with that name (that individual's spouse and children, More About dialog boxes, etc.) will then be associated with the *new* name you entered. You will quickly end up with brothers married to their sisters-in-law or brothers-in-law! (See Figures 3-13 and 3-14 in this chapter.)

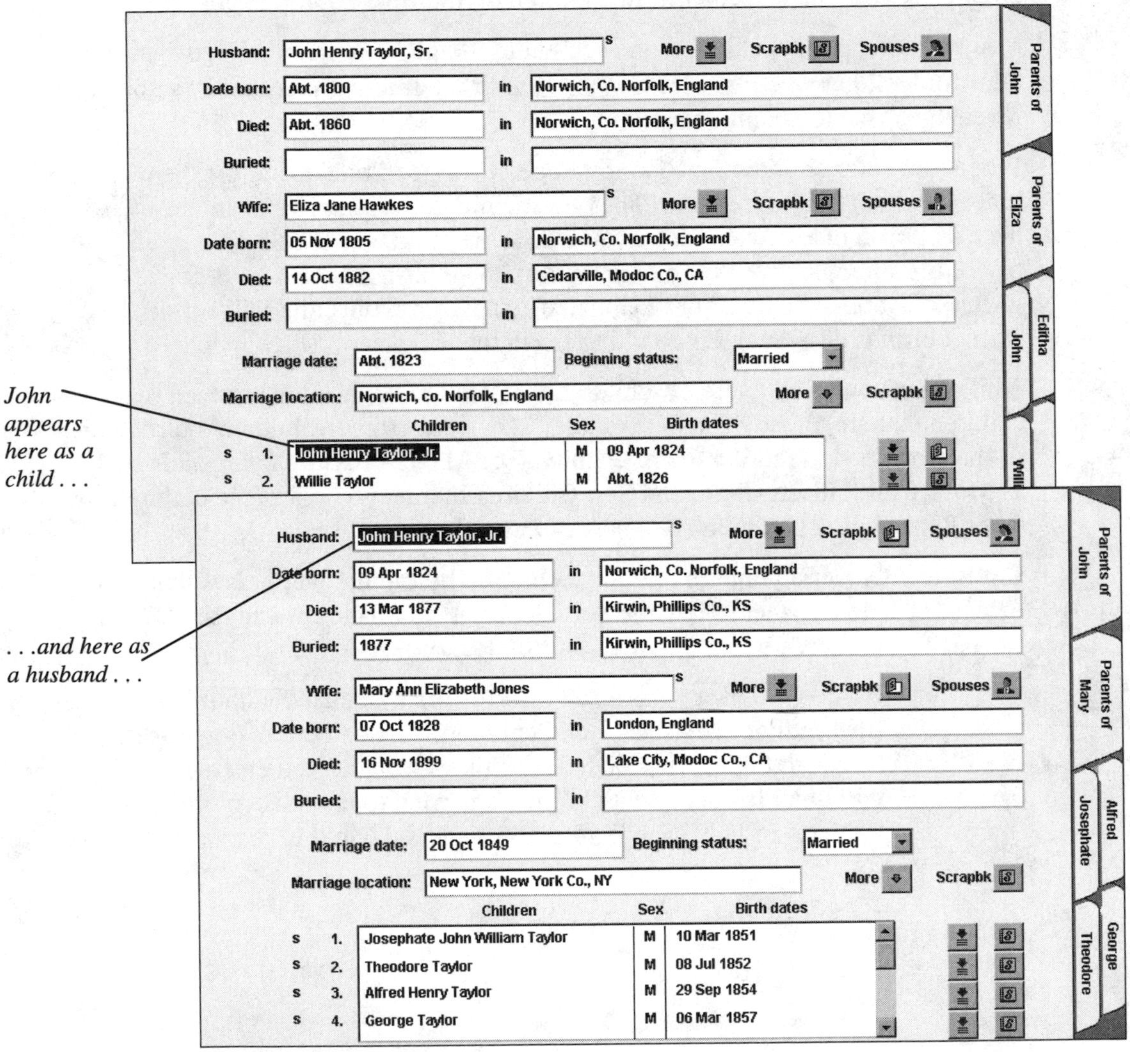

John appears here as a child . . .

. . .and here as a husband . . .

Husband:	John Henry Taylor, Sr.		More	Scrapbk	Spouses
Date born:	Abt. 1800	in	Norwich, Co. Norfolk, England		
Died:	Abt. 1860	in	Norwich, Co. Norfolk, England		
Buried:		in			
Wife:	Eliza Jane Hawkes		More	Scrapbk	Spouses
Date born:	05 Nov 1805	in	Norwich, Co. Norfolk, England		
Died:	14 Oct 1882	in	Cedarville, Modoc Co., CA		
Buried:		in			

Marriage date: Abt. 1823   Beginning status: Married

Marriage location: Norwich, co. Norfolk, England   More   Scrapbk

		Children	Sex	Birth dates		
s	1.	John Henry Taylor, Jr.	M	09 Apr 1824		
s	2.	Willie Taylor	M	Abt. 1826		

Tabs: Parents of John | Parents of Eliza | Editha | John | Willi

Husband:	John Henry Taylor, Jr.		More	Scrapbk	Spouses
Date born:	09 Apr 1824	in	Norwich, Co. Norfolk, England		
Died:	13 Mar 1877	in	Kirwin, Phillips Co., KS		
Buried:	1877	in	Kirwin, Phillips Co., KS		
Wife:	Mary Ann Elizabeth Jones		More	Scrapbk	Spouses
Date born:	07 Oct 1828	in	London, England		
Died:	16 Nov 1899	in	Lake City, Modoc Co., CA		
Buried:		in			

Marriage date: 20 Oct 1849   Beginning status: Married

Marriage location: New York, New York Co., NY   More   Scrapbk

		Children	Sex	Birth dates		
s	1.	Josephate John William Taylor	M	10 Mar 1851		
s	2.	Theodore Taylor	M	08 Jul 1852		
s	3.	Alfred Henry Taylor	M	29 Sep 1854		
s	4.	George Taylor	M	06 Mar 1857		

Tabs: Parents of John | Parents of Mary | Alfred | Josephate | George | Theodore

Figure 3-13. If you type over names…

. . .but if you change the order in which John and Willie are listed by typing over their names. . .

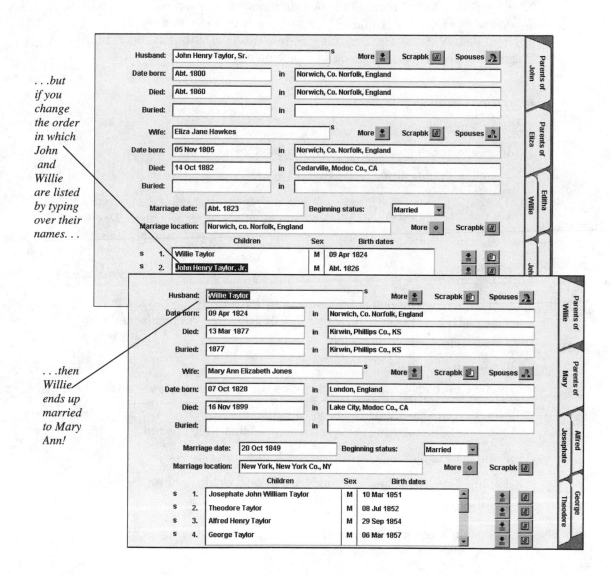

. . .then Willie ends up married to Mary Ann!

Figure 3-14. ... you might not like the results!

Rearranging Children

There are three commands you can use to rearrange the individuals in the "Children" list on a Family Page: Insert Child, Move Child, and Sort Children. Insert Child lets you add a new child between two existing children in a "Children" list. With Move Child you can move a child from one location to another within the same "Children" list. (If you need to move a child to a different Family Page, see "Detaching a Child from the Wrong Parents" in Chapter 6.) Sort Children lets you sort the children by birth order.

Inserting Children

To insert a new child:

1. Place the cursor on the row where you want the new child's name.

2. From the **People** menu, select **Insert Child**.

   The child whose name the cursor is on moves down (as do the children below), leaving the cursor at the beginning of a new, empty line. You may now enter the new child's name, sex, and birth date on the empty line.

Moving Children

You cannot move a child to a different Family Page using the Move Child command. To move a child to another Family Page, see "Detaching a Child from the Wrong Parents" in Chapter 6.

To move a child within a "Children" list:

1. In the **Children** list, place the cursor on the child you want to move.

   Note: To exchange two adjacent children in a "Children" list, select the lower child as the one to move, then move that child upward.

2. From the **People** menu, select **Move Child From**.

   Family Tree Maker displays a message asking you to confirm the move.

3. Click **OK**.

4. In the **Children** list on the same Family Page, place the cursor on the row where you want the child to end up.

5. From the **People** menu, select **Move Child To**.

    The other children on the list move down, and the individual you moved ends up in the row that you selected in step 4.

Sorting Children by Birth Order

To sort the children on a Family Page by birth order:

1. Go to the Family Page where you want to sort the children.

2. From the **People** menu, select **Sort Children**.

    Family Tree Maker tells you that it is sorting the children.

3. Click **OK** to continue.

    When the children are sorted, the oldest child's information appears at the top of the list, and the youngest child's information appears at the bottom. Twins or triplets stay in the order in which you entered them.

    Note: If a date field is blank, that child will sort at the top of the list. If a date field contains a question mark, that child will sort at the bottom of the list. If you don't know the exact birth date of a child, but know that the child was born before or after another child, use a "Before" or "After" date prefix so that the child sorts in the correct order. See Figure 3-6 in this chapter for information about entering estimated dates.

Entering Information About Other Relatives

Family Tree Maker automatically creates Family Pages for the parents and children of every individual you enter on the current Family Page. However, it doesn't automatically create Family Pages for the cousins, great-uncles, and so on. To enter family information about other relatives, you first must fill in the Family Pages of the individuals that link those relatives to the individuals that are already in your Family File.

For example, to enter information about your paternal uncle's family, you first fill in your father's Family Page, and then fill in his father's (your grandfather's) Family Page. On your grandfather's Family Page you'll enter your uncle as a child. You can then go directly to your uncle's page from your grandfather's page and enter his family information.

In other words, you can get to any relative's family by going through a parent, spouse, or child of someone already in your Family File. Once you have created a Family Page for a relative, you can go directly to their Family Page in other ways (see Chapter 4, "Moving Around").

Entering Intermarriages

You may find that somewhere in your family two cousins got married or two brothers married two sisters. Family Tree Maker allows you to enter these individuals twice without duplicating all of their information. In these cases, Kinship reports will show multiple relationships between some individuals. These individuals may also appear in trees more than once.

To enter an intermarriage:

1. On the Family Pages where the individuals appear as children, enter all of their information.

2. Go to the Family Page of one of the individuals. Enter only the name and birth date of their spouse. Don't enter the spouse's parents twice!

    Make sure that the names and birth dates match the ones you entered in step 1 *exactly*. Family Tree Maker compares the Family Pages and finds the duplicate entries.

3. When Family Tree Maker asks if the two individuals are the same, click **Yes**. If it doesn't ask, make sure the names and birth dates are identical.

    Family Tree Maker displays the Merge Individuals dialog box.

4. Click **Merge**.

    Family Tree Maker "links" the two individuals together.

Adding Individuals Whose Family Link is Unclear

You can use the Add Unrelated Individual command to add an individual to your Family File when you're not sure of their relationship to your family.

To use the Add Unrelated Individual command:

1. From the **People** menu, select **Add Unrelated Individual**.

    Family Tree Maker displays a blank Family Page.

2. Enter the individual's name, birth date, and death date.

    Note: Because this individual is not currently related to anyone in your file, you need to use the Index of Individuals to navigate to any other Family Page. See "Opening the Index of Individuals" in Chapter 4 for instructions.

Unrelated individuals do *not* appear in trees or Kinship reports until you attach them to the rest of the family. When you find the link between the individual and the rest of your family, use the Attach Spouse or Attach Child command, (see "Linking Children to Their Parents" in Chapter 6), to connect them to your family.

Recording Sources for Your Information

One of the first commandments of genealogy is to thoroughly document the sources of your family information. That way you can return to the source if you need to, and you have a record of which sources you've already checked. Once you've entered source information, you can include it in your trees and reports (see Chapter 9, "Customizing Your Family Information"). You can also view and print a Bibliography report listing all of your sources, and a Documented Events report that lists the events in your Family File which you've documented with sources.

If you are not sure how to document your sources, consult the Genealogy "How To" Guide on the Help menu (see "The 'How-To' Guide" in Chapter 1). You may also want to check the genealogy books at your local library, or ask a local genealogy society for information.

If you are planning to submit your Family File to the World Family Tree (see "The World Family Tree Project" in Chapter 12), we want to especially encourage you to document your sources. This way, others who use your file will have an easier time verifying the information that it contains.

You can record source information for all the fields listed below.

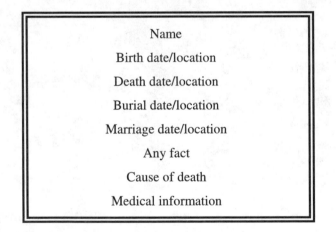

Name

Birth date/location

Death date/location

Burial date/location

Marriage date/location

Any fact

Cause of death

Medical information

Figure 3-15. Fields for which you can enter source information

To record source information for a field:

1. Place your cursor in the field for which you want to enter source information.

   Note: Each set of date and location fields (such as birth date and birth location) has its own set of source information.

2. From the **View** menu, select **Source**, or press [Ctrl] + [S].

   Family Tree Maker displays the Source-Citation dialog box.

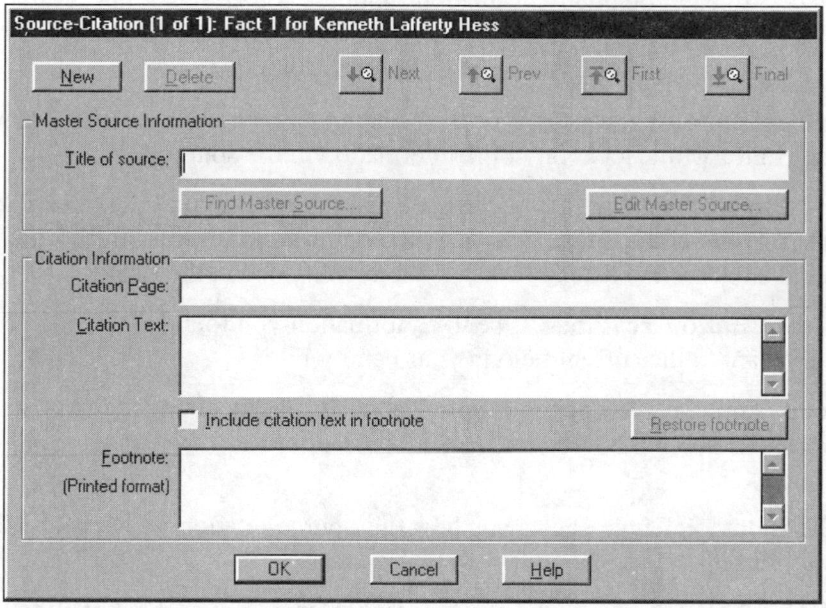

Figure 3-16. Source-Citation dialog box

3. In the **Title of source** field, type the name of the source, or click the **Find Master Source** button to choose from a list of existing sources.

   The source is the document or resource where you found the information. For example, if you found marriage information in a church register, type the name of this document in this field. If your source of information was an individual, type that individual's name in the field.

Make sure, however, that your names are descriptive so that you can tell the difference between similar documents. For example, many of your birth dates may come from birth certificates. If you simply enter `birth certificate` in the "Title of source" field, you can't tell the difference between your mother's birth certificate and grandmother's birth certificate. So your source titles should look more like this: `birth certificate for Jane Smith`.

Note: When you add a new source, you can click **Edit Master Source** to enter detailed information about the source including: Author/Originator, Publication facts, Source media, Call number, Source location, Comments, and Source quality.

4. In the **Citation Page** field, type the page number, record number, or a brief description of the location of the information in the source.

   For instance, you would type the page number where you found the marriage information in this field. If your source of information was an individual, you could type the date the conversation took place in the field.

5. In the **Citation Text** field, type the information you found in the source that is relevant to the current field in your Family File.

   For example, if you are documenting a death date/location, and your source is a letter, you might type the relevant passage exactly as it appears in the letter.

   The "Footnote" field shows you how this source-citation will appear when you print it.

Note: You can change the footnote text by typing over the default footnote text. If you later change your mind and want to return to the original footnote text, then click **Restore Footnote** to undo your footnote changes.

6. If you wish to include the citation text in your footnote, select the **Include citation text in footnote** check box.

7. At this point, you have the following options:

   New — Click this button if you want to add another source-citation for the same field. This button saves the current entry and clears the screen for the next entry. For example, if you just documented an individual's death date from the Social Security Death Index, and you also have a death notice from the newspaper, you can document the newspaper source as well.

   Delete — Click this button to delete the current source-citation.

   Next — If you've already entered other source-citations for this field, you can click this button to move forward to the next entry.

   Prev — If you've already entered other source-citations for this field, you can click this button to move back to the previous entry.

   First — If you've already entered other source-citations for this field, you can click this button to jump to the first entry.

   Final — If you've already entered other source-citations for this field, you can click this button to jump to the last entry.

8. After you finish entering and viewing sources for this field, click **OK**.

   Family Tree Maker returns you to the field for which you recorded sources and places an "s" next to that field indicating that you have recorded source information for this field.

Chapter 4

MOVING AROUND

Entrepreneurs Earle Huntington Hastings and the young Gordon proudly show off one of their side businesses, a Wells Fargo delivery franchise. A turn-of-the-century Los Angeles constable, Earle Hastings also owned a soda fountain. Kevin Hastings, Gordon's grandson, inherited good business sense and is the Product Manager for the Family Archives Unit of Banner Blue.

MOVING AROUND

A complete family tree is, of course, made up of more than just one nuclear family on one Family Page. This means that once you've filled out your first Family Page, you need to fill out more Family Pages with information about other family members. Family Tree Maker makes it easy for you to move between different Family Pages so that you can quickly see and edit them.

Remember, don't be afraid to experiment. If you get lost, you can press ⌑F1 at any time to get on–screen Help.

Note: Be sure that you're not creating a new Family File for each new Family Page. All of your Family Pages should be in the same Family *File* so that the information contained in them can be printed in the same family tree. The only exception to this is if you're creating a Family File for someone who is completely unrelated to your family, such as a neighbor.

MOVING BETWEEN CLOSELY RELATED INDIVIDUALS

You can display the Family Pages of the parents and children of the husband and wife on the current Family Page by clicking the tabs on the right side of the screen. There's also an index of all the individuals in your Family File that you can use to find and display any Family Page instantly, no matter how many Family Pages you have.

Every individual appears on at least two Family Pages: as a child on his or her parents' Family Page and also as a husband or wife (or unmarried adult) on another Family Page. When you enter an individual on one page, Family Tree Maker automatically copies that individual onto the other page to make it easy for you to add new information to your Family File (see Figure 4-1).

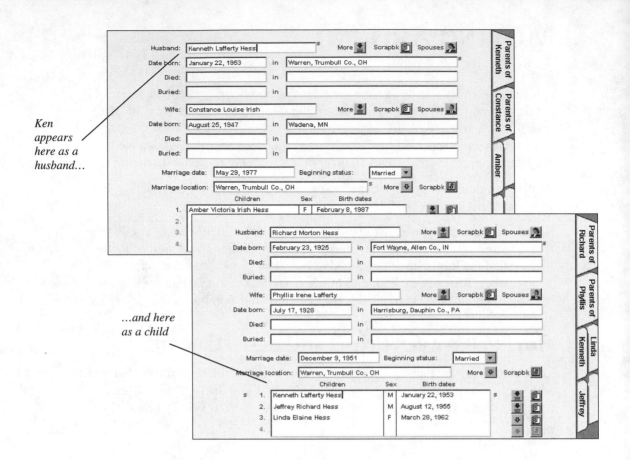

Ken appears here as a husband...

...and here as a child

Figure 4-1. An individual is on two Family Pages

An individual appears on more than two Family Pages if he or she has had more than one spouse or more than one set of parents. For each additional spouse, there is an additional Family Page where you can enter that spouse's name and the names of any children from that marriage. For information about entering additional marriages for an individual, see "Other Spouses" in this chapter. For information about entering additional sets of parents for an individual, see "Other Parents" in this Chapter.

Parents' Family Page

If you are on a Family Page and you want to see the current wife's parents, click the tab on the right side of the screen that says "Parents of <wife>," as shown in Figure 4-2. You can also press F4. Family Tree Maker will display a Family Page with the wife listed as a child, and "Husband" and "Wife" fields where her parents should be.

If you are on a Family Page and you want to see the current husband's parents, click the tab on the right side of the screen that says "Parents of <husband>." You can also press F5. Family Tree Maker will display a Family Page with the husband listed as a child, and "Husband" and "Wife" fields where his parents should be.

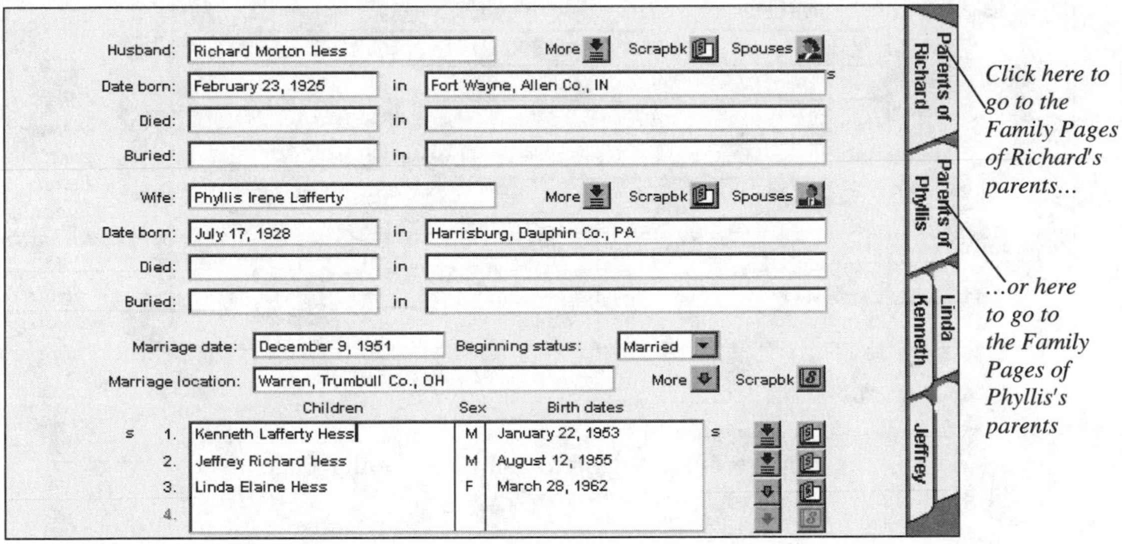

Click here to go to the Family Pages of Richard's parents...

...or here to go to the Family Pages of Phyllis's parents

Figure 4-2. Moving to an individual's parents' Family Page

Child's Family Page

To see the Family Page of a child, click the tab on the right side of the screen labeled with that child's name. You can also click the child's name in the "Children" list, and then press ⌕F6⌕. Family Tree Maker will display a Family Page with the child listed either as a husband or wife, and a "Children" list where his or her children should be (see Figure 4-3).

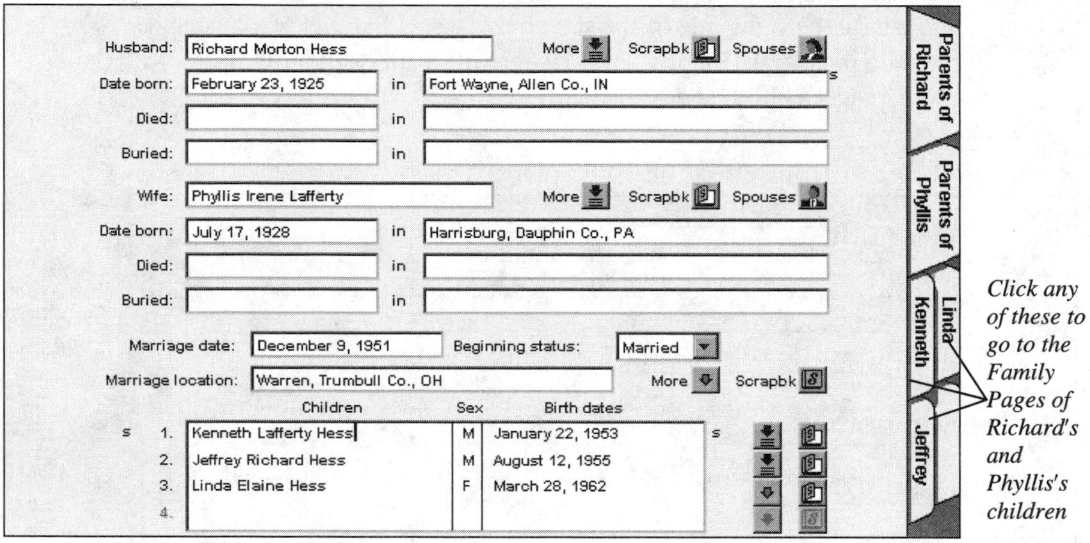

Figure 4-3. Moving to a child's Family Page

Sibling's Family Page

A **sibling** is an individual's brother or sister. To see the Family Page of a husband's or wife's sibling:

1. Click the tab for the husband's or wife's parents.

   Family Tree Maker displays the Family Page of the parents.

2. On the parents' Family Page, click the tab labeled with the name of the child whose Family Page you want to see (see Figure 4-4).

   If the child whose Family Page you want to see is not visible in the "Children" list, use the scroll bar on the right side of the list to scroll through the children.

If you press [F8] when the cursor is in either the "Husband" or "Wife" field, Family Tree Maker goes to the Family Page of the husband's or wife's next sibling. (The "next" sibling is the sibling that is listed directly below the individual in the "Children" list on their parents' Family Page.)

If you press [alt] + [F8] when the cursor is in the "Husband" or "Wife" field, Family Tree Maker goes to the Family Page of the husband's or wife's previous sibling. (The "previous" sibling is the sibling that is listed directly above the individual in the "Children" list on their parents' Family Page.)

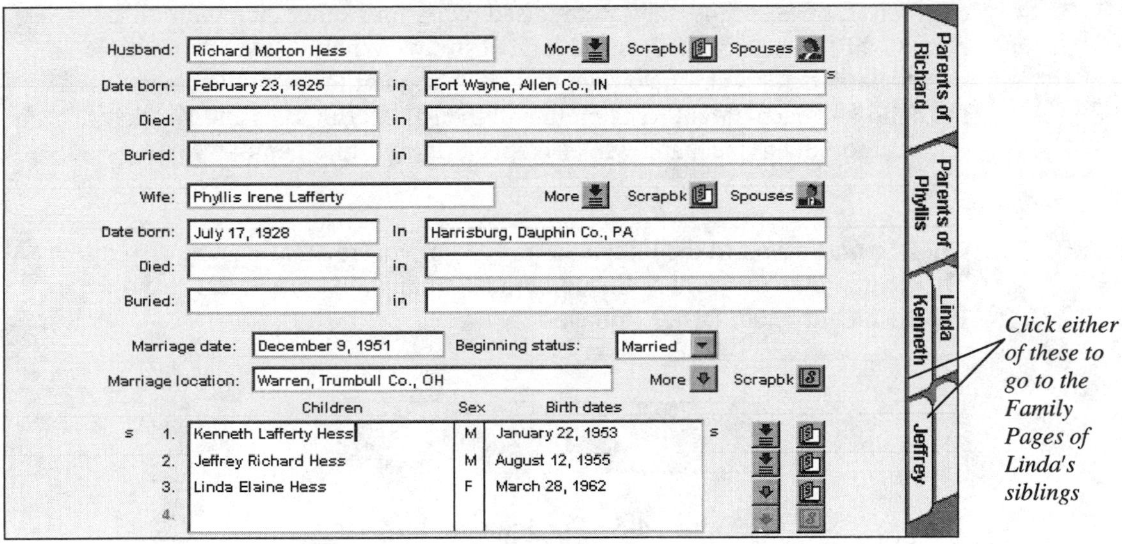

Figure 4-4. Moving to a sibling's Family Page

Other Spouses

When an individual has had more than one marriage, you must create a separate Family Page for each additional spouse. The individual with multiple spouses will then be on multiple Family Pages.

Creating Additional Spouses

To create another spouse for an individual:

1. Display the Family Page containing the individual for whom you want to create another spouse. If the individual has children that you want to appear on the new Family Page with the new spouse, be sure to display the Family Page containing those children.

    Many genealogists prefer to include children only on the Family Page of their birth parents. However, you may want multiple sets of parents for children if, for example, they were raised by parents other than their birth parents, or two sets of parents had joint custody. When you create multiple sets of parents for a child, you can note the nature of the relationship between the child and each parent. The child will then appear in trees and Kinship reports more than once, and will also appear in multiple Family Group Sheets.

2. Click **Spouses** next to the individual for whom you're creating a new spouse. This button is to the right of that individual's name. Alternatively, from the **People** menu, select **Other Spouses**.

Figure 4-5. The Spouses buttons

Family Tree Maker displays the Spouses dialog box. See Figure 4-6.

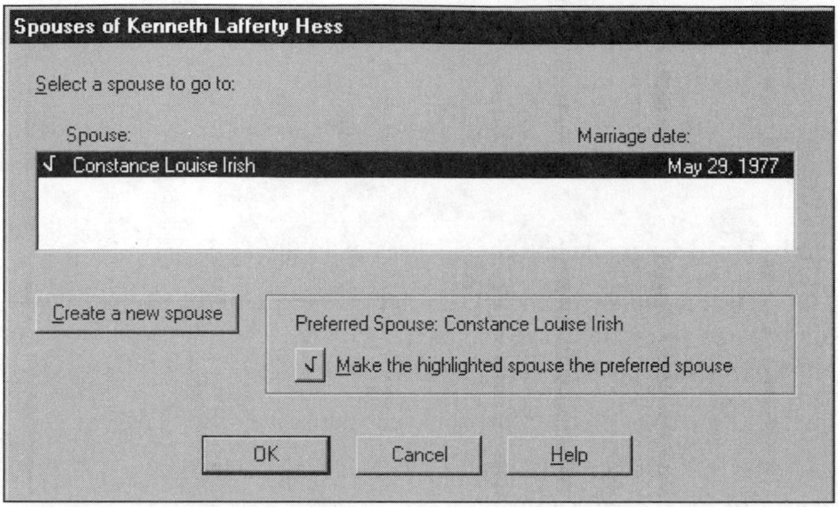

Figure 4-6. The Spouses dialog box

3. Click **Create a new spouse**.

4. If the Family Page you displayed in step 1 contained children, Family Tree Maker asks if you want those children to appear on the new Family Page with the new spouse. Click either **Yes** or **No**.

   If you choose "Yes" the children will appear on the new Family Page and Family Tree Maker creates a step-relationship between the children and the new spouse. If the children actually have different relationships with the new spouse, you can go to each child's Lineage dialog box (see "Entering Nicknames, Titles, and Parental Relationship Information" in Chapter 5) and choose the correct relationship.

5. Family Tree Maker takes you to a new Family Page. It contains the individual you selected in step 1 and any children that you chose to include. You can now enter information about the new spouse and any children that the couple had.

Displaying the Family Pages of Other Spouses

To see a Family Page containing a different spouse:

1. On the Family Page, click **Spouses** next to the individual whose spouses you want to see. Or, click the name of the individual whose spouses you want to see and then press F3.

   Family Tree Maker displays the Spouses dialog box.

2. In the **Select a spouse to go to** list, select the name of the spouse whose Family Page you want to see and then click **OK**. Alternatively, you can double-click the spouse's name.

   Family Tree Maker displays the selected spouse's Family Page.

Selecting the Preferred Spouse

When you go to an individual's Family Page, Family Tree Maker automatically displays the Family Page containing that individual's **preferred spouse**. For example, John has had two spouses, Susan and Mary. Mary is his preferred spouse. When you choose to see John's Family Page, you will see the Family Page that shows Mary as his wife.

Of course, you can still display the Family Pages containing the other spouses, as described in "Displaying the Family Pages of Other Spouses" above.

To select an individual's preferred spouse:

1. On the Family Page, click **Spouses** next to the individual whose spouses you want to see. Or, click the name of the individual whose spouses you want to see and then press F3.

   Family Tree Maker displays the Spouses dialog box.

2. In the **Select a spouse to go to** list, select the name of the spouse that you want to be the preferred spouse.

3. Select **Make the highlighted spouse the preferred spouse**.

4. After you make your selection, click **OK**.

   Family Tree Maker displays the Family Page containing the individual and his or her preferred spouse.

You can change your preferred spouse selection at any time by repeating the four steps above.

Other Parents

When it comes to divorce, remarriage, and other types of special parent-child relationships, many genealogists prefer to include children only on the Family Page of their birth parents. However, with Family Tree Maker you can create multiple sets of parents for each child and then note the special nature of the relationships between the parents and the child. When you create multiple sets of parents for a child, the child will appear in trees and Kinship reports more than once, and will also appear in multiple Family Group Sheets.

Creating Additional Parents

To create an additional set of parents for a child:

1. Display the Family Page containing the child for whom you want to create another set of parents. The child must be displayed in the "Children" list, not in a "Husband" or "Wife" field.

   You can use either the Index of Individuals, or Find Individual, to quickly go to the correct Family Page (see "Moving Around in the Index of Individuals" or "Locating Individuals in Your Family File" in this chapter).

2. Click the child's name, and then from the **People** menu, select **Other Parents**.

   Family Tree Maker displays the Other Parents dialog box.

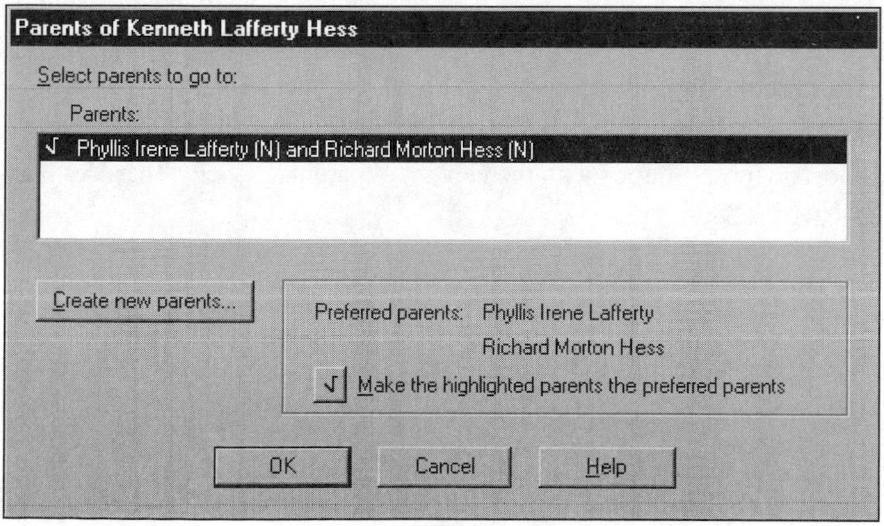

Figure 4-7. The Other Parents dialog box

3. Click **Create new parents**.

   Family Tree Maker displays the Create New Parents dialog box.

Figure 4-8. The Create New Parents dialog box

4. Select one of the three option buttons, **Two new parents**, **Another father**, or **Another mother**, depending on which parent(s) you need to create.

5. Click the appropriate **Relationship with** drop-down list(s) and choose the word that describes the relationship between the new parent(s) and the child.

   Please note that a child can only have one natural mother and one natural father. You must choose a different relationship for any additional parents.

6. After you make your selections, click **OK**.

7. If the child has siblings, Family Tree Maker asks whether you want to associate those siblings with the new set of parents. Click either **Yes** or **No**.

If you choose "Yes," Family Tree Maker adds any siblings that have the same preferred parents (see "Selecting the Preferred Parents" in this section). Family Tree Maker also gives the siblings the same relationship to the new parent(s), unless the siblings would then have too many natural parents. In this case Family Tree Maker gives them a step-relationship. If the children actually have different relationships, you can go to each child's Lineage dialog box and choose the correct relationship (see "Entering Nicknames, Titles, and Parental Relationship Information" in Chapter 5).

8. Family Tree Maker displays a new Family Page with children in the "Children" list. Depending on which option button you selected in step 4, either the "Husband" or the "Wife" field may be filled in already. Enter information about this set of parents in the **Husband**, **Wife**, and other fields.

   If either the husband or wife already exists elsewhere in your Family File, Family Tree Maker will ask you to verify the relationships.

Displaying the Family Pages of Other Parents

To see a Family Page containing another set of a child's parents:

1. On the Family Page, select the child whose Other Parents dialog box you want to see.

2. From the **People** menu, select **Other Parents**.

   Family Tree Maker displays the Other Parents dialog box.

3. In the **Parents** list, select the names of the parents whose Family Page you want to see and then click **OK**. Alternatively, you can just double-click the parents' names.

   To the right of the names of each set of parents are codes indicating the relationship between the parents and the child. This will help you distinguish between the different sets of parents.

   Family Tree Maker displays the Family Page containing those parents.

Selecting the Preferred Parents

An individual's **preferred parents** are the parents that Family Tree Maker will display in Ancestor trees.

To select an individual's preferred parents:

1. On the Family Page, select the child whose Other Parents dialog box you want to see.

2. From the **People** menu, select **Other Parents**.

    Family Tree Maker displays the Other Parents dialog box.

3. In the **Parents** list, select the names of the parents that you want to be the preferred parents.

4. Select **Make the highlighted parents the preferred parents**.

5. After you make your selection, click **OK**.

    Family Tree Maker displays the Family Page containing the individual and his or her preferred parents.

You can change your preferred parents selection at any time by repeating the five steps above.

MOVING TO ANYONE IN YOUR FAMILY FILE

The **Index of Individuals** lists the names, birth dates, and death dates of every individual in your Family File. You can use this list to quickly see information about anyone in your Family File; instructions begin on the next page. You can also move around your Family File by clicking in trees and other views (see "Navigating With Your Mouse" in Chapter 8). Finally, you can use the Find command to search for any individual or information in your Family File (see "Locating Individuals in Your Family File" in this chapter).

Opening the Index of Individuals

To display the Index of Individuals, from the **View** menu, select **Index of Individuals**. Alternatively, you can press [F2], or use the **Index** toolbar button. The individuals are listed alphabetically by last name, with birth and death dates on the right.

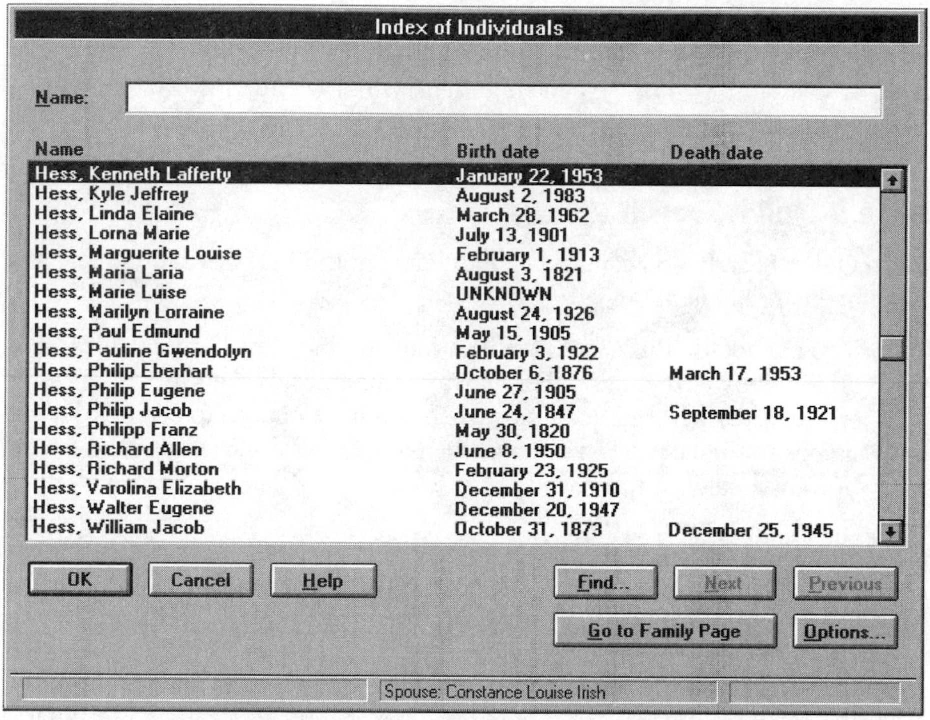

Figure 4-9. The Index of Individuals

Note: Depending on your choice of options, (see "Index of Individuals Options" in this chapter) individuals with nicknames (aka's) may appear in the index twice, one entry for each of their names.

You cannot print the Index of Individuals itself, but you can create and print a report that contains the same information as the Index of Individuals. To create and print a report, see "Displaying Reports" in Chapter 8.

Moving Around in the Index of Individuals

There are three ways to scroll up and down through the names in the Index of Individuals. Each of these methods is described below.

Using the Navigational Keys

You can use ⬆️, ⬇️, PgUp, and PgDn to move up and down through the Index of Individuals. If you press ⬆️ or ⬇️, the highlight will move up or down by one name. If you press PgUp or PgDn, the highlight will move up or down by a full screen's worth of names.

Doing a Quick Search

With a Quick Search, you can find an individual in the Index of Individuals just by typing his or her name.

Note: You cannot use this search feature when the Index of Individuals is arranged by birth dates rather than by last names, when it is sorted alphabetically from Z to A, nor when you have chosen to use married names for females. To rearrange the names, see "Rearranging the Index of Individuals" in this chapter.

To use the Quick Search feature:

1. Click the **Name** field at the top of the Index of Individuals.

2. Start typing the last name of the individual you want to find.

    With each character you type, you get closer to the name you want to find. You can type part or all of the name, as long as you start with the Last name, followed by a comma, the First name, and the Middle name.

Using Find Name

To use the Find Name command in the Index of Individuals:

1. Click **Find**, located at the bottom of the Index of Individuals dialog box.

    Family Tree Maker displays the Find Name dialog box.

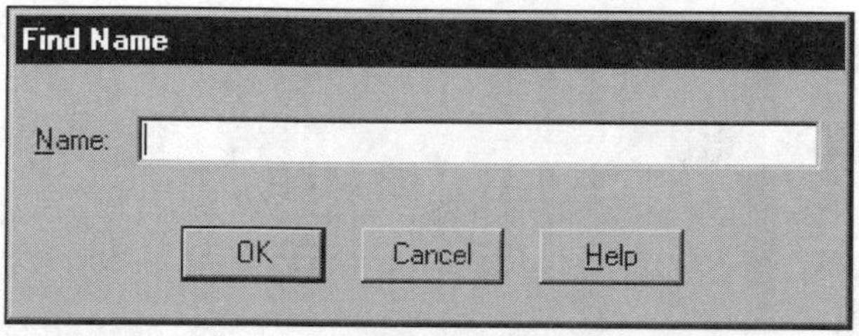

Figure 4-10. The Find Name dialog box

2. Type an individual's name.

    If you're not sure of the exact name, type any part of the name. Family Tree Maker will find any name containing those same letters. For example, if you type **hess**, Family Tree Maker will find "Kenneth Hess," "Hessel Smith," "George Chess, III," and so on.

3. Click **OK** to begin searching.

    Family Tree Maker highlights the name of the first individual meeting your request. If there are no matches, Family Tree Maker displays a message telling you this.

4. If you want to continue searching through the list of names, click **Next** to move to the next name that meets your request.

    Once you have moved past the first match in the list, you can also click **Previous** to go back to previous matches.

    Note: If you didn't find the name you were looking for, try typing a smaller portion of the name. You can search for any part of a name. For example, you could type **sm** to look for the last name "Smith."

Index of Individuals Options

To change the way the list of names appears in the Index of Individuals:

1. Click **Options**, located at the bottom of the Index of Individuals dialog box.

    Family Tree Maker displays the Index of Individuals Options dialog box .

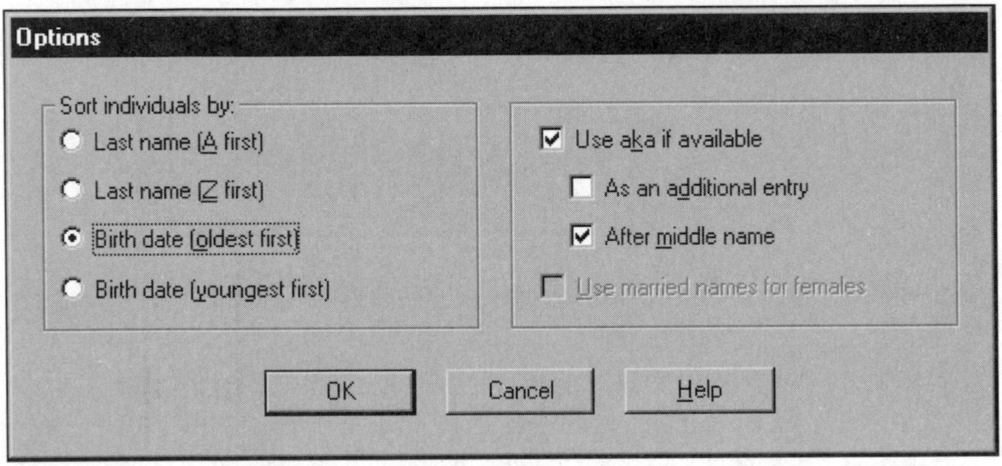

Figure 4-11. The Index of Individuals Options dialog box

2. From the "Sort individuals by" section, select the option button for the type of sorting you prefer.

    Note: You can only use the Quick Search feature when "Last name (A first)" is selected.

    In former versions, Family Tree Maker always added aka's to the Index of Individuals list as additional (duplicate) names. Now you may select from the following options:

3. From the "aka and married names" section, select from the following as desired:

    Use aka if available — Select this check box if you want to display aka's in the Index of Individuals.

    As an additional entry — If you select this check box, aka's will appear as a separate (duplicate) name.

    After middle name — If you select this check box, aka's will appear as part of the person's name, and will not be duplicated in the list.

You can also choose how Family Tree Maker displays the names of women in the Index of Individuals:

Use married names for females — If you select this check box, women will be listed in the Index of Individuals by their married names. Please note that if you have chosen to sort by **Birth date**, this option will be disabled.

Note: You can select to have a woman use her maiden name as a married name, and enter an aka or nickname, all on the More About Lineage page. For more information, see "Entering Nicknames, Titles, and Parental Relationship Information" in Chapter 5.

4. After you make your selections, click **OK**.

Family Tree Maker applies your selections and returns you to the Index of Individuals.

Note: The **Quick Search** feature is disabled when the Index of Individuals is sorted by Birth date. For more information, see "Doing a Quick Search" in this chapter.

Moving to Other Views from the Index of Individuals

Once you find the name of the individual that you are looking for, you can do one of two things:

- Click **Go to Family Page** to see the Family Page containing the individual whose name is highlighted. That individual will be shown as a husband or wife on the Family Page.

  If the individual has been married more than once, Family Tree Maker shows you the Family Page containing the preferred spouse (see "Selecting the Preferred Spouse" in this chapter.)

- Click **OK** to go to the **current view** of the individual whose name is highlighted. The "current view" is the view that you were in before you opened the Index of Individuals. For example, if you were previously looking at an Ancestor tree, clicking **OK** in the Index of Individuals would take you to an Ancestor tree for the individual whose name is highlighted. Or, if you were previously looking at a Family Page, clicking **OK** in the Index of Individuals would take you to the Family Page containing the individual whose name is highlighted.

LOCATING INDIVIDUALS IN YOUR FAMILY FILE

Using **Find Individual**, you can quickly locate anyone in your Family File. You can search for individuals using almost any type of information, including names, dates, comments, items in Scrapbooks, and even phrases in the Notes dialog box. You can also search for individuals using parts of information. For example, you can type "jo" and find the name "Jonathan."

Find Individual is also useful for finding groups of individuals. For example, you could locate everyone in your Family File that has the same last name or birthplace. When Family Tree Maker finds an individual for you, you can edit that individual's information and then continue the search without needing to tell Family Tree Maker what to search for again.

Searching by Name

To search for an individual in your Family File by name, go to any Family Page and then:

1. From the **Edit** menu, select **Find Individual**.

   Family Tree Maker displays the Find Individual dialog box.

2. Click the **Search** drop-down list and select **Name**.

3. In the **for** field, type the name of the individual you wish to find.

   If you're not sure of the exact name, type any part of the name. Family Tree Maker will find any name containing those same letters. For example, if you type **hess**, Family Tree Maker will find "Kenneth Hess," "Hessel Smith," "George Chess, III," and so on.

   Note: Searching the Name field will also find **Alternate** names. But please note that if you contribute a file to the World Family Tree that includes Alternate names, those names will not be indexed in the World Family Tree.

4. Click **Find next** to start the search.

   Family Tree Maker displays the Family Page of the first individual who matches your request. If no matches are found, Family Tree Maker displays a message telling you so.

   If you like, you can edit this Family Page and then continue your search by reopening the Find Individual dialog box and clicking **Find next**. (To reopen the dialog box, from the **Edit** menu, select **Find Individual**.)

5. Click **Find next** to continue your search.

   Continue clicking **Find next** until you're done searching or until Family Tree Maker runs out of matches. To go back to previous matches, you can click **Find previous**.

6. To quit the search, click **Cancel**.

   If you didn't find the individual you wanted, try typing a smaller portion of their name. For example, type `sm` to look for the last name "Smith."

7. If you want to go through the same search again, click **Restart Search**.

   Family Tree Maker goes back to the beginning of the Family File and searches through it again.

Searching for Other Items

Family Tree Maker can search for dates, locations, sources, and comments — almost any information that you can enter into your Family File. In addition, you can locate parentless, childless individuals and individuals who were merged or who were not merged (see "Appending and Merging Information" in Chapter 13).

To search for information other than a name:

1. Go to any Family Page and then:

2. From the **Edit** menu, select **Find Individual**.

   Family Tree Maker displays the Find Individual dialog box.

3. Click the **Search** drop-down list and choose the item you want to find.

   For example, if you wanted to find an individual with a specific birth date, you would select "Birth date."

4. In the **for** field, type the information that you want to find.

   For example, if you search with the "Birth date" field and want to find individuals born in October, you would type `October` Or, if you want to find individuals born before October of 1988, you would type `<October 1988` See Figure 4-12 for more tips.

   If the item you want to find has specific value options (such as "male," "female," and "unknown"), Family Tree Maker displays a drop-down list in the "for" field. In this case, just select what you want to find.

5. Click **Find next** to start the search.

   Family Tree Maker displays the Family Page of the first individual who matches your request. If no matches are found, Family Tree Maker displays a message telling you so.

   If you like, you can edit this Family Page and then continue your search by reopening the Find Individual dialog box and clicking **Find next**. To reopen the dialog box, from the **Edit** menu, select **Find Individual**.

6. Click **Find next** to continue your search.

   Continue clicking **Find next** until you're done searching or until Family Tree Maker runs out of matches. To go back to previous matches, you can click **Find previous**.

7. To quit the search, click **Cancel**.

   If you didn't find the Family Page you were looking for, try typing a smaller portion of the information. For example, you could type 1988 to find "October, 1988."

8. If you want to go through the same search again, click **Restart Search**.

   Family Tree Maker goes back to the beginning of the Family File and searches through it again.

Searching Tips

- Don't worry about punctuation when searching for names.

- You can use any allowable date format (see Figure 3-6 in Chapter 3). If you search for a date range, Family Tree Maker will find all dates which fall within that range and any ranges which overlap or match exactly the range you searched for.

- To find and fill in the empty fields in your Family File, simply type = instead of a name, date, comment, etc. in the **for** field. For example, to find all empty marriage date fields, pick "Marriage date" from the **Search** field and type = in the **for** field.

- To search for a specific date, but not in any particular field, select "Any and all date fields" from the **Search** field.

- To search for a specific set of words, but not in any particular field, select "Any and all text fields" from the **Search** field.

- If you want to search for numbers, you can use the operators >, <, >=, <=, and X...Y, just as they are used with dates in Figure 4-12.

You type this...	Family Tree Maker finds this...
=	All places where the field is empty
!=	All places where the field contains information
10/2/1988	All occurrences of October 2, 1988, including any date ranges which encompass this date
<10/2/1988, or BEFORE 10/2/1988, or BEF 10/2/1988	All dates before October 2, 1988, including dates entered as "Before October 2, 1988"
<=10/2/1988	The date October 2, 1988 and all dates before it, including dates entered as "Before October 2, 1988"
>10/2/1988, or AFTER 10/2/1988, or AFT 10/2/1988	All dates after October 2, 1988, including dates entered as "After October 2, 1988"
>=10/2/1988	The date October 2, 1988 and all dates after it, including dates entered as "After October 2, 1988"
ABOUT 10/2/1988, or CIRCA 10/2/1988, or EST 10/2/1988	All dates entered as "About October 2, 1988," "Circa October 2, 1988," or "Est October 2, 1988"
10/2/1988..10/2/1990, or >=10/2/1988..<=10/2/1990	All dates between October 2, 1988 and October 2, 1990 including those two days and any date ranges which overlap with this range
>10/2/1988..<10/2/1990	All dates between October 2, 1988 and October 2, 1990 not including those two days
UNKNOWN or ?	All dates entered as "Unknown" or "?"

Figure 4-12. Searching for date

Chapter 5

ENTERING DETAILED INFORMATION

Ed Mortensen, an engineer for Family Tree Maker, is the great-great-grandson of John Henry Taylor, Jr. (standing, left). As a First Class Fireman in the Union Navy, John witnessed the historic Civil War naval battle between the Ironclads, the Merrimac and the Monitor. Also pictured here (c. late 1880s) are John's wife, Mary Ann Elizabeth (Jones) Taylor (seated, left), his mother, Eliza Jane (Hawkes) Taylor, and his eldest son, Theodore Taylor.

ENTERING DETAILED INFORMATION

The **More About** dialog boxes provide a place for you to record additional information about the individuals in your Family File. Each individual has five More About dialog boxes: the Facts dialog box, the Address dialog box, the Medical dialog box, the Lineage dialog box, and the Notes dialog box. With these dialog boxes, you can keep track of special events, such as baptism or immigration, track your family's medical history, and record all the details that paint a complete picture of an individual's life. Each marriage also has a Facts dialog box and a Notes dialog box so you can record special information about the marriage and the couple.

In addition, each individual and each marriage have a **Scrapbook**. In Scrapbooks, you can electronically store any type of information, including photos and other scanned images, video, sound, text, and other OLE objects. With space for up to 16,000 items per individual and per marriage, you can create an unforgettable collection of family information — all stored neatly on your computer! Instructions begin with "Scrapbooks: The Basics" in this chapter.

Don't be afraid to experiment while using Family Tree Maker. Remember that if you get lost or have any difficulties, you can press ⌐F1⌐ at any time to get on-screen help.

To display an individual's or marriage's More About dialog boxes:

1. Go to the Family Page containing the individual or marriage whose More About dialog boxes you want to see.

2. On the Family Page, place the cursor either on the name of the individual or on the marriage whose More About dialog boxes you want to see.

3. From the **View** menu, select **More About**. From the submenu, select the name of a More About dialog box.

    Family Tree Maker displays the dialog box that you selected.

To display More About dialog boxes you can also click the **More** button on the Family Page next to the individual's name or next to the marriage.

Each More About dialog box has two parts:

- On the left, there's an area where you can record information about the individual or marriage.

- On the right, similar to a Side Toolbar, there are buttons that you can click to move to the four other More About dialog boxes. For example, to enter medical information, you would click **Medical**. These buttons appear on each of the More About dialog boxes, so it's easy to move from one dialog box to another. You can also move to the other More About dialog boxes using the **View** menu, as you did in step 3.

You'll always know whose More About dialog boxes you're working on because the top of the dialog box displays the individual's name.

To return to the Family Page from any More About dialog box, from the **View** menu, select **Family Page**.

Note: You can print the information in the More About dialog boxes. See Chapter 10, "Printing Your Family Information."

ENTERING FACTS

Family Tree Maker lets you enter facts about an individual's life, such as special events, personal characteristics, or favorite activities just to name a few examples. A Fact is generally composed of three fields: one for a Fact name, one for a Date, and one for a Comment/Location. The Facts page contains all of the facts for an individual, including the **Born** and **Died** events that are entered on the Family Page.

To display the More About Facts page:

1. From the **View** menu, select **More About**. From the submenu, select **Facts**.

    Family Tree Maker displays the More About Facts page for the selected individual. This page always shows a new, empty line of fact fields at the top of the list.

    Note: The **Name**, **Born** and **Died** events displayed on this page are "linked" to the same information on the Family Page. Changing this information on either page affects the way both are displayed.

2. From the empty **Fact Name** field, use the pull-down menu to select a predefined fact name, or enter one of your own by typing it into the empty field. Entering a fact name is *required* before additional information can be entered in either the Date, or Comment/Location fields.

   Note: Typing into a second Name field is how to record alternate name information, such as hyphenated married names. For example, if John Smith and Alice Carson became John and Alice Carson-Smith, you would enter the couple's birth names on their Family Pages and their hyphenated married names in the More About Lineage dialog box.

3. Click the **Date** field and enter a date for this event if you wish. See "Preferences for Dates and Measures" in this chapter for information about valid date formats.

4. Click the **Comment/Location** field and enter a comment or the location for this fact (see "Entering Locations" and "Fastfields," both in Chapter 3).

   Note: For best success when creating maps, enter the comment followed by a slash mark "/," then the location. Family Tree Maker will look for the location information to display in maps after the slash, or after the final slash if there is more than one, in the Comment/Location field.

5. Click the final field in this Fact line: the **Preferred** check box.

   When selected, this date/location is the one that is preferred and will be displayed for all facts with the same Fact Name, both in the family page, and in all reports and trees (see "Adding Alternate Facts" in the next section).

6. Press **Enter** to leave the fact line.

   Family Tree Maker sorts the new fact into the Facts list.

   Note: You can choose to sort facts by Fact Name or Date depending on your selection in the Facts Page dialog box. See "Preferences for Sorting the Facts Page" in Chapter 3.

Adding Alternate Facts or Names

As you add facts to your Family File from varying sources, there is a good chance that you will find conflicting information regarding some facts or names. Depending on the source, there may be a disagreement about the date, location, spelling, or some other detail. Family Tree Maker allows you to record and display differing information as an *alternate* fact or name, until you can confirm, by your later research, which is correct.

To add an alternate fact or name:

Follow the steps for "Entering Facts" in the previous section. After you have completed the steps and clicked Enter, Family Tree Maker sorts the new fact or name into the Fact List. Because the list is sorted alphabetically, alternate facts will appear sequentially in the Fact list.

Note: When you display a view with an alternate fact or name, a small "**a**" is placed at the end of that field indicating that alternate information has been recorded. When displaying a Family Page, only those individuals whose name appears in the Husband or Wife fields will show the "**a**" designation.

You can change which fact is the preferred fact, that is, the one that appears wherever the primary date/location is displayed in a view. Also, you can choose to display all dates and locations for a fact (see "Date and Fact Options," in Chapter 9).

Alternate Names will not be displayed in Reports and Trees, however, you can generate a report that shows only those facts where alternate data with the same fact name exists. See the Alternate Facts report described in "Displaying Reports," in Chapter 8.

Special Note about Changing Name Labels

If you have information to add to your Family File (perhaps imported from another family member) that uses a fact label you don't want to use, you can simply highlight that fact name in the first column of the More About Facts page (see Figure 5-1) and then type your preferred name over it. For example, a fact called "Other name" or "Name 2" could be highlighted and typed over with the label you wish to use.

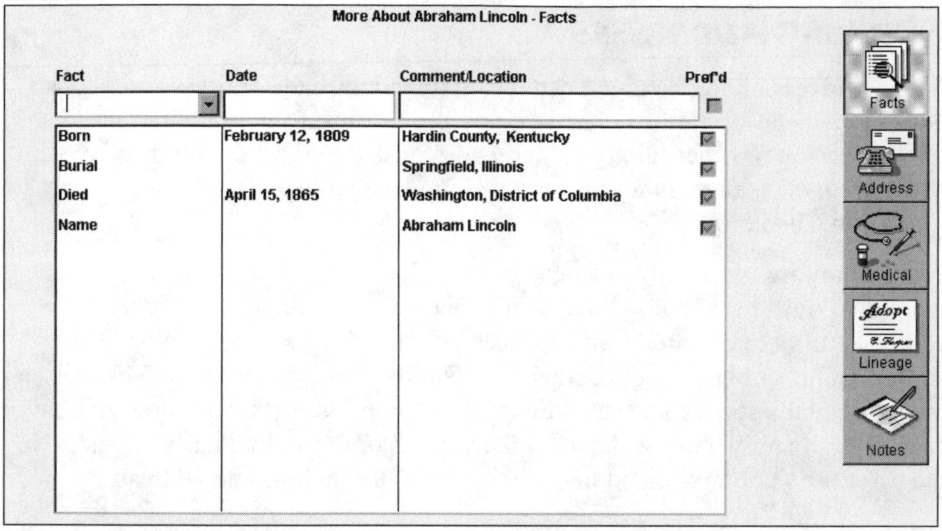

Figure 5-1. The Facts dialog box

Family Tree Maker can include information from the Facts dialog box in your trees and other documents. If Family Tree Maker needs to shorten these fields during printing, it will either abbreviate or truncate them. However, if while selecting items to include, you select the "Word wrap" check box in the Options dialog box, Family Tree Maker will not need to abbreviate or truncate the text in that field (see "Selecting Items to Include," in Chapter 9).

The "Comment/Location" fields can hold up to 256 characters. If you want to enter longer stories or biographical sketches to store separately from your trees, see "Entering Stories and Notes," in this chapter.

ENTERING ADDRESSES

In the **Address** dialog box, you can record an individual's address and phone number. This information is handy if you're planning to send invitations to a family reunion or other family gathering, because this is where Family Tree Maker gets the addresses for printing mailing labels. See "Displaying Labels and Cards," in Chapter 8.

For the purpose of mailing labels, you do not have to type an address into each individual's Address dialog box. This is because individuals can "inherit" addresses from their parents and spouses. If an individual does not have an address in his or her Address dialog box, Family Tree Maker first checks to see if the individual's spouse has an address. If the individual's spouse does not have an address, Family Tree Maker uses the address of the individual's parents. If the parents do not have an address either, the individual has no address.

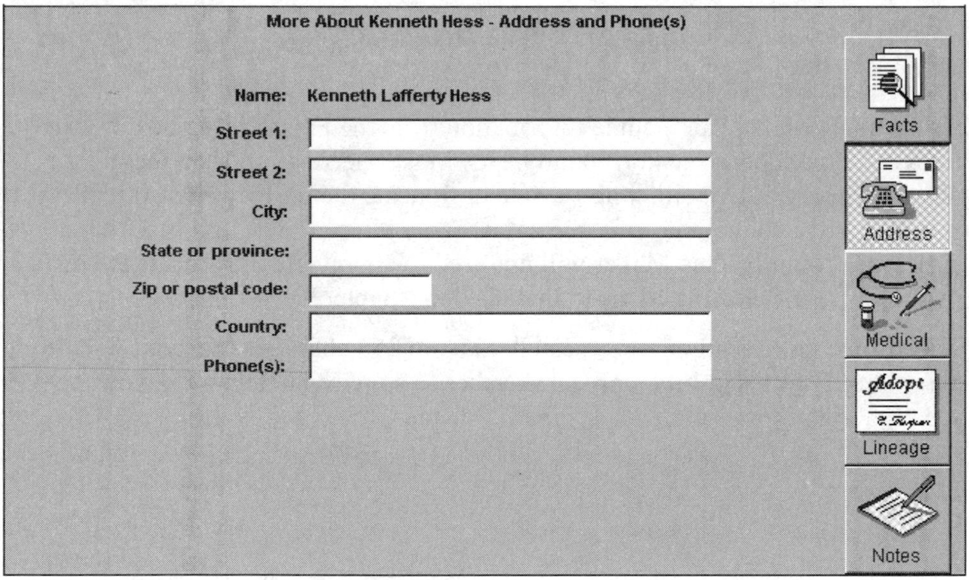

Figure 5-2. The Address dialog box

Street 1 *and* **Street 2** — Type the house or apartment number and street name in the "Street 1" field. You only need to use the "Street 2" field if the address is particularly long.

Phone(s) — You can enter more than one phone number in this field. Use whatever method you prefer to separate them, such as a comma, semicolon, or the word "or."

ENTERING MEDICAL INFORMATION

The **Medical** dialog box contains fields for recording physical and medical information about an individual, including height, weight, cause of death, and medical information. (See Figure 5-3.) If the individual has more information than will fit here, you can use the Notes dialog box to record additional medical information. You can also use the Facts dialog box if you want to record the dates of important medical events.

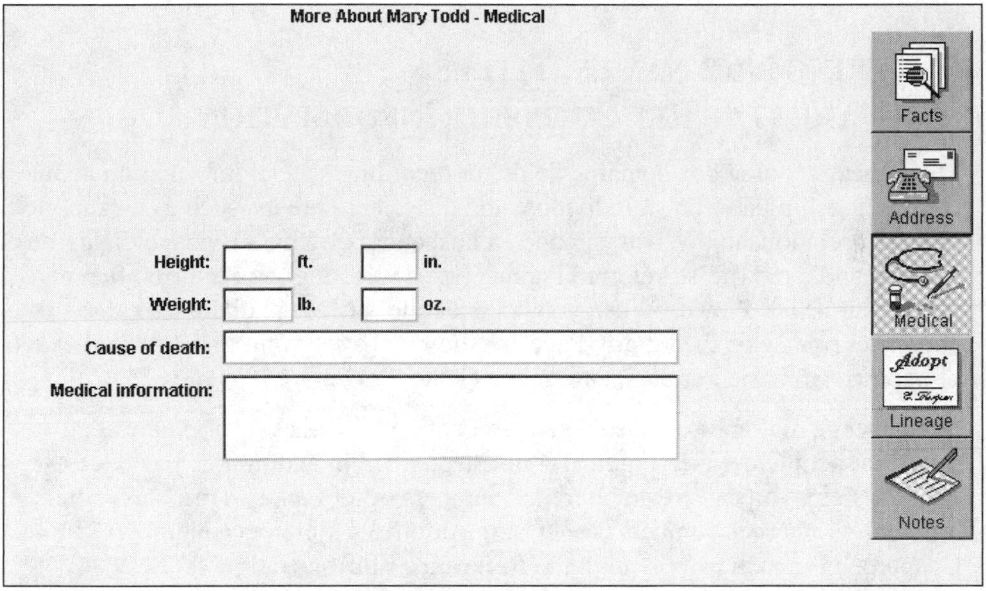

Figure 5-3. The Medical dialog box

Height — Use this field to record an individual's adult or current height. If your system is set for Metric units, enter the height in meters. If your system is set for English units, enter the height in feet and inches.

Note: For information about changing your system from Metric units to English units, see "Preferences for Dates and Measures," in Chapter 3.

Weight — Use this field to record an individual's adult or current weight. If your system is set for Metric units, enter the weight in kilograms. If your system is set for English units, enter the weight in pounds and ounces.

Cause of death — Use this field to record the cause of an individual's death.

Medical information — You can enter any type of medical information about the individual in this field. You might want to record diseases, allergies, injuries, surgeries, or serious illnesses that the individual experienced during his or her life.

ENTERING NICKNAMES, TITLES, AND PARENTAL RELATIONSHIP INFORMATION

The **Lineage** dialog box contains fields for recording special information about the relationship between an individual and his or her parents, such as an adoption or a step-relationship. When you open a husband's or wife's Lineage dialog box, the husband's or wife's Preferred Parents (see "Selecting the Preferred Parents" in Chapter 4) are shown. When you open a child's Lineage dialog box, the parents currently on the Family Page are shown. If you want to display other sets of parents, from the **People** menu, select **Other Parents**.

The Lineage dialog box is also where you enter nicknames (aka's) or special titles that people use (see Figure 5-4 in Chapter 5). In addition, if you have a filing system, you can create reference numbers or let Family Tree Maker create *automatic* reference numbers (see "Using Automatic Reference Numbers" in Chapter 5) for each individual in the **Reference number** field.

Title (Dr., Rev., Col., etc.) — You can select default titles for everyone, such as "Mr.," "Mrs.," and "Ms.," using the Titles dialog box (see "Preferences for Titles" in Chapter 3). However, some individuals in your Family File may go by a special title, such as "Dr." or "Reverend." When an individual has a special title, enter it in the **Title** field in the Lineage dialog box. For all other individuals, leave this field blank.

This person is also known as (aka) — This field is where you enter nicknames. You can print nicknames in family trees and other documents, so it's important to use this field correctly.

In the Family Page, make sure you enter the individual's full name. For example: **Gerald Charles Jansen**. Then in the Lineage dialog box you would enter only the nickname **Bud**. Entering the aka/nickname, *and* the last name, would cause the last name to appear twice when displayed in some aka formats (Gerald Charles "Bud Jansen" Jansen).

If you want to use nicknames rather than given names in printed documents, you need to indicate this to Family Tree Maker. For more information about including nicknames in your trees, reports, and other views, see "Name Options" in Chapter 9.

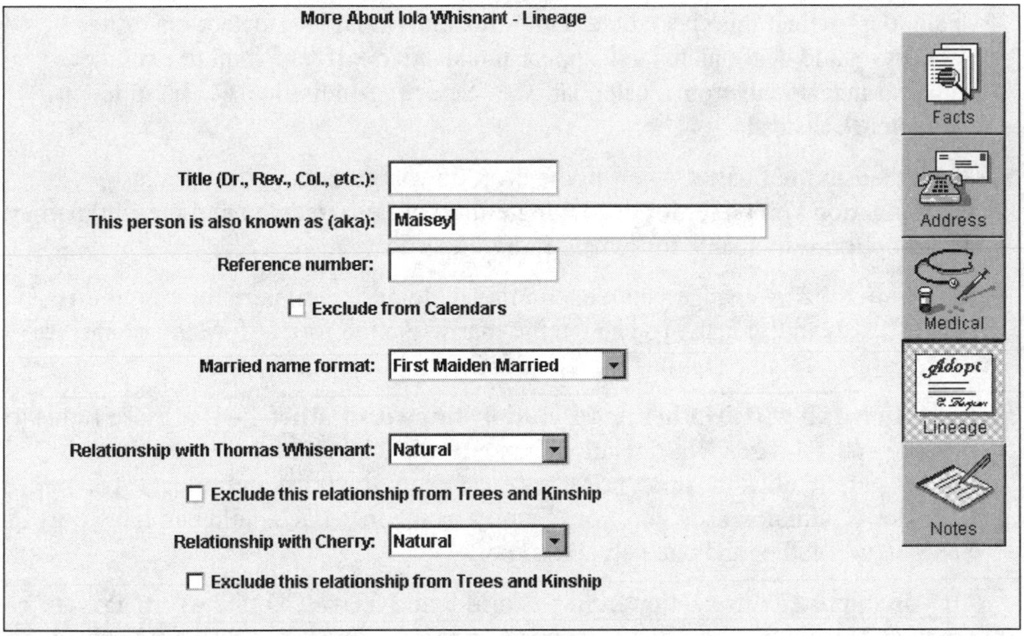

Figure 5-4. The Lineage dialog box

Reference number — This field can contain any numbers or letters that you choose. You might incorporate this number as part of your own filing system, but its use is entirely optional. If you would like, Family Tree Maker can assign reference numbers automatically (see "Selecting Automatic Reference Number Preferences" in Chapter 1).

> **Note:** Family Tree Maker can create Ahnentafel (standard) numbers automatically when you print Ancestor trees. They have nothing to do with what you enter in the "Reference number" field. See "Name Options" in Chapter 9 for information about Ahnentafel numbering.

Exclude from Calendars — If you don't want this individual to appear in calendars, select this check box. Only this individual is affected; his or her ancestors and descendants *will* appear in calendars. If you want to exclude several individuals from a calendar, see "Selecting Individuals to Include" in Chapter 9, instead.

Married name format — From the drop-down list, choose the format combination you prefer for displaying either, or both, maiden and married names. This option is available for female individuals only.

> **Note:** Any change you make in this dialog box will pertain only to this individual. To change the married name format for all women, see "Name Options" in Chapter 9.

Relationship with Mother *and* **Relationship with Father** — Use these fields to record special parent/child relationships. If a special relationship exists with either parent, click the appropriate parent's drop-down list and select "Adopted," "Foster," "Unknown," "Step," or "Family member." Each child can have only one natural father and one natural mother.

If you imported information from a World Family Tree CD, the word "Private" may appear in this drop-down list in some cases. This is to protect the privacy of individuals who may still be living. For your own purposes, it's better not to use this term. If you submit your Family File to the World Family Tree Project (see "The World Family Tree Project" in Chapter 12) "Private" will be selected automatically where necessary.

Exclude this relationship from Trees and Kinship — There may be occasions when you want to exclude certain relationships from a tree or Kinship report. If you select this check box for the relationship between a parent and a child, it means the following:

- In Ancestor trees, the child will appear in the tree, but the child's maternal and/or paternal ancestors will not appear in the tree, depending on which parent's check box(es) you select.

- In Descendant trees, checking either check box will exclude the child and any of the child's descendants. The child's siblings and their descendants will appear in the tree.

- In Kinship reports, the child will appear, but the child's maternal and/or paternal ancestors will not appear in the tree, depending on which parent's check box(es) you select.

Note: Selecting this check box will *not* exclude individuals from the All-in-One tree.

ENTERING STORIES AND NOTES

The **Notes** dialog box is a basic word processor. You can use it to enter and organize virtually any textual information, including a family member's favorite recipes, jokes, or even a short biography. You cannot print information from the Notes dialog box in your trees, but you can print your Notes on separate pages to include in a family book (see Figure 5-5 for an example). Figure 5-6 shows a summary of what you can do in the Notes dialog box.

Note: If you're not familiar with word processors, you'll find it helpful to do Part II of the Tutorial, later in this chapter.

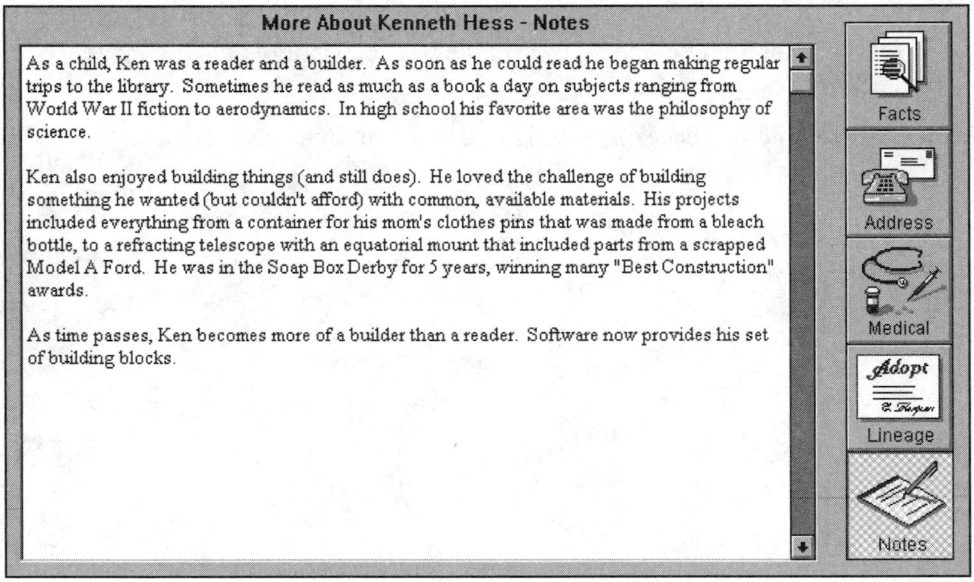

Figure 5-5. The Notes dialog box

To do this...	Turn to this section...
Use your mouse or keyboard to move the cursor anywhere in your text	"Moving Around in the Notes Dialog Box" in this chapter
Insert new text, delete old text, type over existing text, and reverse editing commands	"Editing Information" in Chapter 3
Rearrange text by cutting it from one place and pasting it to another	"Cutting, Copying, and Pasting" in Chapter 3, and "Moving or Copying Text from One Notes Dialog to Another" in this chapter
Avoid retyping information by copying it from one place to another	"Cutting, Copying, and Pasting" in Chapter 3, and "Moving or Copying Text from One Notes Dialog to Another" in this chapter
Change the text in the Notes dialog box to a different font, size, or style	"Formatting Text in the Notes Dialog Box" in this chapter
Print the text in the Notes dialog box	Chapter 10, "Printing Your Family Information"
Get information you've typed into another program and insert it directly into the Notes dialog box without retyping	"Importing Text..." in this chapter
Take information you've typed in the Notes dialog box and export it to another program	"Exporting Text..." in this chapter

Figure 5-6. A summary of what you can do in the Notes dialog box

Moving Around in the Notes Dialog Box

You can enter much more text into the Notes dialog box than can appear on the screen at any one time, so to edit your text you need to know how to move up and down through it. The scroll bar on the right side of the screen is the easiest way to do this. Just place the mouse pointer on the scroll box (that's the rectangle in the scroll bar), hold down your primary mouse button, and drag the scroll box up or down.

You can also use your keyboard to move through your text. Figure 5-7 shows which keys to use.

Press this key...	To do this...
←	Move the cursor one character to the left
→	Move the cursor one character to the right
↑	Move the cursor up one line
↓	Move the cursor down one line
Ctrl + ←	Move the cursor one word to the left
Ctrl + →	Move the cursor one word to the right
PgUp	Move up a whole screen's worth of text
PgDn	Move down a whole screen's worth of text
home	Move the cursor to the beginning of the line
end	Move the cursor to the end of the line
Ctrl + home	Move the cursor to the beginning of the Notes
Ctrl + end	Move the cursor to the end of the Notes

Figure 5-7. How to move around in the Notes dialog box

Editing Text in the Notes Dialog Box

You can edit your Notes just like you can edit the text in any word processor. "Editing Information" in Chapter 3 describes how to cut, copy, and paste text, delete information, reverse editing commands, and add extra lines and spaces.

Moving or Copying Text from
One Notes Dialog Box to Another

You can move or copy sections of text from one individual's Notes dialog box to another individual's Notes dialog box.

To perform this operation, start with the individual who has the text you want to move or copy:

1. Display that individual's Notes dialog box.

2. Highlight the text you want to move or copy.

   To highlight text with a mouse, place the mouse pointer in front of the first character that you want to select. Press and hold the primary mouse button while you drag the mouse until the last character you want to select is highlighted. Then, release the mouse button.

3. From the **Edit** menu, select **Cut** if you wish to move the text or select **Copy** if you wish to copy this text to another Notes dialog box.

4. From the **View** menu, select **Index of Individuals**.

   Family Tree Maker displays the Index of Individuals.

5. Select the individual to whom you want to transfer the text and then click **OK**.

   Family Tree Maker displays the Notes dialog box for that individual.

6. Position your cursor where you want to insert the text. If you want to use the new text to *replace* a section of existing text, highlight that section of text.

7. From the **Edit** menu, select **Paste Text**.

   Family Tree Maker pastes the text from the Clipboard into this individual's Notes and repositions any existing text, if necessary.

   Since the Clipboard is not erased until you use the Copy or Cut command again, you can paste the same text as many times as you like.

Finding Text in the Notes Dialog Box

Using the Find command, you can locate any text in a Notes dialog box.

To find text in a Notes dialog box:

1. Make sure you are in the Notes dialog box that you want to search.

2. From the **Edit** menu, select **Find**.

3. In the **Find what** field, type the text that you want to locate.

   If you type the letters `the` Family Tree Maker locates any word with "the" in it, including "there," "these," and "other," as well as "the." If you only want to find the whole word, and not pieces of other words, select the **Match whole word only** check box. If you only want to find words with the same capitalization as the text in the "Find what" field, select the **Match case** check box.

4. Click **Find next** to start the search.

   Family Tree Maker scrolls through the Notes, and when it locates the text, the cursor stops on the text. You can click **Find next** to look for additional occurrences of the text or **Cancel** to quit the search.

5. If you didn't start searching at the top of the Notes, Family Tree Maker asks if you want to continue the search from the top. Click **Yes** to continue searching from the top or click **No** to quit the search. Click **Cancel** when you want to close the Search dialog box.

Formatting Text in the Notes Dialog Box

When you make formatting choices in the Notes dialog box, you are formatting all of the notes for this one individual. You cannot format individual words or lines. In addition, the formatted text only appears on printed copies of the notes, not on the screen.

To format text in a Notes dialog box:

1. From the **Format** menu, select **Text Font, Style, & Size**.

   Family Tree Maker displays a message telling you that your formatting choices will appear only when you print.

2. Click **OK** to clear the message and continue.

   Family Tree Maker displays the Text Font, Style, & Size dialog box.

3. Make your formatting selections from the drop-down lists on the right side of the dialog box.

   The "Sample" field shows what your choices will look like.

4. After you make your selections, click **OK** to return to the Notes dialog box.

Copying Text from
Another Windows Program into a Notes Dialog Box

If you have family stories in another Windows program, you can copy them to the Clipboard and then paste them into the appropriate Notes dialog boxes. If you want to transfer information from a DOS program into Family Tree Maker, see "Importing Text from Another Program into a Notes Dialog Box," on the next page.

To transfer text from another Windows program into Family Tree Maker:

1. In the other Windows program, copy the information to the Clipboard.

    If you need assistance with this, please consult the manual that came with the other program.

2. In Family Tree Maker, go to the Notes dialog box where you want to place the information.

3. Position your cursor where you want to insert the text. If you want to use the new text to *replace* a section of existing text, highlight the section of text you want to replace.

4. From the **Edit** menu, select **Paste**.

Since the Clipboard is not erased until you use the Copy or Cut command again, you can paste the same information as many times as you like.

Importing Text from
Another Program into a Notes Dialog Box

If you've written paragraphs of family information using another software program, such as a word processor, you may be able to import that information into the Notes dialog box to avoid retyping it. To do this, the other program must be able to export, or transfer, your information to an **ASCII** file. ASCII files are generic text files that many programs can read and create. DOS programs create "PC-8" ASCII files, while Windows programs create "ANSI" ASCII files. Check the manual of your other program to see if and how you can export your information to an ASCII file. Look under "ASCII," "PC-8," "ANSI," or "Export" in the index of the other program's manual.

After you create an ASCII file in another program, you can import its contents into an individual's Notes dialog box.

Importing Note Text

1. Go to the Notes dialog box where you want to place the text.

2. Position the cursor where you want to insert the information.

3. From the **File** menu, select **Import Text File**.

   Family Tree Maker displays the Import Text File dialog box.

4. In the **Look in** drop-down list, select the drive where the file you want to import is located.

   In the box below the "Look in" field, Family Tree Maker displays a list of all the files and folders on the selected drive.

5. Double-click the folder containing the file you want to import.

6. Select the correct file type from the **File of type** drop-down list.

   In general, DOS programs create ASCII (PC-8) files, and Windows programs create ASCII (ANSI) files.

7. In the box below the "Look in" field, click the file you want to import.

8. Click **Open**.

   Family Tree Maker inserts a copy of the text into the Notes dialog box.

   Note: To export your Notes to an ASCII file for use in another program, see "Exporting Text from the Notes Dialog Box into Another Program," in this chapter.

Exporting Text from the Notes Dialog Box into Another Program

You can export the text from a Notes dialog box and bring it into another program, such as a word processor. To do this, you create an ASCII text file with Family Tree Maker and then open or import it into the other program. ASCII files are generic text files that many programs can read and create. DOS programs create "PC-8" ASCII files, while Windows programs create "ANSI" ASCII files. Check the manual of your other program to see if it can read, or import, ASCII files. Look under "ASCII," "PC-8," "ANSI," or "Import" in the index.

Exporting Note Text

1. Go to the Notes dialog box that has the text you want to export.

2. From the **File** menu, select **Export Notes**.

    Family Tree Maker displays the Export Notes dialog box.

3. In the **Save in** drop-down list, select the drive where you want to place the file you're creating.

    In the box below the "Save in" field, Family Tree Maker displays a list of all the files and folders on the selected drive.

4. Double-click the folder where you want to place the file you're creating.

5. Select the correct file type from the **Save as type** drop-down list.

    In general, DOS programs create ASCII (PC-8) files, and Windows programs create ASCII (ANSI) files.

6. Type a file name in the **File name** field.

7. Click **Save**.

    Family Tree Maker creates an ASCII file.

ENTERING BRIEF MARRIAGE FACTS

The Marriage Facts dialog box lets you enter facts about a couple's marriage in much the same way as the Facts dialog box lets you enter facts about an individual (see "Entering Facts" in this chapter). For example, you may wish to document an engagement, an annulment, or the date a divorce was filed or finalized.

To display the Marriage Facts dialog box for a marriage:

1. Go to the Family Page of the couple whose Marriage Facts dialog boxes you want to see.

2. Place the cursor in one of the marriage fields.

3. From the **View** menu, select **More About**. From the submenu, select **Facts**.

    Family Tree Maker displays the Marriage Facts dialog box for the selected individual. This page always shows a new, empty line of fact fields at the top of the list.

4. From the empty **Fact Name** field, use the pull-down list to select a predefined fact name, or enter one of your own.

Entering a fact name is *required* before additional information can be entered in either the "Date" or "Comment/Location" fields.

5. Click the **Date** field and enter a date for this event if you wish. See "Preferences for Dates and Measures" in Chapter 3 for information about valid date formats.

6. Click the **Comment/Location** field and enter a comment or the location for this fact (see "Entering Locations," and "Fastfields," both in Chapter 3).

    Note: For best success when creating maps, enter the marriage comment, followed by a slash "/"mark, then the marriage location. Family Tree Maker will look for the location information after the slash, or after the final slash if there is more than one, in the Comment/Location field.

7. Click the **Preferred** check box.

    When selected, this date/location is the one that is preferred and will be displayed for all facts with the same Fact Name, both in the Family Page, and in all reports and trees (see "Adding Alternate Facts" in this chapter).

    Note: Fact names such as "separated" or "divorced" are of a type called **marriage-ending**. Only one fact name is allowed to be "Preferred" in this category.

8. Press **Enter** to leave the marriage fact line.

    Family Tree Maker sorts the new marriage fact into the list of marriage facts.

Note: Family Tree Maker now allows any number of marriage and marriage ending facts. If the marriage has another significant event or date associated with it, you can use these fields to record it. For example, you could record the date of the couple's engagement or of a special anniversary party.

Reference number — This field can contain any numbers or letters that you choose. Or, you may have Family Tree Maker assign reference numbers for you automatically. For more information see "Setting Automatic Reference Number Preferences" in Chapter 1.

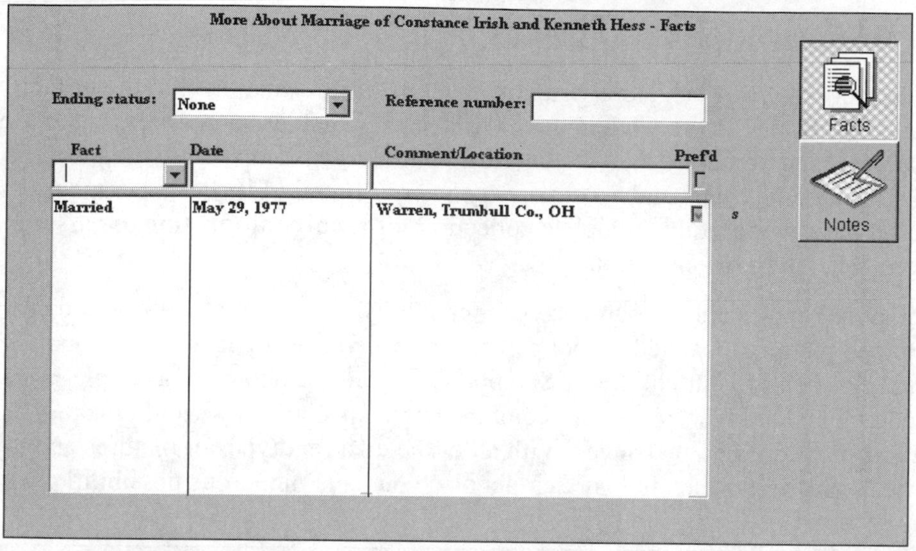

Figure 5-8. More About Marriage Facts dialog box

Using Automatic Reference Numbers

Reference numbers are useful in helping you avoid duplication of information, or documenting facts against the wrong person, especially where two different individuals may share the same name.

You can have Family Tree Maker assign reference numbers to individuals and marriages for you automatically. If you have already entered reference numbers in your Family File, Family Tree Maker will not replace the numbers you assigned with automatic reference numbers. In this case, only individuals and marriages without them will receive automatic reference numbers — including any new individuals and marriages you add to your Family File. For more about this feature, see "Selecting Automatic Reference Number Preferences" in Chapter 1.

Entering Marriage Stories and Notes

To display the Notes dialog box for a marriage, click the Notes button in the More About Marriage Facts dialog box.

A Notes dialog box for a marriage works exactly like a Notes dialog box for an individual. For details, see "Entering Stories and Notes" in this chapter.

To return to the Family Page from the Notes dialog box, from the **View** menu, select **Family Page**.

SCRAPBOOKS: THE BASICS

In Scrapbooks, you can store virtually any type of information about your family, including Kodak Photo CD Pictures; OLE objects such as sound files, video files, text files, and picture files; and non-OLE picture files such as bitmaps and TIFF files. Each individual and each marriage in your Family File has a Scrapbook, so you'll have wonderfully complete collections of family information to pass on from generation to generation.

Scrapbook pages allow you to use your creativity. For example, you could use scanned pictures, scanned school papers, and video files to create childhood pages in each of your children's Scrapbooks. Scanned photos of a couple's wedding and anniversary parties combined with special songs would make a beautiful record of a marriage. With all of the different types of pictures and objects that you can include in Scrapbooks, you have numerous possibilities!

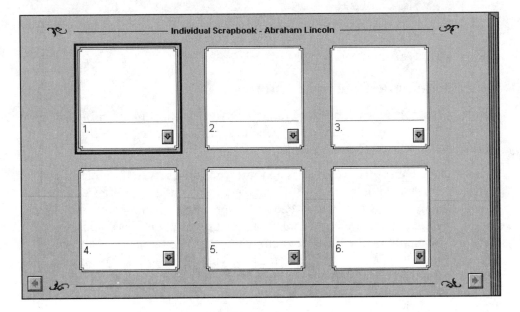

Figure 5-9. An empty Scrapbook page

Opening a Scrapbook for an Individual or Marriage

You can open Scrapbooks from any view. However, we'll first explain how to open Scrapbooks from the Family Page.

To display an individual's or a marriage's Scrapbook:

1. Go to the Family Page containing the individual or the marriage whose Scrapbook you want to see.

    The Index of Individuals and Find Individual are two quick ways to locate an individual's Family Page. See "Moving to Anyone in Your Family File," and "Locating Individuals in Your Family File," in Chapter 4.

2. On the Family Page, place the cursor either on the name of the individual or on the marriage whose Scrapbook you want to see.

3. From the **View** menu, select **Scrapbook**.

    Family Tree Maker displays the individual's or marriage's Scrapbook. If this is the first time you have opened this Scrapbook, you will be on the first page. If you have opened this Scrapbook before, you will be on the same page as when you last closed the Scrapbook.

If you want to open a Scrapbook from a view other than the Family Page, simply do step 3 while you are in that view. Family Tree Maker will display the Individual Scrapbook for the **primary individual**.

The primary individual is the main individual in the view. For example, in a Descendant tree, the primary individual is the individual at the top of the tree. Some views, such as the Report view or the Labels/Cards view, don't have a "main" individual. In these views, the primary individual is the primary individual from the previous view.

Note: If the Scrapbook that Family Tree Maker displays is not for the individual that you want, you can navigate to their Scrapbook easily. From the **View** menu, select **Index of Individuals**, select the individual whose Scrapbook you want to see, and then click **OK**.

What Goes into a Scrapbook?

You can store virtually any type of family information in a Scrapbook — from family photographs and other paper memorabilia that has been scanned, to pictures, and other items that can be pasted to and from the Clipboard. You can also add sound clips, video clips, and other OLE objects, Kodak Photo CD pictures, and text. Once one of these items is stored in a Scrapbook, we refer to it as a **Picture/Object**. If you're uncertain about what these different terms refer to, keep reading; each one is described below.

Note: If you are planning to include large images and video clips in your Scrapbooks, keep the capabilities of your computer in mind. If you only have the minimum system requirements, your machine will run slowly when you work with large images and video clips. In fact, if your machine does not have enough RAM, you may not be able to load particularly large files. In addition, you will need quite a bit of free space on your hard drive to store large images and video clips.

Kodak Photo CD Pictures

A Kodak Photo CD is a CD-ROM disc containing pictures that came from your undeveloped film, negatives, or old photos. Placing your pictures on a Kodak Photo CD is easy to do and a great way to prepare family photos for use with Family Tree Maker.

To use Kodak Photo CDs, the only special equipment you need is a CD-ROM player on your computer that can read a Kodak Photo CD (many of the early CD-ROM players cannot). If you have one of these CD-ROM players, Family Tree Maker can read and import your Photo CD Pictures.

Pictures

Pictures, sometimes called graphics, are electronic images. There are many ways to get pictures:

- Take your undeveloped film, old photos, or negatives to a Kodak processor and have the images placed on a Kodak Photo CD.

- Create, scan, or purchase pictures that you can store on your hard disk in a graphics file. You can create your own pictures using a graphics software program. The next section describes scanning. To purchase pictures in a software package, check with your local software dealer.

- Cut or copy an image from another software program, another Scrapbook in Family Tree Maker, or another view in Family Tree Maker and store it temporarily on the Clipboard as a bitmap or metafile.

- Cut or copy an image from any OLE server application and store it temporarily on the Windows Clipboard.

Pictures can be stored in many different file formats. Some common formats are bitmap (.BMP) and Tagged Image File Format (.TIF). When you have pictures in one of these or several other file formats, you can place them into your Family Tree Maker Scrapbooks as described in "Scrapbooks: Inserting Items" in this chapter.

Note: Family Tree Maker uses the industry standard JPEG compression method and does *not* support graphics files that use LZW compression technology.

Scanning

Scanning refers to making an electronic reproduction of a paper item, such as a photograph, newspaper clipping, birth certificate, or diploma. In effect, scanning is a way of making your own pictures, just like those described above in "Pictures." Scanning is a great way to preserve family memorabilia, because scanned images won't fade or become brittle like paper and photographs tend to do after many years. And, once you have a scanned image of an item, you can store it safely on your computer.

To scan an item, you must have a scanner and scanner software (or use one of today's copy services that offer scanning, among other graphics services). Family Tree Maker does not scan items for you, nor can it act as scanning software, although you can scan pictures directly into a Scrapbook. There are many different types of scanners, but most scanners come with their own software. If you are interested in scanning your paper memorabilia, the best thing to do is to talk with your local computer dealer. They should be able to help you choose the scanner that is right for you. Of course, you'll also want to read the manual for the scanner so that you can correctly create electronic images to place in your Scrapbooks.

Note: Scanning at more than 100 dpi (dots per inch) will take up unnecessary hard drive space on your system.

Object Linking and Embedding

Object Linking and Embedding (OLE) is a technology that lets you create items in one software program and place them in another software program. For example, you can use video capture software to transfer clips of your home videos onto your computer. Then, with the help of Object Linking and Embedding you can transfer video clips from your video capture software into Family Tree Maker Scrapbooks.

OLE objects are items, such as the video clips described above, that can be transferred from one software program to another. The types of objects you might want to use in Scrapbooks include sound clips, video clips, still images or pictures, and text objects from a word processor, spreadsheet, or database.

An **OLE server** is a software program, such as the video capture software described above, that creates OLE objects. Any Windows 3.1 (or higher) compatible program *can* be an OLE server. Not all are, so it is important to read the box carefully before making a purchase. Most software manufacturers will advertise OLE server capability if they have it, or you can call the manufacturer to ask before purchasing.

An **OLE client** is a software program, such as Family Tree Maker, into which OLE objects can be placed. Think of it in terms of a restaurant: the server creates the food and serves it to the client, and the client eats (or stores) it. For a more thorough description of Object Linking and Embedding, see the index of your Microsoft Windows User's Guide.

Text

While the Notes dialog box is generally where you store text, there may also be cases when you want to store text in the Scrapbook. For example, if your child used a word processor to write a report for school or a letter to grandma, you might want to save the word processor file in the Scrapbook.

To store text (word processor files) in the Scrapbook, you cannot just use the Edit menu to copy and paste it into the Scrapbook. Instead, you need to treat the text as an OLE object. For more information about OLE objects, see the section above titled, "Object Linking and Embedding (OLE)."

Setting Defaults for Picture Resolution and Compression

You can set a default degree of compression and resolution for any pictures that you bring into Scrapbooks. Even if you set a default, you can change the settings for individual pictures at any time.

To set default levels of compression and resolution for pictures:

1. From the **File** menu, select **Preferences**. From the submenu, select **Pictures/Objects**.

   Family Tree Maker displays the Pictures/Objects dialog box.

2. You can now select the default compression and/or resolution. Each of your options is described below.

   Degree of Compression — Select the option button corresponding to the degree of compression that you want for your picture. Higher ratios give you a greater loss in picture quality, but the pictures will take up less space on your hard disk. (Family Tree Maker uses the industry standard JPEG compression method and does *not* support LZW compression.) Lower ratios give you pictures with less loss in quality, but will take more disk space. The "1:1" setting will not reduce the quality of your picture at all, but will take up the most space on your hard disk. In general, the "recommended" setting is a good balance between quality loss and disk space.

Photo CD — This option is only available for Kodak Photo CD Pictures. Select the option button corresponding to the resolution that you want for your picture. "Resolution" refers to the size of your picture. A higher resolution will create a larger picture, and a larger picture will be sharper and have more detail. If the default resolution that you choose here is not available for one of the images that you import, Family Tree Maker will import it at the next available lower resolution.

Choosing resolutions higher (larger) than the recommended "256 x 384" will use up large amounts of your hard disk space. In addition, you may not be able to load a picture at a very high resolution if your computer does not have a sufficient amount of RAM (memory).

3. After you make your selections, click **OK**.

Family Tree Maker remembers and applies your selections until you change them again.

SCRAPBOOKS: INSERTING ITEMS

There are five different ways to insert items into a Scrapbook. The method that you use will depend on what it is that you want to insert. Use Figure 5-10 to help determine which method you should use in each case.

When you are ready to insert a new item, you can place it either between two Pictures/Objects or to the immediate right of the last Pictures/Object. To insert an item between two Pictures/Objects, select the Picture/Object on the right and then use a command from the Pictures/Objects menu to insert the new item. When you insert an item after the last Picture/Object in the Scrapbook, you cannot leave empty spaces between the last Picture/Object and the new item. The new item must be inserted directly after the last Picture/Object.

When you have...	Use this menu choice...
A photo or document that you have not yet scanned	Picture/Object: Insert Picture from Scanner/Camera, see "Insert Picture/Object from Scanner/Camera in this chapter
Photos stored on a digital camera	Picture/Object: Insert Picture from Scanner/Camera, see "Insert Picture/Object from Scanner/Camera in this chapter
A Kodak Photo CD Picture	Picture/Object: Insert Photo CD Picture, see "Picture/Object: Insert Photo CD Picture" in this chapter
A graphic file, such as a scanned image or clip art, stored on your computer's hard disk. Compatible file formats include (*.BMP), (*.PCX), (*.TIF), (*.JPG), (*.WMF), (*.PSD), (*.FPX), and (*.JFF). **Note**: Family Tree Maker does *not* support graphics files that use LZW compression technology	Picture/Object: Insert Picture from File, see "Picture/Object: Insert Picture from File" in this chapter
An OLE object in a file (Also use this method when you want to create a new OLE object and then insert it into the Scrapbook)	Picture/Object: Insert Object, see "Picture/Object: Insert Object" in this chapter
Items that you have cut or copied to the Clipboard, such as an Ancestor tree, or even a Picture/Object that you are copying from one Scrapbook to another	Edit: Paste, see "Edit: Paste" and "Edit: Past Special" in this chapter
OLE objects on the Clipboard, such as pictures, text, video, and sound	Edit: Paste or Edit, see "Edit: Paste and Edit: Paste Special" in this chapter

Figure 5-10. Commands for inserting items into Scrapbooks

Picture/Object: Insert Photo CD Picture

Using the Insert Photo CD Picture command on the Pictures/Objects menu, you can insert pictures from Kodak Photo CD-ROM discs. When you insert pictures, keep the capabilities of your computer in mind. If you insert large picture files, your machine may run slowly. In fact, if your machine does not have enough RAM, you may not be able to load particularly large files. In addition, you will need quite a bit of free space on your hard drive to store large images and video clips.

To insert a Kodak Photo CD picture into a Scrapbook:

1. In the Scrapbook, select the area where you want to insert the picture.

    If you insert a picture when an empty Picture/Object area is selected, the picture goes into that Picture/Object area. If you insert a picture when an occupied Picture/Object area is selected, Family Tree Maker moves the existing Pictures/Objects to the right and inserts a new area for the new picture.

2. From the **Picture/Object** menu, select **Insert Photo CD Picture**.

    Family Tree Maker displays the Insert from Photo CD dialog box. You have several options.

    You can use your computer keyboard to move around and select pictures in this dialog box. Figure 5-11 shows which keys work as selection and navigation keys. Your other options are described below.

    Find — Use this button to go to a particular picture on the Photo CD. Simply type the number of the picture in the **Find photo number** field and then click **OK**. Family Tree Maker returns you to the Insert from Photo CD dialog box and selects the picture with that number.

    View — Use this button to display the currently selected picture at full size in the View Picture dialog box. In the View Picture dialog box you can use the scroll bars and the **Zoom** buttons to get a better look at your picture. The choices that you make here do not change the picture; they are only for display purposes. Click **OK** in the View Picture dialog box to return to the Insert from Photo CD dialog box.

    Resolution — Use this button to change the resolution and compression settings used to store this picture. In most cases, you do not need to change the compression and resolution. However, if you want to alter them, go ahead and do it now. See "Controlling Picture Resolution and Compression" in this chapter for instructions.

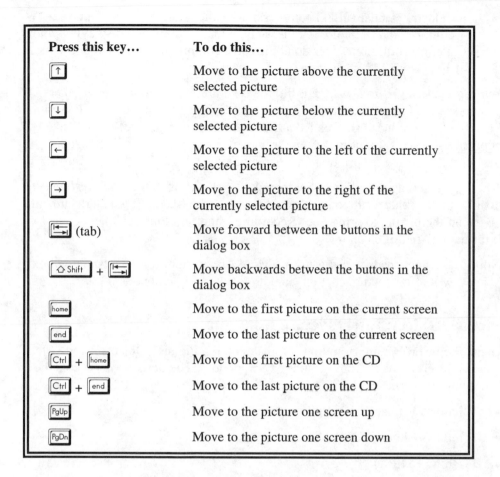

Press this key…	To do this…
⬆	Move to the picture above the currently selected picture
⬇	Move to the picture below the currently selected picture
⬅	Move to the picture to the left of the currently selected picture
➡	Move to the picture to the right of the currently selected picture
⮆ (tab)	Move forward between the buttons in the dialog box
⇧ Shift + ⮅	Move backwards between the buttons in the dialog box
home	Move to the first picture on the current screen
end	Move to the last picture on the current screen
Ctrl + home	Move to the first picture on the CD
Ctrl + end	Move to the last picture on the CD
PgUp	Move to the picture one screen up
PgDn	Move to the picture one screen down

Figure 5-11. Moving the cursor in the Insert from Photo CD dialog box

3. Click **OK** in the Insert from Photo CD dialog box when you are ready to insert a picture.

   Family Tree Maker displays the Edit Picture dialog box where you can select editing options. The editing options fall into three categories: rotating, flipping, and cropping. See "Editing Pictures/Objects" in this chapter for instructions on using this dialog box.

Note: If you want to edit a picture, this is the best time to do it. This is because Family Tree Maker compresses images for storage unless you select 1:1 compression. Once you place a picture in the Scrapbook, Family Tree Maker must decompress and recompress it each time you edit it. Decompressing and recompressing a picture multiple times reduces the quality of the picture. (Family Tree Maker uses the industry standard JPEG compression method, and does *not* support LZW compression technology.) Please note that printing and displaying your picture at different sizes do not involve compression and will not reduce the quality of your picture.

When you click **OK** to leave the Edit Picture dialog box, Family Tree Maker compresses and saves the picture in your Family File. The picture displays in the Scrapbook at a reduced size, called a **thumbnail**. The thumbnail's small size allows you to see several images on the screen at once. The real, full-sized images will be used for printing and displaying.

After you insert a picture into a Scrapbook, use the More About Pictures/Objects dialog box to create a caption and to tell Family Tree Maker in which documents you want the picture to print. See "Recording Important Picture/Object Information" in this chapter.

Note: Changes made to captions in a More About Pictures/Objects dialog box will affect picture captions in both Books and Scrapbooks.

Picture/Object: Insert Picture from File

Using the Insert Picture from File command on the Pictures/Objects menu you can insert pictures from files into a Scrapbook. The Scrapbook accepts the following file formats:

- Windows Bitmap (*.BMP)
- Windows MetaFile (*.WMF)
- FlashPix (*.FPX)
- Photoshop (*.PSD)
- ZSoft Image (*.PCX)
- Tagged Image Format (*.TIF)
- JPEG Interchange Format (*.JPG, *.JFF)

When you insert pictures, keep the capabilities of your computer in mind. If you insert large picture files, your machine may run slowly. In fact, if your machine does not have enough RAM, you may not be able to load particularly large files. In addition, you will need quite a bit of free space on your hard drive to store large images.

Inserting a Picture/Object from File

1. In the Scrapbook, select the frame/area where you want to insert the picture.

    If you insert a picture with an empty Picture/Object area selected, the picture goes into that Picture/Object area. If you insert a picture with an occupied Picture/Object area selected, Family Tree Maker moves the existing Picture/Object to the right and inserts a new Picture/Object area for the new picture.

2. From the **Picture/Object** menu, select **Insert Picture from File**.

    Family Tree Maker displays the Insert Picture dialog box.

3. Click the **Look in** drop-down list and select the drive containing the picture file you want to insert. If you don't know the location of your file, follow the instructions in "Finding Files," in Chapter 13.

    In the box below the "Look in" field, Family Tree Maker displays a list of all the files and folders on the selected drive.

4. Double-click the folder containing the file you want to insert.

5. Click the **Files of Type** drop-down list and select the format of the file that you want to open.

6. In the box below the "Look in" field, select the name of your file, and then choose from the following options:

    Preview Picture — Select this check box to display the picture at reduced size in the "Preview" field.

    View — Use this button to display the picture at full size in the View Picture dialog box.

    Compression — Use this button to change the compression used to store this picture. See "Controlling Picture Resolution and Compression" in this chapter for a description of this dialog box. In most cases, you do not need to change the compression.

7. Click **Open** in the Insert Picture dialog box.

Family Tree Maker displays the Edit Picture dialog box where you can select editing options. The editing options fall into three categories: rotating, flipping, and cropping. See "Editing Pictures/Objects" in this chapter for instructions on using this dialog box.

Note: If you want to edit a picture, this is the best time to do it. This is because Family Tree Maker compresses images for storage unless you select 1:1 compression. After you place a picture in the Scrapbook, Family Tree Maker decompresses and recompresses it each time you edit it. Decompressing and recompressing a picture multiple times reduces the quality of the picture. (Family Tree Maker uses the industry standard JPEG compression and does *not* support LZW compression technology.) Please note that printing and displaying your picture at different sizes do not involve compression and do not reduce the quality of your picture.

When you click **OK** to leave the Edit Picture dialog box, Family Tree Maker compresses and saves the picture in your Family File. The picture displays in the Scrapbook at a reduced size, called a thumbnail. The thumbnail's small size allows you to see several images on the screen at once. The real, full-sized images will be used for printing and displaying.

Insert Picture/Object from a Scanner or Digital Camera

Many home computer users today have their own scanners or digital camera devices for capturing images of all kinds. Family Tree Maker allows you to scan your documents or photos directly into a Scrapbook.

To insert a document into a Scrapbook:

1. In the destination Scrapbook, select the picture frame where you want to insert your scanned document.

2. From the **Picture/Object** menu, select **Insert Picture from Scanner/Camera**.

   Family Tree Maker displays the Select Scanner or Camera dialog box, showing all the Twain-compliant devices installed in your computer.

3. Highlight the device you want to use and click **Select**.

   Family Tree Maker closes the dialog box and opens your scanning device software.

   Note: Scanning at resolutions above 100 dpi will take up unnecessary hard drive space on your system.

4. Scan your image as usual, then click "**Final**" (or whatever commits the previewed image on your scanner). Family Tree Maker will automatically display your scanned image in the **Edit Picture** dialog box.

5. Select any editing options you wish (see "Editing Pictures/Objects" in this chapter), then click **OK**.

    Family Tree Maker inserts your scanned picture into the Scrapbook.

Adding Captions to Pictures

After you insert a picture into the Scrapbook, use the More About Pictures/Objects dialog box to create a caption and to tell Family Tree Maker in which documents you want the picture to print. For more information, see "Recording Important Picture/Object Information" in this chapter.

Picture/Object: Insert Object

With the Insert Object command, you can insert existing OLE objects into the Scrapbook. In addition, you can create new OLE objects and then insert them into the Scrapbook. OLE objects include pictures, text, spreadsheets, sound clips, and video clips. When you insert pictures, video, or sound files, keep the capabilities of your computer in mind. If you insert large files, your machine may run slowly. In fact, if your machine does not have enough RAM, you may not be able to load particularly large files. In addition, you will need quite a bit of free space on your hard drive to store large images and video clips.

Inserting Existing OLE Objects into the Scrapbook

To insert an *existing* OLE object with the Insert Object command:

1. In the Scrapbook, select the area into which you want to insert the object.

    If you insert an OLE object when an empty Picture/Object area is selected, the OLE object goes into that Picture/Object area. If you insert an OLE object when an occupied Picture/Object area is selected, Family Tree Maker moves the existing Picture/Object to the right and inserts a new Picture/Object area for the new OLE object.

2. From the **Picture/Object** menu, select **Insert Object**.

    Family Tree Maker displays the Insert Object dialog box.

3. Select the **Create from File** option button.

4. In the **File** field, type the path and name of the file containing the OLE object that you want to insert into the Scrapbook.

    For example, if you had a file called "sound.wav" in the "windows" folder on your C:\ drive, you would type `C:\windows\sound.wav`

    If you do not remember the exact name and location of your file, click **Browse** to display the Browse dialog box. In the Browse dialog box, use the **Look in** field to locate your file. Click **Open** to return to the Insert Object dialog box after you have the correct file and folder name.

    If you want to display an icon in the Scrapbook instead of the OLE object itself, select the **Display As Icon** check box. You may want to do this if you are pasting a text file or some other object that isn't attractive when it's shrunk down to fit into the Picture/Object area.

    When you select this option, you can change the appearance of the icon by clicking **Change Icon**. In the Change Icon dialog box, you can either type the file name for the new icon in the **From File** field, or search for an icon file by clicking **Browse**. Click **OK** to return to the Insert Object dialog box after you have the correct file and folder name.

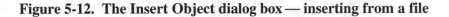

Insert Object

Create New:

● Create from File: File:
c:\windows\sound.wav

Browse...

OK

Cancel

Help

☐ Display As Icon

Result

Inserts the contents of the file as an object into your document so that you may activate it using the application which created it.

Figure 5-12. The Insert Object dialog box — inserting from a file

5.   When the correct file name is in the **File** field, click **OK**.

Family Tree Maker places the OLE object in the Scrapbook.

After you insert an OLE object into the Scrapbook, use the More About Pictures/Objects dialog box to create a caption and to tell Family Tree Maker in which documents you want the item to print (see "Recording Important Picture/Object Information" in this chapter). You can also edit an OLE object after it's in the Scrapbook (see "Editing OLE Objects" in this chapter).

Creating and Inserting New OLE Objects into the Scrapbook

To create a *new* OLE object to insert into a Scrapbook:

1.   In the Scrapbook, select the area where you want to insert the object.

If you insert an OLE object with an empty Picture/Object area selected, the OLE object goes into that Picture/Object area. If you insert an OLE object with an occupied Picture/Object area selected, Family Tree Maker moves the existing Picture/Object to the right and inserts a new Picture/Object area for the new OLE object.

2.   From the **Picture/Object** menu, select **Insert Object**.

Family Tree Maker displays the Insert Object dialog box.

3.   Select the **Create New** option button.

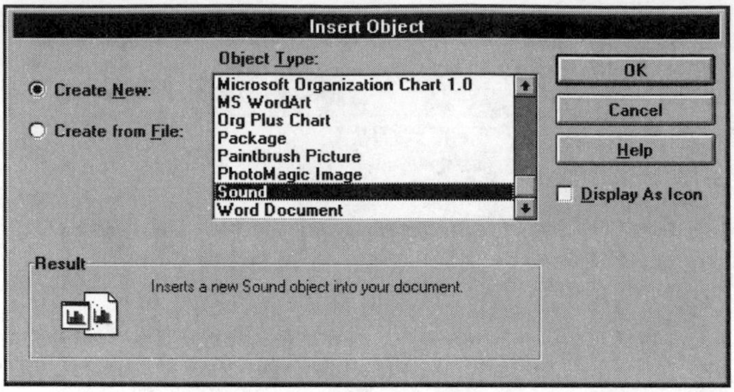

Figure 5-13. The Insert Object dialog box — creating a new file

4. In the **Object Type** scrolling list, click the name of the OLE object that you want to insert into the Scrapbook.

    Microsoft Windows opens the software program in which you can create the OLE object.

5. In the other software program, create the OLE object.

    If you need instructions for that program, please refer to its manual.

6. After you finish creating the new OLE object, from the **File** menu of that software program, select **Exit and Return to Family Tree Maker**.

    Microsoft Windows closes the software program and returns to Family Tree Maker. (Windows may also ask if you want to update or save your information; answer **Yes** or **OK**.) Family Tree Maker places the OLE object in the Scrapbook.

After you insert an OLE object into the Scrapbook, use the More About Picture/Object dialog box to create a caption and to tell Family Tree Maker in which documents you want the item to print (see "Recording Important Picture/Object Information" in this chapter). You can also edit an OLE object after it's in the Scrapbook (see "Editing OLE Objects" in this chapter).

Edit: Paste and Edit: Paste Special

With the Paste command you can insert items that you have cut or copied to the Clipboard, such as items from other software programs, Pictures/Objects from other Scrapbooks, and OLE objects like pictures, sound clips, video clips, and word processor documents. You can also insert OLE Objects with the Paste Special command. When you insert OLE objects with the Paste Special command, you have slightly more control over the process.

When you insert pictures, video, and sound, keep the capabilities of your computer in mind. If you insert large files, your machine may run slowly. In fact, if your machine does not have enough RAM, you may not be able to load particularly large files. In addition, you will need quite a bit of free space on your hard drive to store large files.

To paste an item from the Clipboard into a Scrapbook:

1. Make sure that the item you want to paste is on the Clipboard.

    In general, to copy an item to the Clipboard, you first select that item. Then from the **Edit** menu, select **Copy**. If the item is in a software program other than Family Tree Maker, the process may be slightly different. Please refer to that software program's manual for instructions. The item must either be a metafile or an OLE Object to be pasteable into Scrapbooks.

2. In the Scrapbook, select the area into which you want to paste the item.

    If you paste an item from the Clipboard when an empty Picture/Object area is selected, the item will be pasted into that Picture/Object area. If you paste an item from the Clipboard when an occupied Picture/Object area is selected, Family Tree Maker moves the existing Picture/Object to the right and inserts a new Picture/Object area for the new item.

3. From Family Tree Maker's **Edit** menu, select either **Paste** or **Paste Special**.

    If you are using the Paste command, skip the remaining two steps and read the paragraphs after step 5. If you are using the Paste Special command, continue with step 4.

4. Family Tree Maker displays the Paste Special dialog box. In the **As** list, click the data type corresponding to the OLE object that you want to paste into the Scrapbook.

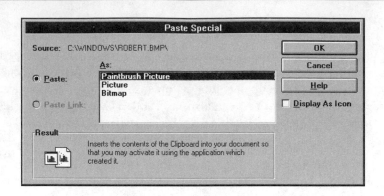

Figure 5-14. The Paste Special dialog box

If you want to display an icon in the Scrapbook instead of the OLE object itself, select the **Display As Icon** check box. You may want to do this if you are pasting in a text file or some other object that isn't attractive when it's shrunk down to fit into the Picture/Object area.

When you select this option, you can also change the appearance of the icon by clicking **Change Icon**. In the Change Icon dialog box, you can either type the file name for the new icon in the **From file** field, or search for an icon file by clicking **Browse**. Click **OK** to return to the Paste Special dialog box after you have the correct file path and name.

5. Click **OK**.

Family Tree Maker places the OLE object in the Scrapbook.

After you paste an item into a Scrapbook, use the More About Picture/Object dialog box to create a caption and to tell Family Tree Maker in which documents you want the item to print (see "Recording Important Picture/Object Information" in this chapter).

You can also edit and change the compression of an item after it's in the Scrapbook (see "Editing Pictures/Objects" and "Controlling Picture Resolution and Compression," both in this chapter). To edit an OLE object, see "Editing OLE Objects" in this chapter.

SCRAPBOOKS: WORKING WITH PICTURES/OBJECTS

Once you have Pictures/Objects in your Scrapbooks, there are many things you can do with them. For example, you can display pictures at full size or play videos and sounds. You can even play a whole Scrapbook at once in a "slide show." You can also edit Pictures/Objects, and store information about them in the More About Picture/Object dialog box. All of these functions are described in the following sections.

Recording Important Picture/Object Information

Each Picture/Object has its own More About Picture/Object dialog box. This dialog box is for recording captions and other important information about your Pictures/Objects, such as what they are and when they were created. Another important function of this dialog box is that you use it to select the types of documents in which you want your Pictures/Objects to print, and whether you want to include each Picture/Object when you play the Scrapbook.

To record captions and other information about your Pictures/Objects:

1. Select the Picture/Object you want to record information about.

2. From the **Picture/Object** menu, select **More About**. You can also press Ctrl + M or click the downward-pointing arrow next to the Picture/Object.

   Family Tree Maker displays the More About Picture/Object dialog box. A reduced-size image of your Picture/Object displays in the upper-right corner of the dialog box. Make sure that it's the Picture/Object you want to record information about. You now have several options:

   Caption — Type a caption for your Picture/Object in this field.

   Note: Any changes to captions in this dialog box will affect both Scrapbooks and Books.

   Category — Type a category of your own creation in this field. Categories are useful when it's time to print or search for a Picture/Object. For example, if you want to look at all the Pictures/Objects related to childhood birthdays and you give all the childhood birthday Pictures/Objects the category "Childhood Birthday," you can locate all of these birthday pictures easily.

Put some thought into the categories you create — you will find that it pays off when you print documents that include Pictures/Objects. Think about the types of documents you might want to print in the future. Will you want family trees containing a portrait of each individual as an adult? How about creating special anniversary address labels that contain each couple's wedding picture? Thinking about the types of documents that you might want to print will help you create your categories.

Depending on the number of Pictures/Objects that you place in Scrapbooks, you may want your categories to be fairly specific. For example, if you have several different portraits for each individual, you wouldn't want to put them all in the category "Portrait." Instead, it would be a good idea to create categories such as "Portrait-Childhood," "Portrait-Teen," and so on.

In general, you will want to base your categories on the event that the Picture/Object portrays. For example, "Wedding-Reception" and "Wedding-Ceremony" for wedding pictures. "Graduation," "Bar Mitzvah," "Thanksgiving," and "Vacation" are other examples. To get an idea of how categories work, you may want to see the section "Picture/Object Options" in Chapter 9.

Date of origin — Type the date on which the original item was created. For pictures, you would type the date when the photograph was taken.

Type — Click this drop-down list and select the type that applies to the currently selected Picture/Object. If the currently selected Picture/Object is a Kodak Photo CD picture or a picture inserted from a file, Family Tree Maker has already selected the type for you.

Description — Type a description of the Picture/Object in this field. You can include more detailed information than in the caption.

Include in show — Select this check box if you want Family Tree Maker to include this Picture/Object when you play the Scrapbook. For more information about playing Scrapbooks, see "Playing a Scrapbook" in this chapter.

Include in printed Scrapbook — Select this check box if you want Family Tree Maker to print this Picture/Object when you print the Scrapbook. Items that you might not want to print include sound clips, because they will only print as icons.

Preferred Picture/Object #1 - #3 for trees — To make it easier to select Pictures/Objects to print in trees, Family Tree Maker allows you to select the three Pictures/Objects that you are most likely to print for an individual. You can designate your three choices using the "Preferred Picture/Object for trees" check boxes.

For example, if you picked each individual's birthday photo as the "Preferred Picture/Object #1 for trees" and told Family Tree Maker to include "Preferred Picture/Object #1 for trees" when you printed a tree, the tree would contain each individual's birthday photo.

Please note that for each individual's Scrapbook, you can only designate one Picture/Object as the "Preferred Picture/Object #1 for trees." The same holds for "Preferred Picture/Object #2 for trees" and so on. This means that if you already have selected one picture as the "Preferred Picture/Object #1 for trees" and then select it for a second picture, the first picture is no longer the "Preferred Picture/Object #1 for trees."

Although Family Tree Maker only allows you to designate three "preferred" Pictures/Objects for trees, you can include any other Picture/Object in a tree. You will simply use Categories, described above, when it is time to print.

Preferred Picture/Object for Labels/Cards — To make it easier to select Pictures/Objects to print on labels or cards, Family Tree Maker allows you to select the Picture/Object that you are most likely to print for an individual. You can designate your choice using the "Preferred Picture/Object for Labels/Cards" check box.

All the same rules apply to "Preferred Picture/Object for Labels/Cards" as for "Preferred Picture/Object for trees" described above.

Preferred Picture/Object for Fam Grp Sheets — To make it easier to select Pictures/Objects to print on Family Group Sheets, Family Tree Maker allows you to select the Picture/Object that you are most likely to print for an individual. You can designate your choice using the "Preferred Picture/Object for Fam Grp Sheets" check box.

All the same rules apply to "Preferred Picture/Object for Fam Grp Sheets" as for "Preferred Picture/Object for trees" described above.

CD#, Picture#, Resolution — When the currently selected Picture/Object is a Kodak Photo CD picture, Family Tree Maker displays this information.

Finding Pictures/Objects in a Scrapbook

Using the Find Picture/Object command, you can locate a Picture/Object in the Scrapbook that is currently open. If you want to search all of the Scrapbooks in your Family File, you must use the Find Individual command. See "Locating Individuals in Your Family File" in Chapter 4.

To find a Picture/Object in a Scrapbook:

1. Make sure you're in the Scrapbook that you want to search.

2. From the **Edit** menu, select **Find Picture/Object**.

    Family Tree Maker displays the Find Picture/Object dialog box.

3. Click the **Search** drop-down list and select the name of the field that you want to search.

4. In the **for** field, type the information that you want to find.

    If the field that you are searching only has certain legal values (such as "yes" or "no"), Family Tree Maker will display a drop-down list in the "for" field. In this case, just click the item that you want to search for.

5. Click **Find next** to start the search.

    Family Tree Maker goes to and selects the first Picture/Object that matches your request. If no matches are found, Family Tree Maker tells you so.

    If you like, you can edit this Picture/Object and then continue your search by clicking **Find next**.

6. Click **Find next** to continue your search.

    Continue clicking **Find next** until you're done searching or until Family Tree Maker runs out of matches. To go back to previous matches, you can click **Find previous**.

7. To quit the search, click **Cancel**.

    If you didn't find the Picture/Object you were looking for, try again with a less restrictive request. For example, search for a portion of a caption rather than a complete caption.

Moving Around in a Scrapbook

One way to move around in a Scrapbook is with your mouse. Just move the mouse pointer to the Picture/Object you want to select and then click the primary mouse button.

To turn Scrapbook pages with the mouse, click the page-turning buttons in the lower-right and -left corners of your screen. When you're on the first page of a Scrapbook, the backward page-turn button will not work. When you're on the last page of a Scrapbook, the forward page-turn button will not work.

You can also use your computer keyboard to move around in a Scrapbook. Figure 5-16 shows which keys work as navigation keys.

Displaying Pictures at Full Size

Although pictures appear in Scrapbooks at a reduced size, called a **thumbnail**, you can display them at full size. (This only applies to non-OLE pictures.)

To display a non-OLE picture at full size:

1. In the Scrapbook, select the Picture/Object that you want to display.

2. From the **Picture/Object** menu, select **View**. You can also double-click the Picture in the Scrapbook.

    Family Tree Maker displays the View Picture dialog box. Use the **Zoom** buttons to display your picture at larger or smaller sizes. When your whole picture is not visible in the dialog box, Family Tree Maker places scroll bars on the bottom and right sides of the picture. You can use these scroll bars to display different sections of your picture.

3. Click **OK** to close the View Picture dialog box.

    Family Tree Maker returns you to the Scrapbook view.

Press this key...	To do this...
↑	Move to the Picture/Object above the currently selected Picture/Object
↓	Move to the Picture/Object below the currently selected Picture/Object
←	Move to the Picture/Object to the left of the currently selected Picture/Object. Family Tree Maker turns the page if the next Picture/Object is on the next page.
→	Move to the Picture/Object to the right of the currently selected Picture/Object. Family Tree Maker turns the page if the Picture/Object is on the previous page.
⇆ (tab)	Move to the next Picture/Object. Family Tree Maker turns the page if the next Picture/Object is on the next page.
⇧ Shift + ⇆	Move to the previous Picture/Object. Family Tree Maker turns the page if the Picture/Object is on the previous page.
home	Move to the first Picture/Object on the current page
end	Move to the last Picture/Object on the current page
Ctrl + home	Move to the first Picture/Object on the first page of the Scrapbook
Ctrl + end	Move to the last Picture/Object on the last page of the Scrapbook
PgUp	Move to the previous page in the Scrapbook
PgDn	Move to the next page in the Scrapbook
Ctrl + M	Display the More About Picture/Object dialog box for the currently selected Picture/Object

Figure 5-15. Keys to move and select Pictures/Objects in a Scrapbook

Playing OLE Objects

After you place OLE objects in a Scrapbook, you can "play" them. For example, you can listen to sound files and watch video files.

To play an OLE object:

1. Double-click the Picture/Object that you want to play.

   What happens after you double-click depends on the OLE object's server. In most cases, video and sound files will play. Picture files will most likely appear at full size and spreadsheets will open.

2. If the OLE server opened, you can return to Family Tree Maker by closing the server. From the **File** menu of the server, select **Exit and Return to Family Tree Maker**.

   Note: If the program does not have a menu choice, such as "Exit and Return" or "Update," refer to that program's manual for instructions.

Playing a Scrapbook

Once you have Pictures/Objects in a Scrapbook, you can easily create a "slide show" to display each of the Pictures/Objects in sequence. All you need to do is indicate which Pictures/Objects you want to include in the show and for how long you want each Picture/Object to appear on the screen.

To play the Pictures/Objects in a Scrapbook sequentially:

1. Open the Scrapbook for which you want to create a show. Do *not* go into Scrapbook Print Preview.

2. Open the More About Picture/Object dialog box for each of the Pictures/Objects that you want to include in the show. You can do this by clicking the downward-pointing arrow next to each Picture/Object. Make sure that the **Include in show** check box is selected for the Pictures/Objects you want in the show, and deselected for the Pictures/Objects you do *not* want in the show.

3. Make sure that the Pictures/Objects are in the order in which you want them to appear in the show. If not, you can move them (see "Moving or Copying Pictures/Objects Between Scrapbooks" in this chapter, or "Sorting a Scrapbook" on the next page).

4. From the **Picture/Object** menu, select **Play Scrapbook**.

Family Tree Maker displays the Play Scrapbook dialog box.

5. Enter a number in the **Time between Pictures/Objects** field.

You can enter from 1 to 999. The number that you enter is the number of seconds for which Family Tree Maker will display each picture on the screen during the show.

6. Click **OK**.

Family Tree Maker begins the show. Each Picture/Object is centered on the screen for the number of seconds that you selected. Pictures/Objects that can be "played," such as sounds and videos, are played. If you click on the screen while a picture is displayed, Family Tree Maker will skip the time delay and move on to the next Picture/Object.

Sorting a Scrapbook

You may want the Pictures/Objects in your Scrapbooks in a particular order. You can choose the order quickly and easily with Family Tree Maker's sorting feature. When you choose a sorting order, it only affects the Scrapbook that is currently open.

To sort a Scrapbook:

1. From the **Format** menu, select **Sort Scrapbook**.

Family Tree Maker displays the Sort Scrapbook dialog box.

2. Click the option button for the type of sorting you prefer.

You can sort by captions, categories, or dates. For captions or categories, Family Tree Maker sorts alphabetically, beginning with the first word.

3. Click **OK** after you make your selection.

Family Tree Maker sorts the current Scrapbook and returns you to the Scrapbook view.

Editing Pictures/Objects

You can edit a picture both as you insert it into a Scrapbook and after inserting it into the Scrapbook. If you want to edit an OLE object, see "Editing OLE Objects," in this chapter.

Editing a Picture as You Place it in a Scrapbook

When you place a picture in a Scrapbook, Family Tree Maker automatically displays the Edit Picture dialog box. If you would like to edit your picture, this is the best time to do it. Instructions for rotating, flipping, and cropping are below.

When you click **OK** to leave the Edit Picture dialog box, Family Tree Maker compresses and saves the picture in your Family File. The picture displays in the Scrapbook at a reduced size, called a thumbnail. The thumbnail's small size allows you to see several images on the screen at once. The real, full-sized images will be used for printing and displaying.

After you insert a picture into a Scrapbook, use the More About Picture/Object dialog box to create a caption and to tell Family Tree Maker in which documents you want the picture to print (see "Recording Important Picture/Object Information" in this chapter).

Editing a Picture after Placing it in a Scrapbook

Editing a picture after placing it in the Scrapbook involves decompressing and recompressing it. Unless you selected 1:1 compression when you initially imported the picture, repeated decompression and recompression reduce the quality of the picture. (Family Tree Maker uses the industry standard JPEG compression method, and does *not* support LZW compression technology.) For this reason, Family Tree Maker asks you to retrieve the original picture before you edit it. See "Preparing to Edit a Picture," on the next page. Please note that printing and displaying your pictures at different sizes do not involve compression and do not reduce the quality of your picture.

Preparing to Edit a Picture

If you are currently in the process of placing a picture in the Scrapbook and the Edit Picture dialog box is already open, you can skip these instructions. Only use these instructions when you are editing a picture that was previously inserted into the Scrapbook.

To open a picture for editing:

1. In the Scrapbook, select the picture that you want to edit.

2. From the **Picture/Object** menu, select **Edit**.

3. Family Tree Maker asks if you want to open and edit the original file. In general, editing the original file will give you the best quality picture. If you click **Yes**, go to step 4. If you click **No**, Family Tree Maker displays your picture for editing. Skip the remaining steps and begin editing now.

   Note: If the picture is either black and white, a Kodak Photo CD picture, stored with 1:1 compression, or was pasted into Family Tree Maker, you will not need to get the original file. Skip the remaining steps and begin editing now.

4. Family Tree Maker displays the Insert Picture dialog box. Select the name of your file.

5. Click **OK**.

   Family Tree Maker displays your picture in the Edit Picture dialog box. To rotate, flip, or crop the picture, follow the instructions that begin on the next page.

Rotating a Picture

Sometimes when you scan a picture, newspaper clipping, or other paper memorabilia, the image turns out sideways or upside down. Rotating enables you to reorient pictures that are sideways or upside down.

To rotate a picture:

1. If the picture is not open, see the previous section, "Preparing to Edit a Picture."

2. Click one of the three following buttons:

   Rotate L — Use this button to rotate the picture ninety degrees to the left (counter-clockwise).

   Rotate R — Use this button to rotate the picture ninety degrees to the right (clockwise).

   180 — Use this button to rotate the picture 180 degrees.

3. After you finish editing the picture, click **OK**.

   Family Tree Maker places the newly rotated picture into the Scrapbook. If you have placed this picture in other Scrapbooks, Family Tree Maker asks if you want to change all copies of the picture. Click **No** if you only want to change the copy in this Scrapbook.

Flipping Pictures

Flipping is for adjusting pictures that are backwards.

To flip a picture:

1. If the picture is not open, see "Preparing to Edit a Picture" in this chapter.

2. You can flip the picture using two different buttons:

   Mirror — Use this button to flip the picture so that it is right-to-left instead of left-to-right.

   Flip — If the items in your picture are upside down instead of right side up, use this button to flip the picture.

3. After you finish editing the picture, click **OK**.

Family Tree Maker places the newly flipped picture into the Scrapbook. If you have placed this picture in other Scrapbooks, Family Tree Maker asks if you want to change all copies of the picture. Click **No** if you only want to change the copy in this Scrapbook.

Cropping Pictures

Cropping pictures allows you to perfect them for your Scrapbook. When you crop a picture, you select the area of the picture that you want to place in the Scrapbook. For example, you can remove empty background space so that the picture focuses on the people. Or, you can use a family photograph to make individual portraits of each family member.

To crop a picture:

1. If the picture is not open, follow the instructions in "Preparing to Edit a Picture," in this chapter.

2. Move the cursor onto the image.

    The cursor becomes a crosshair (large plus sign).

3. Position the crosshair over the exact spot where you want the top-left corner of the cropped picture to be.

    If you want to select a very small portion of the picture, click **Zoom In** to enlarge the picture on the screen. This will allow you to select the cropping area more accurately. If you want to select a large portion of the picture when your picture does not fit inside the Edit Picture dialog box, you can click **Zoom Out**.

4. Press and hold the mouse button while you drag diagonally to the exact spot where you want the lower-right corner of the cropped picture to be, then release the mouse button.

    The area inside the box is what will remain after the picture is cropped. If you do not like the position of the box, simply repeat steps 2 and 3 to create a new box.

5. When you have a box around the area you want to keep, click **Crop**.

    Family Tree Maker deletes the part of the picture that you chose to crop, and shows you the cropped picture. If you want to remove even more of the original picture, repeat steps 2, 3, and 4. If you feel that you have cropped too much of the picture, click **Cancel** to start again.

6. After you finish editing the picture, click **OK**.

Family Tree Maker permanently crops the picture and places the newly cropped version in the Scrapbook. If you have placed this picture in other Scrapbooks, Family Tree Maker asks if you want to change all copies of the picture. Click **No** if you only want to change the copy in this Scrapbook.

Editing OLE Objects

Family Tree Maker does not control the editing of OLE objects. Instead, you edit the objects in the software program that originally created the object.

To edit an OLE object:

1. Select the Picture/Object, and then from the **Picture/Object** menu, select **Edit**.

   Microsoft Windows opens the software program in which the Object was originally created. If Family Tree Maker cannot find the correct software program, check to see that you have not deleted the software program or moved it to a new location.

2. Edit the object as needed.

   Please refer to the manual for that software program for instructions.

3. From the **File** menu of that software program, select **Exit and Return to Family Tree Maker**.

   Note: If the program does not have a menu choice such as "Exit and Return" or "Update," refer to that program's manual for instructions.

   Microsoft Windows closes the program and returns you to Family Tree Maker. (Windows may also ask if you want to update or save your information; answer **Yes** or **OK**, unless you don't want to save your changes.) Family Tree Maker places the OLE object in the Scrapbook.

Controlling Picture/Object Brightness and Contrast

The Brightness and Contrast controls allow you to change the shading in the non-OLE pictures that you have placed in your Scrapbooks. If the color in an individual picture isn't quite right, you can change that picture's contrast. If all of your pictures tend to print too darkly, you can change the brightness for all of the pictures at once.

Changing the Contrast for a Single Picture/Object

To change the contrast setting for a single Picture/Object:

1. Select the Picture/Object whose contrast you want to change.

2. From the **Picture/Object** menu, select **Contrast**.

    Family Tree Maker displays the Contrast dialog box.

3. Click and drag the **Contrast** scroll box to change the contrast.

4. Click **OK**.

    Family Tree Maker returns you to the Scrapbook.

Changing the Brightness for All Pictures/Objects in a View

When you change the brightness setting for all Pictures/Objects at once, you are changing it for a specific view, not for all views. For example, if you are printing an Ancestor tree and you change the brightness setting while you're in the Ancestor tree view, every Ancestor tree that you print afterwards will have the same brightness setting. However, Descendant trees would not have this brightness setting. If you wanted your Descendant trees to have the same brightness setting as your Ancestor trees, you would need to switch to the Descendant Tree view and change the brightness setting there, too.

To change the brightness setting for all Pictures/Objects in a view:

1. Make sure you are in a view that can print Pictures/Objects, such as the Scrapbook view or the Ancestor Tree view.

2. From the **File** menu select **Print Setup**.

   Family Tree Maker displays the Print Setup dialog box.

3. Click **Brightness**.

   Family Tree Maker displays the Brightness dialog box.

4. Click and drag the **Contrast** scroll box to change the contrast.

5. Click **OK**.

   Family Tree Maker returns you to the Print Setup dialog box.

6. Click **OK** to close the Print Setup dialog box.

Controlling Picture Resolution and Compression

Selecting the degree of compression for your color and grayscale pictures lets you control the tradeoff between the quality of your pictures and the amount of disk space they take up. Black-and-white pictures are always compressed because compression does not change their quality. You cannot change the compression of black-and-white pictures. You can also control the resolution of Kodak Photo CD pictures.

You can change the compression of a picture from several places:

- From the Insert Picture dialog box when you are placing a picture into a Scrapbook from a file.

- From the Insert from Photo CD dialog box when you are placing a new Photo CD Picture in the Scrapbook.

- From the Change Compression/Resolution dialog box whenever you are in the Scrapbook.

In addition, if you want to set a default compression or resolution for all pictures that you place in the Scrapbook in the future, see the topic "Selecting Defaults for Picture Resolution and Compression" in this chapter.

To change compression or resolution for color or grayscale images:

1. Select the picture whose compression or resolution you want to change.

2. Open the Compression/Resolution dialog box. How you open this dialog box depends on your current location:

   If you are in the Import Picture dialog box, click **Compression**.

   If you are in the Import from Photo CD dialog box, click **Resolution**.

   If you are in a Scrapbook, select a color or grayscale image, and then from the **Picture/Object** menu, select **Compression/Resolution**. If Family Tree Maker displays a message telling you to get the original picture, click **OK**. Then, in the Insert Picture dialog box, click either **Compression** or **Resolution**.

3. You can now change the compression and/or resolution. Each of your options is described on the next page.

Degree of Compression — Select the option button corresponding to the degree of compression that you want for your picture. Higher ratios reduce the picture's quality, but the picture takes up less space on your hard disk. (Family Tree Maker uses the industry standard JPEG compression method and does *not* support LZW compression technology.) Lower ratios retain more of the picture's quality, but the picture takes up more disk space. The "1:1" setting will not reduce the quality of your pictures at all, but it will take up the most space on your hard disk.

In general, the "Recommended" setting is a good balance between quality loss and disk space. However, if you're importing a file that contains a lot of text, such as a scanned article or birth certificate, you may want to use a compression that's lower than the recommended level. It will make the text easier to read.

Picture resolution — This option is only available for Kodak Photo CD pictures. Select the option button corresponding to the resolution that you want for your picture. "Resolution" refers to the size of your picture. A higher resolution will create a larger picture, and a larger picture will be sharper and more detailed. If a particular resolution is not available for the image you are currently working with, the option button will be grayed out.

Choosing resolutions higher (larger) than the recommended "256 x 384" will use up large amounts of your hard disk space. In addition, you may not be able to load a picture at a very high resolution if your computer does not have a sufficient amount of RAM (memory). You only need to use high resolutions when you want to print large, very high-quality images on a high-quality printer or when you plan to crop a small part of the picture.

Disk Space Needed — This shows the approximate amount of disk space needed to store the current picture. Each time you change one of the options in this dialog box, the numbers in the "Disk Space Needed" field will change. Note that this is an approximation; the actual size may vary slightly when the picture is actually compressed.

4. Click **OK** after you make your selections.

    Family Tree Maker changes the compression and/or resolution of the picture and places it in the Scrapbook.

Moving or Copying Pictures/Objects Between Scrapbooks

You can move or copy Pictures/Objects within a Scrapbook and also from one Scrapbook to another, as long as the two Scrapbooks are in the same Family File. When you edit a Picture/Object that is in more than one Scrapbook, you can choose whether or not your edits affect all copies of the Picture/Object or just the copy in the current Scrapbook.

To move or copy a Picture/Object, start with the Scrapbook containing the Picture/Object you want to move or copy:

1. Select the Picture/Object that you want to move or copy.

2. From the **Edit** menu, select **Cut Picture/Object** to remove the Picture/Object from this location. Select **Copy Picture/Object** to copy the Picture/Object to another Scrapbook.

   If you want to place the Picture/Object in a new location in the *same* Scrapbook, select the new location and then from the **Edit** menu, select **Paste Picture/Object**. You can skip the rest of these steps.

   If you want to place the Picture/Object in a *different* Scrapbook, continue with step 3.

3. Go to the Family Page containing the individual or the marriage whose Scrapbook you want to paste the Picture/Object into.

   Use the Index of Individuals or Find Individual to locate the correct Family Page (see "Moving to Anyone in Your Family File" and "Locating Individuals in Your Family File" in Chapter 4).

4. On the Family Page, place the cursor either on the name of the individual or on the marriage whose Scrapbook you want to open.

5. From the **View** menu, select **Scrapbook**.

   Family Tree Maker displays the individual's or marriage's Scrapbook.

6. Select the area where you want to paste the Picture/Object.

7. From the **Edit** menu, select **Paste Picture/Object**.

    Family Tree Maker pastes the Picture/Object from the Clipboard into the Scrapbook and repositions any existing Pictures/Objects if necessary.

Since the Clipboard is not erased until you use the Copy or Cut command again, you can paste the same Picture/Object or caption as many times as you like.

Removing Pictures/Objects from a Scrapbook

You cannot delete a Picture/Object by selecting it and attempting to insert a new Picture/Object in its place. This will only move the Picture/Object that you wanted to delete to the right and create a space for the new Picture/Object.

To remove Pictures/Objects from the Scrapbook:

1. Select the Picture/Object that you want to remove.

2. Press `delete` or `←BkSp` to permanently remove the Picture/Object from the Scrapbook. Or, from the **Edit** menu, select **Cut Picture/Object** to cut the Picture/Object to the Clipboard.

    Family Tree Maker displays a confirmation dialog box. If you really want to delete the Picture/Object, click **Yes**. Otherwise, click **No**.

    Family Tree Maker removes the Picture/Object from the Scrapbook, as well as any More About information associated with it. The Pictures/Objects remaining in the Scrapbook move to the left to fill up the empty space.

If you accidentally delete the wrong Picture/Object, from the **Edit** menu, select **Undo** immediately.

Note: For more information about making your file smaller after removing Pictures/Objects, see "Compacting Family Files" in Chapter 13.

Chapter 6

FIXING MISTAKES IN YOUR FAMILY FILE

As a kindergartner, Claire LaBeaux enjoyed school and riding horses. She
later went on to figure skate competitively and is now the Public
Relations Manager for Family Tree Maker.

FIXING MISTAKES IN YOUR FAMILY FILE

From time to time you may find that you've accidentally married someone to the wrong individual or given someone the wrong parents. You may even discover that an individual, or an entire branch of individuals, doesn't belong in your Family File at all. This section shows you how to find and correct these types of mistakes, and more.

CHECKING YOUR FILE FOR ERRORS

Because collecting your family information involves tracking down so many dates, names, and other facts, there may be occasions when the information in your Family File is incomplete or inaccurate. While Family Tree Maker cannot determine the accuracy of specific biographical information, it can identify conflicting facts. We encourage you to use the error checking features so that your family information is as accurate as possible.

Note: Family Tree Maker also has a Spell Check feature to check for spelling errors in More About Notes and Text items in Books. See "Using Spell Check" in this chapter for more information.

Family Tree Maker does some error checking automatically, while other types of error checking you initiate yourself. The three techniques are described below.

Data Entry Checking — Screens information as you enter it, finding problems such as inconsistencies in birth and death dates. This method helps you catch errors immediately, while the information is fresh in your mind (see "Data Entry Checking" in this chapter).

The Find Error Command — Searches your Family File for possible errors and fixes them as they are found. This method looks at all of the information in your Family File, not just the information you are currently entering (see "The Find Error Command" in this chapter).

Data Errors Report — Prints a report of the possible errors in your file. You can then use the report to review your Family File and fix the mistakes. Although this method takes the most time because you must search your file manually to locate the errors listed in the report, it is the most thorough method (see "Data Errors Reports" in this chapter).

Data Entry Checking

When the Data Entry Checking feature is on, Family Tree Maker checks information as you enter it on the Family Page. When Family Tree Maker finds information that seems incorrect or conflicts with other information in your Family File, it prompts you to take a closer look at it and fix it, if necessary. For certain types of errors, such as entering titles in a name, Family Tree Maker always prompts you to fix these errors, even when the Data Entry Checking feature is off. For instructions on turning Data Entry Checking on and off, see "Data Entry Checking Preferences" in Chapter 3.

Data Entry Checking in Family Tree Maker searches for many different types of mistakes in names and dates. For a list of the errors that Family Tree Maker can find with Data Entry Checking, see "Error Types" in this chapter. When Family Tree Maker locates a possible error, it displays a dialog box so that you can either fix the error or skip over it if it is not an error. There are five different types of dialog boxes, but they all work in fundamentally the same way. Figure 6-1 shows an example of an error dialog box that you might see when the Data Entry Checking feature is on.

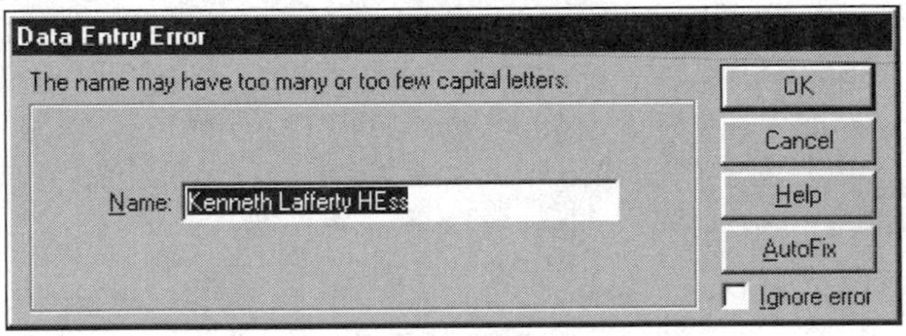

Figure 6-1. The Name Capitalization error dialog box

In this example, Family Tree Maker believes that you capitalized too many letters in the name. To fix the error, you could retype the name correctly and then click **OK**. Alternatively, you could click **AutoFix**. In this case, Family Tree Maker attempts to fix the error for you. When you click **AutoFix**, the button name changes to **Undo** so that you can reverse the change if Family Tree Maker makes a change you don't want.

If the name actually is capitalized correctly, you would select the **Ignore error** check box. This prevents Family Tree Maker from displaying this error in other places in your Family File and in subsequent searches.

The Find Error Command

Using the Find Error command is similar to spell-checking a word processing document: you go through the file from beginning to end and fix mistakes as you come across them. For a list of the errors that you can locate with the Find Error Command, see "Error Types" in this chapter.

To check your Family File with the Find Error Command:

1. Go to the Family Page view.

2. From the **Edit** menu, select **Find Error**.

    Family Tree Maker displays the Find Error dialog box. Each of your options is described below.

    Errors to find in search — Select the check boxes for the types of errors that you want Family Tree Maker to locate.

    Reset all ignored errors — If you previously chose to ignore some errors by selecting the "Ignore error" check box, described in step 3, click this button to include those errors in all future searches.

3. Click **OK** when you've made your selections.

    Family Tree Maker begins searching your Family File for errors and displays an error dialog box similar to the one shown in Figure 6-2.

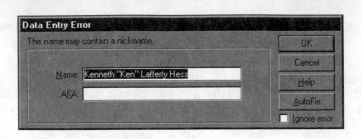

Figure 6-2. The AKA in name error dialog box

In this example, Family Tree Maker believes that you entered a nickname in the "Name" field on the Family Page, instead of in the "AKA" field in the Lineage dialog box.

The "Name" field shows the name on the Family Page and the "AKA" field shows the nickname in the Lineage dialog box. If you click **AutoFix**, Family Tree Maker attempts to extract the nickname from the "Name" field and place it in the "AKA" field. You could also type the names correctly, or if this really isn't an error, you would select the **Ignore error** check box.

4. Either fix the error manually, fix it automatically by clicking **AutoFix**, or skip over it by selecting the **Ignore error** check box.

When you select "Ignore error," Family Tree Maker flags that error so that it will not show up as an error in other places in your Family File and in subsequent searches.

5. Click **Find next** when you want to move to the next error, or click **Close** when you want to quit searching.

When you reach the end of the search, Family Tree Maker returns you to a Family Page.

Data Errors Report

A Data Errors report can show you places in your Family File where there might be mistakes. It is very thorough in its checking, but in order to fix the mistakes, you have to go into your file and manually locate the errors listed in the report.

You create and print a Data Errors report in the Report view. For instructions, see "Displaying Reports" in Chapter 8. For a list of the errors that you can find with the Data Errors report, see "Error Types" below.

Error Types

This section lists the types of errors that Family Tree Maker can locate for you: name errors, date errors, and other types of errors. Each error message is listed in bold and is followed by a brief explanation and a suggestion for correcting it. Please note that Family Tree Maker does not search for some of these errors with all three types of error checking. This information is also included in the descriptions below the error messages.

Name Errors

"Possible misplaced dash in the name"
Available with all three types of error checking.
Family Tree Maker has found a name with either two dashes in a row or a dash at the beginning or end of the name. Verify the spelling of the name and then delete any extra dashes.

"There may be a title in the name field"
Available with all three types of error checking.
You may have typed an individual's title, such as "Dr." or "Reverend" in the "Name" field on the Family Page instead of in the "Title" field in the Lineage dialog box (see "Entering Nicknames, Titles, and Parental Relationship Information" in Chapter 5). Verify the spelling of the name, remove any titles, and type the titles in the "Title" field in the Lineage dialog box.

"The name may contain an illegal character"
Available with all three types of error checking.
Family Tree Maker found a name containing one or more of the following characters: ~ ! @ # $ % ^ & * _ + = | : ; " < / ( ) [ ] { } 1 2 3 4 5 6 7 8 9 0. You may also have typed a "?" at the beginning of a name, or a name may contain three or more consecutive "\\\" (backslash) characters. Verify the spelling of the name and then delete any illegal or extra characters.

"Possibly used married instead of maiden name"
Available with all three types of error checking.
Family Tree Maker has found a Family Page where the surname for both the husband and the wife is the same. Even though women usually assume their husbands' last names, most genealogists record women with their maiden (or family) surname instead of their married surname. Using this standard is helpful for tracking maternal lineage and for distinguishing between a man's sisters and spouses. Replace the married name with the maiden name.

"The name may have too many or too few capital letters"
Available with all three types of error checking.
Family Tree Maker has found a word containing more than one uppercase letter. (Family Tree Maker understands surnames such as "Mac Donnell," "De Long," and "Von Trapp." Verify the spelling of the name and then switch any extra uppercase letters to lowercase letters.

"The name may contain a nickname"
Available with all three types of error checking.
You may have typed an individual's nickname in the "Name" field on the Family Page instead of in the "aka" field in the Lineage dialog box (see "Entering Nicknames, Titles, and Parental Relationship Information" in Chapter 5). Verify the spelling of the name, remove any nicknames, and type the nicknames in the "aka" field.

Date Errors

"Born when parent <name> was under 13"
Available only with Data Errors reports.
According to the dates in your Family File, this individual was born before one (or both) of the parents reached age 13. Verify the birth dates, then make sure you have the correct relationship between the mother and child.

"<child's name> birth date is after <mother's name> death date"
Available with all three types of error checking.
According to the dates in your Family File, this individual was born after the death date of his or her mother. Verify the birth and death dates, then make sure you have the correct relationship between the mother and child.

"<child's name> birth date occurred too long after <father's name> death date"

Available with all three types of error checking.

According to the dates in your Family File, this individual was born more than 10 months after the death date of his or her father. Verify that the child is the natural child of the father and that the birth and death dates are correct.

"Death date is before birth date"

Available with all three types of error checking.

This individual's death date indicates that he or she died prior to the birth date. Check to see if you entered these two dates in reverse order.

"<Name's> marriage to <name> occurred before age 13"

Available with Data Errors reports and Find Errors command.

This individual was twelve years old or younger on the date of his or her marriage. Consult a municipal record for the marriage to ensure that you're using the most reliable source. Also double-check your original source for the marriage date and the birth dates of both spouses.

"Event date is empty"

Available only with Data Errors reports.

Family Tree Maker has found a date field that contains no text or numbers. Since events always correspond to a date, this indicates a gap in your research. If you do not know an exact date, you can use an estimated date (see "Entering Dates" in Chapter 3) or type `unknown` in the date field. Please note that this error message does not include the "Fact" fields in the Facts dialog box.

"Death date more than 120 years after birth date"

Available with all three types of error checking.

Your Family File indicates that this individual had a life span of more than 120 years. Verify both the birth and death dates, making sure that the correct century is entered. If you do not have an exact death date for an individual, but do know that the individual is deceased, use an estimated death date (see "Entering Dates" in Chapter 3).

"<child's name> birth date more than 20 years after the marriage date of <name> and <name>"

Available only with Data Errors reports.

Family Tree Maker has found an individual who was born more than 20 years after his or her parents were married. Verify both the birth and marriage dates, as well as the relationship between the parents and the child.

"<child's name> birth date before the marriage date of <name> and <name>"

Available only with Data Errors reports.

Family Tree Maker has found an individual who was born before his or her parents were married. Verify both the birth and marriage dates, as well as the relationship between the parents and the child.

"Not in birth order in the children list"

Available only with Data Errors reports.

Family Tree Maker found a Family Page where this child does not appear in his or her birth order. See "Sorting Children by Birth Order" in Chapter 3.

"Mother older than 50 at the time of child's birth"

Available with the Find Error Command and Data Entry Checking.

Family Tree Maker has located a woman who was at least 50 years old on the birth date of one of her children. The listed child might instead be a grandchild, or there could be a special circumstance such as adoption.

Other Errors

"Is this <name> the same as <name>?"

Available with Data Entry Checking and Data Errors reports.

Family Tree Maker has found two people with identical names, sexes, and birth dates. Make sure that the individuals actually are distinct people. If you accidentally created more than one record for the same individual, you can eliminate the excess record by merging the information. See "Merging Duplicate Individuals" in this chapter.

"No parents, no children, and no spouses"

Available only with Data Errors reports.

Make sure you haven't omitted the individuals to whom this individual is related. If you don't yet know who they are, you'll at least know where to start your research! In some instances, you may have inadvertently unlinked an individual in order to fix a relationship mistake. For more information, see "Changing Relationships in Your Family File," in this chapter.

"<Fieldname> may have incorrect capitalization"

Available only with Data Errors reports.

Family Tree Maker has found a field where you have typed information in all capital letters. Check the capitalization.

Using Spell Check

There's no need to worry about embarrassing typos detracting from your beautiful family books because spell check can proofread the text in your Notes and Books for you.

To use the spell check:

1. Decide which items you want to spell check and then switch to the appropriate view.

To spell check...	Switch to this view...
All notes and text items in the current Family File	Family Page, Tree, or Report
All text items in a book	Book Outline for that book
A specific text item in a book	The Text Item window for that item
A note for a specific individual or marriage	The More About Note dialog box for that note

Figure 6-3. A summary of where to use Spell Check

2. From the **Edit** menu, select **Spell Check**.

   Family Tree Maker opens the Spell Check dialog box and begins checking the text based on the current view selection.

3. If Family Tree Maker detects a potential spelling error, it displays the error in the **Not in dictionary** field.

   Family Tree Maker scrolls to the potential error and highlights it in the document. To specify which types of words Family Tree Maker views as errors, see "Selecting Spell Check Preferences" in Chapter 1.

   Note: If the dialog box is covering the word you want to view, click and drag the title bar of the Spell Check dialog box to a corner of the screen while holding the mouse button down.

At this point you can do one of the following:

Correct the error — Select a word from the **Suggestions** list and then click the **Change** button, or type the correct spelling in the **Change to** field and then click the **Change** button.

Add the word to the dictionary — Click the **Add** button to accept the current spelling and to add it to your dictionary. Once you add the word to your dictionary, Family Tree Maker will not treat it as an error during future spell checks.

Ignore the error for the rest of this spell check — Click the **Ignore** button to accept the current spelling and to ignore all instances of this word in the current spell check session.

Stop spell checking your file — Click the **Close** button to interrupt the spell check and return to the view where the last spelling correction was made.

4. If you checked only one item, Family Tree Maker asks if you want to check other items in your Family File. Click **Yes** to continue spell checking or **No** to return to the view where the last spelling correction was made.

5. After Family Tree Maker checks the last item, a dialog appears to inform you that the spell check is complete. Click **OK** to return to the view where the last spelling correction was made.

REMOVING AN INDIVIDUAL FROM YOUR FAMILY FILE

If you find that you've added an individual to your Family File by mistake, you can use the **Delete Individual** command to remove him or her. You can only delete one individual at a time using this command.

Note: If you've made a mistake entering a single piece of information, such as an incorrect date or location, you don't need to use Delete Individual; just type over the incorrect information. Do *not* type over an individual's *name* unless you are just changing the spelling. If you need to *move* an individual to a different Family Page, use the Attach and Detach commands described later in this chapter.

To delete an individual:

1. Go to the Family Page of the individual whom you want to delete and place the cursor on the individual's name.

2. From the **People** menu, select **Delete Individual**.

Family Tree Maker asks you to confirm the deletion.

Note: It's important to remember that the Delete Individual command severs all ties that the deleted individual created between any other individuals in your tree. This means that when you've deleted an individual, you may have to reconnect other individuals in your tree. For example, if you delete a single parent, you've disconnected all of that parent's children from the rest of their relatives. Since children are related to other family members only through the parental connection, you must re-attach children to a parent to reestablish their family ties. See "Linking Children to Their Parents," in this chapter, for instructions.

DELETING A GROUP OF INDIVIDUALS

With the **Delete Individuals in (Tree/Report)** command, you can permanently remove multiple individuals from your Family File all at once.

To use this command, you must first create a document containing the group of individuals that you want to delete. This allows you to visually double-check that the correct individuals are in the group, and then you delete the individuals.

To delete a group of individuals from your Family File:

1. Display either a report or tree containing the group of individuals you want to delete.

   Note: This feature is not available in all views.

   See Chapter 8, "Displaying Your Family Information," and Chapter 9, "Customizing Your Family Information" for more information.

2. After you display your document, review it carefully to make sure that it contains the correct set of individuals.

   Note: You don't have to worry about what information appears in the document, because Family Tree Maker will delete all information associated with the individuals in the document.

3. From the **People** menu, select **Delete Individuals in (Tree/Report)**.

   Family Tree Maker displays a confirmation dialog box.

4. Click **Yes** to delete the individuals, or click **No** to keep them in your Family File.

CHANGING RELATIONSHIPS IN YOUR FAMILY FILE

The following four commands allow you to change relationships in your Family File without removing anyone permanently.

Detaching a Child from the Wrong Parents

If a child in your Family File appears with the wrong parents, you can use the **Detach Child** command to separate the child from those parents. If the individual you are detaching has children, those children will remain with the individual after he or she is detached. Only the relationship between the individual that you detach and his or her parents will be severed.

To detach a child from his or her parents:

1. Go to the Family Page containing the set of parents and the child that you want to detach from each other.

   Note: You must be on the Family Page where the individual is in the "Children" list. If you're on a page where the individual appears as a husband or wife, click the tab for the individual's parents. This tab is on the right side of your screen.

2. Place the cursor on the child you want to detach.

3. From the **People** menu, select **Fix Relationship Mistakes**.

4. From the **Fix Relationship Mistakes** submenu, select **Detach Child**.

   Family Tree Maker asks you to confirm the detachment.

   If the child has siblings, Family Tree Maker asks if the siblings should be detached as well. If you select "Yes," Family Tree Maker will detach all siblings from the parents at once and they will remain together as siblings. If you select "No," Family Tree Maker will only detach the selected individual.

To reattach this individual elsewhere in the tree, see "Linking Children to Their Parents" in this chapter.

Detaching Incorrect Spouses

If Family Tree Maker shows two individuals as married when they actually never had this type of relationship, use the **Detach Spouse** command to separate them from each other. If these spouses have children listed on their Family Page, the children will remain with the spouse who is not being detached. Use the **Detach Child** command (see "Detaching a Child from the Wrong Parents" in this chapter) if you also need to detach the children from the remaining spouse.

Do not use this command if a couple divorces. Instead, record a divorce in the More About Marriage dialog box for that couple (see "Entering Brief Marriage Facts" in Chapter 5). In addition, if an individual remarries, you can create a new Family Page containing the new couple (see "Other Spouses" in Chapter 4).

To detach someone from an incorrect spouse:

1. Go to the Family Page containing the individual you want to detach.

    Note: You must be on the Family Page where the individual appears as a husband or wife, not as a child. If you're on a page where the individual is in the "Children" list, click the tab with the individual's name on it. This tab is on the right side of your screen.

2. Place the cursor on the spouse you want to detach.

3. From the **People** menu, select **Fix Relationship Mistakes**.

4. From the **Fix Relationship Mistakes** submenu, select **Detach Spouse**.

    Family Tree Maker asks you to confirm the detachment.

If the individual you are detaching has children, the children will remain with the spouse who was not detached.

To reattach this individual elsewhere in the tree, see "Linking Individuals by Marriage" in this chapter.

Linking Children to Their Parents

If an individual and his or her parents are in your Family File, but the individual does not appear on the parents' Family Page, use the **Attach Child** command. You only need to use this command when both the child and parents are already in your Family File. If one of them is not in the Family File, just type his or her name on the appropriate Family Page (see "Entering Family Information" in Chapter 3 for more information).

To attach a child to his or her parents:

1. Go to the Family Page where you want the individual to appear as a child (the page that shows the child's parents as spouses).

2. From the **People** menu, select **Fix Relationship Mistakes**.

3. From the **Fix Relationship Mistakes** submenu, select **Attach Child**.

   Family Tree Maker displays a list of everyone in your Family File.

4. Click the name of the individual whom you want to attach as a child.

   If you click the name of an "illegal" individual, Family Tree Maker displays an error message and asks you to select another individual. An "illegal" individual is someone that, for logical reasons, could not possibly be the child of the individual. For example, you could not attach an individual's mother as the individual's child.

5. Click **OK**.

6. If the child has siblings, Family Tree Maker asks whether you want to associate those siblings with the new set of parents. Click either **Yes** or **No**.

   If you choose "Yes," Family Tree Maker attaches any siblings that have the same preferred parents.

7. If the child already has another set of parents, Family Tree Maker displays the Set Relationship dialog box. Click the drop-down list next to each parent's name and select the word that describes the relationship between the parent and the child.

Family Tree Maker gives the individual's siblings the same relationship to the new parent(s), unless the siblings would then have too many natural parents. In this case Family Tree Maker gives them a step- relationship. If the children actually have different relationships, you can go to each child's Lineage dialog box (see "Entering Nicknames, Titles, and Parental Information" in Chapter 5) and choose the correct relationship.

8. Click **OK** after making your selections.

Family Tree Maker displays the Family Page.

Linking Individuals by Marriage

If a married couple in your Family File isn't listed on a Family Page as husband and wife, you can use the **Attach Spouse** command to join them. You only need to use this command if both spouses are already in your Family File, but are not shown as married to each other. If only one of the individuals is already in your Family File, just enter the other spouse's name on that individual's Family Page (see "Entering Family Information" in Chapter 3 for more information).

Note: Before you can attach a spouse, you must have an opening for him or her on the Family Page. If two spouses are already on the Family Page, you will need to create a spot for the new one that you're attaching (see "Other Spouses" in Chapter 4).

To attach two individuals as spouses:

1. Go to the Family Page where one of the individuals appears in the "Husband" or "Wife" field.

   Note: You must be on the Family Page where the individual to whom you want to attach a spouse appears as a husband or wife, not as a child. If you're on a page where the individual is shown in the "Children" list, click the tab for that individual's Family Page. The tab is on the right side of your screen.

   In order to ensure that the children from this marriage will appear on the same Family Page as their parents, make sure that you are on the Family Page where the children and one of the parents appear. That way, Family Tree Maker knows to keep the children with the marriage you are creating.

2. From the **People** menu, select **Fix Relationship Mistakes**.

3. From the **Fix Relationship Mistakes** submenu, select **Attach Spouse**.

   Family Tree Maker displays a list of everyone in your Family File.

4. Click the name of the individual that you want to attach as a spouse.

   If you click the name of an "illegal" individual, Family Tree Maker displays an error message and asks you to select another individual. An "illegal" individual is someone who, for logical reasons, could not possibly be the spouse of the individual. For example, you can't attach someone as a spouse if doing so would make this person his or her own parent.

5. Click **OK**.

   Family Tree Maker asks you to confirm your selection.

MERGING INDIVIDUALS

On occasion, you may find duplicate individuals in your Family File. Duplicate individuals are individuals who appear in your file twice. Duplicate individuals can result from combining files, from appending a World Family Tree pedigree to your Family File, or from accidentally entering the same person twice.

Family Tree Maker provides commands to help you find and merge duplicate individuals. When you merge two records for an individual, Family Tree Maker lets you keep both pieces of information for most fields that contain differing information. An Exceptions report is created for any information that was not merged.

The sections that follow explain how to find and merge individuals using these Family Tree Maker commands:

Merge Duplicate Individuals — Searches your entire Family File for duplicate individuals and shows you the duplicates. You can review the duplicates in a report before you begin merging them. You can also choose which individuals to merge and which individuals to keep separate. If you suspect that you have many duplicates in your file, and you want to see a report of them, select this command.

Merge Specific Individual — Enables you to select two individuals to merge. You can use this command to merge any two individuals in your Family File — even individuals that Family Tree Maker doesn't recognize as duplicates.

Merging Duplicate Individuals

The Merge Duplicate Individuals command helps you find duplicate individuals in your Family File. With this command, Family Tree Maker searches your Family File for duplicate individuals. You can then print a report of these duplicates, and if you choose to do so, you can review the duplicates and merge the individuals you believe to be duplicates.

To use the Merge Duplicate Individuals command:

1. From the **People** menu, select **Merge Duplicate Individuals**.

    Note: Family Tree Maker will display a Caution message advising you to backup your Family File (which we strongly recommend) before proceeding.

    Family Tree Maker displays the Merge Duplicate Individuals dialog box which gives you information about your file.

Figure 6-4. The Merge Duplicate Individuals dialog box

2. Select one of the following options:

    Display merge report — Display a list showing whether any of the individuals in your Family File is an exact or possible match with someone else in your Family File. See "Displaying a Merge Report" in Chapter 13 for details on using this option. *Read this report carefully before you begin any merging operations.* This will help you avoid making mistakes.

Merge matching individuals — Review the exact matches and possible matches one-by-one and decide which to merge.

Cancel — Quit the merge without reviewing duplicate individuals.

Note: If you have not already looked at the Merge Report, Family Tree Maker asks if you want to view it. Click **Yes** to see it, or click **No** to move on.

Family Tree Maker displays the Merge Individuals dialog box where you can compare the information associated with the "possible match" individuals — individuals who may exist in two places, but whose information differs slightly.

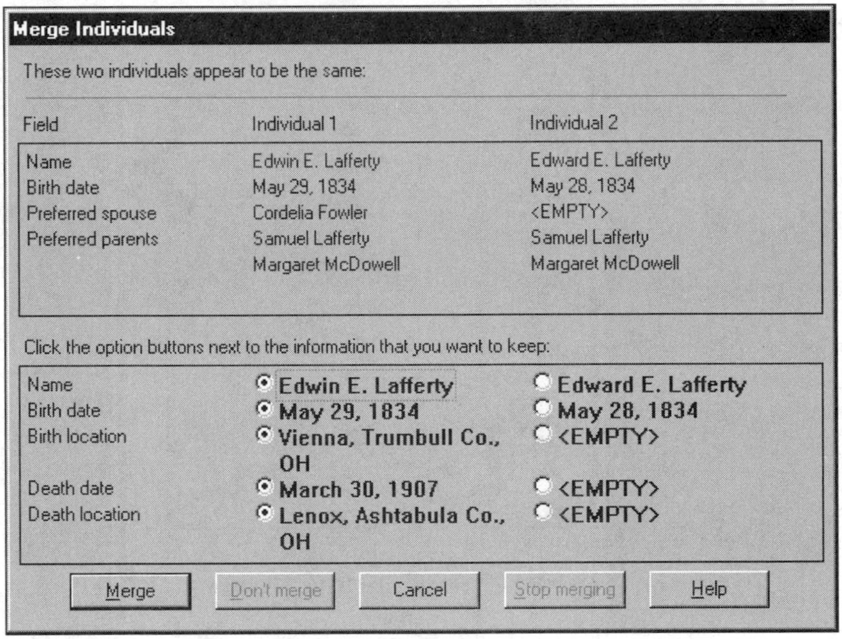

Figure 6-5. The Merge Individuals dialog box

3. Look through the information in the second and third columns. The lines at the top of the dialog box contain names of parents and spouses to help you identify the individual. This information is for reference only, and Family Tree Maker will not merge or discard it.

If you think that the information in the two columns belongs to the same individual, click **Merge**. If you think that it belongs to two separate individuals, click **Don't Merge**.

When you click "Merge," Family Tree Maker combines the information from the two records. If there are two sets of data for a given fact, Family Tree Maker creates an "alternate" fact for it (see "Adding Alternate Facts" in Chapter 5). Family Tree Maker joins together differing Notes and Scrapbooks. If there isn't enough room for both sets of Notes or Scrapbook pages, Family Tree Maker will include all of the first individual's information and as much of the second individual's as it can fit. In addition, if two mothers or two fathers have a "Natural" relationship with the individual, one of the relationships is changed to "Unknown."

When you click "Don't Merge," Family Tree Maker does not merge the two individuals. Instead, both individuals remain in your Family File as they are now.

Repeat step 3 with the next set of information.

Note: If at any time you want to discontinue merging information and save the merges you already completed, click **Stop merging**. If you do not want to save any of your merges, click **Cancel** instead. Family Tree Maker will return you to a Family Page.

If there is no more information to compare, Family Tree Maker either displays a Merge Report (if all items were merged successfully), or an Exceptions Report (if there were items which could not be merged).

4. Click **OK** when you are done viewing or printing the reports.

Family Tree Maker will return you to a Family Page.

5. Print some trees and reports *before* you quit Family Tree Maker. Check the documents to make sure that you didn't make any mistakes when merging the individuals. If you did make mistakes, you can reverse the merge by going to the **Edit** menu and selecting **Undo** *before* you quit Family Tree Maker. You cannot reverse a merge after quitting and restarting Family Tree Maker.

Merging Specific Individuals

The Merge Specific Individuals command enables you to select two individuals in your Family File and to merge them. Use this command to merge two individuals that Family Tree Maker doesn't recognize as duplicates with the Merge Duplicate Individuals command. For example, you may not have entered enough information about one of the individuals for Family Tree Maker to conclude that they're the same individual. Use this command only when you are certain that the two individuals are really the same.

To merge specific individuals:

1. Go to the Family Page of one of the individuals you want to merge.

2. From the **People** menu, select **Merge Specific Individuals**.

   Family Tree Maker displays a dialog box showing a list of the individuals in your Family File.

3. Click the name of the individual you want to merge with the individual you chose in step 1. If you need help finding the name you want, see "Moving Around in the Index of Individuals" in Chapter 4.

4. Click **OK** to continue.

   Family Tree Maker displays a message asking if you really want to merge these two individuals.

5. Click **Yes** to continue, or **No** to cancel the merge.

   When you click "Yes" Family Tree Maker may display additional questions about these two individuals. Click **Yes** or **No** as appropriate.

   If Family Tree Maker can complete the merge, it displays the Merge Individuals dialog box (see Figure 6-5).

   If you click the name of an "illegal" individual, Family Tree Maker displays an error message and asks you to select another individual. An "illegal" individual is someone that, for logical reasons, could not possibly be the same individual. For example, you can't merge two individuals if doing so would make the individual his or her own parent.

   Note: The "Don't Merge" and "Stop Merging" buttons are not available with the Merge Specific Individuals command.

6. Look through the information in the second and third columns. The lines at the top of the dialog box contain names of parents and spouses to help you identify the individual. This information is for reference only, and Family Tree Maker will not merge or discard it.

If you think that the information in the two columns belongs to the same individual, click **Merge**. If you do not want to merge these individuals, click **Cancel** instead.

If there were items that could not be merged, Family Tree Maker displays an Exceptions report. If all items were merged successfully, Family Tree Maker displays a Family Page.

Note: If there are two sets of Notes or two Scrapbooks for that individual, Family Tree Maker joins them together. If there isn't enough room for both sets of Notes or Scrapbook pages, Family Tree Maker will include all of the first individual's information and as much of the second individual's as it can fit. In addition, if two mothers or two fathers have a "Natural" relationship with the individual, one of the relationships is changed to "Unknown."

7. When you finish merging, print some trees and reports *before* you quit Family Tree Maker. Check the documents to make sure that you didn't make any mistakes when merging the individuals. If you did make mistakes, you can reverse the merge by going to the **Edit** menu and selecting **Undo** *before* you quit Family Tree Maker. You cannot reverse a merge after quitting and restarting Family Tree Maker.

Chapter 7

RESEARCHING YOUR FAMILY FROM HOME

Very little is known about Luigi Cirio, an Italian citizen who lived
in the 1800s. Tracing records in Italy is one of the challenges
facing his great-great-granddaughter, Doreen DeSalvo, an
amateur genealogist and the User Interface Designer for
the Banner Blue Division of Brøderbund.

RESEARCHING YOUR FAMILY FROM HOME

As many family historians can tell you, genealogy is an enjoyable but time-intensive pursuit. In the past, you would have had to spend a good portion of that time at libraries and other resources, hunting and searching through numerous indexes before you could determine if a record containing the information you needed even existed. But with the FamilyFinder Center, Family Tree Maker has consolidated its powerful research tools and Internet and CD-based resources into one easy-to-find location.

THE FAMILYFINDER CENTER: HOME BASE

The **FamilyFinder Center** is where you begin (and maintain) your research efforts, whether you are just beginning to examine your family history or are continuing research begun in previous versions of Family Tree Maker. The FamilyFinder Center comprises search tools, "how-to" hints, and convenient Web links to a growing number of Internet resources that will have you quickly conducting high-quality, personalized research into your family's history from the comfort of your home.

What are the FamilyFinder Search and FamilyFinder Report?

After establishing your first family file with the **Start-up Wizard** (see Chapter 1, Program Setup), or opening one from a previous version of Family Tree Maker, you will want to perform a **FamilyFinder Search.** If you have Internet capability, take advantage of our precision matching technology that analyzes not only names, but compares dates and family relationships as well. This ability to cross check and confirm different kinds of information results in a conveniently organized **FamilyFinder Report** that places only the highest probability names into their own 5-Star Matches section. There are additional sections for World Family Tree, Internet, and Family Archive CD matches as well.

What are Internet Resources?

From the FamilyFinder Center, you also have easy access to many additional Internet resources dedicated to serving genealogists of all levels. **Family Tree Maker Online**, **GenealogyLibrary.com**, **Family Finder Agents**, and **GenForum Message Boards** are just some of the online features and resources that we will discuss later in this chapter.

What are the Research Journal and the Genealogy "How-To" Guide?

After you perform a FamilyFinder Search (and the results of that search are displayed in your FamilyFinder Report), you need a way to focus your future research plans and track your progress. The customizable **Research Journal** (with its enclosed **"To Do"** List) is the perfect tool for that job and will prove to be an indispensable aid as you perform the research necessary to confirm the leads generated by FamilyFinder Search. If you find yourself considering what steps to take next, remember to consult the online **Genealogy "How-To" Guide**. It has tips and hints to help you decide how to proceed, no matter where you are in your research.

THE FAMILYFINDER INDEX AND FAMILY ARCHIVES

If you are not Internet-ready at this time, you can still find name matches by searching the **FamilyFinder Index,** found on the installation CDs that came with Family Tree Maker. The resulting FamilyFinder Report will show name matches found in the ever-growing collection of **Family Archive** CDs.

Depending on the number of CDs included with your version of Family Tree Maker, you may be able to begin searching for matches right away (see "Using the FamilyFinder Index and the Family Archives" in this chapter). Your FamilyFinder Index search may also locate and identify additional Family Archives, such as census or marriage records, or other CDs that contain potential matches. See "Ordering Family Archive CDs" in this chapter for information on how to order them directly from Family Tree Maker.

You can also find the Family Archives at selected libraries. Check with your local branch for more information about their CD index collection.

USING THE FAMILYFINDER CENTER

The **FamilyFinder Center** is where you begin researching your family history. All the search, report, and reference power of Family Tree Maker can be accessed from here. First, the **FamilyFinder Search**, with its highly accurate matching capabilities, researches and analyzes a vast amount of information, providing you with a segmented and prioritized **FamilyFinder Report**. This powerful feature will be the cornerstone of your research efforts. In this chapter we will show you how to take advantage of the leads provided in the improved FamilyFinder Report, as well as the many Internet resources available through **Family Tree Maker Online** and our easy-to-use Web links. You will also learn about the **FamilyFinder Index** and how it is used to search the expanding Family Archive CD library, allowing you to identify useful records, learn what they contain, and where they are located. In addition, you will learn how to save time and preserve the accuracy of your research findings by copying information from the **Family Archives** directly to your Family File.

To view the FamilyFinder Center:

1. From the **View** menu, select **FamilyFinder**. Then, from the submenu, select **FamilyFinder Center**.

    Family Tree Maker displays the FamilyFinder Center screen.

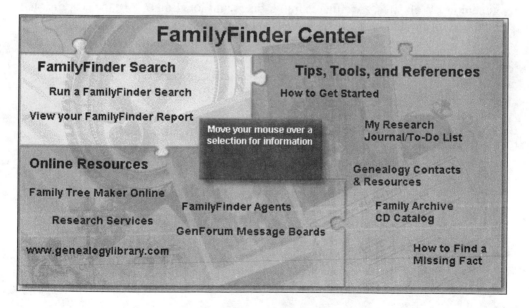

Figure 7-1. The FamilyFinder Center

2. As you slide your mouse pointer over the text links, they change color and a brief description appears in the center of the screen. Click any of these links to go to the corresponding location.

THE FAMILYFINDER SEARCH AND THE FAMILYFINDER REPORT

The FamilyFinder Search is where to begin your research. When you perform a FamilyFinder Search, the FamilyFinder Index (or optionally the Internet) is searched for some, or all, of your relatives at once, depending on the options you select. When the search is completed, the resulting potential matches are displayed in the FamilyFinder Report. If you choose an online (Internet) search, the very best matches will be placed in a 5-Star Matches section. The remaining categories, World Family Tree Matches, Other Family Archive CD Matches, and Internet Matches will contain the rest of the search results.

What is 5-Star Matching?

How does the FamilyFinder Report know which matches are most likely part of your family tree? Many factors are considered when comparing individuals in your family file with those found in the Family Archives or at various Internet genealogy Web sites. Are there similar dates and locations? Are there additional matches for related individuals such as spouses? For example, if a couple appears as married in a World Family Tree or Marriage CD *and* in your Family File, then the probability of a valid match is greatly increased. The FamilyFinder Report then ranks the potential matches with a 5-star system to rate their quality, and assigns only those with a high probability of being the same people, the highest 5-Star Match rating.

Note: 5-Star Matches are the result of precision matching (comparing information other than names only) and are only available as a result of Internet-based FamilyFinder Searches.

The Family Page Match Alert

When an individual is listed in the 5-Star Matches portion of the FamilyFinder Report, a star is placed next to their name on their Family Page. A blue star indicates a new match, a yellow star identifies previous matches, and a gray star appears for matches that have been checked (marked as Done) in the FamilyFinder Report.

- Click the star that appears on an individual's Family Page to see a FamilyFinder Report showing only matches for that individual (or members of their same clan).

- To change the number of stars a potential match must earn in order to be considered a high-quality match, see "FamilyFinder Preferences" in this chapter.

FamilyFinder Report

This shows CDs and genealogy-related Internet sites that may have information on people in your file.

Stars indicate confidence in each match: ★★★★★ Highest ★ Lowest

Click on folders to open or close: 📁 New Matches 📁 Previous Matches

Last updated July 29, 1999. Source: Online. To update the report, Click here

5-STAR MATCHES

5-star ranking indicates source that is virtually certain (95% chance or better) to hold information about your family members.

DONE	QUALITY	MATCH	SOURCE	
☑	★★★★★	📁 Lincoln, Abraham and 8 others	CD 701: World Family Tree: Vol. 1	Tree 3203
☑	★★★★★	📁 Lincoln, Abraham and 9 others	CD 701: World Family Tree: Vol. 1	Tree 3204

WORLD FAMILY TREE MATCHES

Each World Family Tree entry is an entire family file contributed by a family researcher like yourself. Most include 100 or more individuals.
(Click here for information on contributing to the World Family Tree.)

📁 **Top 10 World Family Tree Matches**

DONE	QUALITY	MATCH	SOURCE	
☑	★★★	📁 Lincoln, Abraham	CD 701: World Family Tree: Vol. 1	Tree 3203

Figure 7-2. The FamilyFinder Report

As you use the FamilyFinder Report, keep these things in mind:

- Previous users of Family Tree Maker should update their FamilyFinder Reports. Improved matching will likely result in more accurate matches.

- Though the 5-Star rating virtually insures a match, all matches are *potential* matches. You should investigate each one to verify that the matching name is actually part of your family tree.

- The number of individuals you include in your search may affect the number of stars Family Tree Maker assigns to a potential match. For example, if you search on a husband and a wife, and both are found on a marriage CD, they may score more stars than if you searched on just one of the spouses.

- The FamilyFinder Report does not include matches based on first name initials. For example, the FamilyFinder Report will not consider "M. Johnson" a match for "Mary Johnson", but the Search Expert will (see "Using the Search Expert" in this chapter).

- If there are errors in your Family File (such as titles in the "Name" field) the FamilyFinder Report may not find your relatives. We recommend that you check your Family File for errors before you use the FamilyFinder Report. See "Checking Your Files for Errors" in Chapter 6 for instructions.

- The special key combination, **Control + Alt + Shift + Down Arrow** can be used to delete a FamilyFinder Report if you find that it is too large or difficult to use. However, be aware that you *cannot* be in the FamilyFinder Report itself when using this quick-key combination.

  Note: If you use this delete option and then create another FamilyFinder Report, any matches that you had previously marked "Done" will appear as new, unmarked matches.

CREATING OR UPDATING THE FAMILYFINDER REPORT

The FamilyFinder Report is organized into the following four sections:

5-Star Matches — If you select an Online search for your first FamilyFinder Report, or if you update an existing report online, only the best matches appear in this section.

Note: If there are no 5-star matches, or if they have been checked off (Done), this section will not appear.

World Family Tree Matches — This section contains possible matches found on the World Family Tree CDs that rated 4-stars or less.

Other Family Archive CDs — This section contains potential matches found on CDs other than the World Family Tree.

Internet Matches — This section provides clickable links to individual genealogy-related Web sites.

Note: If a category contains more than 10 matches, only the top 10 will be shown. The rest will be placed in a separate folder called Other Matches.

When opening a FamilyFinder Report created in a previous version of Family Tree Maker, you will be reminded to update it. Matches in the updated FamilyFinder Report may show some changes in ranking due to improved matching technology.

To create or update a FamilyFinder Report:

1. From the **View** menu, select **FamilyFinder**. Then, from the submenu select **FamilyFinder Search/Report**.

   If you have created a FamilyFinder Report in a previous version of Family Tree Maker, it will be shown here.

   Note: If you've added or removed individuals, dates, or locations since your last FamilyFinder Report, you may want to update your FamilyFinder Report to include those changes.

2. From the **Edit** menu, select **Create New FamilyFinder Report**. If you have already created a FamilyFinder Report, the menu will only show **Update FamilyFinder Report**.

   Family Tree Maker displays the FamilyFinder Search dialog box.

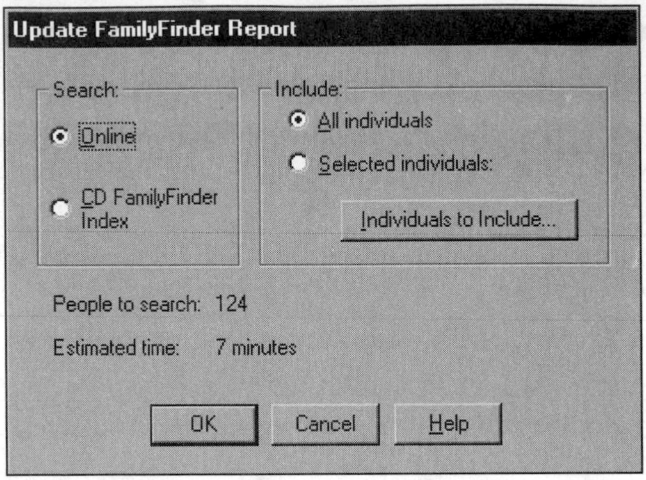

Figure 7-3. The FamilyFinder Search dialog box

3. Select one of the following **Search** options.

    Online — The online searches are faster, more comprehensive, and more up-to-date than the CD searches. For more information, see the next section, "The Online Search Option."

    CD — These CDs come with your Family Tree Maker program and provide an index to all of the Family Archives available at the time of production. For more information, see "The CD Search Option" later in this chapter.

Please note that if the current Family File contains no FamilyFinder Report, or only one created prior to this version of Family Tree Maker, the options in the following step will not appear in the dialog box.

4. Select one of the following **Include** options:

    All individuals — This option looks for information on all individuals in your Family File. Although searches on large numbers of people take more time, they provide the most accurate results.

    Selected individuals — This option looks for information about specific individuals. For example, you could limit your search to only your maternal ancestors.

If you select Selected individuals, click **Individuals to Include** to display the Individuals to Include dialog box. See "Selecting Individuals to Include" in Chapter 9 for more detailed information.

Family Tree Maker displays a message at the bottom of the dialog box indicating how many individuals are in the group you selected, and approximately how long it will take to search for these individuals.

5. After you make your selections, click **OK**.

Note: If you selected the **Online** option, continue with the next section, "The Online Search Option." If you selected **CD FamilyFinder Index**, proceed to "The CD Search Option" in this chapter.

The Online Search Option

If you select the **Online** option when creating or updating your FamilyFinder Report, Family Tree Maker opens your browser and connects you to Family Tree Maker Online. The FamilyFinder Search starts to run and a progress meter displays in the Family Tree Maker window.

The progress meter indicates approximately how many minutes it will take to complete the process. If you don't want to wait for the report to finish, simply click the **Cancel** button and run the search at a later time.

Note: If you are connecting to Family Tree Maker Online for the first time, follow the on-screen instructions to complete the online registration.

1. You can continue to explore the Family Tree Maker Online Web site while you wait for the FamilyFinder Search to finish downloading new matches.

2. To review the status or your search, Press ⌥ + ⇥ (tab), or click the Family Tree Maker button on the Windows taskbar to view the progress meter.

When the FamilyFinder Search has been completed, you may view some of the matches, or close your browser and disconnect from your online service.

For more information, see "Using Family Tree Maker Online" in this chapter.

The CD Search Option

If you select the CD FamilyFinder Index option when creating or updating the FamilyFinder Report:

1. Family Tree Maker prompts you to insert one of the FamilyFinder Index CDs if it is not already in the drive, and then displays the FamilyFinder Search status dialog box.

2. Wait for Family Tree Maker to prompt you to insert the next FamilyFinder Index CD, and then insert that CD in your computer's CD-ROM drive.

Family Tree Maker completes the search and displays the FamilyFinder Report on your screen.

Displaying Items in the FamilyFinder Report

To select specific items to display in your FamilyFinder Report:

1. From the Contents menu, select **Items to Display**.

   Family Tree Maker displays the Items to Display in FamilyFinder Report dialog box.

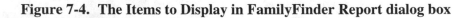

Figure 7-4. The Items to Display in FamilyFinder Report dialog box

2. From the **Show items marked** section, select either **Done**, **Not Done**, or **Both Done and Not Done**. Use this option to select which check boxed items you want to display — complete, incomplete, or both.

3. From the **Show these FamilyFinder Report matches** section, select one of the following:

   All matches — This option displays all matches found in the FamilyFinder Report.

   Selected Individuals — This option allows you to choose matches only for specific individuals. If you select this option, click **Choose** to display the Individuals to Include dialog box.

   Make your selections, then click **OK** to return to the Items to Display dialog box.

   Selected Family Archive CDs — This option allows you to show only those matches found in the Family Archive CDs of your choice. If you select this option, click **Choose** to display the Family Archives to Include dialog box.

   Make your selections, then click **OK** to return to the Items to Display dialog box.

   Show only 4- and 5-star matches — This option allows you to display only the highest-ranking matches in your report.

4. After making your selections from the options listed above, click **OK**.

   Family Tree Maker displays the FamilyFinder Report according to your preferences.

Sorting Items to Display in the FamilyFinder Report

You may want items in your FamilyFinder Report to appear grouped by quality, category or some other option. Some items may be sorted a second time for easier follow up and tracking.

To sort the FamilyFinder Report:

1. From the **Format** menu, select **Sort**.

    Family Tree Maker displays the Sort FamilyFinder Report dialog box.

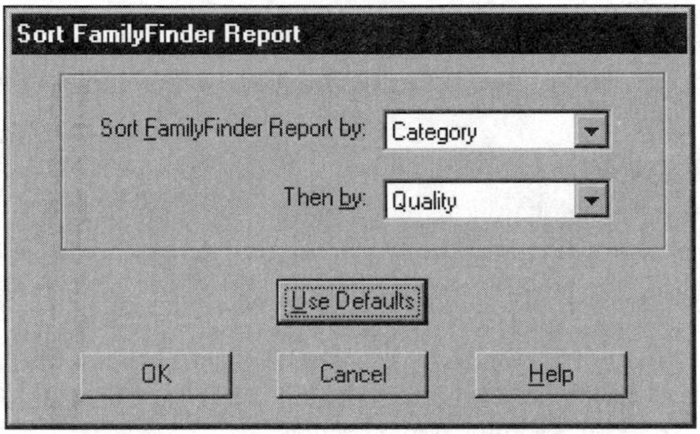

Figure 7-5. The Sort FamilyFinder Report dialog box

2. The pull-down lists allow you to sort on two different levels. Select from the following options:

    Sort . . .by — First you can select from among "Category," "Family Archive CD," "Individual," or "Quality."

    Note: If you selected Category as your first sort option, then the FamilyFinder Report is split into separate sections for World Family Tree, Family Archive CD, and Internet matches (plus 5-star matches, if any). Otherwise, only the 5-star matches will have a separate section.

    Then by — This is your second level sorting option. From the pull-down menu, select from among "Family Archive CD," "Individual," "Quality," or "nothing."

Note: If you selected Category as your first sort option, then your second level sort option is performed within each section.

3. After you make your selections, click **OK**.

Family Tree Maker sorts the FamilyFinder Report according to your selections and returns you to the current report.

Special Note about the FamilyFinder Report

Additional information about the FamilyFinder Report:

- Click the folder next to a match to display additional information. The file folder expands and collapses each line.

- Click the information in the **Possible Matches** column to jump to that site on the Internet or to display information about the CD containing the match.

- The next time you run or update the report, it will reflect the current date and new matches will appear with blue stars in the "New Matches" section of the report. Matches from previous searches will move to the "Based on your previous searches" section.

- Clicking on link-formatted (colored and underlined) text takes you to another view: your browser, the Genealogy "How-To" Guide, or a dialog box.

You can also customize your report as described in "Adding a Title, Footnote, or Date and Time Stamp," "Formatting Text," and "Choosing Styles for Boxes, Lines, and Borders" in Chapter 9.

USING FAMILY TREE MAKER ONLINE TO FIND INFORMATION ABOUT YOUR FAMILY

Another good resource for finding information about your family is the Family Tree Maker Online Web site. Below we describe some of the ways our Web site can help you. Internet Web sites are constantly being changed and updated, so be sure to visit often at **http://www.familytreemaker.com** to make sure you have the very latest information available.

For details about using Family Tree Maker Online, please see "Using Family Tree Maker Online" in this chapter.

Locate Your Ancestors

Internet FamilyFinder — Quickly search genealogy sites across the Internet for your ancestors. We provide direct links to the pages containing possible matches.

Genealogy SiteFinder — Search or browse through categorized links to locate Web sites that interest you.

FamilyFinder Index — Access the most up-to-date Family Archive index to see which CDs might contain information about your ancestors.

Record Lookup Service — Order photocopies and scanned records right from your home computer!

Share with and Learn from Others

Home Pages — Create a home page to share information about your ancestors or search others' home pages to find connections to your family. Home pages can include text, a box-style tree, up to five reports, and even a book!

Message Boards — Ask questions, post family queries, and help others with your knowledge and experience.

Get Research Help and Hints

Professionally-Written Articles — Find information on a wide variety of research topics.

Online University — Brush up your research skills with our fun, self-paced genealogy class.

Biography Assistant — Writing your family stories has never been so easy!

USING FAMILY TREE MAKER ONLINE

Family Tree Maker Online is the Family Tree Maker Internet Web site where you can access valuable genealogical resources to speed your research. Here, you can get expert answers to your Family Tree Maker and genealogy questions. Share tips, tricks, and success stories with other Family Tree Maker customers and family history enthusiasts, help develop future versions of Family Tree Maker, and stay informed about Family Tree Maker and other products. In addition, as a Family Tree Maker user, you are exclusively entitled to post classified ads, create a home page with information from your Family File, and more. These services are provided free of charge through December 31, 2000.

Visiting the Family Tree Maker Online Web Site

Before you begin, make sure your Web browser and Internet Service Provider (ISP) software are set up correctly (see "Changing Your Online Setup" in this chapter).

To visit Family Tree Maker Online:

1. Start your Family Tree Maker software if it is not already running. In addition, be sure your modem is on and connected to your phone line (or cable modem).

2. From the **Internet** menu, select **Go Online**.

   Your Web browser opens, and you may hear dialing and beeping noises. If this is your first time using an Internet Service Provider, you may need to answer some setup questions before you continue. If you have already set up your Internet account, you may still need to type a user name and password to access the Internet.

Note: If your Web browser does not open, or you see the screen in Figure 7-6, refer to "Family Tree Maker Online Problems" in the Troubleshooting appendix.

After a few moments, Family Tree Maker displays a registration form. We offer registered users the following special benefits: setup Online FamilyFinder Report Agents to search the Internet for every name in your file — and then email you when they find new information. You can also add a Family Tree Maker book to your home page. But, you have to register before you can take advantage of these features.

Note: This is different than registering your Family Tree Maker software. Even if you have already registered your Family Tree Maker software, you must sign up with Family Tree Maker Online so that we can assign you a Family Tree Maker Online user number. This unique user number ensures that you are the only one who can create and modify your home page and post messages to the message board in your name.

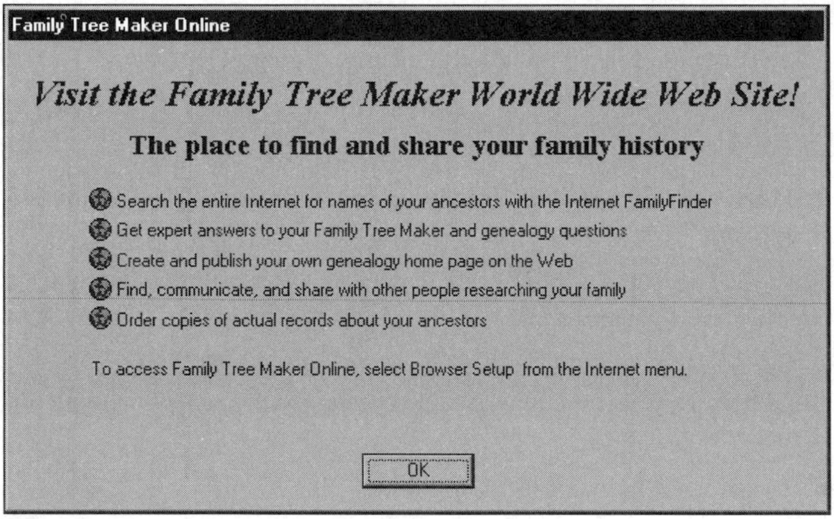

Figure 7-6. Family Tree Maker Online invitation dialog box

3. Follow the instructions on the screen to complete the Family Tree Maker Online registration form.

Closing Your Browser to Save Money

An important thing to know about your Web browser is how to close it after you finish so that you do not incur unnecessary phone or Internet access charges. You can do this by selecting **Exit** from the Web browser's **File** menu. When you open Family Tree Maker Online, your Family Tree Maker software does not shut down, but is still running in the background. This means that you can press $\boxed{\text{alt}}$ + $\boxed{\leftrightarrows}$ (Tab) and go work in it again while Family Tree Maker Online is still running. Family Tree Maker Online and your Web browser will not shut down when you go back into Family Tree Maker. When you want to return to Family Tree Maker Online, from the **View** menu, select **Online** again.

However, if you pay an hourly fee for Internet access, you probably won't want to open Family Tree Maker Online and then let it run while you do work in Family Tree Maker that can be done offline — that could be expensive! It's probably best to open Family Tree Maker Online, find the information you want, and then close it by exiting your Web browser. When you exit your Web browser (by selecting the **File** menu and then clicking **Exit**), Family Tree Maker reappears.

Note: Depending on your setup, you may need to close both your browser and the connection to your service provider.

Changing Your Online Setup

If you install a new Web browser or move your current Web browser to a different location, you must tell Family Tree Maker about the change.

From the **Internet** menu, select **Browser Setup**, and then just follow the on-screen instructions. You don't even have to exit Family Tree Maker.

The FamilyFinder Agents

The first time you run an online version of the FamilyFinder Search, Family Tree Maker automatically creates an "agent" that continues to search for information about your family, even after you end your online session. If necessary, you can change the email address where you receive notices from the agent, and if you don't want to use an agent at all, you can disable it.

To change agent options:

1. From the **FamilyFinder Center**, select **FamilyFinder Agents**.

    Family Tree Maker opens your browser and connects you to Family Tree Maker Online.

2. Follow the instructions on the screen to change the agent options.

MORE ONLINE RESOURCES

Spend some time exploring the text links in this section of the FamilyFinder Center. Here are some brief descriptions of the kinds of information and resources available to help you in your family history research

Research Services — Click this link to go to the Research Services page of www.familytreemaker.com where you will find links to resources providing professional help in tracking your ancestors.

The Genealogy Library — Click this link to go to www.genealogylibrary.com where you will find hundreds of rare books and resources at your fingertips.

FamilyFinder Agents — Click this link to go to the Agent screen of www.familytreemaker.com where you can set up an automated agent to scour the Internet and report new finds back to you via email.

GenForum Message Boards — Click this link to go to the online GenForum message boards where you can read and post messages for thousands of other genealogy researchers.

TIPS, TOOLS, AND REFERENCES

This section of the FamilyFinder Center provides convenient reference links and tools to make your family history research as easy and productive as possible. Spend some time exploring each section for tips and ideas to keep you focused and motivated.

The Research Journal and To Do List

After you have performed a FamilyFinder Search and created a FamilyFinder Report, you need a way to track your progress as you confirm which name leads are actual family members. With its built-in "To Do" list, the Research Journal is the ideal tool to keep you focused and organized while you continue investigating your family history. Create, categorize, and sort your personal To Do items, monitor your research progress as you mark those To Do items as "Done," and plan future research — all from this convenient and easy-to-use tool.

To access the Research Journal, from the **View** menu, select **FamilyFinder**. Then, from the submenu, select **Research Journal**.

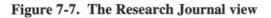

| File | Edit | View | Books | People | Picture/Object | Contents | Format | Internet | Help |

My Research Journal

Instructions: Use this list to track your family tree to-do list and your accomplishments.
Press Ctrl-t from any Family Tree Maker screen to add an item to this list.

Click here to create a new to-do item.

Done	Priority	To Do	Category	Date
☑	! ! ! ! !	Find tips to trace your family in the Genealogy How-to Guide		
☐	! ! ! ! !	Visit Family Tree Maker Online		
☐	! ! ! !	Karen's Canada Trip	Canada	August 1999
☑	! !	Follow up with Reg	Ruby's Birthday	September 1999
☐	! ! ! !	Aunt Janet's Report	Reunion	November 1999
☐	! ! !	The Reunion	Canada	April 2000
☐	! ! ! ! !	Keith's Pictorial	Graduation	June 2000

Figure 7-7. The Research Journal view

The following sections describe the Research Journal features.

Instructions — Offers a reminder that you can press the quick-key combination of "**Ctrl + t**" from any Family Tree Maker screen to add a new "To Do" item to the Research Journal.

Click Here to create a new To Do item — This line is always at the top of the Research Journal. Click the underlined Click Here command to display the Create a New To Do item dialog box.

The Done check box — Click these check boxes to mark items as done, or completed, allowing you to generate lists that show only those items that still need action. Click a second time to remove the check mark. See "Displaying Items in the Research Journal" in this chapter.

Priority — The Research Journal uses exclamation points (with 5 being the highest) to rate the priority of an item. You can set your own priority rating for the To Do items you create. See "Adding New To Do Items" in this chapter.

To Do — This is where you log your list of action items and ideas for future research to keep you focused, motivated, and on track.

Category — This column displays the categories you have assigned (if any) to your custom To Do items.

Date — Any dates you may have entered for To Do items will be displayed in this column. These could be deadlines, dates of entry, or dates of completion.

RESEARCH JOURNAL OPTIONS

The Research Journal makes it easy for you to keep track of a variety of different kinds of information. The following sections describe how to add, edit, delete, and sort items in the Research Journal and the To Do list.

Adding New To Do Items

To add a new To Do item to the Research Journal:

1. Click the underlined **Click Here to create a new To Do item** text at the top of the Research Journal view.

   Family Tree Maker displays the New To Do Item dialog box.

   Note: You can also use the quick-key combination **Ctrl + T** to display a New To Do Item dialog box.

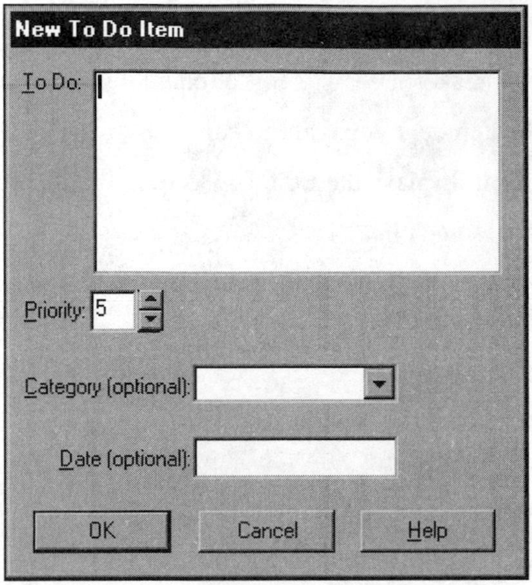

Figure 7-8. The New To Do Item dialog box

2. Enter your To Do item information. You can enter up to 250 characters.

3. Choose a **Priority** setting by using the up/down arrows to display a number between 1 and 5 (with 5 as the highest priority).

4. If you wish, you may find it helpful to type a **Category** of your own creation to help organize your future research. Perhaps you might want a category name based on a specific event, like a special family trip or upcoming reunion, a specific surname, or a meaningful geographical location. Once you've typed it, Family Tree Maker adds it to the drop-down list.

5. The **Date** is also optional. Use it to track your choice of entry, deadline, or completion dates.

6. Click **OK** to close the To Do item dialog box.

Editing To Do Items

The Research Journal makes it easy to edit or change your custom To Do items:

1. Double click the item text you want to edit.

    Family Tree Maker displays the Edit To Do Item dialog box.

2. Make your changes and click **OK**.

    The Edit To Do Item dialog box closes and you are returned to the Research Journal view.

Deleting To Do Items

To delete individual To Do items:

1. Select (highlight) the item you want to remove.

2. Press the **Delete** key on your keyboard.

    The selected To Do item is deleted and you are returned to the Research Journal view.

Displaying Items in the Research Journal

Use the Items to Display dialog box to customize the To Do list by category, selecting only those items you want to display. Perhaps you only want to see completed To Do items, or just those that share the same category. Whatever your particular need, the Items to Display dialog box lets you control the size and focus of your Research Journal.

To select items you want to display in the Research Journal:

1. From **Contents**, select **Items to Display**.

    Family Tree Maker displays the Items to Display in Research Journal dialog box.

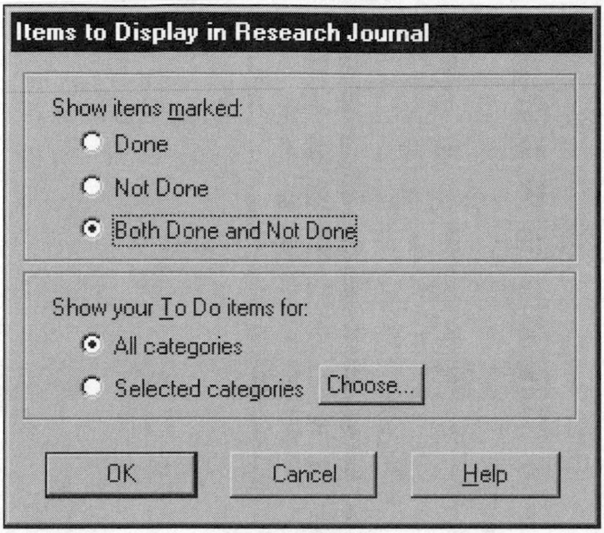

**Figure 7-9. The Items to Display in Research Journal
dialog box**

2. From the **Show items marked** section, select either **Done**, **Not done**, or **Both Done and Not Done**. Use this option to select which check boxed items you want to display — completed, incomplete, or both.

3. From the **Show your To Do items for** section, select from the following:

   All categories — Select this option to display all available categories of To Do items in the Research Journal.

   Selected categories — Select this option if you want to display only specific categories of items in the Research Journal.

   If you select Selected categories, click **Choose**. Family Tree Maker displays the **Categories to Include** dialog box. You can move the categories you want to show in the Research Journal from the left side of the dialog box to the right side, then click **OK**. Please note that To Do items without categories are always shown.

4. After you've selected your options, click **OK**.

   The Research Journal displays the available items according to your preferences.

Sorting Items to Display

You may want items you've entered for your customized To Do list to appear in a particular order. You can choose the order quickly and easily with the Research Journal's sorting feature.

To sort your Research Journal To Do items:

1. From the **Format** menu, select **Sort**.

    Family Tree Maker displays the Sort Research Journal dialog box.

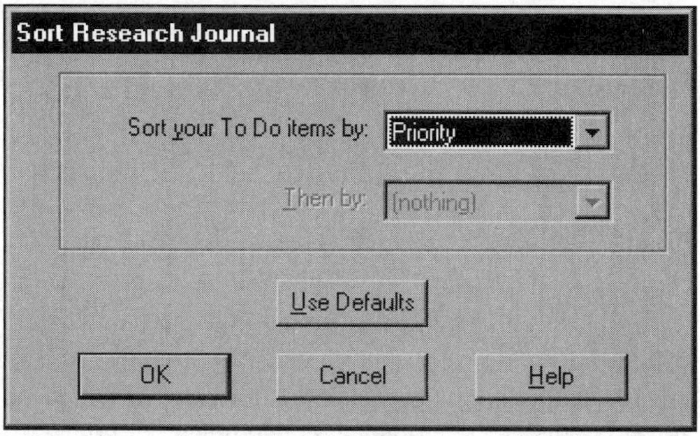

Figure 7-10. The Sort Research Journal dialog box

2. In the **Sort your To Do items by** window, use the pull-down list to select the sorting option from among "Category," "Date," or "Priority."

    The **Then by** sorting option is not available for the Research Journal.

3. After you make your selections, click **OK**.

    Family Tree Maker sorts according to your selection then returns you to the Research Journal.

More FamilyFinder Center Tips, Tools, and References

Take some time to explore the remaining links in the FamilyFinder Center. As your research progresses, you will find many useful, time-saving hints and ideas to make your journey an enjoyable one.

Genealogy Contacts and Resources — Click here to go to the "Genealogy research directory" page of the Genealogy "How To" Guide. You will find links to national, state and county information, plus international, ethnic, and religious resources. There is even a bibliography of suggested readings.

Family Archive CD Catalog — Click here to go to a listing of all the Family Archive and World Family Tree CDs available at the time of the release of this version of Family Tree Maker. Any of these CDs can be ordered from the Family Tree Maker Online home page, www.familytreemaker.com.

International Form Letters — Click here to go to the "Form letters and other aids" page of the Genealogy "How To" Guide. Here, you can generate helpful form letters in five different languages: English, Italian, German, Spanish, and French. These letters clearly state the information you are requesting, requiring only that you add postage and mail them.

How to Find a Missing Fact — Click here to go to the "Step-by-step guide to finding family information" page of the Genealogy "How To" Guide. There you will find a list of the facts common to genealogical research and how to go about locating them. At the bottom of the page, you will also find a useful guide called "Keys to successful genealogical research."

USING THE FAMILYFINDER INDEX
AND THE FAMILY ARCHIVES

Family Archives are an expanding collection of CDs that contain information from a variety of sources, such as federal and state census records, marriage records, actual family trees, and Social Security death indexes for over 220 million people. If you think of a Family Archive as a "book" with "pages," then the FamilyFinder Index is the master index to all of the Family Archives; it helps you find the right "book" in the library.

Use the FamilyFinder Index as you would any index to look for information that resides on the Family Archive CDs.

Where can I get the FamilyFinder and Family Archives?

You already have the FamilyFinder Index — it is contained on the installation CDs that came with your Family Tree Maker program. Some versions of Family Tree Maker also contain additional selected Family Archives. If, while using the FamilyFinder Index, you find information about your family in Family Archives that did not come with Family Tree Maker, you can purchase these Family Archives from The Learning Co.

Ordering Family Archive CDs

Purchasing Family Archives for use in your home enables you to locate ancestors without ever leaving your computer. You save rental and copy fees as well as avoiding the restrictions and time limits that libraries often impose on computer use — and your computer is open whenever you're ready.

Visit Family Tree Maker Online (www.familytreemaker.com) for more information on how to conveniently order special CD bundles and for news on the latest additions to the Family Archives.

You can also find the Family Archives at selected libraries. Check with your local libraries for more information about their CD collection.

What Can I Do with the Family Archives Information?

Software programs (just like books and movies) are protected by U.S. copyright laws and international treaties. The pamphlet included with each Family Archive CD describes the acceptable use policy for this information. Please read the pamphlet carefully before you use the CD, and use the Family Archives responsibly.

Opening Family Archives and the FamilyFinder Index

To open the FamilyFinder Index or a Family Archive:

1. Insert a FamilyFinder Index or Family Archive CD in your computer's CD-ROM drive.

2. From the **View** menu, select **FamilyFinder**, then from the submenu, select **View CD**.

   Family Tree Maker displays the Introduction page of the FamilyFinder Index or Family Archive. If this is the first time that you have opened a particular Family Archive, you will see a license agreement. Please read it carefully, and then click **OK** to display the content of the CD.

Moving Around in Family Archives and the FamilyFinder Index

Both the Family Archives and the FamilyFinder Index have labeled tabs along the right side of the screen. You can click these tabs to turn to the Introduction, Contents, Index, and Information pages. You always know which page you are on because each page has a title at the top, such as "FamilyFinder Index — Index."

ALL ABOUT INTRODUCTION PAGES

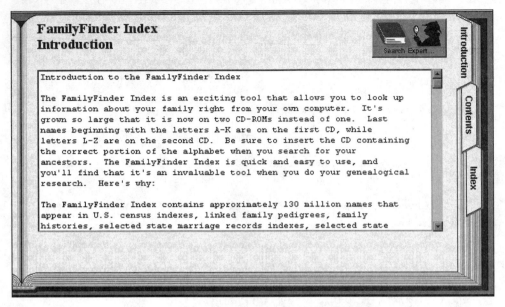

FamilyFinder Index
Introduction

Search Expert...

Introduction
Contents
Index

```
Introduction to the FamilyFinder Index

The FamilyFinder Index is an exciting tool that allows you to look up
information about your family right from your own computer.  It's
grown so large that it is now on two CD-ROMs instead of one.  Last
names beginning with the letters A-K are on the first CD, while
letters L-Z are on the second CD.  Be sure to insert the CD containing
the correct portion of the alphabet when you search for your
ancestors.  The FamilyFinder Index is quick and easy to use, and
you'll find that it's an invaluable tool when you do your genealogical
research.  Here's why:

The FamilyFinder Index contains approximately 130 million names that
appear in U.S. census indexes, linked family pedigrees, family
histories, selected state marriage records indexes, selected state
```

Figure 7-11. A sample Introduction page

Introduction pages give you general information about the contents of the
FamilyFinder Index and the Family Archives. They also provide you with
important information about how to search in different types of records.
Understanding this information can help you research your family tree more
effectively.

Printing a Family Archive CD
Introduction Page

In Family Tree Maker, you can select text in the Introduction page of a Family
Archive CD and print it. This may come in handy if you want to print an
enrollment form for a genealogy society or some other information that describes
the source from which you gathered your family history.

To print a Family Archive CD Introduction page:

1. Insert the Family Archive CD in your CD-ROM drive.

2. From the **View** menu, select **FamilyFinder**, then select **View CD**.

   Family Tree Maker displays the FamilyFinder view.

3. Click the **Introduction** tab.

   Family Tree Maker displays the Introduction page for the current Family Archive CD.

4. Highlight the text you want to print.

5. From the **Edit** menu, select **Copy Selected Text**.

   Family Tree Maker copies the selected text to the Windows Clipboard.

6. Turn on your printer and make sure it is ready to print.

7. From the **File** menu, select **Print Selected Text**.

   Family Tree Maker prints the selected text.

   Note: Since Family Tree Maker places the Introduction Page on the Clipboard, you can also paste this information into a text item in a book, into a word processor, or into many other applications.

ALL ABOUT INDEX PAGES

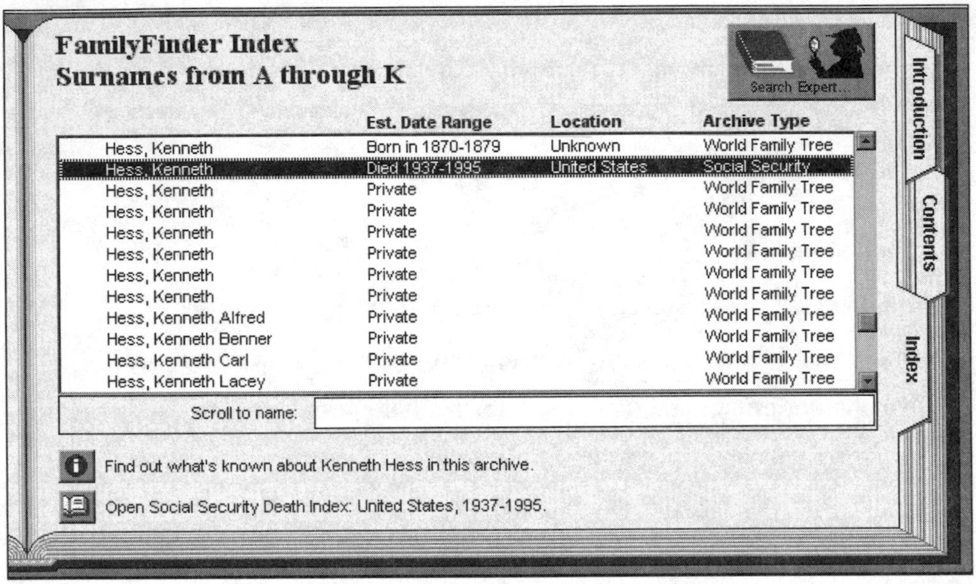

Figure 7-12. A sample Index page

The Index page in the FamilyFinder Index lists all the names from all the Family Archives — more than 220 million names! To see what you'll find in the Family Archive containing a name, click a name and then click **Find out** in the lower-left corner. To open a particular Family Archive, see "Opening Family Archives from within the FamilyFinder Index" in this chapter.

The Index page of a Family Archive shows the name of every individual in that particular Family Archive. To display a record about a particular individual, click a name and then click **Turn to** in the lower-left corner.

To scroll through an index, use the scroll bar, and the arrow keys on your keyboard. To jump from one section of the index to another, click the **Scroll to name** field and start typing the last name of the individual you want to find. With each character you type, you get closer to the name. Type part or all of the name in this order: Last name, First name Middle name. To do a complete search, use the Search Expert. See "Using the Search Expert" in this chapter.

ALL ABOUT CONTENTS PAGES

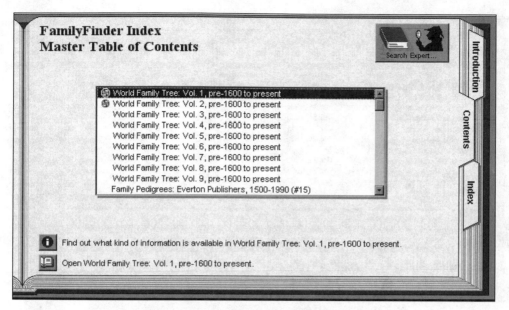

Figure 7-13. A sample Contents page

The Contents page in the FamilyFinder Index lists all of the Family Archives that are referenced in the FamilyFinder Index. To see what type of information a Family Archive contains, click the Family Archive name and then click **Find out** in the lower-left corner.

In most cases, the Contents page in a Family Archive is similar to the contents page of a book; it tells you how the information is divided into sections and chapters. You can use the Contents page to go to information that interests you. To turn to a specific page, click the section and chapter that you want to see and then click **Turn to** in the lower-left corner. The "Turn to" icon on a Family Archive Index page looks the same as the "Open" icon shown on the FamilyFinder Index page above.

ALL ABOUT FAMILY ARCHIVE INFORMATION PAGES

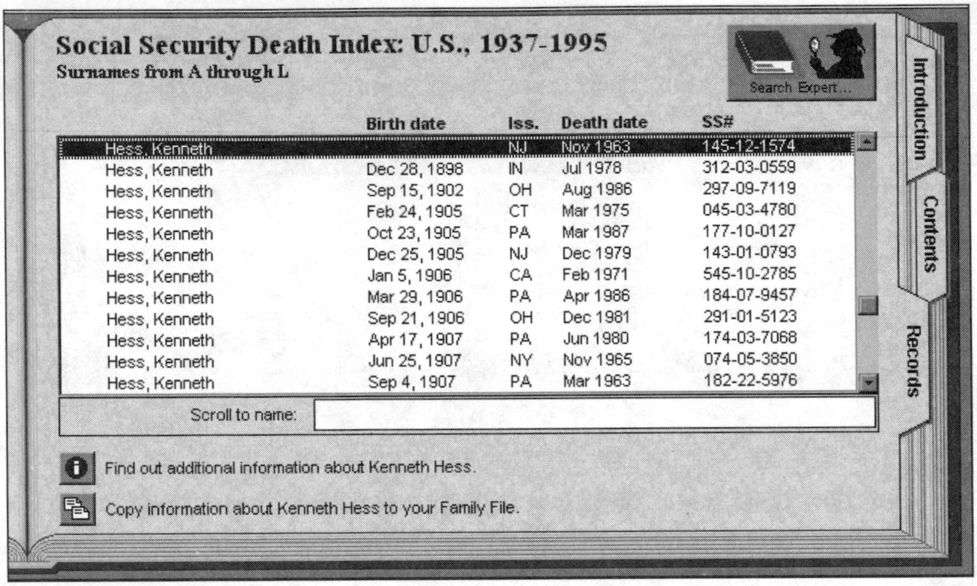

Figure 7-14. A sample Information page

Information pages come in four different varieties:

- **Data** — Family Archives consist of information from marriage records, death records, and much more. In most cases you can copy this information directly into your Family File. When a Family Archive field contains too much information to fit in the allotted space, Family Tree Maker places an ellipsis button (**...**) to the right of it. Click the button to see the rest of the information.

- **Text** — Family Archives contain paragraphs of information from books, such as genealogies. You can scroll through the pages in this Family Archive to look for information that you want to copy to the Notes dialog box on an individual's Family Page.

- **Image** — Family Archives contain scanned images of records or books, such as military records. You can read these images to get family information, print the images, and copy the images to the Clipboard or into Family Tree Maker Scrapbooks.

- **World Family Tree** — archives contain family trees that were submitted to the World Family Tree Project by Family Tree Maker customers just like you (see Figure 7-19). You can view and print them on Family Pages or in trees, reports, Family Group Sheets, and more. When you find a connection to your family, you can append or merge these family trees into your Family File. World Family Tree Archives work in a slightly different way than the other Family Archives, so you'll see separate sets of instructions for them throughout this chapter.

Scrolling Through the Information Pages

When you want to browse through the information in a Family Archive, you can use the scroll bars, the "Scroll to name" field, or the "Go To" command. Instructions for the "Scroll to name" field and the "Go To" command are below. Please note that the "Scroll to name" field is only available when the information in the Family Archive is organized alphabetically. The "Go To" command is only available for Text and Image Family Archives. When you want to do a thorough search for a name, see "Using the Search Expert" in this chapter.

To scroll with the "Scroll to name" field:

1. Click the **Scroll to name** field.

2. Type the last name of the individual you want to find.

   With each character you type, you will get closer to the name you want. You can type part or all of the name, as long as it is in the following order: Last name, First name Middle name.

To use the "Go To" command:

1. From the **Edit** menu, select **Go To**.

   Family Tree Maker displays the Go To dialog box.

2. In the **Section** and **Chapter** lists, click the title of the section and chapter you want to view.

3. In the **Page number** field, type the number of the page you want to see.

4. Click **OK**.

   Family Tree Maker displays the page you requested.

Opening Family Archives from Within the FamilyFinder Index

When you search in the FamilyFinder Index, Family Tree Maker automatically places a magnifying glass next to each match. If you own the Family Archive containing the match, you can open that Family Archive from within the FamilyFinder Index. This way, you don't have to respecify the search that you began in the FamilyFinder Index.

If you do not own a Family Archive containing a particular match, you can get purchasing information by highlighting the match and clicking **How to order** in the lower-left corner.

If you own a Family Archive that you haven't used yet, you still see "How to order" in the lower-left corner. Once you view a Family Archive, **How to order** changes to **Open**, and a CD icon appears to the left of the archive title on the FamilyFinder Index Contents page (see Figure 7-13). To use the Family Archive for the first time, follow the steps below.

Opening a Family Archive for the First Time

1. From the FamilyFinder Index, do a search using the **Search Expert**. See "Searching for Information" in this chapter.

2. Insert the Family Archive into your CD-ROM drive.

   Family Tree Maker opens the Family Archive and displays the Introduction page.

Opening a Family Archive Again

1. Do a search using the Search Expert. See "Searching for Information" in this chapter.

2. Click the matching name you want to view. This name must have a magnifying glass next to it.

3. Click **Open** in the lower-left corner.

4. Insert the correct Family Archive into your CD-ROM drive when Family Tree Maker asks you to do so.

Family Tree Maker opens the Family Archive and displays the page containing the first match.

Selecting and Deselecting
Index Entries for Printing and Copying

When you see entries that interest you in the FamilyFinder Index, in a World Family Tree Archive, or in other selected Family Archives, you can print them or copy them to the Clipboard. You can create a list of several entries that interest you. To create a list of entries, you select them by placing check marks next to them. These lists can be handy when you order or use Family Archives. The table below describes how to select index entries.

To do this...	Do this...
Select a single entry	Highlight the entry and press the spacebar, or from the **Edit** menu, select **Select Entry**
Deselect a single entry	Highlight the entry and press the spacebar, or from the **Edit** menu, select **Deselect Entry**
Select all matching entries	From the **Edit** menu, select **Select Matching Entries**
Deselect all matching entries	From the **Edit** menu, select **Deselect Matching Entries**
Deselect all entries that are currently selected	From the **Edit** menu, select **Deselect All**

Figure 7-15. Selecting and deselecting index entries

After you make your selections, you can either print the entries in a list or copy the list to the Clipboard. The list will include the selected individuals' names, as well as the information listed to the right of their names, such as the Family Archive number and date range. Instructions for printing and copying begin on the next page.

Printing Selected Entries

To print selected entries:

1. Turn on your printer.

2. From the **File** menu, select **Print Selected Entries**.

    Note: Family Tree Maker may display a message reminding you how to format the text; click **OK** to clear the message. (For instructions, see "Formatting Text" in Chapter 9.)

    Family Tree Maker displays the Print dialog box where you can select printing options. See "Printing a Single Document" in Chapter 10, if you need more information.

3. After you select your printing options, click **OK**.

    Family Tree Maker prints the list.

Copying Selected Entries to the Clipboard

To copy selected entries to the Clipboard:

1. From the **Edit** menu, select **Copy**.

    Family Tree Maker places a list of the names on the Clipboard.

2. You can now use the **Paste** command to insert the contents of the Clipboard wherever you like. In most cases, you probably want to open a Windows word processor or spreadsheet and paste the text in there.

If you need help with another Windows program, please refer to that program's manual.

USING THE SEARCH EXPERT

You use the View CD view in Family Tree Maker to display the FamilyFinder Index. This view includes a "find" tool called the Search Expert. You type the name of the person you want to find in the Search Expert and it looks for that name in the FamilyFinder Index. When a matching name is found, it tells you which Family Archive contains more information about the name. Reading the information in that Family Archive will help you determine if you've actually found your ancestor, or just someone with a similar name. When you do find one of your ancestors, you can add information from the Family Archive directly to your Family File.

If you also want to see the actual record, the Family Archive can help you find it. For example, the Family Archive tells you on which microfilm roll you can find a specific census record. Then, you can go to a library or National Archives branch and ask for that roll.

When you use Family Archives, you can also use the Search Expert to search for information such as dates, locations, and other text. For example, you can search for all people born on a particular date in the state of New York. The type of information you can search for varies depending on the type of information in the Family Archive.

For more control over what the Search Expert looks for, see "FamilyFinder Preferences" in this chapter.

Searching for Information

You can begin a search from any page in the FamilyFinder Index or a Family Archive. If you're working with a World Family Tree Archive, you can begin a search from either the Index or Introduction page. See "Using the FamilyFinder Index and the Family Archives" in this chapter.

To search for information:

1. Click **Search Expert**.

    Family Tree Maker displays the Search Expert dialog box.

2. To find someone in your Family File, click **Search for Someone from your Family File**. When you select this option, Family Tree Maker will use the information in your Family File, such as birth dates, death dates, married names, maiden names, and nicknames to help find matches for the individual. To find matches for any other name, click **Search for Someone NOT from your Family File**.

    If you're working with a Family Archive and decide that instead of searching only this Family Archive, you want to search all Family Archives simultaneously, click **Search all archives**. Family Tree Maker will ask you to insert the FamilyFinder Index and will then display the FamilyFinder Index Search Expert.

    Note: With some Family Archives you will see a "Find" field instead of the search choices described above. In this case, type up to four words in the **Find** field and indicate how many words apart you want these words to appear in the **Find these words within** field. For example, even if you want to find a name, such as John Sweeney, by typing his name in the "Find" field and choosing six words apart, Family Tree Maker will find him in a case like this: "The Sweeney family, Robert and Mary (parents), John, Rachel, and William (children)…"

3. Now you must tell Family Tree Maker what to search for.

    If you chose "Search for Someone from your Family File" in step 2, Family Tree Maker displays a list of the individuals from your Family File. Select a name from the list, or type a name in the **Scroll to name** field.

If you type this...	You find this...
Last	Entries with that word in the surname
First Last *or* Last, First	Entries with the first name and surname
, First	Entries with that word in the first name
, First Middle	Entries with the first and middle name
Last, First Middle *or* First Middle Last	Entries with the first, middle, and surname
?????	All five letter names or words. Each question mark represents a letter. Use any number of question marks and include any letters you are sure about. For example, Sm??? finds all five letter names that begin with Sm. (This type of search can take hours and is available only in name and generic fields.)
*	Any name or word regardless of the number of letters. Combine this symbol with other letters to narrow the search. For example if you don't know whether a name is spelled Smith or Smythe, type Sm* to find both spellings. Or to find a name that begins with "S" and ends with "ski," type S*ski. (This type of search can take hours and is available only in name and generic fields.)
Year	Any date in that year
Month and Year	Any date in that month of that year
Year - Year	Any date between the beginning of the first year and the end of the second year

Figure 7-16. Field formats for the Search Expert

If you chose "Search for Someone NOT from your Family File" in step 2, Family Tree Maker displays a dialog box containing the fields that you can search on the CD in your CD-ROM drive. Type the information you want to find using the search field formats shown in Figure 7-16.

4. Click **Start search**.

    Family Tree Maker displays a status box while it conducts the search and then places a magnifying glass to the left of the matches and highlights the best match. When a record contains too much information to fit in the allotted space, Family Tree Maker places an ellipsis button (**...**) to the right of it. Click the button to see the rest of the information.

    If the Family Archive contains images, Family Tree Maker places a magnifying glass next to the page number below the image.

    If there are no matches, FamilyFinder displays a message telling you this. You may want to read "What if I Can't Find My Ancestor's Name?" in Appendix B, "Troubleshooting."

    The current matches remain marked until you begin another search, leave the FamilyFinder view, or select the **Clear Search** command from the **Edit** menu.

What can you do with these matches? Figure 7-17 lists your options and indicates where you can find more information about each option.

To do this...	See this Chapter 7 section...
Navigate through the matches	"Navigating Through Matching Entries"
Select and deselect entries to print or copy to the clipboard	"Selecting and Deselecting Index Entries for Printing and Copying"
Find out more about a Family Archive that contains a match	"Getting More Information About a Match"
Display the information associated with the match	"Using the FamilyFinder Index and the Family Archives"
Copy matching information to an existing individual in your Family File	"Copying Information from Family Archives to Your Family File"
Create a new individual in your Family File and add matching information to the new individual's Family Page	"Adding New Information from Family Archives to Your Family File"
Display the family tree containing a match from a World Family Tree Archive	"Turning to a World Family Tree Pedigree"
Add a World Family Tree Pedigree to your Family File	"Merging a World Family Tree Pedigree with a Family File"
Display an image at different sizes	"Displaying Images"
Copy images to the Clipboard	"Copying Images"
Select images for printing	"Printing Images"

Figure 7-17. What you can do with matching entries

Navigating Through Matching Entries

In some cases, the Search Expert will find so many matches that you'll need some tips to wade through them. The table below describes how to navigate through the matches.

To do this...	Do this...
Move forward to the next matching entry	Click **Next matching name**
Move backwards to the previous matching entry	Click **Previous**
Jump to the very first matching entry	Click **First**
Jump to the very last matching entry	Click **Final**

Figure 7-18. Ways to navigate through matching entries

You can also press `PgUp` or `PgDn`, use the scroll bars, and use the "Scroll to name" field to move through the FamilyFinder Index and look at names other than the matches, if you like.

FamilyFinder Preferences

You can choose whether or not the Search Expert uses **Soundex codes** to find possible matches. Soundex is a method of coding surnames based on their *consonant sounds*, rather than their spellings. For example, a Soundex search would find names that sound alike even when they are spelled differently, such as "Story," "Storey," and "Storie." Using Soundex codes can help you find records that you may otherwise not know to look for. Please note that Soundex searching may generate a high number of matches and may not be available in all Family Archives.

Note: For Marriage Family Archives, Soundex codes are available only for the first spouse and not for the second spouse. So, if you want to find the husband's name, enter his name in the first spouse field, if you want to find the wife's name, enter her name in the first spouse field.

To choose preferences for searching:

1. From the **File** menu, select **Preferences**. From the submenu, select **FamilyFinder**.

   Family Tree Maker displays the FamilyFinder Preferences dialog box.

2. Select from the following options:

   Use Soundex ... — Select this check box if you want to find similar sounding names, such as "Smyth," or "Smythe" for "Smith."

   Show when...out of date — Select this check box if you want to see a reminder when your FamilyFinder Report is out of date.

   Show star on Family Page for...matches — Select this check box if you want to see a star displayed on your Family Page indicating potential matches. Use the drop-down menu to select the number of stars a match must earn in order to qualify to appear on your Family Page when this option is selected.

3. After you make your preference selections, click **OK**.

   Family Tree Maker returns you to the current view.

The Soundex Calculator

For those whose research takes them into areas that can take advantage of it, Family Tree Maker incorporates a calculator that will automatically generate the Soundex code for any name. The Soundex calculator can be accessed from any tree, report, or calendar view.

To use the Soundex Calculator:

1. From the **People** menu, select **Soundex Calculator**.

   Family Tree Maker displays the Soundex Calculator dialog box.

2. In the **Name** field, type the name for which you want the Soundex code.

   Family Tree Maker automatically calculates the code as you type the name.

   Note: You may also click **Choose** to display the Index of Individuals dialog box. Highlight the name you wish, and then click **OK** to return to the Soundex Calculator.

3. Click **Close** to exit the Soundex Calculator and return to the current view.

Getting More Information About a Match

To find out what information a Family Archive contains about a match, highlight the match and click **Find out** in the lower-left corner. Family Tree Maker displays the More About dialog box. It summarizes what type of information is available in the Family Archive. For more details about the Family Archive, click **Archive info**. For purchasing information, click **To order** in the lower- left corner.

Turning to a World Family Tree Pedigree

When you're in a World Family Tree Archive, you see a number to the far right of each name. This is the number of the tree in which you can find that name. Also listed are the individual's birth date, death date, and the state, country, or geographic area of their birth, death, or marriage, if available. Follow the steps below to view Family Pages for the individuals in a World Family Tree Pedigree.

To view a pedigree in a World Family Tree Archive:

1. From the Index page, click **Turn to** in the lower-left corner.

    Family Tree Maker goes into a special **World Family Tree mode**. This mode lets you look at Family Pages, trees, and reports for the World Family Tree Pedigree.

    When you open a pedigree, Family Tree Maker displays a Family Page from the pedigree. As shown in Figure 7-19, the Family Page in World Family Tree mode looks very similar to a regular Family Page. The main differences are that it has a different background color than the regular Family Pages and it has a different toolbar. In addition, the title bar at the very top of your screen will say, for example, "World Family Tree - Pedigree #3034" instead of listing the name of your Family File.

2. To look at the information in a World Family Tree Pedigree, you have the following options:

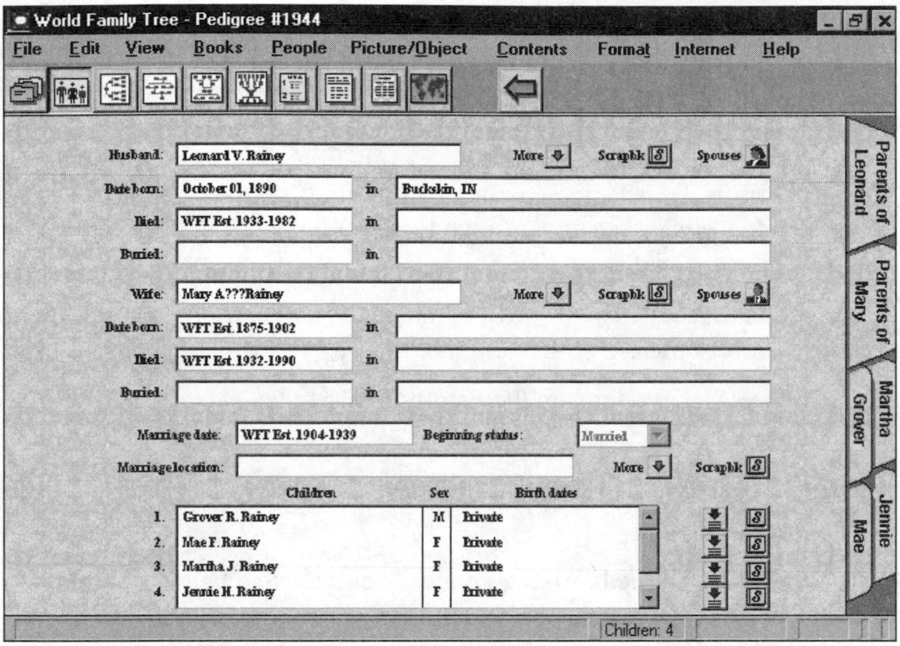

Figure 7-19. Family Tree Maker in World Family Tree mode

- Move between Family Pages by clicking the tabs along the right side of the screen.

- Display reports and different types of trees by clicking the toolbar buttons or using the commands on the **View** menu (see Chapter 8, "Displaying Your Family Information").

- Customize trees and reports using the commands on the **Contents** and **Format** menus. For example, you can control which individuals and information appear in a tree (see Chapter 9, "Customizing Your Family Information").

- Print trees, reports, and other documents using the **Print** command on the **File** menu. See "Printing a Single Document" in Chapter 10.

Note: You cannot edit the information in a World Family Tree pedigree. While you are in World Family Tree mode, the editing commands on the pull-down menus are not available, and you cannot change the information in fields. If you find a link to your family, you can merge the pedigree with your Family File. See "Merging a World Family Tree Pedigree with a Family File" in this chapter. After you add the pedigree to your own Family File, you can edit the information there.

3. When you are ready to exit World Family Tree mode, from the **View** menu, select **FamilyFinder**.

   Family Tree Maker returns to the FamilyFinder Index view.

Copying Information from Family Archives to Your Family File

Copying information directly from a Family Archive into a Family File is much faster than copying it by hand, and it eliminates potential transcription errors. The instructions below show you how to copy information about an individual who is already in your Family File. To learn about copying information about an individual who is *not* in your Family File, see "Adding New Information from Family Archives to Your Family File" in this chapter. For instructions on copying images, see "Copying Images" in this chapter.

Before you begin with the steps below, confirm that the information is part of *your* family tree, and that you have the correct Family File open.

To copy information to a Family File:

1. Click the record that you want to copy into your Family File.

   Family Tree Maker highlights the record.

2. Click **Copy information about** in the lower-left corner.

   Note: This command is not available with all Family Archives. If you do not see the "Copy information about" icon in the lower-left corner, you will need to type the information in your Family File to copy it.

   Family Tree Maker displays the Copy Information to Family File dialog box.

3. Click **Copy to someone already in your Family File**.

   Family Tree Maker displays the Index of Individuals.

4. Highlight the individual into whose record you want to place the information, and then click **Copy information**.

    Family Tree Maker displays the Facts to Import dialog box.

5. After you make your selections in the Fields to Import dialog box, click **OK**.

    Family Tree Maker adds the information to appropriate fields in your Family File. When available, Family Tree Maker adds a description of the Family Archive where you found the information to the corresponding source-citation field (see "Recording Sources for Your Information" in Chapter 3).

6. If some of the fields already contain information, Family Tree Maker displays the Merge Individuals dialog box. There you can choose whether to keep the information that was already in your Family File, or to replace it with the information from the Family Archive (see "Merging Matches with Confirmation" in Chapter 13).

    Family Tree Maker returns to the Family Archive's Information page.

Adding New Information
from Family Archives to Your Family File

While researching your family, you may find matching information about someone who is not yet in your Family File. You can add this person and copy the information directly from a Family Archive in a single step. To learn how to copy information about an individual who is already in your Family File, see "Copying Information from Family Archives to Your Family File" in this chapter. For information about copying images, see "Copying Images" also in this chapter.

Before you begin the steps below, be sure you have the correct Family File open.

To add new information to a Family File:

1. Click the record that you want to add to your Family File.

    Family Tree Maker highlights the record.

2. Click **Copy information** in the lower-left corner of the screen.

    Family Tree Maker displays the Copy Information to Family File dialog box.

3. Click **Create a new individual to copy to**.

   Family Tree Maker tells you that it is adding a new individual to your Family File.

4. Click **Copy information to a new individual in your Family File**.

   Family Tree Maker displays the Choose Sex dialog box.

5. Select the option button corresponding to the sex of the individual listed in the dialog box and then click **OK**.

   Family Tree Maker displays the Facts to Import dialog box.

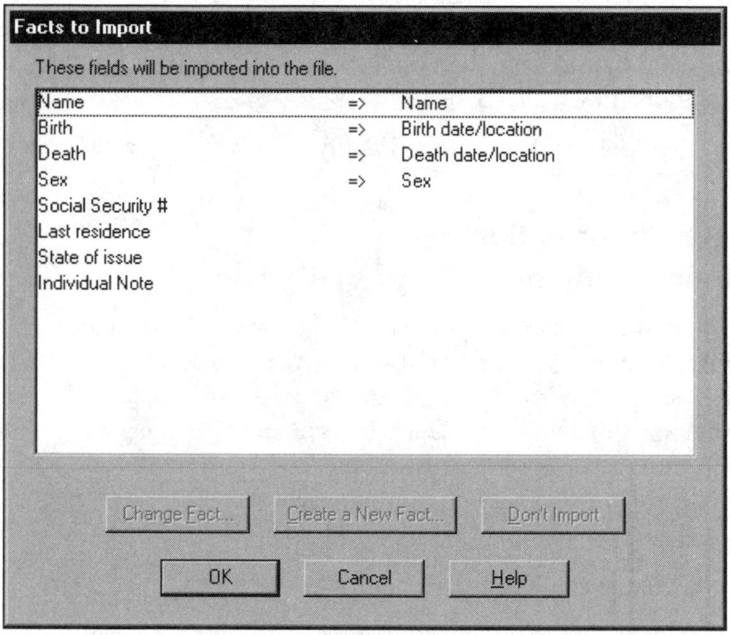

Figure 7-20. The Facts to Import dialog box

6. After you verify the selections in the Facts to Import dialog box, click **OK**.

   Family Tree Maker adds the individual to your Family File and returns to the Family Archive's Information page. When available, Family Tree Maker adds a description of the Family Archive where you found the information to the corresponding source-citation field (see "Recording Sources for your Information" in Chapter 3).

   Note: The individual(s) you created will not be linked to anyone else in your Family File. To create links with other individuals, see either

"Linking Children to Their Parents" or "Linking Individuals by Marriage" in Chapter 6.

Merging a World Family Tree Pedigree with a Family File

If you decide that a World Family Tree pedigree has a link to your family, you can append or merge the pedigree into your Family File. If you have more than one Family File, open the correct one before you start merging.

To merge a World Family Tree pedigree into a Family File:

1. Go to a Family Page in the pedigree that you want to merge into your Family File.

2. From the **People** menu, select **Merge Pedigrees**.

    Family Tree Maker displays a message reminding you to back up your files before you begin the merge.

3. If you have a current backup of your Family File, click **OK** to continue. If you do not have a current back up, click **Cancel** and follow the instructions in "Backing Up Your Family File" in Chapter 13.

    When you click **OK**, Family Tree Maker displays the Individuals to Include dialog box.

4. For more information see both "Selecting Individuals to Include" and "Appending and Merging Information," in Chapter 13.

Displaying Images

When you display an image from an Image CD, you can change the size of the image on the screen. Changing the size of the image on the screen will not change the size of the printed image. There are two ways to display an image at a different size:

*   You can make the text in the image larger by clicking **Zoom In** or smaller by clicking **Zoom Out**.

- You can increase the size of the viewing area and see more of the image at once by clicking **View**. Family Tree Maker will display the image in the View dialog box. You can move from image to image by clicking the **PrevPg** and **NextPg** buttons, and you can use **Zoom In** and **Zoom Out** to change the size of the text in the image. However, most menu commands and toolbar buttons are unavailable while you are in the View dialog box. To close the View dialog box and return to the Image page, click **Go Back**.

Copying Images

To copy an image from an image CD to the Clipboard:

1. Display the image that you want to copy.

2. Click **Copy this image to the Clipboard**.

   If you want to paste the image to a Windows word processor or graphics program, skip the remaining steps. If you are copying the image to a Scrapbook, continue with step 3.

3. Go to your Family File.

4. Use the **Index of Individuals** to select the individual to whose Scrapbook you want to add the image.

5. From the **View** menu, select **Scrapbook**.

   Family Tree Maker displays the Scrapbook for the selected individual.

6. From the **Edit** menu, select **Paste Picture/Object**.

   Family Tree Maker adds the image to the individual's Scrapbook. In addition, Family Tree Maker adds a sentence of source information to the "Description" field in the image's More About dialog box (see "Recording Important Picture/Object Information" in Chapter 6). This sentence gives information about the Family Archive from which you copied the image.

Printing Images

To print an image:

1. Display the image that you want to print.

2. From the **Edit** menu, choose **Select Image**.

   Family Tree Maker places a printer icon in the upper-left corner of the dialog box.

Figure 7-21. A printer icon

3. Repeat step 2 for any additional images that you want to print.

4. After you select all of the images you want to print, from the **File** menu, select **Print**.

   Family Tree Maker asks you to confirm that you want to print all of the images you have selected.

5. Click **OK** to print them.

Each image is printed on a separate page. At the bottom of each page, Family Tree Maker prints source information about the Family Archive from which you copied the image.

Chapter 8

DISPLAYING YOUR FAMILY INFORMATION

Terashi (Ted) Nomura and his wife Junko Nakazato moved to the United States shortly after their wedding in Tokyo, Japan on May 12, 1960. Their daughter, Tina, is Project Supervisor for the World Family Tree Project.

DISPLAYING YOUR FAMILY INFORMATION

Creating beautiful family trees is one of the easiest and most rewarding aspects of using Family Tree Maker. You create a tree by choosing to display your family information as a tree. Just as you can choose to display your information on a Family Page, you can also choose to display trees, reports, and other views such as maps, calendars, labels and cards, Scrapbooks, and Timelines.

After you display a tree, report, or other view, you can customize the display and then print the information you see on your screen. This chapter describes how to display trees, reports, and other views. For information about customizing and printing your information, see Chapter 9, "Customizing Your Family Information" and Chapter 10, "Printing Your Family Information."

DISPLAYING TREES

You can display five different types of trees: **Ancestor trees**, **Descendant trees**, **Outline Descendant trees**, **Hourglass trees,** and **All-in-One trees**. The next few pages describe each tree type and how to display it.

Ancestor, Descendant, and Hourglass trees may be displayed or printed in either **Standard** or **Fan** styles. Standard trees display relatives as branches from the primary individual. Fan trees, display relatives in concentric circles around the primary individual (see "Displaying Fan Trees" in this chapter). The All-in-One tree is unique because it allows you to see every member of your Family File in one continuous tree.

Ancestor Trees

An Ancestor tree shows an individual's ancestors including his or her parents, grandparents, great-grandparents, and so on. It does not show the individual's aunts, uncles, nieces, nephews, or cousins. In a Standard Ancestor tree, the selected individual (also called the **primary individual**) appears in the leftmost box of the tree and the individual's ancestors form branches above and below the primary individual. Figure 8-1 shows a Standard Ancestor tree. See "Displaying Fan Trees" later in this chapter for information about Ancestor Fan trees.

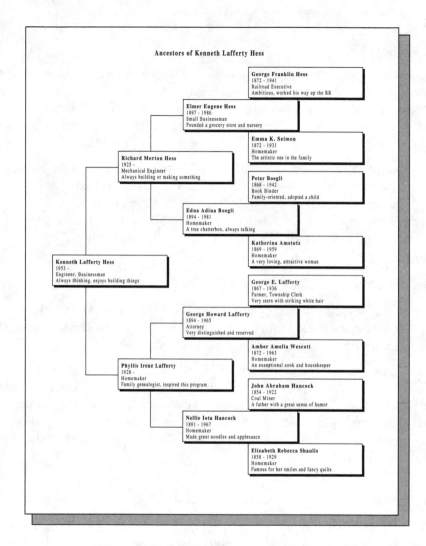

Ancestors of Kenneth Lafferty Hess

George Franklin Hess
1872 - 1941
Railroad Executive
Ambitious, worked his way up the RR

Elmer Eugene Hess
1897 - 1986
Small Businessman
Founded a grocery store and nursery

Emma K. Seimon
1872 - 1931
Homemaker
The artistic one in the family

Richard Morton Hess
1925 -
Mechanical Engineer
Always building or making something

Peter Boegli
1868 - 1942
Book Binder
Family-oriented, adopted a child

Edna Adina Boegli
1894 - 1981
Homemaker
A true chatterbox, always talking

Katherina Amstutz
1869 - 1959
Homemaker
A very loving, attractive woman

Kenneth Lafferty Hess
1953 -
Engineer, Businessman
Always thinking, enjoys building things

George E. Lafferty
1867 - 1936
Farmer, Township Clerk
Very stern with striking white hair

George Howard Lafferty
1894 - 1965
Attorney
Very distinguished and reserved

Amber Amelia Wescott
1872 - 1963
Homemaker
An exceptional cook and housekeeper

Phyllis Irene Lafferty
1928 -
Homemaker
Family genealogist, inspired this program

John Abraham Hancock
1854 - 1922
Coal Miner
A father with a great sense of humor

Nellie Iota Hancock
1891 - 1967
Homemaker
Made great noodles and applesauce

Elizabeth Rebecca Shaulis
1858 - 1929
Homemaker
Famous for her smiles and fancy quilts

Figure 8-1. A Standard Ancestor tree

To display an Ancestor tree:

1. Select the **primary individual** by highlighting his or her name on a Family Page or in another view.

2. From the **View** menu, select **Ancestor Tree**. From the submenu, select **Standard** as the tree style. Please note that both Fan trees and Vertical Ancestor Trees are both discussed later in this chapter.

   Family Tree Maker displays the Ancestor Tree view.

3. From the **Format** menu, select **Tree Format**.

   Family Tree Maker displays the dialog box shown in Figure 8-2.

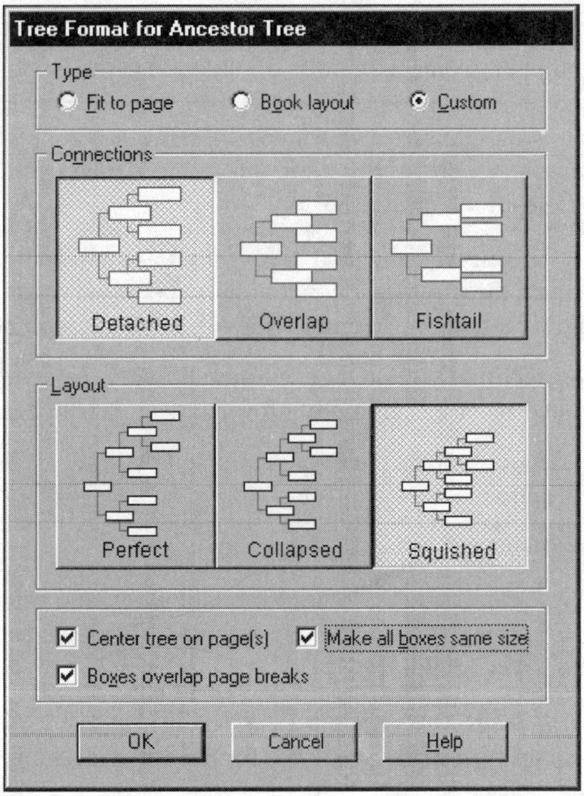

Figure 8-2. Tree Format for Ancestor Tree dialog box

4. Select one of the **Type** option buttons described below.

    Fit to page — is a one-page Ancestor tree that allows you to display up to 6 generations on one page. Because Fit to Page Ancestor trees are limited to one page, you have limited control over your tree's appearance. For example, Family Tree Maker controls things like the tree's layout, font size, number or generations, and the amount of information that prints in the boxes.

    Note: Some style options, such as increasing the font size or adding Items to Include, may make your tree too big to fit on one page.

    Book layout — is an Ancestor tree that is divided into pages. Each page contains cross-references to the previous and next page so that you can easily include your trees in a family book.

    Note: If you plan to create a family book, choose the Book layout option. If you choose any other layout option, Family Tree Maker will automatically convert your tree to the Book layout when you add your tree to a book. For more information about books see Chapter 10, "Creating Family Books."

    Custom — is an Ancestor tree that gives you complete control over its appearance, from the information that it contains to the color and size of the text. In addition, a Custom Ancestor tree can have any number of pages.

5. Click the **Connections** and **Layout** buttons showing the style that you prefer. Tighter styles allow you to fit more information on each page.

    Note: The Layout buttons are only available if you select "Custom" as the Type option.

6. Select the following check boxes if desired.

    Center tree on page(s) — This check box allows you to center your tree between the left, right, top, and bottom margins (available for Book layout and Custom trees only).

    Make all boxes same size — This check box allows the tree's boxes to vary in size — which saves space (available for Custom trees only).

    Boxes overlap page breaks — This check box allows boxes to overlap page breaks (available for Custom, detached-style trees only).

7. After you make your selections, click **OK**.

    Family Tree Maker returns you to the Ancestor Tree view. You can either print your tree right away (see Chapter 10, "Printing Your Family Information"), or customize it (see Chapter 9, "Customizing Your Family Information") and then print.

Vertical Ancestor Trees

The Vertical Ancestor Tree differs from the standard Ancestor tree by centering the primary individual at the bottom of the tree, with his or her ancestors branching upward in a "V" shape.

To create a Vertical Ancestor tree:

1. Select the **primary individual** by clicking his or her name on the Family Page or any other view.

2. From the **View** menu, select **Ancestor Tree**. From the submenu, select **Vertical** as the style.

    Family Tree Maker displays the Vertical Ancestor Tree view.

    Note: The Vertical Ancestor tree will display the spouse of the primary individual, but there is no option to include siblings in this tree.

3. From the **Format** menu, select **Tree Format**.

    Family Tree Maker displays the **General** tab of the Tree Format for Ancestor Tree dialog box.

4. Select one of the **Type** option buttons described below.

    Book layout — results in a Vertical Ancestor tree that is divided into pages with cross-references to both previous and subsequent pages that contain information about particular individuals in your tree.

    Note: If you plan to include this tree in your family book, choose the **Book layout** option. If you choose the **Custom** option, Family Tree Maker will automatically convert your tree to **Book layout** if you add it to a book. For more information, see Chapter 11, "Creating Family Books."

    Custom — results in a Vertical Ancestor tree that allows boxes to spread over multiple pages. Use this option to display a single continuous tree or wall chart.

5. Select the following check boxes as desired.

    Center tree on page(s) — Select this check box if you want to center your tree between the left, right, top, and bottom margins.

    Make all boxes the same size — Select this check box if you want to make all boxes a uniform size. Some space is saved if this box is *not* selected.

    Boxes overlap page breaks — Select this check box if you want to allow boxes to overlap page breaks.

6. Click the **Layout** tab.

    Family Tree Maker displays the layout options for your tree. Tighter styles allow you to fit more information on each page.

7. After you make your selection, click **OK**.

    Family Tree Maker returns you to the Vertical Ancestor tree view. You may now print your tree right away, or customize it and then print. For more information, see Chapter 10, "Printing Your Family Information," or Chapter 9, "Customizing Your Family Information."

Descendant Trees

A **Descendant tree** shows an individual's children, grandchildren, great-grandchildren, and so on. In a Standard Descendant tree, the primary individual appears at the top of the tree and the descendants appear in branches below the individual. Because Descendant trees include so many individuals, they can grow to numerous pages very quickly. A Standard Descendant tree is shown in Figure 8-3. For information about Descendant Fan trees, see "Displaying Fan Trees" in this chapter.

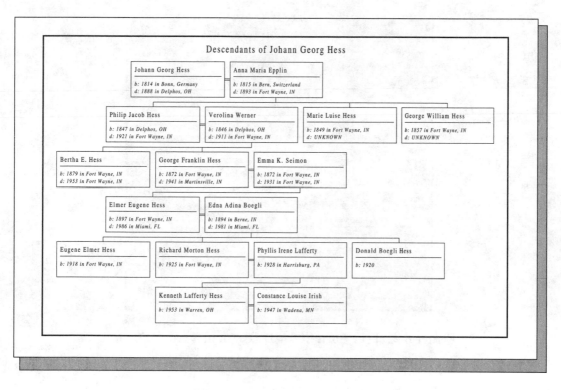

Figure 8-3. A Standard Descendant tree

To display a Descendant tree:

1. Select the **primary individual** by highlighting his or her name on a Family Page or in another view.

2. From the **View** menu, select **Descendant Tree**. From the submenu, select **Standard** as the tree style. For more information on the Fan style, see "Displaying Fan Trees" later in this chapter.

3. From the **Format** menu, select **Tree Format**.

   Family Tree Maker displays the dialog box shown in Figure 8-4.

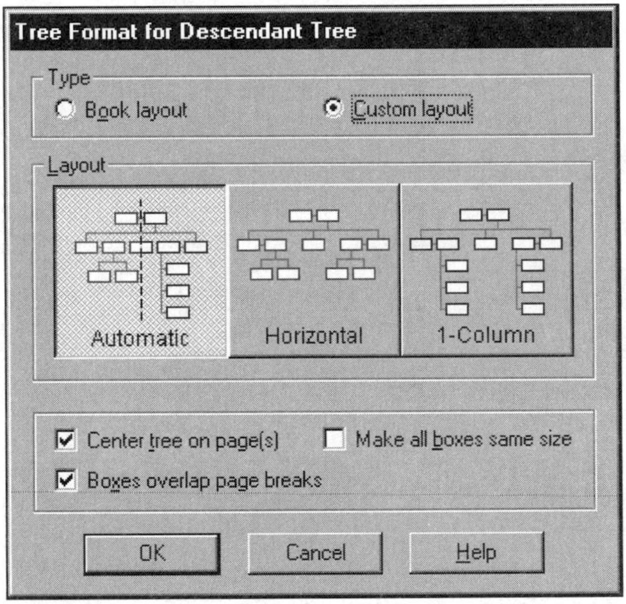

Figure 8-4. Tree Format for Descendant Tree dialog box

4. Select one of the **Type** option buttons described below.

   Book layout — is a Descendant tree that is divided into pages. Each page contains cross-references to the previous and next page so that you can easily include your tree in a family book.

   Note: If you plan to create a family book, choose the Book layout option. If you choose any other layout option, Family Tree Maker will automatically convert your tree to the Book layout when you add your tree to a book. See Chapter 11, "Creating Family Books" for more information about Books.

   Custom — is a Descendant tree that gives you complete control over its appearance, from the information that it contains to the layout and size of the text. In addition, a Custom Descendant tree can have any number of pages.

5. If you chose "Custom" in step 4, click the **Layout** button showing the style that you prefer.

6. Select the following check boxes if desired.

   Center tree on page(s) — This check box allows you to center your tree between the left, right, top, and bottom margins.

   Make all boxes same size — Deselecting this check box allows the tree's boxes to vary in size — which saves space (available for Custom Descendant trees only).

   Boxes overlap page breaks — This check box allows boxes to overlap page breaks.

7. After you make your selections, click **OK**.

   Family Tree Maker returns you to the Descendant tree view. You can either print your tree right away (see Chapter 10, "Printing Your Family Information"), or customize it (see Chapter 9, "Customizing Your Family Information") and then print.

Hourglass Trees

Hourglass trees combine both the ancestors and descendants of the primary individual into a single view. The Hourglass tree displays an individual's ancestors in the top portion of the tree, while the descendants appear in the bottom portion.

To display an Hourglass tree:

1. Select the **primary individual** by clicking his or her name on a Family Page or in another view.

2. From the **View** menu, select **Hourglass Tree**. From the submenu, select **Standard** as the tree style. For more information on the Fan style, see "Displaying Hourglass Fan Trees" later in this chapter.

3. From the **Format** menu, select **Tree Format**.

    Family Tree Maker displays the **General** tab of the Tree Format for Hourglass Tree dialog box.

4. Select one of the **Type** option buttons described below.

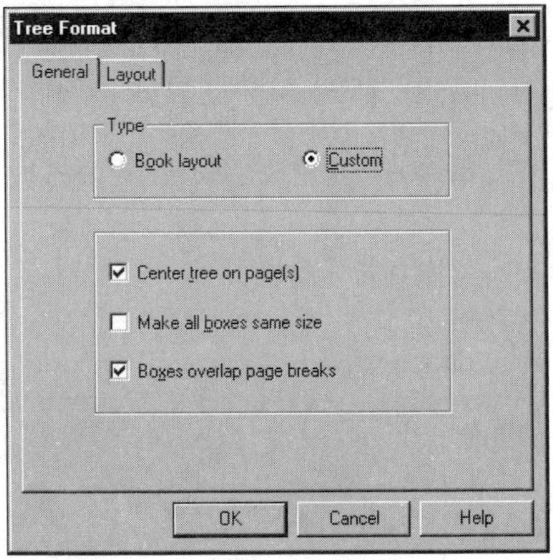

Figure 8-5. Tree Format for Hourglass Tree dialog box

> **Book layout** — is an Hourglass tree that is divided into pages. Each page contains cross-references to the previous and next page so that you can easily include your trees in a family book.

Note: If you plan to create a family book, choose the Book layout option. If you choose any other layout option, Family Tree Maker will automatically convert your tree to the Book layout when you add your tree to a book. See Chapter 11,"Creating Family Books" for more information about Books.

Custom — is an Hourglass tree that allows greater control over its appearance, from the information that it contains to the color and size of the text. Select this to produce larger, wall-chart style trees.

5. Select the following check boxes as desired.

Center tree on page(s) — this check box allows you to center your tree between the left, right, top, and bottom margins.

Make all boxes the same size — this check box allows you to make all boxes a uniform size. Some space is saved if this box is *not* selected.

Boxes overlap page breaks — this check box allows boxes to overlap page breaks if necessary.

6. Click the **Layout** tab.

Family Tree Maker displays the layout options for the ancestor and descendant portions of the Hourglass tree. Tighter styles allow you to fit more information on each page.

7. After you make your selections, click **OK**.

Family Tree Maker returns you to the Hourglass Tree view. You can either print your tree right away (see Chapter 10, "Printing Your Family Information") or customize it (see Chapter 9, "Customizing Your Family Information") and then print.

All-in-One Trees

The **All-in-One** tree is unique among all other display formats, because it allows you to show every member of your Family File in one continuous tree.

Family Tree Maker will automatically arrange the tree's layout to make the best use of space, but you are still able to customize the tree's appearance by choosing from a range of options.

To create an All-in-One tree:

1. Select the **primary individual** by clicking his or her name on the Family Page or in another view.

2. From the **View** menu, select **All-in-One Tree**. Or, from the toolbar, click the **All-in-One Tree** button.

   Family Tree Maker displays the All-in-One Tree view.

Family Tree Maker automatically applies certain settings to the All-in-One tree in order to ensure its compactness. For example, the tree will always appear in a condensed layout, with the tree centered on the page. Boxes will overlap page breaks — to do otherwise would dramatically increase the size of the tree. Each box will be sized to accommodate the amount of information displayed in it.

To enhance legibility and make the best use of space, the All-in-One tree will display siblings where they fit best, rather than in strict birth order. This setting may be changed in the All-in-One tree options dialog box (see "All-in-One Tree Options" in Chapter 9).

You can either print your tree right away (see Chapter 10, "Printing Your Family Information") or customize it (see Chapter 9, "Customizing Your Family Information") and then print.

Outline Descendant Trees

An **Outline Descendant tree** contains the same type of information as a Descendant tree: an individual's children, grandchildren, great-grandchildren, and so on. However, instead of showing each individual in a box, the individuals are in outline form. Each individual's information is on a separate line, and each generation is indented slightly more than the one before it. Each descendant's spouse is directly beneath him or her and is marked with a plus sign (+). This type of tree can fit many generations on a single page. Figure 8-7 shows a sample Outline Descendant tree.

To display an Outline Descendant tree:

1. Select the **primary individual** by highlighting his or her name on a Family Page or in another view.

2. From the **View** menu, select **Outline Descendant Tree**.

3. From the **Format** menu, select **Tree Format**.

   Family Tree Maker displays the Tree Format dialog box.

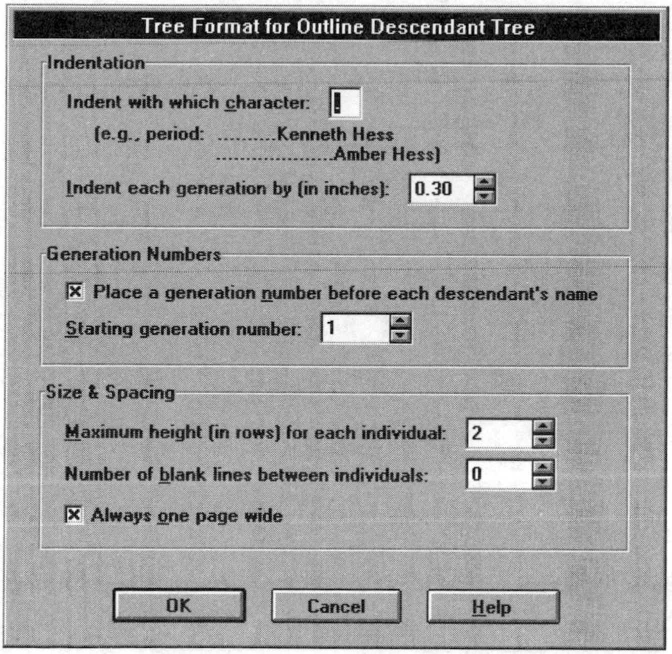

Figure 8-6. The Tree Format for Outline Descendant Tree dialog box

```
1 Thomas Sprunger  1645 - UNKNOWN
.. +Regina Buergi  1649 - UNKNOWN
......... 2 Hans Sprunger  1668 -
................... 3 Deiter Sprunger
........................ +Elizabeth Neuenschwander
............................... 4 Christian Amstutz  1772 -
.................................... +Katherina Nussbaum  1773 -
............................................. 5 Johannes Ulrich Amstutz  1817 - 1869
.................................................. +Elisabeth Sprunger  1832 - 1902
.......................................................... 6 Katherina Amstutz  1869 - 1959
.............................................................. +Peter Boegli  1868 - 1942
.......................................................... 6 Lena Amstutz  1860 -
.......................................................... 6 Marianna Amstutz  1861 -
.......................................................... 6 Jakob U. Amstutz  1862 -
.......................................................... 6 John J. Amstutz  1864 -
.......................................................... 6 Japhet Amstutz  1865 -
.......................................................... 6 Elisabeth U. Amstutz  1867 -
.......................................................... 6 Twin Amstutz  1867 -
.......................................................... 6 Jakob Sprunger  1830 -
.......................................................... 6 Katharina Sprunger  1833 -
.......................................................... 6 David Sprunger  1836 -
.......................................................... 6 Marianna Sprunger  1838 -
............................................. 5 Elisabeth Amstutz  1797 -
............................................. 5 Johannes Amstutz  1800 -
............................................. 5 Christian Amstutz  1802 -
............................................. 5 Regina Amstutz  1803 -
............................................. 5 Anna Amstutz  1804 -
............................................. 5 Durs Dorsey Amstutz  1805 -
............................................. 5 Michael Amstutz  1807 -
............................................. 5 Jakob Amstutz  1808 -
............................................. 5 Kathrine Amstutz  1810 -
............................................. 5 Magdalena Amstutz  1815 -
............................... 4 Johann Amstutz  1771 -
............................... 4 Michael Amstutz  1779 -
......... 2 Hans Sprunger  1668 -
......... 2 Hans Peter Sprunger  1669 -
......... 2 Barbara Sprunger  1671 -
......... 2 Catharina Sprunger  1673 -
......... 2 Sebastian Sprunger  1675/76 -
......... 2 Salomon Sprunger  1676/77 -
......... 2 Salmon Sprunger  1679/80 -
```

Figure 8-7. An Outline Descendant tree

4. Select the **Indentation** options you prefer.

    Indent with which character — In Outline-style trees, each generation is indented slightly more than the generation above it. Some people find it easier to distinguish between generations with leader dots (........) extending from the left margin of the page to each individual's name. If you want leader dots in your tree, enter a period (.) in this field. If you want to indent with a character other than leader dots, enter that character in this field. Leave it blank if you don't want anything at all.

    Indent each generation by — To increase or decrease the size of each generation's indentation, click the up arrow or down arrow in this field. A larger number creates a wider tree, and a smaller number creates a narrower tree. When you change the size of the indentation, it changes for all generations in the tree.

5. Select the **Generation Numbers** options you prefer.

    Place a generation number before each descendant's name — Generation numbers can help you see who belongs to each generation and are especially helpful when your tree is very long. To include generation numbers, select this check box.

    Starting generation number — Normally, "1" is the first generation number in a tree. If you are creating a series of several trees, you can enter a number up to 9999 in this field.

6. Select the **Size & Spacing** options you prefer.

   Maximum height (in rows) for each individual — If you include a lot of information for an individual, it may not fit on a single line. To allow an individual's information to wrap over more than one line, enter a number greater than one in this field. To limit each individual to one line only, enter "1" in this field.

   Number of blank lines between individuals — Blank lines between each individual can make outline-style trees easier to read, but they will also limit the amount of information you can fit on a page. To include blank lines between each individual, enter a number greater than zero in this field.

   Always one page wide — If an individual's information is too wide to fit on one page, Family Tree Maker can reduce the size of the text to fit the information on one page. Select this check box to keep the tree only one page wide. If you select this check box and the text is too small to read, increase the number in the **Maximum height (in rows) for each individual** field to allow the information to wrap onto multiple lines.

7. After you make your selections, click **OK**.

   Family Tree Maker returns you to the Outline Descendant Tree view. You can either print your tree right away (see Chapter 10, "Printing Your Family Information"), or customize it (see Chapter 9, "Customizing Your Family Information") and then print.

DISPLAYING FAN TREES

Fan trees display relatives in an expanding circle around a primary individual, offering a style alternative to Family Tree Maker's standard Ancestor, Descendant, and Hourglass trees. Of course, just like all other trees, you can customize the fonts, colors, and borders, as well as the information to include in each box (see Chapter 9, "Customizing Your Family Information").

To display a Fan tree:

1. Select the **primary individual** by clicking his or her name on a Family Page or in another view.

2. From the **View** menu, select **Ancestor Tree** or **Descendant Tree**. From the submenu, select **Fan** as the tree style. Family Tree Maker displays your tree choice in the Fan view.

   For Hourglass Fan trees see "Displaying Hourglass Fan Trees" in this chapter.

3. From the **Format** menu, select **Fan Tree Format**.

Family Tree Maker displays the Format for Fan Tree dialog box.

4. Select one of the **Type** option buttons described below.

Fit to page — Select this option if you want to limit your Fan tree to one page. This is useful if you want to include your Fan tree in a Family Tree Maker Book, or simply reduce its size. See Chapter 11, "Creating Family Books" for more information about Books.

Note: Because a Fit to Page Fan tree is limited to one page, you have limited control over your tree's appearance. For example, Family Tree Maker controls the number of generations in your tree, the tree's shape, font size, and border style, and the amount of information that prints in each box. If you choose this option, most of the other format options are disabled.

Custom — Select this option if you want complete control over your Fan tree's appearance, from the information that it contains to the color and size of the text. A Custom Fan tree can have any number of pages.

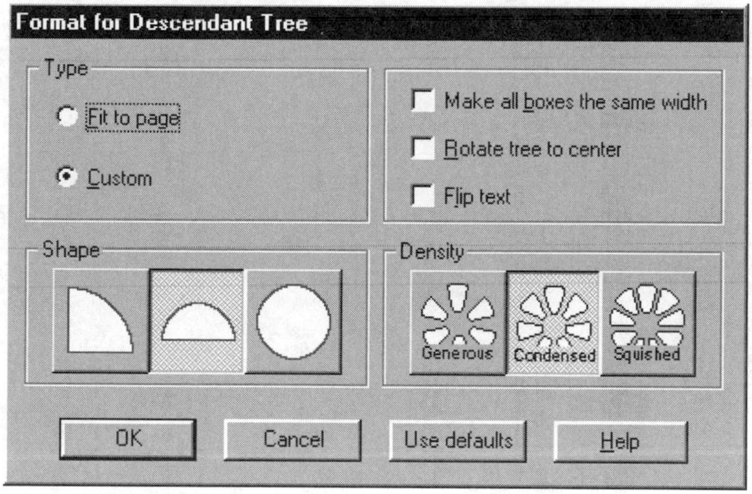

Figure 8-8. Format for Ancestor Fan Tree dialog box

5. Click the **Shape** and **Density** buttons that show the styles you prefer. Tighter styles allow you to fit more information on each page.

6. Select the following check boxes as desired.

    Make all boxes the same width — Select this check box if you want all the boxes to be the same size as the widest box on your tree. Deselect this check box if you want to save space and allow the width of the tree's boxes to vary in size.

    Rotate tree to center — Selecting this check box allows the branches of your tree to form uniform angles from the center of the tree. If this check box is not selected, the branches will align with the bottom of the page.

    Flip text — Selecting this check box allows the text on the right side of the page to face right, and the text on the left side of the page to face left. This enables you to read the text without turning the page upside down.

7. After you make your selections, click **OK**.

Family Tree Maker returns you to the Fan Tree view. You can either print your tree right away (see Chapter 10, "Printing Your Family Information"), or customize it (see Chapter 9, "Customizing Your Family Information") and then print.

DISPLAYING HOURGLASS FAN TREES

Because the Hourglass tree displays both ancestor and descendant information, the Format dialog box in Hourglass Fan view offers some different options.

To display an Hourglass Fan tree:

1. Select the **primary individual** by clicking his or her name on a Family Page or in another view.

2. From the **View** menu, select **Hourglass Tree.** From the submenu, select **Fan**.

    Family Tree Maker displays the Hourglass Fan tree.

3. From the **Format** menu, select **Tree Format**.

    Family Tree Maker displays the **General** tab of the Tree Format for Hourglass Tree dialog box.

4. Select one of the **Type** option buttons described below.

    Fit to page — Select this option if you want to limit your Hourglass Fan tree to one page. This is useful if you want to include it in a Family Tree Maker Book, or simply reduce its size. See Chapter 11, "Creating Family Books" for more information about Books.

    Note: Because a Fit to Page Hourglass Fan tree is limited to one page, you have limited control over its appearance. For example, Family Tree Maker controls the number of generations in your tree, its shape, font size, and border style, and the amount of information that prints in each box. If you choose this option, most of the other format options are disabled.

    Custom — Select this option if you want complete control over your Hourglass Fan tree's appearance, from the information that it contains to the color and size of the text, and more. A Custom Hourglass Fan tree can have any number of pages. For more, see Chapter 9, "Customizing Your Family Information."

5. Click the **Shape** button showing the style that you prefer.

    Note: Clicking the third (far right) Shape button allows Family Tree Maker to assign the larger portion of the tree to the group (ancestors or descendants) which contains the larger number of individuals.

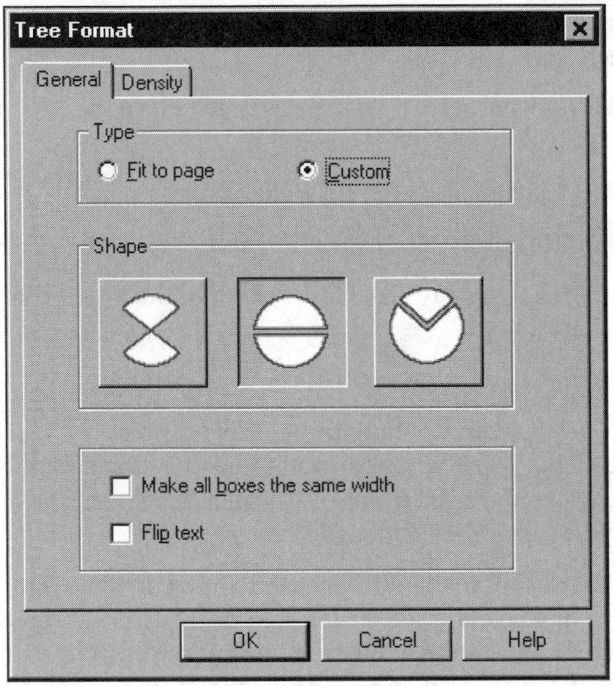

**Figure 8-9. The Tree Format for Hourglass Fan Tree,
General tab dialog box**

6. Select the following check boxes as desired.

Make all boxes the same width — Select this check box if you want all the boxes to be the same size as the widest box on your tree. Deselect this check box if you want to save space and allow the width of the tree's boxes to vary in size.

Rotate tree to center — Selecting this check box allows the branches of your tree to form uniform angles from the center of the tree. If this check box is not selected, the branches will align with the bottom of the page.

Flip text — Selecting this check box allows the text on the right side of the page to face right, and the text on the left side of the page to face left. This enables you to read the text without turning the page upside down.

7. Click the **Density** tab. Family Tree Maker displays the Format for Hourglass Tree dialog box shown in figure 8-10.

    Click the button with the picture of the density setting you prefer. Having the choice of density settings is convenient if you have a large number of either ancestors or descendants.

8. After you make your selections, click **OK**.

    Family Tree Maker returns you to the Hourglass Fan Tree view.

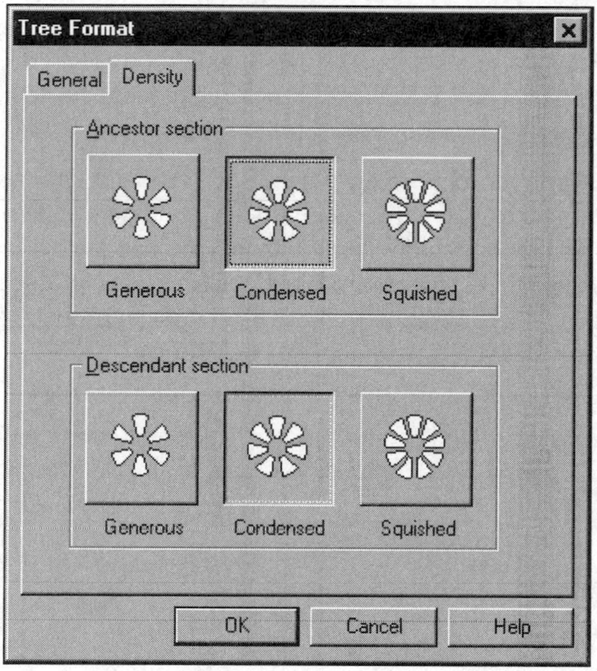

Figure 8-10. The Tree Format for Hourglass Fan Tree, Density tab dialog box

DISPLAYING REPORTS

Family Tree Maker creates a few different types of reports: **Standard reports**, **Custom reports**, **Genealogy reports**, and **Family Group Sheets**. To learn about the contents of these reports and how to display them, read the sections that follow.

Displaying Standard and Custom Reports

With Standard reports, Family Tree Maker chooses the contents, although you can still choose formatting options, such as fonts, borders, and titles. In some cases you can also choose who appears in a Standard report. You can choose from several different types of Standard reports. Standard reports are easy to use because Family Tree Maker does most of the work for you.

With Custom reports, you choose the contents as well as the formatting. Custom reports can contain up to 100 columns of almost any type of information. You also can choose whom to include. For example, you can print a report that contains only the people born before a certain date or in a certain place. Custom reports can be useful or just fun. Be creative — you can probably think of all kinds of facts that you want to know about your family.

Note: If you are planning to create a Kinship report, select the primary individual before you display the report. The primary individual in a Kinship report is the individual to whom everyone else in the report is related. To select the primary individual, highlight his or her name on a Family Page or in another view.

To display a Standard or Custom report:

1.   From the **View** menu, select **Report**.

   Family Tree Maker displays the last report you created.

2.   From the **Format** menu, select **Report Format**.

   Family Tree Maker displays the Report Format dialog box shown in Figure 8-11.

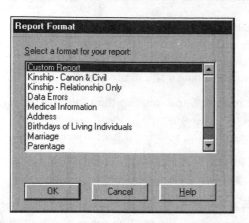

Figure 8-11. Report Format dialog box

3. In the **Select a format for your report** list, select the report format that you want to create. Each format is described below.

    Custom Report — Custom reports enable you to choose the contents, as well as the format of your report. You also can choose to include all of the individuals in your Family File or just a small group. Select this type of report when none of the other reports contain the information that you want.

    Kinship: Canon & Civil — Kinship reports list the names, relationships, and relationship degrees of the primary individual's blood relatives and their spouses, as well as the blood relatives of the primary individual's spouse(s). Adopted children, foster children, and children of unknown status will also appear in Kinship reports unless you choose to exclude them. See "Entering Nicknames, Titles, and Parental Relationship Information" in Chapter 5 for information about excluding individuals.

    The "degree" of a relationship is a legal term. It refers to the number of "steps" between two individuals who are blood relatives. The degree in Civil law represents the total number of steps through the bloodline that separate two individuals. For example, there are two steps from you to your grandparent and then two steps back down to your first cousin, so the degree is four.

The degree in Canon law measures the maximum number of steps from the nearest common ancestor. Your grandparent is the nearest common ancestor between you and your first cousin, so in this case the degree would be two. Canon law is used in most of the United States.

If two individuals are related in more than one way, Family Tree Maker displays each of the relationships in the Kinship report. For example, if two cousins marry, each of the relationships between them would be included.

Kinship: Relationship Only — This type of Kinship report lists each individual's name, birth date, and relationship with the primary individual.

Data Errors — This report helps you locate and fix possible errors in your Family File. A complete listing of the types of errors that it finds can be found in "Error Types" in Chapter 6. Select this type of report when you want to clean up your file. If you're planning to submit your file to the World Family Tree Project (see Chapter 12), you should do this beforehand.

Medical Information — This report lists each individual's name, birth date, and any medical information from his or her Medical dialog box. See "Entering Medical Information" in Chapter 5 for information about the Medical dialog box.

Address — This report lists each individual's name, address, and phone number, if available. The addresses and phone numbers are taken from the individual's Address dialog box. See "Entering Addresses" in Chapter 5 for information about the Address dialog box.

Birthdays of Living Individuals — This report lists each living individual's name, birth date, and age at next birthday. Family Tree Maker uses your computer's internal clock to calculate how old each individual is. Be sure that the clock is set correctly before you generate this type of report. See your Windows User's Guide for instructions on setting the clock.

Marriage — This report lists each couple along with their marriage date and any information you entered about their relationship. If multiple marriage ending facts exist, the report will list all of them.

Parentage — This report lists each individual's name, his or her parents' names, and the nature of the relationship between the individual and each parent. For example, it could show someone as a "Step" relation.

Documented Events — This report lists the events in your Family File that you've documented with sources. It includes both the events and the sources you've entered in the Source-Citation dialog box. See "Recording Sources for Your Information" in Chapter 3 for more about entering sources. If you like, you can also customize this report to include events without sources (see "Documented Events and Facts Options" in Chapter 9).

Bibliography — This report lists the sources of the information in your Family File. This information comes from the Source-Citation dialog box (see "Recording Sources for Your Information" in Chapter 3 for more about entering sources).

If the currently open Family File is in LDS mode (see "Preferences for Labels" in Chapter 3), you have the following additional options:

PAF: Incomplete Individual Ordinances — This report lists each individual in the Family File that is missing at least one of the following dates: birth or christening, death, baptism, endowment, or seal to parents.

PAF: Incomplete Marriage Sealings — This report lists each individual in the Family File that is missing at least one of the following dates: marriage or sealing.

Alternate Facts — This report lists each fact in the Family File for which an alternate (conflicting) fact exists. Every fact in the report is listed with the individual associated with the fact.

4. After you make your selections, click **OK**.

    Family Tree Maker returns you to the Report view. You can either print your report right away (see Chapter 10, "Printing Your Family Information"), or customize it (see Chapter 9, "Customizing Your Family Information,") and then print.

Displaying Family Group Sheets

A Family Group Sheet is a detailed report about a single nuclear family (two parents and their children) including names, birth dates, death dates, marriage dates, and more. You can also include a Picture/Object for each individual, as well as a Picture/Object for the marriage.

To display a Family Group Sheet:

1. Go to the Family Page containing the individual whose Family Group Sheet you want to see.

   Use the Index of Individuals or Find Individual to locate that individual's Family Page. See "Opening the Index of Individuals" and "Locating Individuals in Your Family File" in Chapter 4 for more information.

   Make sure you go to the Family Page of the husband and wife you want to display on your Family Group Sheet. If either of them was married more than once and the Family Page shows a spouse other than the one that you want, click **Spouses** to select the correct spouse.

2. From the **View** menu, select **Family Group Sheet**.

   Family Tree Maker displays the Family Group Sheet.

3. From the **Format** menu, select **Family Group Sheet Format**.

   Family Tree Maker displays the Family Group Sheet Format dialog box.

4. To display a separate page for each individual, select the **Begin each person on a new page** check box. To conserve space and display individuals consecutively, deselect this check box.

   Family Tree Maker returns you to the Family Group Sheet view. You can either print your Family Group Sheet right away (see Chapter 10, "Printing Your Family Information"), or customize it (see Chapter 9, "Customizing Your Family Information") and then print.

Displaying Genealogy Reports

A **Genealogy report** is a detailed listing of family information presented in a narrative format, just like a book. The report includes basic facts about each family member as well as any biographical information you've entered in your Family File.

To display a Genealogy report:

1. Select the **primary individual** by highlighting his or her name on a Family Page or in another view.

   The primary individual will be the first individual in your report.

2. From the **View** menu, select **Genealogy Report**.

3. From the **Format** menu, select **Genealogy Report Format**.

   Family Tree Maker displays the Genealogy Report Format dialog box.

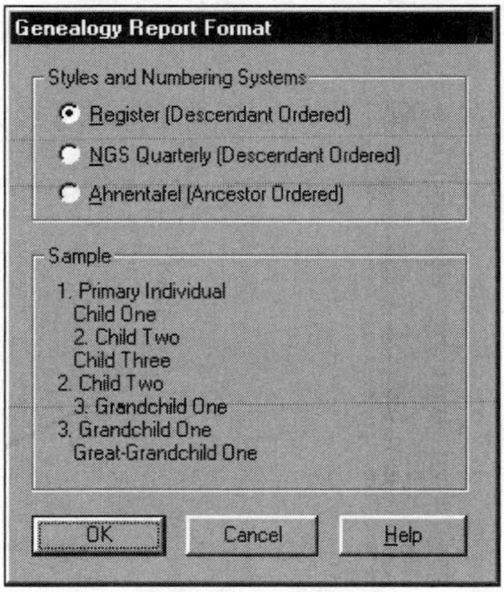

Figure 8-12. The Genealogy Report Format dialog box

4. Select the **Styles and Numbering Systems** option you prefer.

Register — (Descendant Ordered) This format is accepted by the New England Historic Genealogical Society, one of the oldest genealogical societies in the country. The Register format dates back to 1870 and is used to establish "pedigree."

NGS Quarterly — (Descendant Ordered) This format is the preferred genealogical report of the National Genealogical Society. The format dates back to 1912. It is similar to the Register format, but uses slightly different numbering and symbol systems.

Ahnentafel — (Ancestor Ordered) This format lists both the maternal and paternal family lines in the same report. It is not as popular as the other two formats for formal presentations.

Family Tree Maker displays a sample of the selected format in the lower portion of the dialog box.

5. After you make your selections, click **OK**.

Family Tree Maker returns you to the Report view. You can either print your report right away (see Chapter 10, "Printing Your Family Information"), or customize it (see Chapter 9, "Customizing Your Family Information") and then print.

Using the Relationship Calculator

The Relationship Calculator quickly determines how two individuals are related. Just select any two individuals from your Family File, and Family Tree Maker automatically calculates their relationship — including Civil and Canon numbers. For more information about Kinship reporting and definitions of Civil and Canon numbers, see "Displaying Standard and Custom Reports" in this chapter.

To use the Relationship Calculator:

1. From the **People** menu, select **Relationship Calculator**.

Family Tree Maker displays the Relationship Calculator dialog box.

2. To change either individual, click the corresponding **Change** button.

Family Tree Maker displays the Index of Individuals.

3. Select an individual from the list, and then click **OK.**

   Family Tree Maker returns you to the Relationship Calculator and automatically calculates the closest relationship between the selected individuals.

4. Click **Close** to exit the Relationship Calculator and return to the current view.

DISPLAYING MAPS

Family Tree Maker allows you to display family information in the form of a map, with or without an accompanying legend, showing the locations where facts noted in your family file occurred. You can see both what and where milestone events happened in your family history.

The individuals for whom facts are displayed are the same as those listed in the Individuals to Include dialog box (see "Selecting Individuals to Include" in Chapter 9). The *kinds* of facts displayed are listed in the Items to Include dialog box (see "Selecting Information to Include" in Chapter 9).

The *styles* of the legend and map labels are determined by your selections in various Options dialog boxes, such as the Map Format dialog box below, or the Text Font, Style & Size dialog box (see "Formatting Text" in Chapter 9).

To display a Map View:

1. From the **View** menu, select **Map**.

   Family Tree Maker displays a Map view.

   Note: If there are locations that could not be mapped, Family Tree Maker displays a dialog box listing those locations. See "Using Location Check" in this chapter.

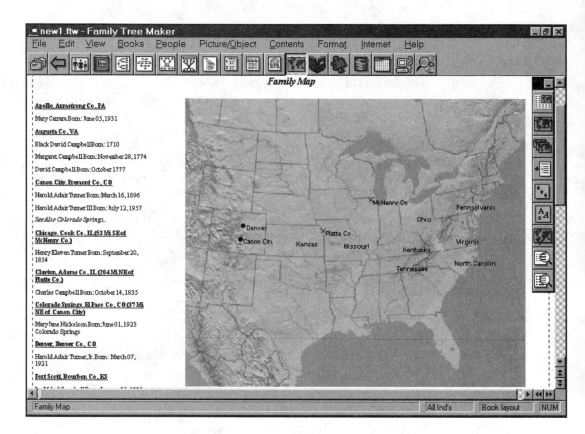

Figure 8-13. A Map View, in Book Layout format,
with legend starting on page with map

2. From the **Format** menu, select **Map Format**.

    Family Tree Maker displays the Map Format dialog box.

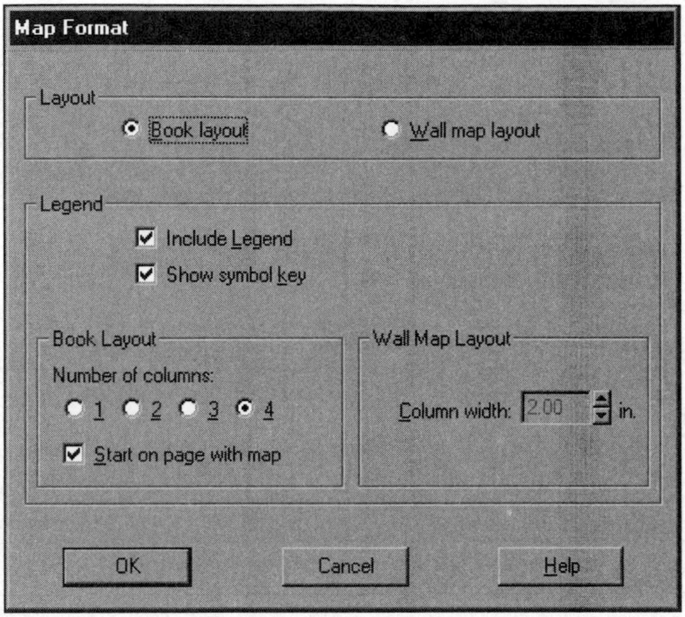

Figure 8-14. The Map Format dialog box

3. Select one of the following **Layout** options:

    Book layout — Select this option to create a map that will fit on a single page.

    Wall map layout — Select this option to create a larger map that requires multiple pages to display.

4. Select from the following **Legend** options:

    Include Legend — Select this check box to include a Legend with your map.

    Show symbol key — Select this check box to display the symbols used to designate towns, cities, large cities, and counties. Symbols will display under the Distance scale if it has also been selected.

5. In the **Book Layout** section, select from the following options as desired:

    Number of columns — Select a number from 1 to 4 to choose the number of columns for your legend.

    Start on page with map — Select this checkbox if you want the legend to begin on the same page as the map. Otherwise, the legend will begin on the following page.

6. From the **Wall Map Layout** section, use the up and down arrows to choose the **Column width** for the legend in your wall map. Note that the unit of measure is the same as selected in step 4 above.

7. After you make your selections, click **OK**.

Family Tree Maker returns you to the Map view.

Note: Once you have created and saved maps, they may also be displayed from a **Book** view.

Displaying Facts and Locations in Legends

Map legends comprise a location, followed by all standard and custom facts for that location (including Name), as entered in the More About Facts and More About Marriage pages. You can select the facts you want to display using the Items to Include dialog box (see "Selecting Information to Include" in Chapter 9). Facts (or locations) from the More About Medical, Lineage, or Notes pages are *not* available to be included in your map legend.

Note: Facts with locations that are not within the area of the displayed map do not appear in either the map or the legend (e.g., a fact located in California won't be displayed, or listed in the legend, for a map of the eastern United States or Europe).

Skipped Locations in Maps

If there is not enough room on the map to display all the locations in the legend, certain ones will be skipped (though the associated fact still appears in the legend).

Locations are displayed, in order, by Nation, State, County, Big City (population greater than 500,000), and finally, City or Town. If there is no more room for a location label without it overlapping another label, then it will be skipped.

Changing the Map Size and Area

The Map Area is that portion of a map view, apart from the legend, where the actual map displays. You can also select (or crop), part of a map image and resize it to create a more customized map view.

To change the size and/or area of your map image:

1. From the **View** menu, select **Map**. Then from the **Format** menu, select **Map Size and Area**.

   Family Tree Maker displays the Map Size and Area dialog box.

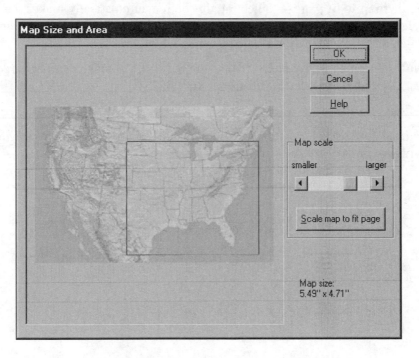

Figure 8-15. The Map Size and Area dialog box

2. Move the cursor onto the thumbnail image shown in the dialog box.

   The cursor becomes a crosshair (large plus sign).

3. Position the crosshair over the exact spot where you want the top-left corner of the cropped map image to be.

4. Press and hold the mouse button while you drag the crosshair diagonally to the exact spot where you want the bottom-right corner of the cropped map image to be, then release the mouse button.

The area inside the box you just created is what will remain of the map after it is cropped. If you want to change the selected area, simply repeat steps 3 and 4 until you are happy with the selection.

5. When you have a box around the area you want to keep, click **OK**.

    Family Tree Maker "crops" the image and displays only your selected area.

6. Make your selection from the following options:

    Map scale — Click on the slider and move left to right to change the map image from its smallest to largest possible size.

    Scale map to fit page — Selecting this option automatically makes the selected map image area as large as possible while still fitting the current page, or simply the largest scale possible, which ever is smaller.

    Note: Cropping the map, and then using the slider to make the map larger will help decrease location "skipping."

7. After you have made your selections, click **OK**.

    Family Tree Maker closes the dialog box and returns you to the Map view with your newly created map image.

Changing Map Images

You can choose different backdrops, or map images, from a list of available backdrops.

To select a different background image for your map:

1. From the **View** menu, select **Map,** then from the **Contents** menu select **Change Maps.**

    Family Tree Maker displays the Change Map dialog box.

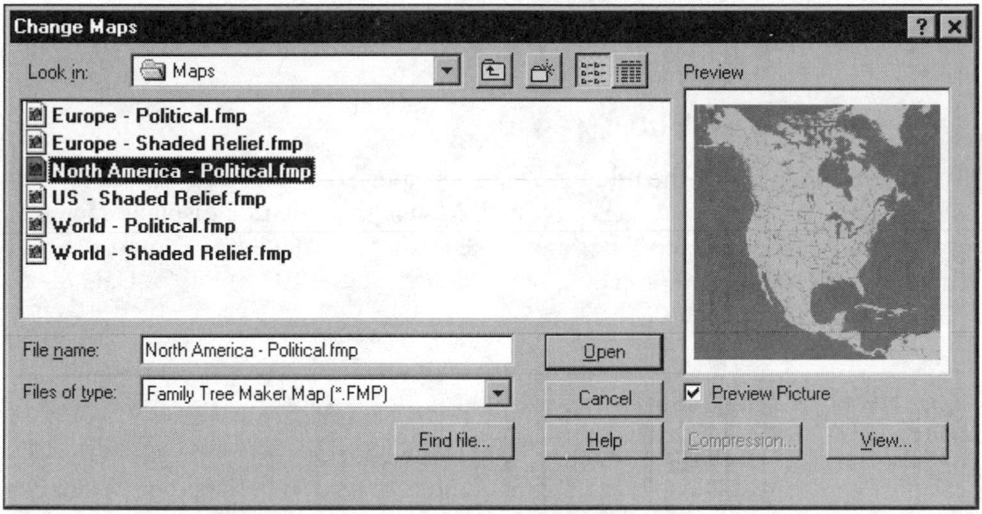

Figure 8-16. The Change Map dialog box

2. From the **Look in** drop-down list, select **C:** as the drive.

    If you installed Family Tree Maker on a drive other than drive C, then select that drive.

    In the box below the "Look in" field, Family Tree Maker displays a list of all the files and folders on the selected drive.

    Note: If you did not install the optional map images on your hard drive at the time you installed Family Tree Maker, they can be found on your program CD-ROM.

3. Double click the **FTW** folder.

    If you installed Family Tree Maker in a folder other than "FTW," select that folder instead.

Family Tree Maker displays a list of all the graphic files in the selected folder. Please note that map image files have the extension ".fmp."

4. In the box below the "Look in" field, click the map image file you want to use.

   Note: Select the **Preview Picture** check box to display the map images at a reduced size in the "Preview" field.

5. When you have selected your map image, click **Open**.

   Family Tree Maker displays the Map Size and Area dialog box. In this dialog box you can crop and scale your map image even further. See "Changing the Map Size and Area" in this chapter.

Displaying a Map Title

As in trees and reports, the title for a map is displayed centered on the page above the map. If you have selected Wall Map layout, the title displays centered over the whole document. Titles are created using the "Title and Footnote" dialog box. For more information, see "Adding a Title & Footnote or Date & Time Stamp" in Chapter 9.

Conflicts in Map Views

Crowding conflicts occur when there is not enough room to display all of the locations listed in the map legend without the map labels overlapping. When this happens, some locations are skipped and do not display on the map. However, this can be changed in the Options for Maps dialog box by allowing location labels to overlap. For more information, see "Map Options" in Chapter 9.

Note: Conflicts can also be reduced by cropping and enlarging the map in the Map Size and Scale dialog box (see Figure 8-15).

Using Location Check

The Location Check operates very much like a word processor's spell check, but instead of checking words against a dictionary, it checks location names against a list of known locations.

When Family Tree Maker discovers a location name that is questionable, you are prompted to use the Location Check. These "ambiguous locations" may share the same names, but actually be different places. For example, there are three cities in California named "Fremont." Sometimes the location in question may be included in such a way that Family Tree Maker cannot confirm it due to misspelling or because the field contains something other than a location.

To use the Location Check:

1. From the **Edit** menu, select **Location Check**.

   Family Tree Maker displays the Ambiguous Location dialog box.

   The upper portion of the dialog box shows the location in question while the field in the lower half shows a list of possible choices.

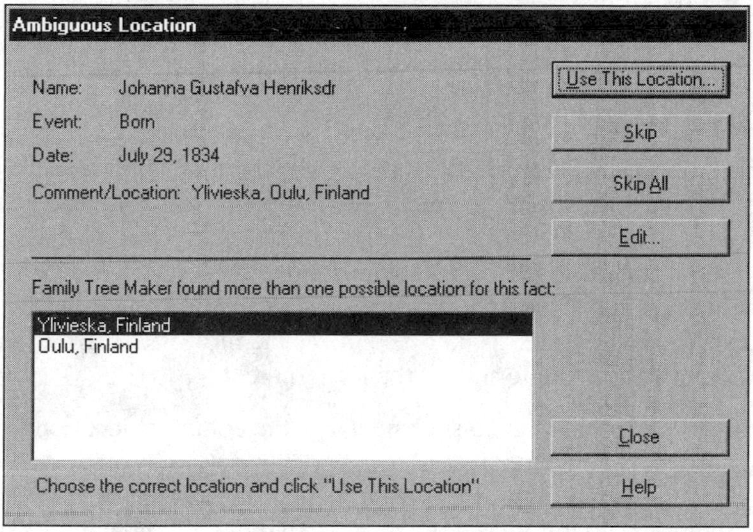

Figure 8-17. The Ambiguous Location dialog box

2. Select (highlight) the location you want to use and then click **Use This Location**.

   Family Tree Maker displays the Confirm Change dialog box.

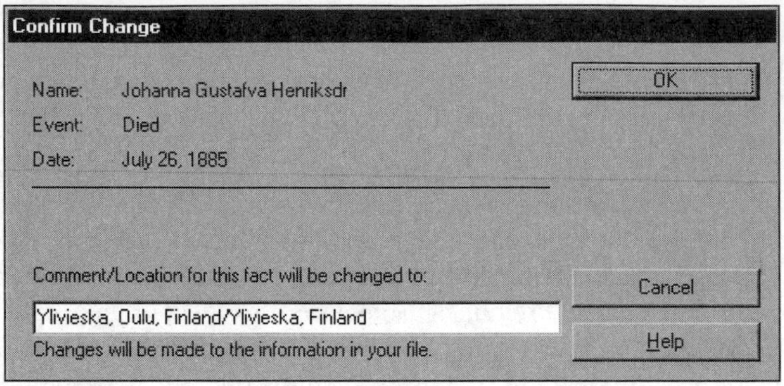

Figure 8-18. The Confirm Change dialog box

> **Note:** Family Tree Maker adds clarifying information without deleting any of your original text.

3. If you agree with the change, click **OK** to apply the change to your Family File and continue to the next ambiguous location, if any. If you want to make a different selection, click **Cancel** to return to the Ambiguous Location dialog box.

Special Notes about Location Check

- To minimize the occurrence of location errors in your More About Fact or Marriage pages, make sure to enter your comment first, followed by a slash "/" and then type the location. Family Tree Maker recognizes the text after the slash, or after the last slash if there is more than one, as the location to use. For example: "Served as a cook/midshipman/in Long Beach, California." Family Tree Maker recognizes the information after the second slash, Long Beach, California, as the location text.

- If a slash "/" appears as the last character in the comment/location field, the comment will be ignored. This allows you to record the comment, but not worry about it being displayed in your map. For example, if you were to type: "I don't want this fact in my map, even though I know it took place in San Francisco, CA/" Family Tree Maker would detect the final slash character and the fact would not be displayed.

- Family Tree Maker recognizes some locations as "major" locations — locations that are so well know that the majority of people would recognize them by a single name — such as, Paris (France), or London (England). If a comment/location field contains a "major" location, with no other names that might cause an ambiguous match, it will be interpreted as the commonly recognized location, bypassing the Ambiguous Location dialog box shown above.

- Family Tree Maker considers all nations as "major." When a nation name appears with no other location indicators such as a city or state, then Family Tree Maker will attribute it to the commonly recognized location. For example: **France**, appearing by itself, will be displayed as the country, even though there is a town in the state of Idaho called France. **Georgia**, appearing by itself, will be displayed as the country, since that is a higher-ranking category than state.

- After nations, the next highest-ranking category is states/provinces. As with nations, all U.S. states and Canadian provinces are considered "major." Any locations containing only a state or province name will be interpreted as that state or province. For example: **Washington** by itself will be recognized as the state (not the city or any of the several Washington counties).

  Note   Family Tree Maker recognizes standard two-letter state and province abbreviations as well as common synonyms, such as CA, Cal., and Calif. for California, or PE and PEI to indicate Prince Edward Island.

- Family Tree Maker recognizes many well-known cities and will automatically identify and display them even if their states or other information is missing. For example: New York City, Chicago, or San Francisco.

- If a location is not being recognized that could be either one or two words, such as Old Town, or LaCross, try spelling it both ways.

Special Note about Multiple Names and Historical Names

In our own lifetimes, locations with great historical relevance have changed their spellings — even their entire names. For instance, locations that have split into many, such as the USSR, could now be mapped as Russia, Ukraine, Lithuania, or others. It is also evident in the case of locations that have combined, such as West and East Germany, now mapped simply as Germany. In general, locations will be listed under the American English spelling of their *current* names. For example:

- **Mandalay, Burma** would be interpreted as Mandalay, Myanmar (new country name)

- **Leningrad, USSR** would be interpreted as St. Petersburg, Russia (new city and country names)

- **Peking, China** would be interpreted as Beijing, China (different city spelling)

DISPLAYING OTHER VIEWS

In addition to family trees, maps, and reports, Family Tree Maker can also display and print timelines, calendars, labels, cards, and Scrapbook pages. This section tells you how to display these views. Displaying your family history in different views can be fun, as well as informative, so don't be afraid to experiment! Remember, if you get lost, you can always press ⌨F1 to get on-screen Help.

Displaying Timelines

Timelines display a horizontal **Life bar** for each individual in the view. One of the unique features of this view is that you can choose to display your family history against a setting of historical milestones. The individuals displayed are the same as those you listed in the Individuals to Include dialog box (see "Timeline Options" in Chapter 9).

To display a Timeline view:

1. From the **View** menu, select **Timeline**.

2. From the **Format** menu, select **Format for Timeline**.

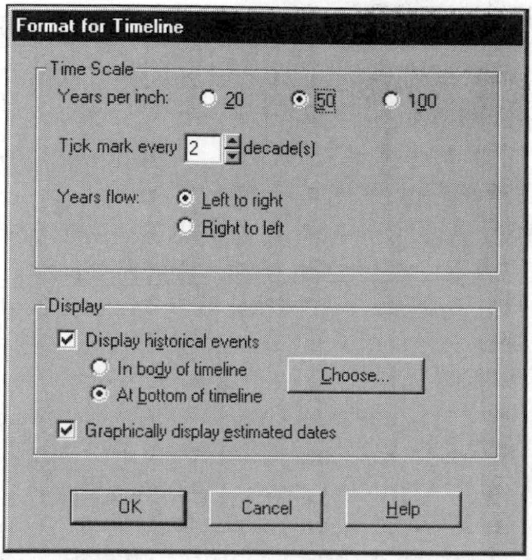

Figure 8-19. The Format for Timeline dialog box

3. Select from the **Time Scale** options described on the next page:

   Years per inch — Sets the number of years displayed, per inch, in the timeline. Choose a larger number for a more compact view.

   Tick mark — Sets the number of decades between tick marks displayed in the timeline. Use the arrows to display a number between 1 and 10.

   Years flow — Sets the way the flow of years is displayed, either left to right (1800 to 1990) or right to left (1990 to 1800).

4. Select from the **Display** options described below:

   Display historical events — Select this check box if you want to display historical events in your Timeline. If you select this check box, choose from one of the options below.

   In body of timeline — This option displays historical events in the body of the timeline.

   At bottom of timeline — This option displays historical events at the bottom of the timeline.

   Note: Click **Choose** to display a list of categories of events that can be displayed in your Timeline. Simply select, or deselect, the check boxes of the categories shown.

Graphically display estimated dates — when checked ON, life bars that contain estimated birth or death dates will display hash marks instead of closed (solid) end-lines. When this option is OFF, all life bars display closed ends.

5. After making your selections, click **OK**.

   Family Tree Maker returns you to the Timeline view. You can either print the Timeline right away (see Chapter 10, "Printing Your Family Information"), or customize it (see Chapter 9, "Customizing Your Family Information") and then print.

Displaying Scrapbooks

Scrapbook pages are great documents to add to family books or other collections of family information. You can display and print Scrapbook pages with as many or as few Pictures/Objects per page as you like. To personalize them, you can add a title and decorative borders, too.

To display a Scrapbook page:

1. Go to the Family Page containing the individual or the marriage whose Scrapbook you want to display.

   The Index of Individuals and Find Individual are two quick ways to locate an individual's Family Page. They are both described in Chapter 4 ("Locating Individuals in Your Family File").

2. On the Family Page, place the cursor either on the name of the individual or on the marriage whose Scrapbook you want to display.

3. From the **View** menu, select **Scrapbook**.

   Family Tree Maker displays the Scrapbook.

4. From the **File** menu, select **Print Preview**.

   Family Tree Maker displays the Scrapbook in a preview window.

5. From the **Format** menu, select **Scrapbook Format**.

   Family Tree Maker displays the Format for Printed Scrapbook dialog box shown in Figure 8-20.

6. Click the layout that you prefer. If you don't like any of the choices, click **Edit** to create a Custom Layout.

   You can either print your Scrapbook right away (see Chapter 10, "Printing Your Family Information"), or customize it (see Chapter 9, "Customizing Your Family Information") and then print.

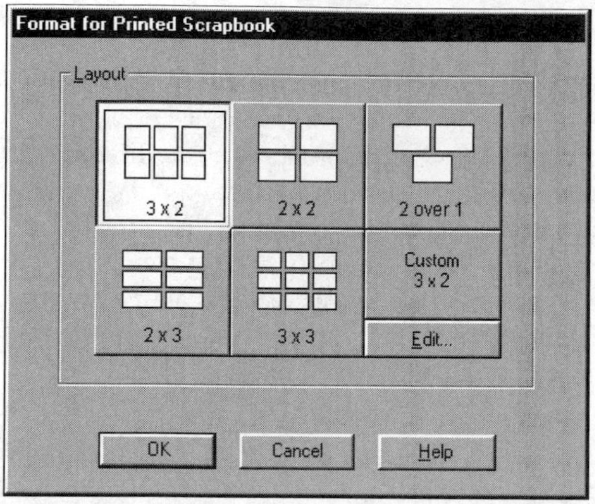

Figure 8-20. The Format for Printed Scrapbook dialog box

7. When you are ready to return to the Scrapbook view, from the **View** menu, select **Scrapbook**.

Displaying Calendars

You can display a calendar to help you keep track of family members' birthdays and anniversaries year-round. If you like, your calendar can also include people's ages and the number of years that they've been married.

To display a calendar, from the **View** menu, select **Calendar**. Family Tree Maker displays a calendar containing your family's birthdays and anniversaries. If the space for a single day is not large enough to show all the events that occurred on that day, then Family Tree Maker prints a second page of that month to hold the overflow.

Note: Your calendar will not include individuals with an empty birth date field or individuals who have only a year in the birth date field.

You can either print your calendar right away (see Chapter 10, "Printing Your Family Information"), or customize it (see Chapter 9, "Customizing Your Family Information") and then print.

Displaying Labels and Cards

Labels and cards have all kinds of valuable uses. For example, you can print address labels when it's time to send out invitations or holiday greetings. If you need to do a family mailing, you can print addresses directly onto postcards. Making "Hello, my name is…" stickers for large family reunions can help everyone get acquainted, and printing rolling index cards or address book pages allows you to keep family phone numbers close at hand. For a list of the different sizes and types of labels and cards that Family Tree Maker can print, look in the Print Setup dialog box from the Labels/Cards view. For instructions on how to access the Print Setup dialog box, see "Setting your Printer options" in Chapter 10.

To display labels and cards, from the **View** menu, select **Labels/Cards**. Family Tree Maker displays a page of basic labels or cards for you.

You can either print your labels and cards right away (see Chapter 10, "Printing Your Family Information"), or customize them (see Chapter 9, "Customizing Your Family Information,") and then print.

CHANGING YOUR DISPLAY OPTIONS

You may find it helpful to adjust your display options for your trees, reports, and other views. As described in the sections that follow, you can zoom, show or hide page lines, use your mouse to change the primary individual, and go to an individual's Family Page. You can also activate Pictures/Objects, either displaying pictures at full size or "playing" OLE objects.

Zooming

With the Zoom command, you can make the selected view appear larger on screen so it's easier to read the text. You can also shrink it down so you can see the whole thing at once. Please note that the Zoom command does not control the size of your view when you print.

To use the Zoom command:

1. From the **View** menu, select **Zoom**.

   Family Tree Maker displays the Zoom dialog box shown in Figure 8-21.

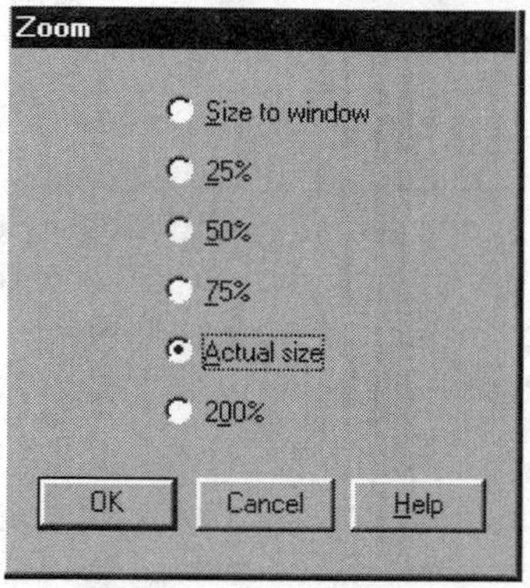

Figure 8-21. The Zoom dialog box

2. Select the option button for the size that you prefer.

   Size to Window — Fits your entire view on the screen.

   25% — Reduces the size of your view to one fourth of its actual size.

   50% — Reduces the size of your view to half of its actual size.

   75% — Reduces the size of your view to three quarters of its actual size.

   Actual Size — Makes the view the approximate size that it is when it prints.

   200% — The largest size at which you can display your information.

3. After you make your selection, click **OK**.

   Family Tree Maker returns to the selected view. When your whole view is not visible on the screen, Family Tree Maker places scroll bars on the bottom and right sides of the view. You can use these scroll bars to display different sections of the view.

Showing Page Lines

You can control whether or not dotted lines indicating page margins appear on the screen. From the **Format** menu, select **Show Page Lines**. If this option has a check next to it, the page lines will be visible. Otherwise, they won't be. Page lines never appear on your printed documents.

Navigating With Your Mouse

You can use your mouse in trees, reports, and other views to do two different things. First, you can navigate through Family Tree Maker by moving to different views and changing the primary individual. Second, you can activate Pictures/Objects, either displaying pictures at full size or "playing" OLE objects. For more information about including Pictures/Objects in your trees, reports, and other views see "Picture/Object Options" in Chapter 9.

Whether you navigate through Family Tree Maker or activate your Pictures/Objects depends on what you click and whether you double-click or single-click. The figure below describes each of the functions.

To do this...	Do this...
Select a new primary individual. You can then use the menus or the toolbar to change to any view.	Click once anywhere in a box, or click an individual's name in an Outline Descendant tree, report, or other view.
Go to the individual's Family Page.	Double-click any text in a box, or double-click an individual's name in an Outline Descendant tree, report, or other views.
Open the OLE server for an OLE Picture/Object and "play" the object. For example, this would play sound and video files.	Double-click a Picture/Object in a box (not available in Outline Descendant trees and reports).
Display a Picture/Object that isn't an OLE object, in the View Picture dialog box.	Double-click a Picture/Object in a box (not available in Outline Descendant trees and reports).

Figure 8-22. Using your mouse in trees, reports, and other views

Chapter 9

CUSTOMIZING YOUR FAMILY INFORMATION

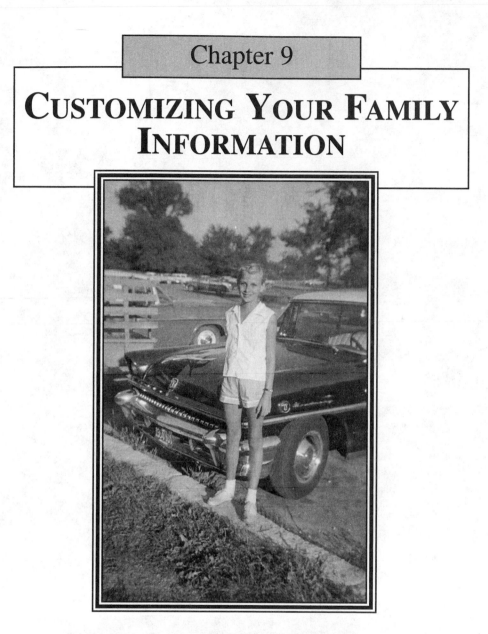

Marjorie (Pakosta) Ewart poses in front of the family car in her hometown of Brookfield, Illinois. Marjorie's son, Michael Vanata, works as an Engineer for Family Tree Maker Online.

CUSTOMIZING YOUR FAMILY INFORMATION

After you enter your information and select a tree, report, or other view, you can customize your views by adding color and borders, changing fonts and font styles, including different types of information, and much more. A complete list is below. You can go through these sections in any order you want, or skip them altogether, so experiment until you find the options that suit your tastes. Then, when you're happy with your tree, report, or other view and ready to print it, see Chapter 10, "Printing Your Family Information."

Your customization options include the following (some options are not available in all views):

- Selecting individuals to include, page 334

- Choosing the number of generations to include, page 344

- Selecting information to include, page 348

- Adding a title & footnote or date and time stamp, page 368

- Adding background pictures to trees, page 370

- Options for All-in-One trees, page 373

- Formatting text, including color, font, size, and style, page 379

- Selecting colors and box, border, and line styles, page 381

- Selecting the width for boxes and Pictures/Objects, page 384

- Choosing column widths and spacing in reports, page 385

- Sorting information, page 387

SELECTING INDIVIDUALS TO INCLUDE

Many Family Tree Maker views allow you to select the individuals you want to see in a particular view — whether on screen, or in print. This section describes how to choose who appears in your current view.

Tree Options

In the Descendant Tree, Hourglass Tree, and Outline Descendant Tree views you can choose to include all descendants or only direct descendants of the primary individual.

To select individuals to include in Descendant, Hourglass, and Outline Descendant trees:

1. Display a Descendant tree, an Hourglass tree, or an Outline Descendant tree (see Chapter 8, "Displaying Your Family Information").

2. From the **Contents** menu, select **Individuals to Include**.

   Family Tree Maker displays the Individuals to Include dialog box.

3. Select one of the options described below.

   All descendants — This option includes all descendants of the primary individual in your Family File. If you select this option, skip to step 7.

   Direct descendants — This option includes only direct descendants between the primary and secondary individual.

4. Click **Change secondary individual**.

   Family Tree Maker displays the Change Secondary Individual dialog box shown in Figure 9-1.

5. Select the name of the secondary individual (the individual that you want at the bottom of your tree) and click **OK**.

   If you have trouble locating the correct individual, you can type his or her name in the **Name** field or click **Find**. For instructions, see "Doing a Quick Search" or "Using Find Name" both in Chapter 4.

6. If you want to include each individual's brothers and sisters, select the **Include siblings of direct descendants** check box. To exclude siblings, leave this check box blank.

7. Click **OK** to close the Individuals to Include dialog box.

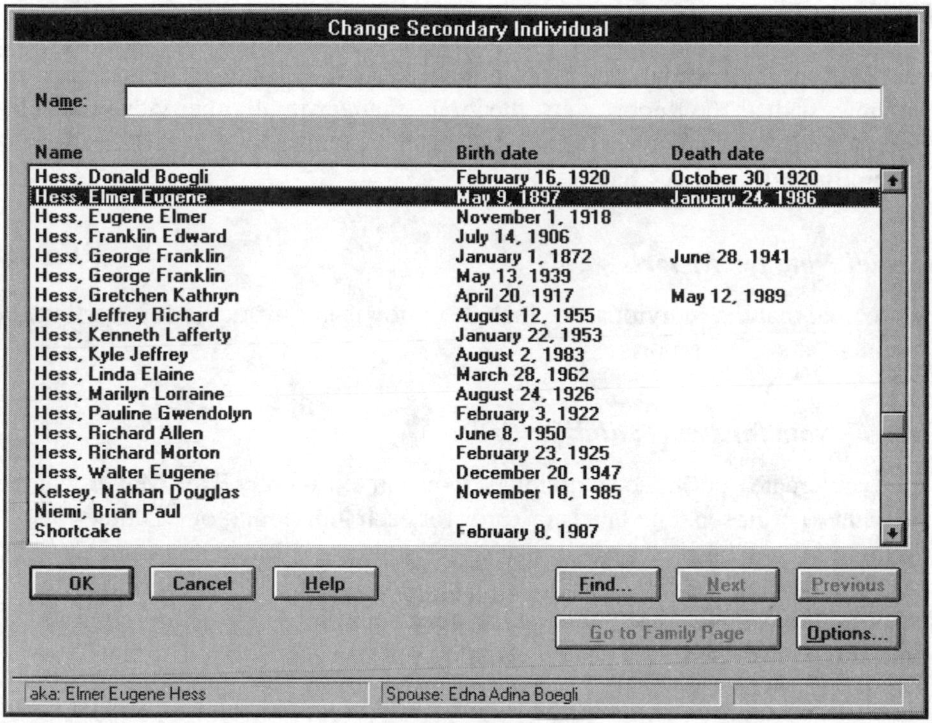

Figure 9-1. The Change Secondary Individual dialog box

Report, Calendar, and Label and Card Options

When you create reports, calendars, labels, and cards, you can use the "Individuals to Include" dialog box to select a group of individuals to display and print. All views in Family Tree Maker, *except* the Research Journal (see "The Research Journal and To Do List" in Chapter 7), share the same Individuals to Include dialog box. The group of individuals you select for one view such as Labels/Cards, is also available to you in the other views that allow you to choose groups: Report, Calendar, and batch print. If you make changes to the group in one view, such as the Report view, the group changes in all other views as well. If you want to create a group of individuals for a specific view, see "Creating Custom Book Items" in Chapter 11.

Special Note for Reports

Please note that the Individuals to Include option is *not* available for Marriage, Parentage, and PAF reports.

Special Note for Labels and Cards

After you create your list of individuals, you can tell Family Tree Maker whether you want to print separate labels or cards for each individual, or whether you want to print one label or card for each household (see "Label and Card Options" in this chapter). For example, if you are printing address labels for holiday cards, you probably want to print only one label per household. If you are printing name tags, however, you probably want to print one for each individual.

As you create your list of individuals, make sure to include *all* of the names you want to appear on a label or card. If you are printing labels or cards for households, and you leave out a member of a household, the information on the label or card may not print as you expect.

To select individuals to include in reports, calendars, labels, and cards:

1. Display a report, a calendar, or labels/cards (see Chapter 8, Displaying Your Family Information).

2. From the **Contents** menu, select **Individuals to Include**.

Family Tree Maker displays the Include dialog box.

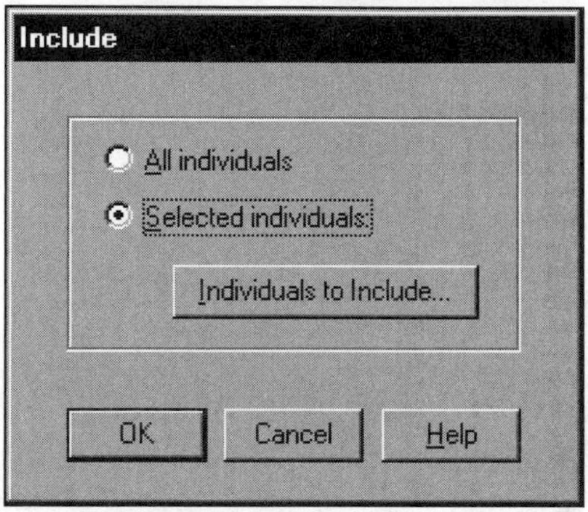

Figure 9-2. The Include dialog box

3. Select one of the options described below.

   All individuals — This option includes all individuals in your Family File. If you select this option, click **OK** and skip the remaining steps.

   Selected individuals — This option includes only the individuals you select. If you select this option, complete the remaining steps.

4. Click **Individuals to Include**.

   Family Tree Maker displays the Individuals to Include dialog box shown in Figure 9-3. The list on the right shows the group of individuals you've selected. The list on the left shows the individuals you can add to the group. Note that the list on the left is in alphabetical order by last name, and that nicknames (aka's) are on different lines than the given names.

   When you add an individual, his or her name is added to the list on the right and the "Number included" increases by one. When you remove an individual, his or her name moves to the list on the left, and the "Number included" decreases by one.

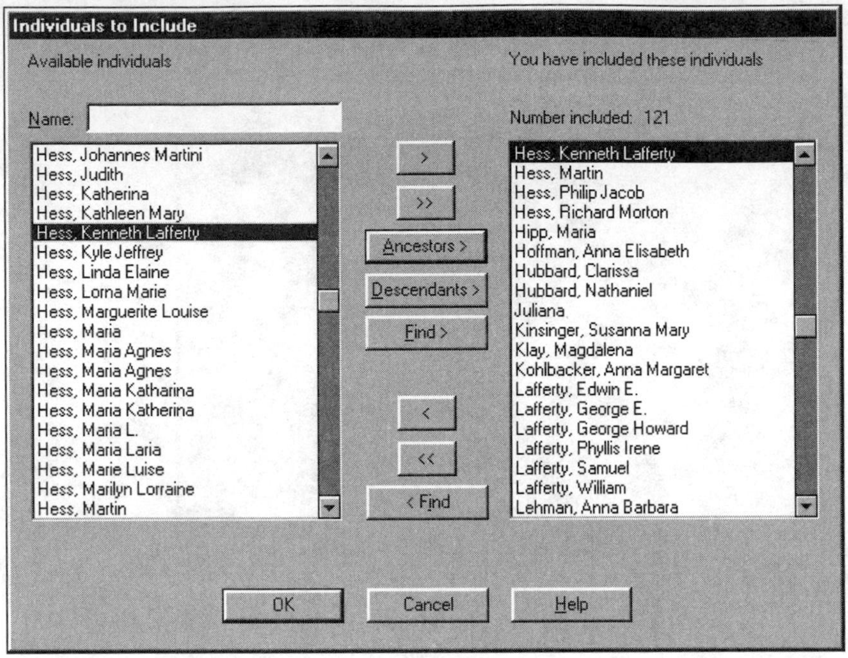

Figure 9-3. The Individuals to Include dialog box

5. Select the individuals to include in your view. Figure 9-4 shows the methods that you can use. You can use any combination of these methods to create your group.

6. After you create the group, click **OK** in the Individuals to Include dialog box.

   Family Tree Maker returns you to the selected view.

To do this...	Follow these steps...
Include individuals one-by-one.	Select an individual in the list on the left and then click [>] (Include).

Or, double-click the individual's name. |
| Include all of the individuals *currently* in your Family File | Click [>>] (Include All).

Note: If you use this button, individuals you add to your Family File later are *not* added to the group. To automatically include all current and future individuals, select the **All Individuals** option in the Include dialog box.. |
Include an individual's ancestors	Select an individual in the list on the left and then click [Ancestors >] (Include Ancestors).
Include an individual's descendants	Select an individual in the list on the left and then click [Descendants >] (Include Descendants).
Choose a category of individuals to include	Click [Find >] (Find and Include). See "Using the 'Find and Include' and 'Find and Remove' Buttons."
Remove individuals one-by-one	Select an individual in the list on the right and then click [<] (Remove).

Or, double-click the individual's name. |
Remove all of the individuals currently in the group	Click [<<] (Remove All).
Choose a category of individuals to remove	Click [< Find] (Find and Remove). See "Using the 'Find and Include' and 'Find and Remove' Buttons."
Include most of the individuals in your Family File	Click [>>] (Include All) and then click [<] (Remove) to remove the few individuals you don't want in the group.

Figure 9-4. Methods for selecting individuals to include

Using the "Find and Include" and "Find and Remove" Buttons

You can use the "Find and Include" and "Find and Remove" buttons to search your Family File for individuals, such as those who were born before a certain date or those who are ancestors of a particular individual, and add them to or remove them from the group.

To search for individuals using the "Find and Include" and "Find and Remove" buttons:

1. Decide which individuals you want to add to or remove from the group. For example, do you want to add your ancestors? Do you want to add the individuals who were merged or appended to your Family File? Do you want to remove all of the individuals who were born before a particular date?

    If you want to add or remove a group of individuals who are relatives of a particular individual, make sure to highlight the name of that individual in the list on the left before moving on to step 2. For example, if you want to add all of your ancestors, you would highlight your name.

2. Click either [Find >] (Find and Include) or [< Find] (Find and Remove).

    Family Tree Maker displays either the Add Individuals or Remove Individuals dialog box. In this dialog box you specify which individuals you want to find and add to or remove from the group.

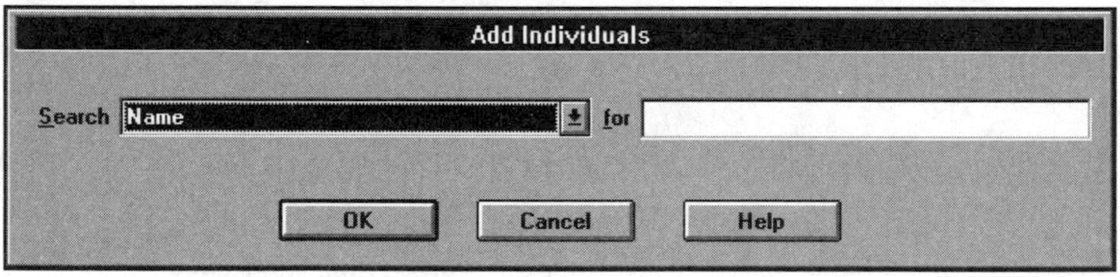

Figure 9-5. The Add Individuals dialog box

3. Click the **Search** drop-down list and select the item you want to find.

    You can use this option to search for people who have something in common. For example, if you want to find all the living relatives of a particular individual, you would search for all individuals in your Family File who do not have a death date. In this case you would select **Death Date** from the Search drop-down list. After you select a field, continue with the following step.

4. In the **for** field, type the information you want to find. If you are searching for information in a field that has certain legal values (such as "male," "female," or "unknown"), Family Tree Maker displays a drop-down list in the "for" field. In this case, select the item you want to find from the list.

    For example, if you chose "Death Date" in step 3, and you want Family Tree Maker to find everyone who is living, then you need to type = (equal sign) in the "for" field. If you are searching a date field, see the Table in Chapter 4 called "Searching for date," (Figure 4-12), for searching tips.

    Note: You can find additional tips on how to create "wild card" searches using the Find Individual dialog box. From the **Edit** menu, select **Find Individual**. From the Find Individual dialog box, click **Help**. From step 2 of the "Tips for Searching" Help screen, click the colored text link **click here** to display a table of tips and ideas for more productive searches.

5. Click **OK**.

    Family Tree Maker searches your Family File for individuals who match your request. If no matches are found, Family Tree Maker tells you so. If you chose to add the individuals, their names are added to the list on the right and the "Number included" increases. If you chose to remove the individuals, their names are removed from the list on the right, and the "Number included" decreases.

Map Options

Selecting individuals to include in maps is similar to selecting them for timelines and calendars in that the Map view is not dependent on a primary individual. Unlike trees, a map does not change when initiated, or called up, from different individuals in your Family File.

To select individuals to include in a Map view:

1. From the **View** menu, select **Map**.

    Family Tree Maker displays the view you selected.

2. From the **Contents** menu, select **Individuals to Include**.

    Family Tree Maker displays the Include dialog box.

3. Select one of the options described below:

    All individuals — This option includes all individuals in your Family File. If you select this option, click **OK** and skip the remaining steps.

    Selected Individuals — This option includes only the individuals you select. If you select this option, complete the remaining steps.

4. Click **Individuals to Include**.

    Family Tree Maker displays the Individuals to Include dialog box. When you add an individual, his or her name moves to the list on the right. When you remove an individual, his or her name moves to the list on the left.

5. After selecting the individuals to include in your view, click **OK**.

    Family Tree Maker returns you to the selected view.

Timeline Options

Timelines are unique in their ability to help you view your family from a historical perspective by plotting the life of each family member against time. You also have the option of including historical milestones in your timelines so you can see the events that helped shape each person's life.

To select individuals to include in a Timeline:

1. Display a Timeline (see "Displaying Timelines" in Chapter 8).

2. From the **Contents** menu, select **Individuals to Include**.

   Family Tree Maker displays the Include dialog box.

3. Select one of the options described below:

   All individuals — This option includes all individuals in your Family File. If you select this option, click **OK** and skip the remaining steps.

   Selected Individuals — This option includes only the individuals you select. If you select this option, complete the remaining steps.

4. Click **Individuals to Include**.

   Family Tree Maker displays the Individuals to Include dialog box. When you add an individual, his or her name moves to the list on the right. When you remove an individual, his or her name moves to the list on the left.

   Family Tree Maker automatically sorts the names in alphabetical order by "Last name (A first)."

5. After selecting the individuals to include in your view, click **OK**.

   Family Tree Maker returns you to the selected view.

CHOOSING THE NUMBER
OF GENERATIONS TO INCLUDE

You can choose the number of generations to include for many trees and reports. The number of generations you can include depends on the type of tree or report you wish to create.

Tree and Genealogy Report Options

Fit to Page Ancestor trees can show up to 6 generations. Descendant trees, Custom Ancestor trees, Hourglass trees, and Genealogy reports can show up to 99 generations while Outline Descendant trees can show up to 250 generations. This option is not available for Direct Descendant and Outline Direct Descendant trees, because those tree types show how two individuals are connected, rather than a specific number of generations.

Remember, the more generations you add, the bigger your tree will be. For example, a 10-generation Ancestor tree can have 512 boxes in its rightmost column because each of us has 512 seventh great-grandparents (assuming no one married a cousin).

Note: The All-in-One tree is unique because it shows both ancestors and descendants. For more information, see "Special Notes for All-in-One Trees" in this Chapter.

To choose the number of generations to include in your tree:

1. Display a Descendant tree, an Ancestor tree, an Outline Descendant tree, an Hourglass tree, an All-in-One tree, or a Genealogy report (see Chapter 8, "Displaying Your Family Information").

2. From the **Contents** menu, select **# of Generations to Show**.

   Family Tree Maker displays the # of Generations to Show dialog box.

3. Select the number of generations you want to include in your tree.

   Note: You can select separate options for both the ancestor and descendant portions of the Hourglass tree.

4. After you make your selection, click **OK**.

   Family Tree Maker returns you to the Tree view.

When you look at a Fit to Page Ancestor tree, you may notice that Family Tree Maker abbreviates some of the names, locations, and biographical information to make the tree fit on a single page. This happens more often with trees that include five or more generations. If your Fit to Page Ancestor tree grows too large to fit on a single page, Family Tree Maker lets you know by displaying a message.

Special Notes for All-in-One Trees

The All-in-One Tree adds a check box to the # of Generations to Show dialog box. Settings you select in this dialog box will also affect the "Show unrelated trees" option (see "All-in-One Tree Options" in this chapter).

To choose the # of generations you want to show in an All-in-One tree:

1. From the **Contents** menu, select **# of Generations to Show**.

   Family Tree Maker displays the # of Generations to Show dialog box.

2. Select one of the options described below:

   Show all generations — Select this check box if you want to show all the generations in your family file. When selected, the spinner controls are disabled, and your All-in-One tree will display up to 99 generations in either direction, regardless of the generation settings. When this check box is deselected, you can choose from the generation settings below.

   Note: Selecting this check box also selects the **Show unrelated trees** check box in the All-in-One tree options dialog box. Conversely, if the **Show unrelated trees** check box is *deselected*, the **Show All Generations** check box will also be deselected.

   Generations of Ancestors — Click the up or down arrows in this field to choose how many generations of ancestors to include in your tree.

   Generations of Descendants — Click the up or down arrows in this field to choose how many generations of descendants to include in your tree.

   Note: If you selected the **Show all generations** check box above, these options will be disabled.

3. After you make your selections, click **OK**.

   Family Tree Maker returns you to the All-in-One tree view.

   Note: A warning message dialog box will appear if more than 10,000 individuals (including duplicates) will be displayed in the tree. Options will be provided for you to reduce the size of your tree.

Kinship Report Options

Family Tree Maker lets you choose how many generations of ancestors and descendants to include in Kinship reports. In addition, you can limit the degrees of cousinship that a Kinship report contains (5th cousins, 6th cousins, 7th cousins, and so on).

To choose the number of generations for a Kinship report:

1. Display a Kinship Report (see Chapter 8, "Displaying Your Family Information").

2. From the **Contents** menu, select **# of Generations to Show**.

   Family Tree Maker displays the # of Generations to Show for Kinship dialog box.

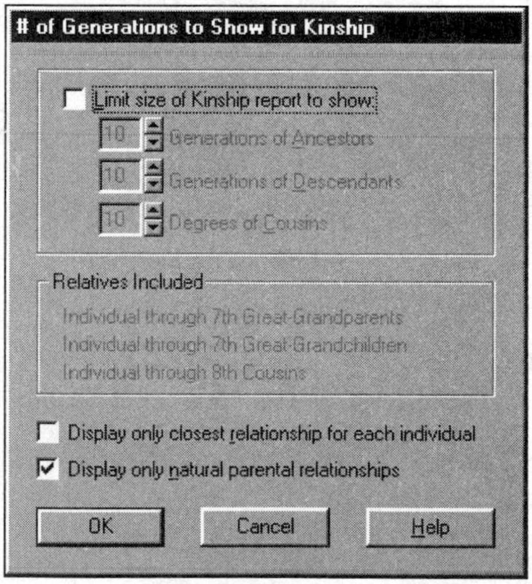

Figure 9-6. The # of Generations to Show for Kinship dialog box

3. **Limit size of Kinship report to show** — Select this check box if you want to limit the number of individuals in your Kinship report. Leave this check box unchecked if you want to include all possible relatives in your Kinship report. When you select this check box, you also have the options described below.

   Generations of Ancestors and **Generations of Descendants** — Click the up or down arrows in these fields to choose how many generations to include. You can choose any number from 1 to 99.

   Degrees of Cousins — Click the up or down arrows in this field to choose how many cousins to include. For example, if you don't want to include individuals more distantly related than 3rd cousins, select "5" in this field. You can choose any number from 1 to 99.

4. Select the following check boxes if desired:

   Display only closest relationship for each individual — The individuals in your Family File can be related in more than one way, especially when intermarriage exists. If you select this check box, Family Tree Maker includes only one relationship between the primary individual and each of the other individuals in the Kinship report.

   Display only natural parental relationships — Select this check box to include only natural parents in the Kinship report.

5. After you make your selections, click **OK**.

   Family Tree Maker returns you to the Kinship report.

SELECTING INFORMATION TO INCLUDE

With Family Tree Maker, you can choose which information to include in your trees, reports, and other views, such as timelines and maps. Each item that you choose appears in either the boxes on your trees, maps, and calendars, or on a line in reports and outline style trees.

Depending on your view, you can choose to include items such as names, dates, facts, addresses, relationship information, and reference numbers. If you have placed Pictures/Objects in Scrapbooks, you can include them in your tree's boxes — for individuals and/or for marriages — and on your labels and cards too. You can include up to 50 items per individual. Remember, however, the more items you include in your view, the fewer individuals fit on a page when you print your information.

Note: The steps that follow apply to all views *except* the Calendar view. See "Selecting Information to Include in Your Calendar" in this chapter for information about the Calendar view.

To select items to include:

1.   Select the view you want to see as described in Chapter 8, "Displaying Your Family Information."

2.   From the **Contents** menu, select **Items to Include**.

Family Tree Maker displays the Items to Include dialog box (see Figure 9-7). It contains two lists: the list on the right shows the items included in your view, and the list on the left shows the items you can add to your view. You can add items to and delete items from the list on the right as often as you like. When you add an item, it moves to the list on the right. When you remove an item, it moves to the list on the left.

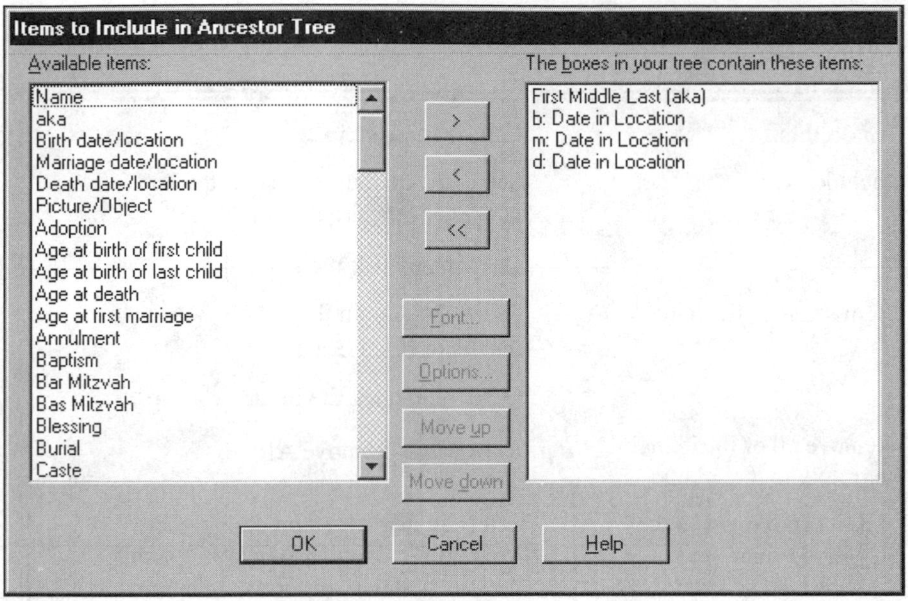

Figure 9-7. The Items to Include in Ancestor Tree dialog box

The items in the lists vary depending on the view you've selected. Some items, such as names and dates, require you to select format options. Family Tree Maker automatically displays a dialog box for you to select these options when it is necessary. You can change the item format by selecting it in the list on the right and then clicking **Options**. For more information about the various format options, see the sections that begin with "Name Options" in this chapter. You can also click **Font** to choose the text size and style for your view (see "Formatting Text" in this chapter).

3. Add, remove, and arrange items using the options described below.

To do this...	Follow these steps...
Include items	Select the item in the list on the left and then click [>] (Include).
	Or, double-click the item..
Remove specific items	Select the item in the list on the right and then click [<] (Remove).
	Or, double-click the item.
Remove all of the items currently in the group	Click [<<] (Remove All).
Arrange the items in the list on the right.	Select an item and then click either **Move up** or **Move down** to move that item up or down one space. The item at the top of the list will appear at the top of the box, or as the first item on the line in Outline-style trees.

Figure 9-8. Methods for creating groups

4. After you make your selections, click **OK**.

   Family Tree Maker returns you to the selected view.

Special Notes for Trees

- With Ancestor trees, you have the option to print the primary individual and the primary individual's spouse in the same box. To do this, select **Spouse (primary individual only)** as an item to print. All of the other individuals' spouses already appear in the tree.

- If you include any marriage information in Ancestor trees, such as "Marriage date/location" or "Marriage Pictures/Objects," it only appears in the husband's box.

- If you include any marriage information in Descendant trees, such as "Marriage date/location" or "Marriage Pictures/Objects," it only appears in the non-bloodline spouse's box.

- When an individual has had more than one spouse, the Outline Descendant tree lists them in the order in which the marriages took place. If Family Tree Maker is not displaying spouses in the correct order, check the marriage dates on the applicable Family Pages. When you do not have an exact marriage date, use approximate dates so that the spouses print in the correct order. For help with estimated dates, see the Table "How to enter estimated dates" (Figure 3-6), in Chapter 3.

- When choosing Items to Include for Hourglass trees and Hourglass Fan trees, your list of items will be applied to both the ancestor and descendant portions of the tree.

Special Notes for Maps

- All built-in and custom facts from the More About Facts page, the Family Page, and the Marriage Facts page (including Name) are available to include in maps.

- Removing Name from the Items to Include list prevents the name from appearing with each fact. This is useful, for example, if you want to create a map for a single individual, such as a biographical map.

- If you click **OK** with no facts selected, or with no facts except Name selected, then no locations will display in either the map or the legend.

- Facts from the More About Medical, Lineage, or Notes pages are *not* available for displaying on a map.

Name Options

When you choose to include names in your view, Family Tree Maker displays the Options: Name dialog box. In this dialog box, you choose the display format for all names in your view.

Note: Not all options are available in all views. Any check boxes that appear grayed out will not function in your particular view. If you are working in the Labels/Cards view, see "Names on Labels and Cards" in this chapter.

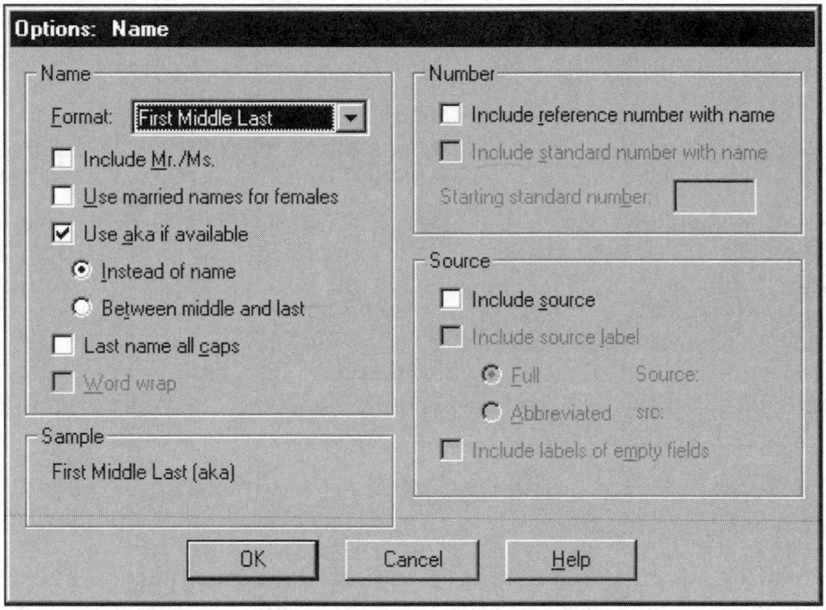

Figure 9-9. The Options: Name dialog box

To select name options:

1. Click the **Format** drop-down list to select a format for the names in your view. For example, you could choose to omit middle names or split names onto two lines. A line split is indicated by "\\".

2. Select any of the following options:

    Include Mr./Mrs./Ms. — Select this check box to include titles in your view. If you entered a title in an individual's Lineage dialog box, Family Tree Maker uses the title you entered instead of Mr./Mrs./Ms. (see "Entering Nicknames, Titles, and Parental Relationships" in Chapter 5). You must also select the "Use married names for females" option for Family Tree Maker to correctly apply the Ms. and Mrs. titles.

    Use married names for females — Select this check box to use women's married names as last names and maiden names as middle names. Otherwise, Family Tree Maker uses women's full maiden names.

    Note: If you want to use married names for females for a single individual only, see "Entering Nicknames, Titles, and Parental Relationship Information" in Chapter 5.

    Use aka if available — Select this box to use aka's (nicknames) and choose either of the following two options:

    - **Instead of name** — Choose this if you prefer to use aka's (nicknames) instead of given names.

    - **Between middle and last** — Choose this if you want to place the aka's between the middle and last names.

    Last name all caps — To print all last names in capital letters, select this check box.

    Word wrap — To allow long name formats to wrap onto two lines, select this check box.

    Include reference number with name — If you use reference numbers in your Family File (see "Entering Nicknames, Titles, and Parental Relationship Information" in Chapter 5), you can include them in front of people's names by selecting this check box.

Include standard numbers with name — If you want Family Tree Maker to calculate Standard (Ahnentafel) numbers for you in Ancestor trees, select this check box and type the number for the primary individual in the **Starting standard number** field.

Include Source — If you documented sources, select this check box to include them in your view. If you entered a source "Title," the title appears, otherwise the source "Footnote" appears.

Include source label — If you choose to include sources in your view, you can also choose whether to include a label with the source reference. To include a label, select the **Include source label** check box, and then select either **Source** or **Src** as the label.

Include labels of empty fields — To include a source label when you did *not* document a source, select this check box.

3. After you make your selections, click **OK**.

    Family Tree Maker returns to the Items to Include dialog box.

Names on Labels and Cards

When you choose to include names on labels or cards, Family Tree Maker displays the Options: Name dialog box shown in Figure 9-10. In this dialog box, you choose the printing format for all names in this set of Labels/Cards.

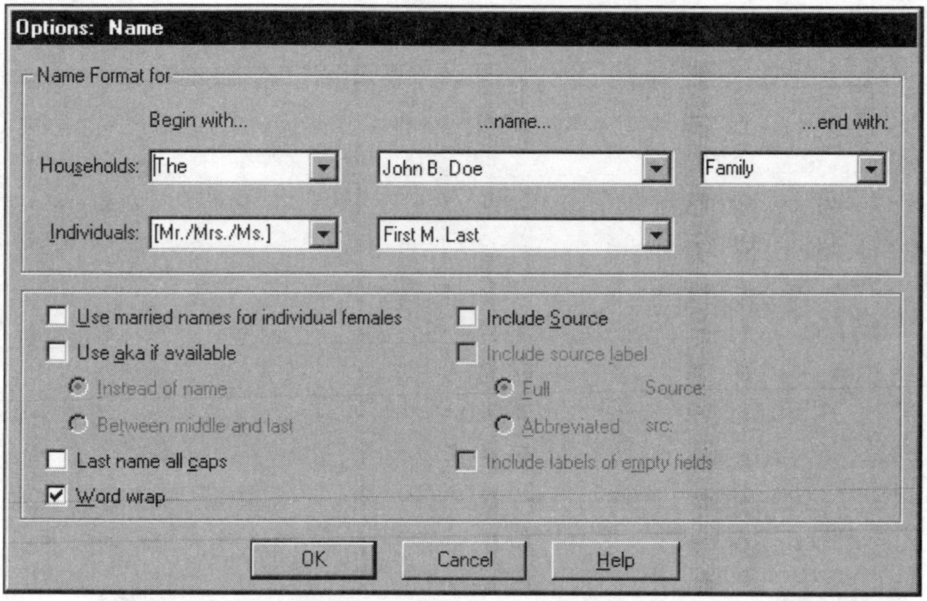

Figure 9-10. The Options: Name dialog box for labels and cards

Note: There may be a few individuals in your Family File who use different titles. For example, some individuals may use the title "Dr." or "Reverend." You can create special titles for those individuals in their Lineage dialog boxes. See "Entering Nicknames, Titles, and Parental Relationship Information" in Chapter 5. However, the majority of the individuals in your Family File get their titles from the Options: Name dialog box.

There are two different name formats that you can set in this dialog box: one when the individuals are printed on a label or card as part of a household, and one when the individuals are printed separately. Each of these name formats has multiple parts that work together to create the whole printed name.

Before you begin making your selections, here are a few examples:

To get	Begin with	name	end with
The John B. Doe Family	The	John B. Doe	Family
John & Jane Doe and Children	(Blank)	John & Jane Doe	And Son/Daughter/ Children
Mr. and Mrs. Doe	Mr. and Mrs.	Doe	N/A
Ms. Jane S. Doe	Mr./Mrs./Ms.	First M. Last name	N/A

Figure 9-11. Name format samples

To select name options:

1. Click the **Households/Begin with** drop-down list. You can either select an item from the list, type your own word(s), or leave the field blank.

   The drop-down list generally uses the titles "Mr." and "Mrs." However, if you prefer different titles, you can change them in the Titles dialog box, (see "Preferences for Titles" in Chapter 3).

2. Click the **Households/name** drop-down list and select an appropriate name format.

3. In the **Households/end with** field, either select an item from the drop-down list or type your own word(s).

   This field is only available for Households.

4. Repeat steps 1 and 2 for the **Individuals** fields.

5. Select any of the following options you want to use:

Use married names for individual females — To use women's married names as last names and maiden names as middle names, select this check box. Otherwise Family Tree Maker uses women's full maiden names.

Use aka if available — Select this box to use aka and choose either of the following two options:

- **Instead of name** — Choose this if you prefer to use aka (nicknames) instead of given names.

- **Between middle and last** — Choose this if you want to place the aka between the middle and last names.

Last name all caps — To print all last names in capital letters, select this check box.

Word wrap — To allow long name formats to wrap onto two lines, select this check box.

Include Source — If you documented sources, select this check box to include them in your view. If you entered a source "Title," the title appears, otherwise the source "Footnote" appears.

Include source label — If you choose to include sources in your view, you can also choose whether to include a label with the source reference. To include a label, select the **Include source label** check box, and then select either **Source** or **Src** as the label.

Include labels of empty fields — To include a source label when you did *not* document a source, select this check box.

6. After you make your selections, click **OK**.

Family Tree Maker returns you to the Items to Include dialog box.

Date and Fact Options

When you choose to include dates or facts that are entered in the More About Facts dialog box, Family Tree Maker displays the Options dialog box for that fact (see Figure 9-12). If you are working in a Report view, Family Tree Maker automatically formats your dates and facts. Please note that not all views have the same options. The date or fact option dialog box in your view may look different from this Marriage date/location example. See "Other Options" in this chapter.

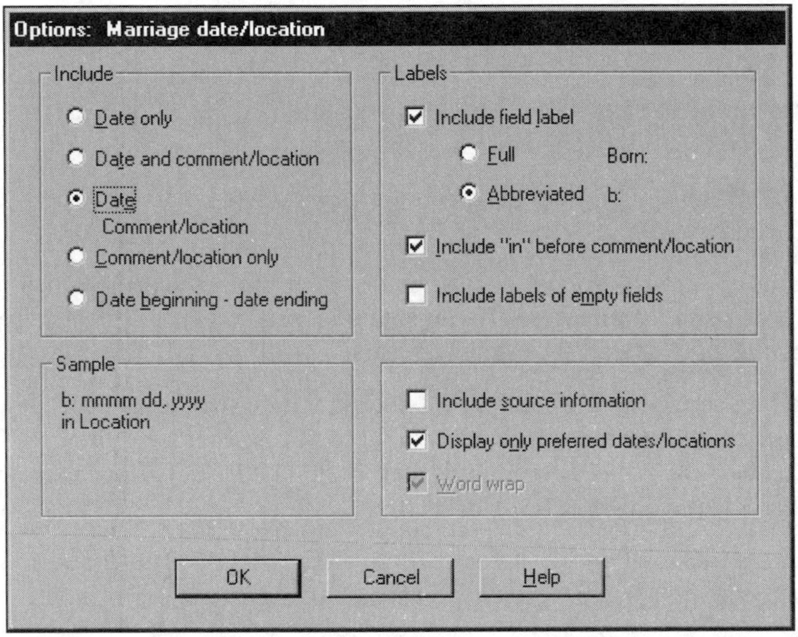

Figure 9-12. The Options: Facts dialog box

To select date and fact options:

1. Select one of the following **Include** options.

    Date only — To include date information and exclude comments and locations, select this option button.

    Date and comment/location — To include date, comment, and location information on a single line, select this option button.

    Date Comment/location — To include date information on one line, and comment and location information on a separate line, select this option button.

    Comment/location only — To include comment and location information and exclude dates, select this option button.

2. Select any of the following **Labels** options.

    Include field label — To include description labels next to the date or fact, select this check box. You can also choose whether to show the **Full** word or an **Abbreviated** version. The text next to these option buttons shows samples of each label type.

    Include "in" before comment/location — To include the word "in" before comments and locations, select this check box.

    Include labels of empty fields — To include descriptions of fields which do not contain any information, select this check box.

3. If you want to include source information for facts in your tree, select the **Include source information** check box.

4. If your "Fact" fields contain more than a few words, select the **Word wrap** check box.

5. After you make your selections, click **OK**.

    Family Tree Maker returns you to the Items to Include dialog box.

Picture/Object Options

When you choose Picture/Object in the Items to Include dialog box, Family Tree Maker displays the Options: Picture/Object dialog box shown in Figure 9-13. This is where you choose which Pictures/Objects appear for each individual in your view. You may not have a Picture/Object for all of the individuals in your view. When this is the case, Family Tree Maker substitutes a graphic (or a blank space) where the Picture/Object would normally appear. When you include Pictures/Objects, it's a good idea not to include too much other information. Otherwise, you won't be able to fit as many generations on a single page.

Note: In addition to the options described below, you can also limit the size of the Pictures/Objects (see "Changing the Width of Boxes and Pictures/Objects" in this chapter).

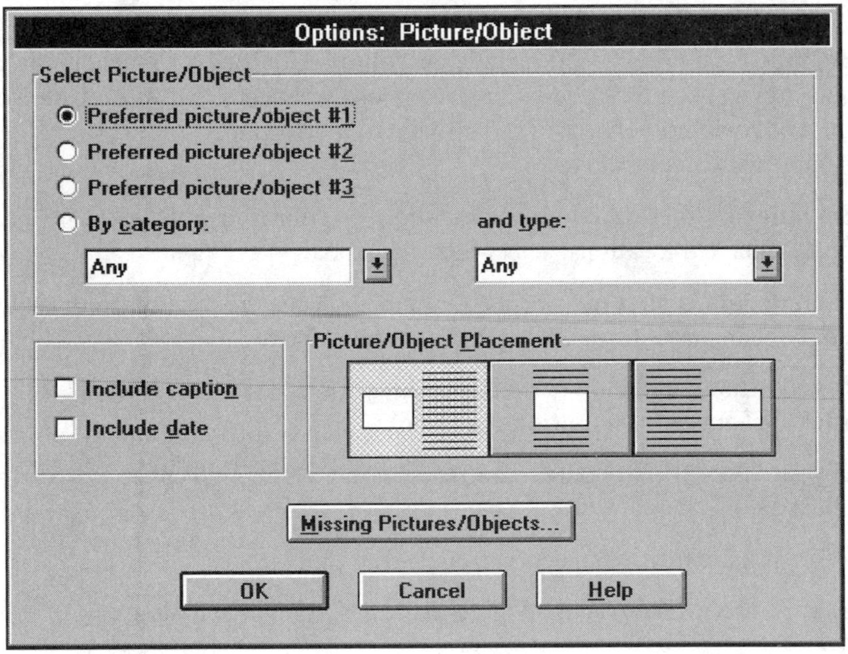

Figure 9-13. The Options: Picture/Object dialog box

To select Picture/Object options:

1. Select one of the following options.

   Preferred Picture/Object — These option buttons correspond to the Picture/Object preferences you selected in the More About Picture/Object dialog boxes. For more information about the More About Picture/Object dialog box, see "Scrapbooks: Working with Pictures/Objects" in Chapter 5.

   By Category and Type — These fields work together to find Pictures/Objects that you assigned to a particular category and type in the More About Picture/Object dialog box. For example, if you choose the category "Birthdays" and the type "Picture," Family Tree Maker searches for Pictures/Objects that fulfill *both* requirements. However, both of the fields have an "Any" option, which, in effect, allows you to search only one of the two fields. If the category that you assigned to a Picture/Object does not appear in the "By Category" drop-down list, just type it into the field. When there is more than one Picture/Object of the category and type that you select, Family Tree Maker uses the first one that it finds.

2. If you want to include the Picture/Object's caption or date, select the **Include caption** or **Include date** check box.

3. Select the **Picture/Object Placement** button that shows the placement you prefer. You can place the Picture/Object to the right or left of the text, or you can center both the text and the Picture/Object in the box.

4. Click **Missing Pictures/Objects**.

   Family Tree Maker displays the Missing Pictures/Objects dialog box.

5. Do one of the following to tell Family Tree Maker how to handle missing Pictures/Objects:

- To use a Family Tree Maker substitute graphic, click the button for the graphic that you want and then click **OK**.

- To substitute a blank space, click the blank space and then click **OK**.

- To use your own picture file as a substitute graphic, click **Choose Picture**. Family Tree Maker displays the Import Picture from File dialog box. The graphic can be in any of the following file formats: Windows Bitmap (*.BMP), ZSoft Image (*.PCX), Tagged Image Format (*.TIF), Windows MetaFile (*.WMF), FlashPix (*.FPX), Photoshop (*.PSD), or JPEG Interchange Format (*.JPG, *.JFF). If you need instructions, see "Picture/Object: Insert Picture from File" in Chapter 5. After you select a picture, click **OK**, then click **OK** a second time to return to the Options: Picture/Object dialog box.

If you do not have Pictures/Objects in each individual's Scrapbook and you want to manually attach photos to your trees after you print them, you can add several blank rows to leave space for the photos. The number of blank rows that you need to add depends on the size of your photos. To insert lines and blank rows in a tree's boxes, select **Line in box** or **Blank row** in the Items to Include dialog box (see "Selecting Information to Include" in this chapter).

Note: Family Tree Maker does not support graphics files that use LZW compression technology.

Standard Number Options

Standard numbers (Ahnentafel numbers) are automatically generated by a formula. The formula states that an individual's father is twice that individual's number, and an individual's mother is twice that individual's number plus 1. If your Ahnentafel number is 1, your father's number is 2, and your mother's is 3.

If you choose to include Standard numbers, Family Tree Maker displays the Options: Standard number (Ahnentafel) dialog box shown in Figure 9-14. Type the starting number for the primary individual; Family Tree Maker calculates the rest of the numbers for you. Since Ahnentafel numbering is calculated based on an individual's position in an Ancestor tree, this option only applies to standard Ancestor trees.

You can also choose to include Reference numbers. Reference numbers are numbers that you can create for your own filing system. You can enter these numbers in the Lineage dialog box (see "Entering Nicknames, Titles, and Parental Relationship Information" in Chapter 5).

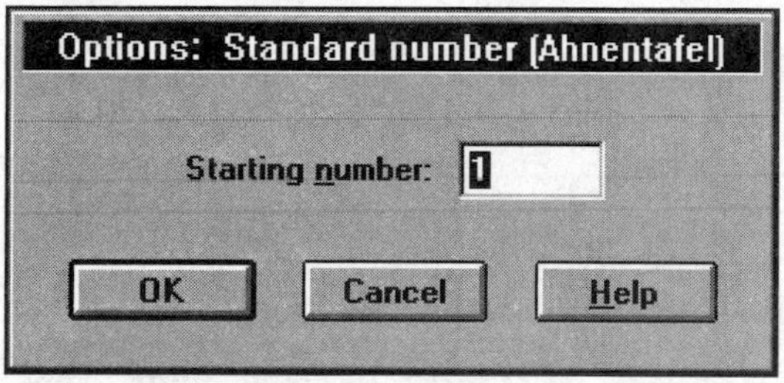

Figure 9-14. The Options: Standard Number dialog box

Special Note for Hourglass Trees & Fan Trees

Standard (Ahnentafel) numbers are unavailable for Hourglass Trees and Fan trees.

Standard Page Options

When you chose the Standard Page option in the Family Group Sheet view, Family Tree Maker displays the Options: Standard Page dialog box shown in Figure 9-15. Use the options in this box to select formatting options for this view.

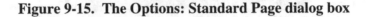

Figure 9-15. The Options: Standard Page dialog box

To select standard page options:

1. To include descriptions of fields that do not contain any information, select the **Include labels of empty fields** check box.

2. To add extra blank rows for other children, select the **Include blank row for additional children** check box.

3. To include all of an individual's spouses, select the **Include all spouses** option button. To include only the preferred spouse, select the **Include preferred spouse only** option button.

4. Click **OK** to return to the Items to Include dialog box.

Standard Page With Pictures/Objects Options

In the Family Group Sheet view, you can choose both the Picture/Object options and the Standard Page options in a single dialog box. This dialog box is called the Options: Standard Page with Pictures/Objects dialog box. For information about the options in this dialog box, see "Picture/Object Options" and "Standard Page Options" in this chapter.

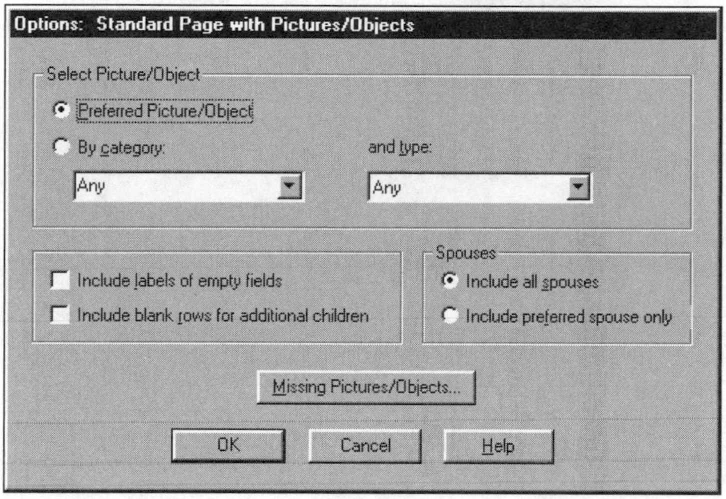

Figure 9-16. The Options: Standard Page with Pictures/Objects dialog

Custom Field Options

In trees and some other views you can choose to include the **Custom field** item. This item enables you to add up to 80 characters of text to each individual's information in the tree. Remember, what you type in this field appears as part of *every* individual's information. Word wrapping allows the text to wrap onto multiple lines if it is too long to fit on one line.

Other Options

Some fields, such as "Phone" have only a simple set of options, such as whether or not to include field labels or use the word wrapping function. Word wrapping allows the text to wrap onto multiple lines if it is too long to fit on one line. Most views have some options that fall into this category.

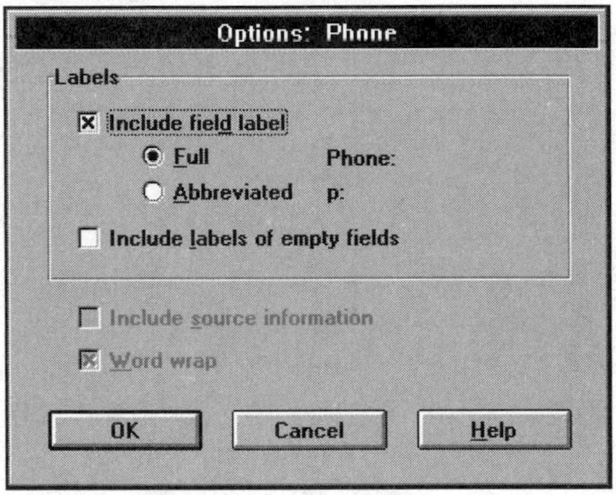

Figure 9-17. The Options: Phone dialog box

Selecting Information to Include in Your Calendar

To choose information to include in your calendar:

1. From the **Contents** menu, select **Items to Include**.

   Family Tree Maker displays the Items to Include dialog box shown in Figure 9-18.

2. Make your **Time Period** selections using the options described below.

   Year — Use the up or down arrow in this field to select a year.

   Month — Click this drop-down list and select **All** if you want to print a full year. Otherwise, select the month that you want to print.

Figure 9-18. The Items to Include for Calendar dialog box

3.   Select any of the following **People** options.

Name format — Click this drop-down list and select the format in which you want each individual's name to appear.

Use married names for female family members — Select this check box to use women's married names as last names and maiden names as middle names. Otherwise Family Tree Maker uses women's full maiden names.

Use aka if available — Select this check box if you want nicknames to appear in the calendar when they are available.

Last name all caps — Select this check box if you want to print all last names in capital letters.

Print only if still alive — Select this check box to exclude information about individuals for whom you have entered death dates or who are more than 120 years old.

4. Select either the **Birthdays**, **Anniversaries**, or **Both** option button according to the type of information you want in your calendar.

5. Select the **Include age for birthdays & years for anniversaries** check box to have Family Tree Maker calculate individuals' ages on their birthdays and the number of years they have been married on their anniversaries. This number appears next to their names. A "?" means there is no information in the associated date field. The word "est," as in "Bonnie Anderson - 85 est," means you entered an estimated date.

   Events that fall on February 29th appear on February 28th if the calendar is not for a leap year.

6. After you make your selections, click **OK**.

   Family Tree Maker returns you to the Calendar view.

Adding a Title, Footnote, or Date and Time Stamp

You can give your view a personal touch by adding a title, footnotes, page numbers, even a time and/or date stamp. The options available vary slightly from view to view, so don't be surprised if your screen varies from the one shown in this section. If you're trying to save space, you might want to skip these options altogether.

To add a title, footnote, or date/time stamp to your view:

1. From the **Contents** menu, select **Title & Footnote**.

   Family Tree Maker displays the Title & Footnote dialog box shown in Figure 9-19.

2. Select the type of **title** you want to include.

   Automatic Title — Family Tree Maker creates a title for you, such as "Ancestors of Jane Smith."

   Custom title — You create your own title by selecting this option button and typing your title in the field provided.

   Print title on every page — To include the title at the top of each page, select this check box. (Available in the Outline Descendant Tree, Report, and Scrapbook views.)

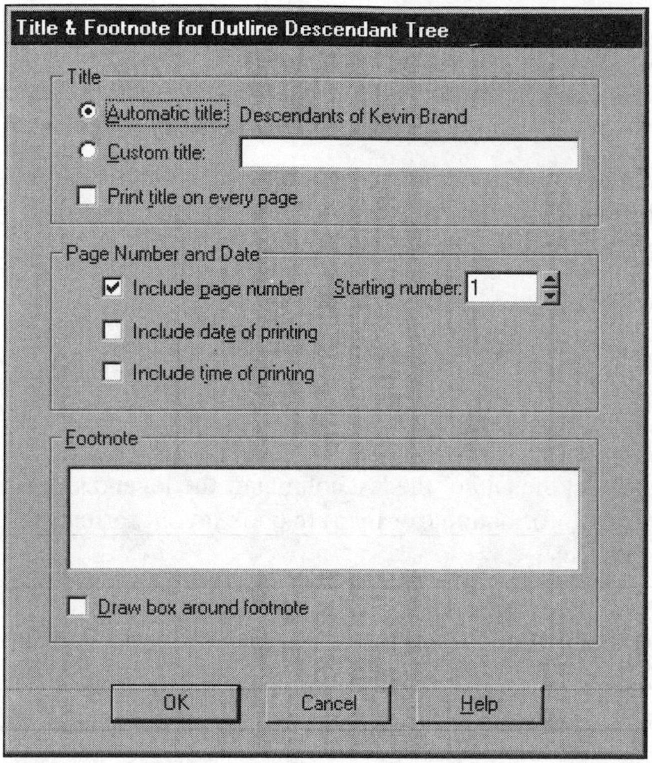

Figure 9-19. The Title & Footnote dialog box

3. To include page numbers in your view, select the **Include page number** check box and then click the up and down arrows on the **Starting number** field to change the starting page number. (Not available in Ancestor Tree, Descendant Tree, or Hourglass Tree views.)

4. To include a Date/Time Stamp in your Reports, Family Group Sheets, and Genealogy Reports, select from the following options:

   Include date of printing — Select this check box to add a date stamp to your report.

   Include time of printing — Select this check box to add a time stamp to your report.

   Note: Both date and time will appear in the lower-right corner of your printout, in the same font used for the page number.

   Date formats can be changed in the **Preferences** dialog box. For more information, see "Preferences for Dates and Measures" in Chapter 3.

5. Type a **Footnote** up to four lines long. It displays in the lower-left corner of your view. You can place a box around it by selecting the **Draw box around footnote** check box. (Not available in the Family Group Sheet, Scrapbook, or Genealogy Report views.)

   Note: In the Family Group Sheet view you can enter **Preparer Information** instead of a footnote. This information appears in the same place as a footnote.

6. After you make your selections, click **OK**.

   Family Tree Maker returns you to the selected view.

Special Note for Map Legends

Footnotes display at the end of the last column of the legend. Page number, Date, and/or Time information (for maps in book layout format) displays at the bottom of each page.

Adding Background Pictures in Trees

Family Tree Maker allows you to place your choice of graphics — from personal photos or scanned images to pre-packaged clip art — behind the text in your family trees.

Family Tree Maker has included a selection of more than 200 ClickArt™ images on the installation CD included with this program. This collection includes images from four of ClickArt's most popular categories, and you can use them to get started. You can also use images from your personal photo CDs. More comprehensive ClickArt graphics collections can be purchased online, at www.broder.com, or by dialing 1-800-223-6985 to place your order by phone. Try adding background pictures to your trees — you'll soon be creating interesting and informative keepsakes for generations to come.

To add a background picture to a currently open tree:

1. From the **Format** menu, select **Background Picture**.

   Family Tree Maker displays the Background Picture dialog box.

2. Click **Choose**.

   Family Tree Maker displays the Insert Picture dialog box.

3. Select an image from the **Insert Picture** dialog box and click **Open**.

   Family Tree Maker displays the Edit Picture dialog box.

If you don't know the location of the file that contains the picture you want to use, follow the instructions in "Finding Files" in Chapter 13.

Note: If you did not choose the option to install the ClickArt images to your hard drive when you installed Family Tree Maker, insert the installation CD now and navigate to the ClickArt folder. Look for the images with a ".**wmf**" extension.

For more information about editing your picture before selecting it as the Background Picture, see "Editing Pictures/Objects" in Chapter 8.

4. Once you are satisfied with the picture, click **OK**.

   Family Tree Maker returns you to the Background Picture dialog box. The "Display picture in background" check box is automatically checked.

5. Select one of the following **Position** options:

   Centered — Select this option to center the picture between the tree's borders.

   Tiled — Select this option to repeat the picture across the entire background until it fills the tree's borders.

6. For additional image options, select the following check boxes as desired:

   Resize picture to fit tree borders — This option controls whether the image stretches, shrinks, or maintains its original dimensions.

   Fade picture — Family Tree Maker allows you to control the density of the background image. You may enter a range from 0 to 100 percent, where 0 is the lightest, and 100 is the darkest possible.

7. Click **OK**.

   Family Tree Maker closes the Background Picture dialog box and the selected image appears as the background image in the tree.

CHOOSING OTHER DISPLAY OPTIONS

Each view has its own set of special display options. To display these special options, from the **Contents** menu, select **Options**, (or select the Options button on the side toolbar). Read the appropriate section below for descriptions of the options. Please note that not all options apply to all views.

Ancestor Tree and Hourglass Tree Options

Label columns as "Parents," "Grandparents," etc. — Column labels (Ancestor trees only) identify each generation of your tree as the parents, grandparents, great-grandparents, etc., of the primary individual. These labels appear at the top of each column and make it easy to understand the tree at a glance. When checked, rows in Hourglass trees will be labeled in both the ancestor and descendant portions of the tree. This does not apply to Fan trees.

Include duplicate ancestors each time they appear — If you have an instance of intermarriage in your family (for example, cousins marrying cousins), you have duplicate individuals in your tree. Select this check box if you want these individuals to print in your tree more than once. For Hourglass trees, this will affect only the ancestor portion.

Note: Each time a duplicated individual is listed, he or she will have a bracketed number next to his or her name, such as [1]. This makes it easier to identify the duplicated individual. If there are several individuals duplicated, the first one will be assigned [1], the second one will be assigned [2], and so on.

Include siblings of primary individual — Usually an ancestor tree doesn't include the siblings of the primary individual. Instead, it only shows the ancestors of the primary individual. However, you can select this option if you wish to include them. Even when you select this option, the siblings do not appear on Fit to Page Ancestor trees if there isn't enough space.

Include empty branches — Printing empty branches is useful when you want to collect more information about your family. You can fill out the boxes by hand and later transfer the information into your computer.

All-in-One Tree Options

Family Tree Maker allows you to choose which groups within your Family File will be displayed in the All-in-One tree view. Read the appropriate sections below for descriptions of the options.

Show unconnected step-family trees — When selected, additional marriages of a person who is not a blood relative of the primary individual (but is related by marriage) will be displayed. For example, if a sister's husband had an additional marriage that included descendants, or ancestry, then the tree for that additional marriage would be included in the All-in-One tree. When deselected, only trees that are part of the primary individual's lineage are displayed.

Show unrelated trees — When selected, trees that are not part of the primary individual's lineage in any way are displayed. For example, if two or more people in the Family File are related to each other, but to no one else, then their tree is displayed. When deselected, only trees that are part of the primary individual's lineage are displayed.

Note: Selections here also affect the "Show all generations" check box found in the **# of Generations to Show** dialog box (see "Choosing the Number of Generations to Include" in this chapter).

Show solitary, unlinked boxes — When selected, people who are not related to anyone else in the Family File (for example, persons added using the "Add Unrelated Individual" command) are displayed. Family Tree Maker places these boxes at the bottom of the tree. When deselected, people who are unrelated to anyone else in the file are not displayed.

Display siblings in order shown on Family Page — When selected, siblings are displayed from left to right on the tree, in the order they are listed on their family page. When deselected, Family Tree Maker will place them in the order that makes the best use of space.

Note: Displaying siblings in the order shown on the Family Page may result in a much larger tree. If you want to conserve paper and space, deselect this check box.

Use thicker line for primary individual's box — When selected, a thicker border is used for the primary individual's box. This makes it easier to identify the primary individual of the tree. When deselected, the primary individual's box appears as determined by the "Box, Line, & Borders" dialog box settings (see "Choosing Styles for Boxes, Lines, and Borders" in this chapter).

Note: Other views in Family Tree Maker allow you to exclude certain relationships by selecting the "Exclude this relationship from trees and Kinship" check box on the "More About Lineage" page. However, the All-in-One tree displays all individuals in the Family File, regardless of their relationship to the primary individual.

Descendant Tree and Hourglass Tree Options

Label rows as "Children," "Grandchildren," etc. — Row labels identify each generation of your tree as the children, grandchildren, great-grandchildren, etc., of the primary individual. These labels appear at the left margin of the page and make it easy to understand the tree at a glance.

Include duplicate descendants each time they appear — If you have an instance of intermarriage in your family (for example, cousins marrying cousins), you have duplicate individuals in your tree. Select this check box if you want these individuals to print in your tree more than once.

Note: Each time a duplicated individual is listed, he or she will have a bracketed number next to his or her name, such as [1]. This makes it easier to identify the duplicated individual. If there are several individuals duplicated, the first one will be assigned [1], the second one will be assigned [2], and so on.

Outline Descendant Tree Options

Print spouses — Select this check box to include descendants' spouses in your Outline Descendant tree. Each descendant's spouse appears directly beneath him or her and is marked with a plus sign (+).

Include duplicate descendants each time they appear — If you have an instance of intermarriage in your family (for example, cousins marrying cousins), you have duplicate individuals in your tree. Select this check box if you want these individuals to print in your tree more than once.

Note: Each time a duplicated individual is listed, he or she will have a bracketed number next to their name, such as [1]. This makes it easier to identify the duplicated individual. If there are several individuals duplicated, the first one will be assigned [1], the second one will be assigned [2], and so on.

Map Options

Allow location labels . . .to overlap — When there is not enough room to display all of the locations listed in the map legend without the map labels overlapping, Family Tree Maker "skips" them, and does not display them on the map, even though they still appear in the legend. Select this check box if you want Family Tree Maker to display all map labels even though they overlap.

Note: Facts with locations other than that displayed in the Map view do not appear in the legend. For example, a fact located in California will not be listed in the legend for a map of the eastern United States.

Label and Card Options

Use Name Format for — When you print labels or cards, you need to decide if you want to print one label or card for each household or for each individual. For example, if you are printing address labels for holiday cards, you probably want to print only one label per household. If you are printing name tags, however, you probably want to print one for each individual.

If you select **Individual**, Family Tree Maker uses the "Individuals" name format you selected in the Options: Name dialog box (see Figure 9-10) and prints a label or card for each individual in your list of Individuals to Include. If you select **Household**, Family Tree Maker uses the "Household" name format you selected in the Options: Name dialog box and prints a label or card for each group of individuals who share the same address. Family Tree Maker is smart enough to adjust the name format for different types of households based on your selections:

- A family, such as parents and children, that shares the same address prints on one label. For example "Mr. and Mrs. Doe and Family."

- A couple sharing the same address prints on one label. For example "Mr. and Mrs. Doe."

- A single individual with a unique address prints alone on a label. For example, "Ms. Doe."

That way, all of your labels or cards have the same basic style, but suit the type of household. The exact name format printed on your labels or cards depends on your selections in the Options: Name dialog box (Figure 9-10).

Print blank rows when fields are empty — When you select this check box, Family Tree Maker inserts a blank row in the label or card when it comes across an empty field.

Genealogy Report Options

Notes — If you've entered notes for individuals or marriages in the Notes dialog boxes, you can choose to include them in your Genealogy report. Select the **Include individual notes** check box to include the notes for individuals. Select the **Include marriage notes** check box to include the notes for marriages.

Source Information — You can choose to include source information for the facts contained in your Genealogy report. If you want the source information to appear at the end of the report for all of the items in the report, select the **Include source information as endnotes** option button. If you want the source information to appear directly after the piece of information to which it refers, select the **Include source information as inline notes** option button. If you prefer to leave the source information out of your Genealogy report, select the **Do not include source information** option button. For more details about entering source information, see "Recording Sources for Your Information" in Chapter 3.

Note: Most genealogy societies require that you include source information if you submit your family pedigree to them.

Generation Numbering — You can choose one of two different methods for numbering the generations in your Genealogy report. Select **Automatically find the oldest ancestor** if you want to begin the generation numbering from the oldest male ancestor in the primary individual's blood line. For example, if you select yourself as the primary individual for the report, and your Family File contains information going back to your father, but no further, then your father would be assigned generation number 1 and you would be assigned number 2. Since you're the primary individual, your Genealogy report would begin the generation numbering with the number 2, next to your name. Select **Assume the primary individual is the immigrant ancestor** if you would like the numbering on your report to start with "1" regardless of how many generations precede the primary individual. The previous generations (older than the primary individual) will be "numbered" A, B, C, D, etc. This is the style of numbering traditionally used for ancestors who did not immigrate to the United States.

Documented Events and Facts Options

Whom to report — You can choose to include three different groups of people in this report. To include only individuals who have at least one source entry associated with their Family Page, select **List individuals and marriages with documentation**. This option is helpful if you want to see a list of all the events you've already documented with sources. To include only individuals who have no source entry associated with their Family Page, select **List individuals with no documentation**. This option is helpful if you want to see a list of all the individuals for whom you need to enter source information. To include everyone in your Family File regardless of whether you've documented sources, select **List all individuals and marriages**.

What to report — You can choose to include three different groups of information in this report. To include only events and facts for which you've entered at least one source entry, select **List events and facts with documentation**. This option is helpful if you want to see a list of all the events you've already documented with sources. To include only events and facts that have no source entry, select **List events and facts without documentation**. This option is helpful if you want to see a list of all the events and facts that you need to verify and document. To include all events and facts in your Family File regardless of whether you've documented sources, select **List all events and facts**.

Printed format — To include the footnote version of your source entry, select **Show footnote format of documentation**. This option may not display all the information you've entered about your sources. To include all of your source information, select **Show complete documentation**.

Bibliography Report Options

Standard Bibliography — Select this option button to display source information using a traditional bibliography format.

Annotated Bibliography — Select this option button to display all the information you entered about your sources.

Include footnotes without referenced sources — Select this check box to include footnotes for source entries that did not include a source title. If you entered sources in a previous version of Family Tree Maker, your source entries will not have a title unless you enter one. To include source entries from a previous version of Family Tree Maker, select this check box.

Scrapbook Options

To change the Scrapbook display options, you must first be in Print Preview mode. To switch to Print Preview mode, select the **Scrapbook** view, and then from the **File** menu, select **Print Preview**.

Note: When you print Scrapbook pages, you may want to exclude some Pictures/Objects. For example, sound clips would appear as icons. To exclude a Picture/Object from a Scrapbook, open the More About Picture/Object dialog box (see "Recording Important Picture/Object Information" in Chapter 5) and deselect the **Include in Printed Scrapbooks** check box. In the Options for Printed Scrapbook dialog box, you can further control which Pictures/Objects print on the Scrapbook pages.

All — To print all the Pictures/Objects you marked for printing, select this option button.

By Category and Type — These fields work together to find Pictures/Objects that you assigned to a particular category and type in the More About Picture/Object dialog box. For example, if you choose the category "Birthdays" and the type "Picture," Family Tree Maker searches for Pictures/Objects that fulfill *both* requirements. However, both of the fields have an "Any" option, which, in effect, allows you to search only one of the two fields. If the category that you assigned to a Picture/Object does not appear in the "By Category" drop-down list, just type it into the field. When there is more than one Picture/Object of the category and type that you select, Family Tree Maker uses the first one that it finds.

FORMATTING TEXT

You can assign a different format to each text item in your view, including the title and footnote. For example, you might want to make the names in your tree bold, or make them larger than the other information in each box. You can also format the text that appears in a map area or legend.

Note: In addition, Family Tree Maker offers 40 different colors that can be used to further customize your trees, timelines, and reports. Just click the drop-down list wherever color options are available and make your selections.

To format text in your view:

1. From the **Format** menu, select **Text Font, Style, & Size**.

   Family Tree Maker displays the Text Font, Style, & Size dialog box shown in Figure 9-20. You can also format text from the Items to Include dialog box (see "Selecting Information to Include" in this chapter). In that case, select the item in the list on the right that you want to format, then click **Font**.

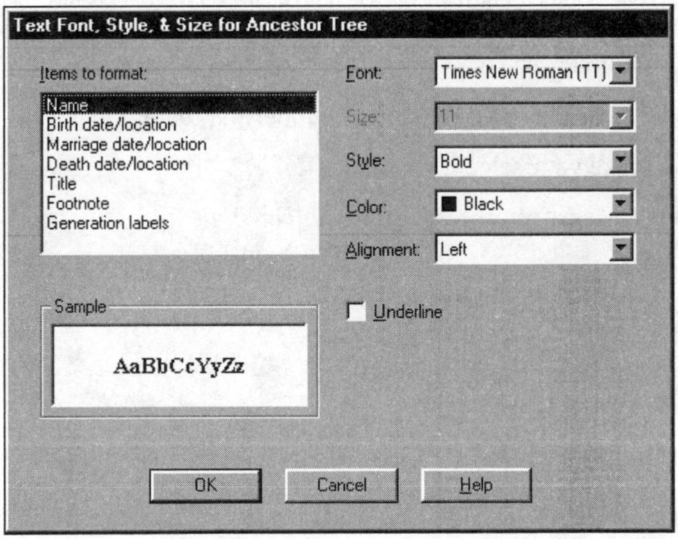

Figure 9-20. The Text Font, Style, & Size for Ancestor Tree dialog box

2. In the **Items to format** list on the left, select an item that you want to format, such as **Name**.

3. Select any of the following formatting options for the item you selected in step 2. Notice that the "Sample" field shows a sample of your formatted text.

   Font — Click this drop-down list to display a list of fonts and then select the name of the font you want.

   Size — Click this drop-down list to display a list of text sizes and then select the size you want.

   Note: The Size option is not available for Fit to Page trees and Family Group Sheets using the LDS format option. Family Tree Maker automatically sizes text in these views.

   Style — Click this drop-down list to display a list of text styles, such as "Bold" or "Italic," and then select the style you want.

   Color — Click this drop-down list to display a list of colors and then select the color you want. If you do not have a color printer, the colors print in shades of gray.

   Alignment — Click this drop-down list to display a list of text alignments, such as "Center," and then select the alignment you want. This option is not available in all views.

   Underline — Select this check box to underline the item.

4. After you make your selections, click **OK**.

   Family Tree Maker returns you to the selected view.

CHOOSING STYLES FOR BOXES, LINES, AND BORDERS

You can add finishing touches to your view by choosing various box, line, and border styles to most Family Tree Maker views. The options available vary from view to view, but you'll use the same methods to customize your Ancestor Tree, Descendant Tree, Hourglass Tree, All-in-One Tree, Calendar, and Labels/Cards views.

Box styles and colors can be changed to differentiate between genders and generations and lines between two selected individuals — even non-natural parental relationships — can be highlighted for easy identification. Spend some time exploring the following dialog box so you can add variety and creativity to your views.

To select box, line, and border styles:

1. From the **Format** menu, select **Box, Line, & Border Styles**.

    Family Tree Maker displays the dialog box shown in Figure 9-21.

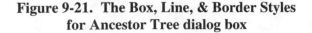

**Figure 9-21. The Box, Line, & Border Styles
for Ancestor Tree dialog box**

2. Switch to either the **Boxes**, **Lines**, or **Borders** tab if the one you want is not showing, and make your selections by clicking the buttons with the pictures of the boxes, lines, and borders that you like. Each view can have only one box, line, and border style.

3. To use the color options, click the color drop-down list for each element — **Outline**, **Fill**, and **Shadow** — and then select a color from the list.

   With a color printer, your view prints in color. With a black-and-white printer, the view prints in shades of gray.

4. After you make your selections, click **OK**.

   Family Tree Maker returns you to the selected view.

Highlighting the Relationships between Two Individuals

To make it easier to see certain relationships within a tree view, Family Tree Maker allows you to choose any two individuals, and then color-code the path that connects them.

1. From the **Format** menu of your tree view, select **Box, Line, & Border Styles**.

   Family Tree Maker displays the Box, Line, & Border Styles dialog box.

2. Select the **Lines** tab.

   Choose from the following options:

   Highlight the relationship between — Select this check box if you want to color code the line that connects two specific individuals in your tree.

   Change — Click either of these two buttons to display the "Index of Individuals" dialog box. Then select a different name from the list and click **OK** to highlight the relationship between the selected individuals.

   Note: In the All-in-One tree, it is possible that you could select two individuals who have no actual relationship between them. Family Tree Maker will tell you if no relationship exists between the selected individuals.

Line color — Click the down arrow to display a drop-down list of 40 color choices.

3. After you make your selections, click **OK**.

    Family Tree Maker returns you to the selected view.

Showing Non-natural Parental Relationships

You can also make it easy to see non-natural parent/child relationships, such as stepchildren.

1. From the **Format** menu of your tree view, select **Box, Line, & Border Styles**.

    Family Tree Maker displays the Box, Line, & Border Styles dialog box.

2. Select the **Lines** tab.

3. Select the **Show non-natural parent/child relationships with dashed lines** check box.

    Family Tree Maker will automatically draw a dashed line to differentiate any non-natural relationships in the tree.

    Note: Parental relationships are specified on an individual's "More About Lineage" page. For more information, see "Entering Nicknames, Titles, and Parental Relationship Information" in Chapter 5.

4. Click **OK**.

    Family Tree Maker returns you to the selected view.

Changing the Width of Boxes and Pictures/Objects

Setting a maximum box and Picture/Object width can help you fit more information on a single page. This option is not available in all views.

To set a maximum width for your boxes and Pictures/Objects:

1. From the **Format** menu, select **Maximum Width for Each Box & Picture/Object**, or in the Labels/Cards view, select **Maximum Width for Picture/Object**.

   Family Tree Maker displays the Maximum Width for Each Box & Picture/Object dialog box.

2. Enter a number in the **Maximum box width** field. To get a smaller tree, enter a smaller number. You can enter any width between .1 and 99.99 inches.

3. Enter a number in the **Maximum Picture/Object width** field. To allow the Pictures/Objects to fit inside their boxes, this number must be slightly smaller than the number in the "Maximum box width" field. If the maximum Picture/Object width is too large, Family Tree Maker displays an error message.

4. After you make your selections, click **OK**.

   Family Tree Maker returns you to the selected view.

   Note: If necessary, Family Tree Maker abbreviates your information to make it fit in the box size you specify. For example, if you select a very long name format, but a small maximum box width, Family Tree Maker may have to change the name format to a smaller one.

CHOOSING COLUMN WIDTHS AND SPACING IN REPORTS

Normally, Family Tree Maker chooses appropriate widths for each column in a report and spaces the columns .25" apart. However, if you prefer, you can choose your own column widths and spacing. These options are available for the following report formats: Medical Information, Addresses, Marriage, Birthdays of Living Individuals, and Parentage.

To select column widths and spacing in reports:

1. From the **Format** menu, select **Maximum Width**.

   Family Tree Maker displays the Maximum Width for Each Column dialog box.

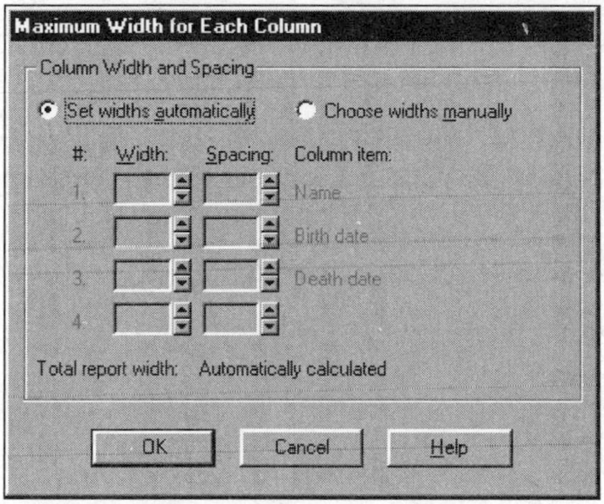

Figure 9-22. The Maximum Width for Each Column dialog box

The numbers on the left side of the dialog box correspond to the columns in your report; "1" is the leftmost column. The "Column item" on the right side of the dialog box tells you what information each column contains. If a column that you want to edit is not visible, use the scroll bar on the left side of the dialog box to scroll through the list.

2. Select one of the following options.

   Set widths automatically — Select this option button if you prefer to have Family Tree Maker choose the widths and spacing for each column. In this case, none of the other options in the dialog box are available.

   Choose widths manually — Select this option button if you prefer to manually set the widths and spacing for each column.

3. If you selected the "Choose widths manually" option in step 2, you can change the following settings.

   Width — Click either the up or down arrow to change how much space a column occupies. If you choose a width that is too narrow for the text in the column, Family Tree Maker tries to abbreviate the text. If the abbreviated text does not fit, it truncates the text.

   Spacing — Click either the up or down arrow to change the distance between a column and the column to the right of it.

   Total report width — This field shows the width of your entire report with the current column widths and spacing selections. To change these numbers, change the numbers in the "Width" and "Spacing" fields.

4. After you make your selections, click **OK**.

   Family Tree Maker returns you to the Report view.

SORTING INFORMATION

For labels and cards, reports, and timelines you can select the order in which the names appear. You can also select the order in which Pictures/Objects are arranged in Scrapbooks. Instructions for using this feature begin below. This feature works slightly differently for different documents, so be sure also to read the special note for the document that you are creating:

To sort your information:

1. From the **Format** menu, select **Sort**.

   Family Tree Maker displays the Sort dialog box.

2. Select the option button for the type of sorting you prefer.

3. After you make your selection, click **OK**.

   Family Tree Maker returns you to the selected view.

Special Note for Labels and Cards, Reports, and Timelines

If you want the individuals to print in the order in which you added them to the group in the Individuals to Include dialog box (see Figure 9-3), select **Don't Sort Individuals**. This is especially useful for printing individuals in an Ancestor or Descendant order.

Special Note for Scrapbooks

When you sort information in the Scrapbook view, it affects only the Scrapbook that is currently open.

Special Note for Custom Reports

Family Tree Maker allows a two-level sort when creating Custom reports. This is helpful because it allows you to choose how you want Family Tree Maker to resolve any ties in the sorting order.

To sort information for a Custom report:

1. From the **Format** menu, select **Sort Report**.

    Family Tree Maker displays the Sort Report dialog box.

2. Click the **Sort by** drop-down list and then select the category you want to use for the first order of sorting.

3. Select the **Order** option button for the type of sorting you prefer, either Ascending (A to Z or 1 to 10) or Descending (Z to A, or 10 to 1).

4. If you want to choose how Family Tree Maker will sort any ties, repeat steps 2 and 3 for the **Then by** section.

5. After you make your selections, click **OK**,

    Family Tree Maker returns you to the selected view.

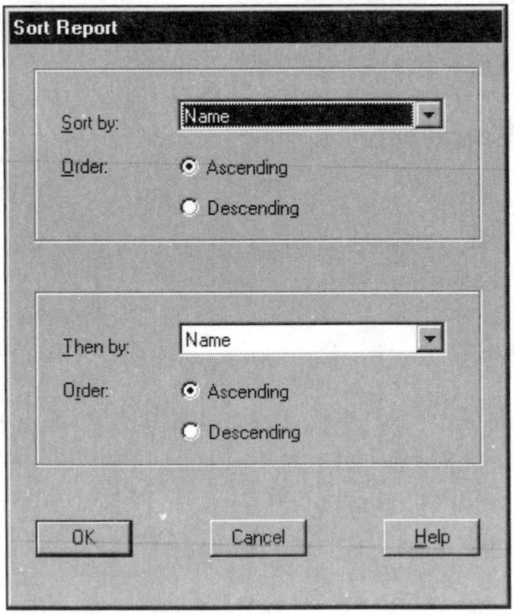

Figure 9-23. The Sort Report dialog box

Chapter 10

PRINTING YOUR FAMILY INFORMATION

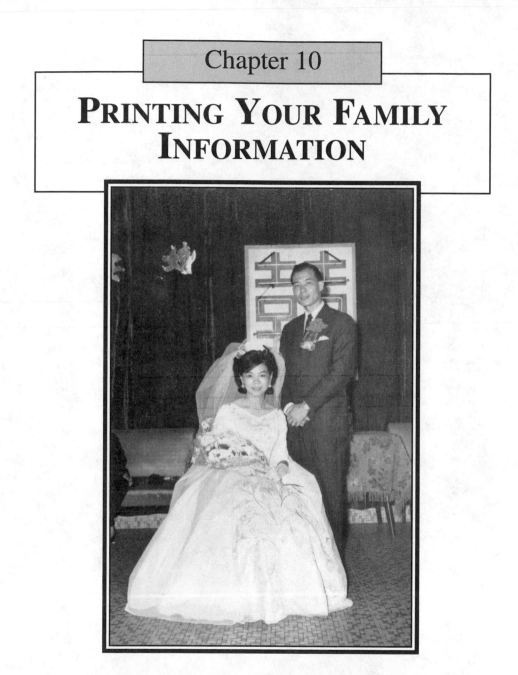

James Lee and Regina Gee sit (and stand) proud on their wedding day in
Hong Kong, China, in August 1964. Their daughter, Brenda Lee, is an
Assistant Product Manager in the Banner Blue Division.

PRINTING YOUR FAMILY INFORMATION

There are three main steps to printing your family information. First, you select and display the view for the document that you want to print (see Chapter 8). Second, you customize the view so that it looks the way you want (see Chapter 9). Third, you print your finished document. It's really quite simple, and this chapter will guide you along the way.

In the first part of this chapter, we explain how to set your printer options. Then we show you how to print a single document, followed by how to print a batch of documents.

SETTING YOUR PRINTER OPTIONS

Normally, you won't have to change your printer settings because Family Tree Maker uses the same settings as your other Windows programs. When you do change your printer settings, you are changing them for a specific view, not for all views. For example, if you change the printer settings while you're in the Ancestor Tree view, every Ancestor tree that you print afterwards will use those same settings until you change them again. If however, you print a Descendant tree, it will not use these settings. If you want your Descendant trees to use the same settings as your Ancestor trees, you need to switch to the Descendant Tree view and change the settings.

With the Print Setup dialog box, you can control the following printer settings: page margins, paper size and orientation, paper source, whether or not your pages overlap, which printer prints your documents, and other printer-specific options. Changing these settings can affect the number of pages needed to print a multiple page document.

Note: Family Tree Maker will use the printer settings you choose for your view when you include that view in a book (see Chapter 11, "Creating Family Books"). If you plan to create a book, you probably want to keep the paper size and orientation the same for all the views in the book — unless you plan to include pages that fold out of the book, or you want the reader to turn the book sideways to read the page.

To change your printer settings:

1. Make sure you're in the view you want to print.

2. From the **File** menu, select **Print Setup**. Or, if you're in the Print dialog box, click **Setup**.

   Family Tree Maker displays the Print Setup dialog box.

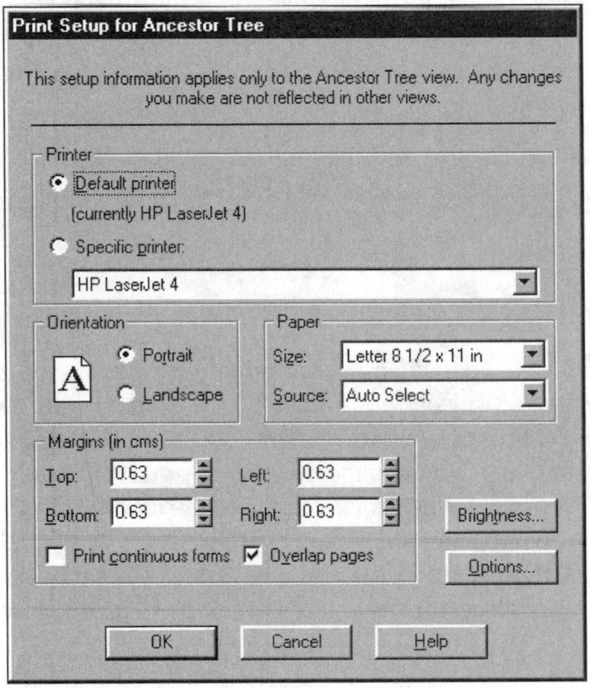

Figure 10-1. The Print Setup dialog box

3. Select the **Printer** you want to use.

   Default printer —The default printer is the printer you normally use with your other Windows programs. You choose the default printer in the Windows Control Panel. To use this printer, select this option button.

   Specific printer — If you wish to use a different printer, select this option button and select a printer from the list.

   Note: If the printer you wish to use is not shown in the "Specific printer" drop-down list, then you need to install that printer's driver. Consult your Microsoft Windows User's Guide for information about installing printer drivers.

4. Select the **Orientation** you want to use.

   Portrait — To print your document with the short edge of the paper at the bottom (as a letter normally prints) select this option button.

   Landscape — To print your document with the long edge of the paper at the bottom (sideways), select this option button.

   Note: Ancestor trees usually take fewer pages in portrait orientation and Descendant trees usually take fewer pages in landscape orientation. This option may not be available for all printers.

5. Select the **Paper** you want to use.

   Size — Click the drop-down list to choose a paper size.

   Source — Click the drop-down list to choose the paper tray.

6. Select the **Margins** settings you want to use.

   Top, Bottom, Left, Right — Click the arrows next to these fields to change the margins on your pages.

   Print continuous forms — If your printer uses a continuous sheet of paper, you can select this check box to print across the perforations in your paper. This does not apply to printers that automatically use single sheets of paper (such as laser printers).

   Overlap pages — If you want information on the edge of one page to be repeated on the edge of the next page so that it's easier to tape pages together, select this check box.

7. If you are printing a color or grayscale images, you can click **Brightness** to adjust the color level for all the Picture/Objects in the current view. Drag the slider in the Brightness dialog box to the left to decrease the brightness or to the right to increase the brightness, and then click **OK** to return to the Print Setup dialog box. (These settings do not affect black-and-white images.)

8. If desired, you can click **Options** to display the Options dialog box. The options available to you depend on your printer. Make your selections from this dialog box, and then click **OK** to return to the Print Setup dialog box.

9. After you make your selections, click **OK**.

   Family Tree Maker returns you to the current view.

PRINTING A SINGLE DOCUMENT

After you finish customizing your tree, report, or other view, you're ready to print. In some cases you may need to adjust the size of your tree before you print it. To do this, see "Controlling the Size of Your Tree" in this chapter before you print. You can also print large trees on oversized paper, see "Printing an Extra-Large Tree on a Large Piece of Paper" in this chapter.

To print your document:

1. Make sure you're in the view you want to print.

    Note: If you go to an individual's Notes dialog box, only the Notes will print. If you go to any of the other More About dialog boxes, you can print the information in all of the More About dialog boxes for that individual, except Notes.

2. Turn on your printer.

3. From the **File** menu, select **Print**.

    Family Tree Maker displays the Print dialog box.

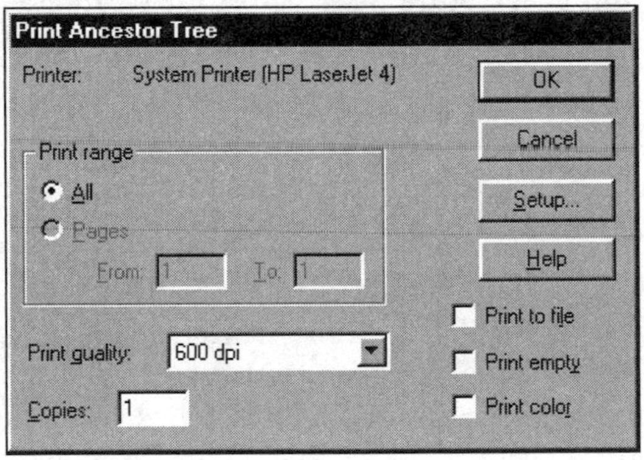

Figure 10-2. The Print dialog box

4. Select from the options described below.

   Note: You can also control items such as paper orientation, paper size, margins, and which printer prints your document. If you want to change any of these items, see "Setting Your Printer Options" in this chapter.

   Print range — Use this option to select the pages you want to print. To print all of the pages, select the **All** option button. To print a range of pages, type the page number of the first page that you want to print in the **From** field and type the page number of the last page you want to print in the **To** field. If you want to print only one page, type the number of that page in both the **From** and **To** fields.

   Print quality — Use this option to select the quality of your printed materials. The higher the print quality you choose, the darker and sharper your printed materials will be. However, items printed in high print quality also take longer to print. If your printer does not support different print qualities, this option will not be available to you.

   Copies — Type the number of copies that you want to print.

   Print to file — If you want to print your document to a file and send it to your printer at a later time, select this check box. This option is especially useful if you want to print your document on a printer or plotter owned by someone who doesn't have Family Tree Maker. When you print, Family Tree Maker will ask for an "Output File Name." For instructions on printing to a file, see "Printing an Extra-Large Tree on a Large Piece of Paper" in this chapter.

   Print empty — Select this check box to print an empty document. For example, you might want to print an empty Ancestor tree to use as a form while you're collecting information about your family. (This option is not available in all views.)

   Print color — If you have a color printer, select this check box to print in color. If you have a black-and-white printer, select this check box to print in grayscale. Deselect this check box if you want to print in black and white.

5. After you make your selections, click **OK**.

   Family Tree Maker prints your document.

Controlling the Size of Your Tree

You can print a tree that contains as much information as you want, as long as it doesn't exceed 800,000 x 800,000 inches! Family Tree Maker prints the tree on as many pages as it takes to show the information and then you can piece the pages together to create one large, beautiful tree.

Note: Some printers limit the size of the document. So check your printer manual for information about the limitations of your printer. In general, it's a good idea to limit a print run to 50 pages. If your tree or report is larger, try printing in smaller batches or "ranges" (see "Print range" on the previous page).

If you want to reduce the size of your tree, experiment with the options in the following two tables. To print a large tree on one sheet of paper, see "Printing an Extra-Large Tree on a Large Piece of Paper" in this chapter.

If Your Tree is Too Tall...

- Choose a date format that includes the date and location on the same line or only prints the date. (See "Selecting Information to Include" in Chapter 9.)

- Include fewer generations in a single tree. Print the tree using the Book layout option, or print multiple trees instead. (See "Choosing the Number of Generations to Include" in Chapter 9.)

- Print fewer items for each individual. (See "Selecting Information to Include" in Chapter 9.)

- Omit borders, titles, and footnotes. (See "Choosing Styles for Boxes, Lines, and Borders," and "Adding a Title and Footnote," both in Chapter 9.)

- Don't use column labels. (See "Choosing Other Display Options" in Chapter 9.)

- Omit empty branches and the siblings of the primary individual. (See "Choosing Other Display Options" in Chapter 9.)

- Select a different font type, a smaller font size, and select "Regular" as the font style. (See "Formatting Text" in Chapter 9.)

- Try switching page orientation to "Portrait." (See "Setting Your Printer Options" in this chapter.)

- For Outline Descendant trees, reduce the number of rows per individual. (See "Outline Descendant Trees" in Chapter 8.)

Figure 10-3. Making tall trees shorter

If Your Tree is Too Wide...

- Choose a date format that separates the date and location onto two lines or only prints the date. (See "Selecting Information to Include" in Chapter 9.)

- Choose a name format that omits middle names, or turn on the text wrap option. (See "Selecting Information to Include" in Chapter 9.)

- Include fewer generations in a single tree. Print multiple trees instead. (See "Choosing the Number of Generations to Include" in Chapter 9.)

- If you print "Fact" fields, shorten the information entered in them (see "Entering Facts" in Chapter 5.)

- Omit borders, titles, and footnotes. (See "Choosing Styles for Boxes, Lines, and Tree Borders," and "Adding a Title and Footnote," both in Chapter 9.)

- Don't use row labels. (See "Choosing Other Display Options" in Chapter 9.)

- Omit empty branches and the siblings of the primary individual. (See "Choosing Other Display Options" in Chapter 8.)

- Select a different font type, a smaller font size, and select "Regular" as the font style. (See "Formatting Text" in Chapter 9.)

- Reduce the width of the boxes with the Maximum Box and Picture/Object Width option. (See "Changing the Width of Boxes and Picture/Objects" in Chapter 9.)

- Try switching the page orientation to "Landscape." (See "Setting Your Printer Options" in this chapter.)

- For Outline Descendant trees, select the "Always One Page Wide" option. (See "Outline Descendant Trees" in Chapter 8.)

Figure 10-4. Making wide trees narrower

Printing an Extra-Large Tree on a Large Piece of Paper

If you have access to a large plotter, you can print your tree on a poster-size piece of paper. To find a plotter, check with engineering and architectural service bureaus in your area. When you find a service bureau that can plot your tree, follow the instructions below:

1. Find out what type of plotter they use and then install that plotter's printer driver in Windows on your computer. For information about installing printer drivers, see your Microsoft Windows User's Guide.

2. Change the settings in Family Tree Maker's Print Setup dialog box so that they match the plotter on which you will print your tree (see "Setting Your Printer Options" in this chapter).

3. Create your tree.

4. Put a floppy disk in your disk drive.

5. From the **File** menu, select **Print**.

    Family Tree Maker displays the Print dialog box.

6. Select the **Print to file** check box. Also select **Print color** if you want the tree to print in color or grayscale and have selected colors while creating your tree.

7. Click **OK**.

    Family Tree Maker displays the Print to File dialog box.

8. Click the **Drives** drop-down list and select the drive where your floppy disk is located, and then in the **File name** field, type a name for the tree.

    For example, if your floppy disk is in drive a:\ and you are creating a tree for the Hess family, you would type something like `A:\hesstree.prn`

9. Click **OK**.

    Family Tree Maker prints your tree to your diskette.

You can now take the floppy disk to a service bureau to print your tree. The service bureau does not need a copy of Family Tree Maker to print your tree. They will simply copy the file directly to their plotter. For example, if their plotter is connected to LPT 1 and your floppy disk is in drive a:\ of their computer, they would type `copy/b A:hesstree.prn LPT1:`

PRINTING A BATCH OF DOCUMENTS

When you want to print a lot of information, you can create a family book or use the Batch Print command. It is available for Family Pages, Family Group Sheets, Notes dialog boxes, and Scrapbooks. The Batch Print command lets you specify what document you want to print, what information it contains, and also provides page-numbering functions.

Note: If you want to print an index for your document(s), use the Books feature instead (see Chapter 11, "Creating Family Books").

Batch printing also comes in handy when you're doing family research. For example, you can batch print a set of Family Group Sheets to send to relatives so that they can verify the information. After printing the Family Group Sheets, you can easily switch to the Labels/Cards view and print mailing labels for the same group of people! This is because Family Tree Maker saves the group that you select in the Individuals to Include dialog box until you change it again.

To select and set up a document for batch printing:

1. Go to the view you want to print.

   Note: If you are printing Scrapbooks or Notes, place the cursor on an individual or a marriage (depending on what you want to print) before you select the view.

2. Use the commands on the **Contents** and **Format** menus to set up the document for printing.

   For example, use the **Items to Include** command to choose which items you want to include in all of the documents. You also might want to format the text in the documents using the **Text Font, Style, & Size** command (see Chapter 9, "Customizing Your Family Information," for specific instructions).

3. Check your printer settings, for items such as paper orientation, paper size, and margins. If you want to change any of these items, see "Setting Your Printer Options" at the beginning of this chapter.

4. From the **File** menu, select **Batch Print**.

   Family Tree Maker displays the Individuals to Include dialog box. In this dialog box you can create a group of individuals to include in the batch print. However, you first need to select a printing order.

5. Click **Sort order**.

    Family Tree Maker displays the Sort Batch Print dialog box.

Figure 10-5. The Sort Batch Print dialog box

6. Select the option button for the type of sorting you prefer and
    then click **OK**.

    If you want individuals to print in the order in which you choose them
    in the Individuals to Include dialog box, select **Don't sort individuals**.

    Family Tree Maker returns you to the Individuals to Include dialog box.
    Now you can choose the individuals to print.

7. Select individuals and add them to, or remove them from, the list on
    the right, and then click **OK**. For specific instructions, see "Selecting
    Individuals to Include" in Chapter 9.

    Family Tree Maker displays the Batch Print dialog box.

8. Make your selections in the Batch Print dialog box. Each option is described below.

Print quality — Use this option to select the quality of your printed materials. The higher the print quality you choose, the darker and sharper your printed materials will be. However, items printed in high print quality also take longer to print. If your printer does not support different print qualities, this option will not be available to you.

Page Numbering — Select the option button for the page numbering scheme that you want for your batch print. If you choose to have page numbers, enter a starting number in the **Starting number** field.

Print color — If you have a color printer, select this check box to print in color. If you have a black-and-white printer, select this check box to print in grayscale. Deselect this check box if you just want to print in black and white. If you have a black-and-white printer, color Pictures/Objects will always print in grayscale.

9. After you make your selections, click **OK**.

Family Tree Maker starts printing the batch.

Printing to RTF (formatted text)

Family Tree Maker lets you copy Genealogy reports, Bibliography reports, and Documented Events reports to the Clipboard and then paste them into word processing applications in a **RTF** (formatted text) format.

While in your choice of Report view:

1. From the **Edit** menu, select **Copy Report**.

Family Tree Maker copies your report to the clipboard.

2. Paste into your word processor and then edit and/or print your report.

Printing a Batch of Documents
in Ancestor or Descendant Order

With batch printing, you can choose which individuals to include in the documents and how to number the pages. You can also select the order in which the documents print — alphabetically, chronologically, or virtually any order you want. Many people like to print their documents in Ancestor or Descendant order, so we're including general instructions here:

To batch print in Ancestor or Descendant order:

1. When you first open the Individuals to Include dialog box, click
    ⟪ (Remove all).

2. Click **Sort order**.

    Family Tree Maker displays the Sort Batch Print dialog box.

3. Select the **Don't sort individuals** option button and then click **OK**.

    Family Tree Maker returns to the Individuals to Include dialog box.

4. Select the individual whose ancestors or descendants you want to add and then click either **Ancestor** or **Descendant**.

5. Click **OK**.

    Family Tree Maker displays the Batch Print dialog box.

6. Make your selections in the Batch Print dialog box.

7. Click **OK**.

    Family Tree Maker begins printing.

Chapter 11

CREATING FAMILY BOOKS

Otis Terpening, the first President of the Michigan Lumberjack Association, posing for a statue honoring the group. His great-grandson, Michael Bilby, served in the United States Army before becoming Controller for the Banner Blue Division of Brøderbund.

CREATING FAMILY BOOKS

In addition to printing trees, reports and other views as individual documents, Family Tree Maker provides everything you need to create a professional looking book. You can include a Title Page, Dedication, Preface, Foreword, Table of Contents, Chapters, Bibliography, and an Index. What's even better is that you can use the views you've already created. Just imagine combining family trees and reports, with a nice Title Page, a Table of Contents, and Scrapbook pictures to create a unique family album that your relatives will cherish for generations.

Using Family Tree Maker's built-in word processor, you can add stories, family anecdotes, chapter introductions, and other descriptive text to complete your book.

CREATING A NEW BOOK

Family Tree Maker lets you create as many as 32 books per Family File with over 500 items in each book. For example, you can create a book about the history of your father's side of the family and a separate book about the history of your mother's side of the family. Or, you can create one book for your family and another book for your spouse's family. The possibilities are endless!

To create a new book:

1. From the **Books** menu, select **New Book**.

    Family Tree Maker displays the New Book dialog box.

2. In the **Book title** field, type the title of the book you want to create.

3. In the **Author** field, type your name, or the name of the person who did most of the genealogical research.

4. Click **OK**.

    Family Tree Maker displays the Books view shown in Figure 11-1 on the next page. Now, you are ready to add items to your book.

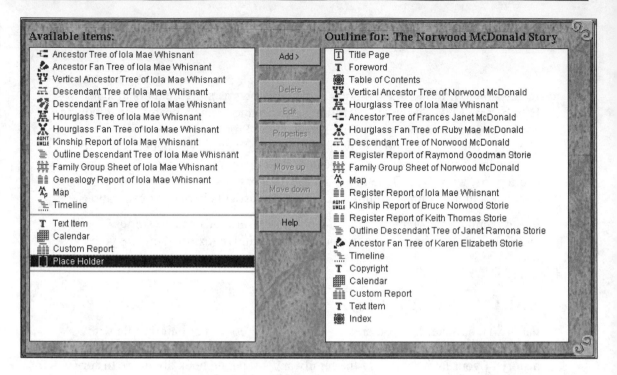

Figure 11-1. The Books view

ALL ABOUT BOOK OUTLINES

The Books view, shown in Figure 11-1, is where you create the outline for your book by collecting trees, reports, and other items and adding them to your book. The "Available items" list on the left side of the screen shows the items you can include in your book, and the "Outline for" list on the right side of the screen shows the items you've already added to your book.

When you create a book, you can add many different types of items. These items fall into three basic categories:

"Standard" book items — Standard book items enable you to add trees, both specific reports, calendars, a Table of Contents, and an Index to your book. In addition to these items, Family Tree Maker automatically adds a Title Page to every book. For details, see "Adding Trees, Reports and Calendars to Your Book" and "Adding a Table of Contents and Index to Your Book," both in this chapter.

Text items — Text items enable you to add your own text and Scrapbook pictures to your book. You can start with a blank page, or choose from a variety of templates. For details, see "Creating Text Items in Your Book" and "Adding Pictures to Your Book," both in this chapter.

Custom book items — Custom book items enable you to add reports that are not part of the standard book item list to your book. For example, if you want to add a bibliography to your book, you can create a Custom book item for a Bibliography report, and then add it to your book. For details, see "Creating Custom Book Items" in this chapter.

Notice that the top portion of the "Available items" list includes standard book items based on the current primary individual. The middle section of the list includes text items and standard book items that do not change when you change the primary individual, such as a Calendar, Table of Contents, and Index. The lower portion of the list includes any custom book items you've created

ADDING TREES, REPORTS, AND CALENDARS TO YOUR BOOK

When you add trees, reports, and calendars to your book, you are actually adding a copy of the view to your book. This means that you can customize these reports using the options on the Contents and Format menus, and Family Tree Maker remembers the options you choose for your book. Don't worry, Family Tree Maker still updates the information in your book items when you change the information in your Family File.

To add items to your book:

1. From the **Available items** list on the left, select the tree, report, or calendar you want to add.

    Trees and reports — Select any of the following trees or reports based on the current primary individual: Ancestor or Ancestor Fan trees, Descendant or Descendant Fan trees, Hourglass or Hourglass Fan trees, Outline Descendant trees, Kinship reports, Family Group Sheets, Genealogy Reports, and Timelines. (If necessary, change the primary individual using the Index of Individuals, just like you do in any other view.)

    Note: When you select Genealogy Report, Family Tree Maker prompts you to choose the report format.

Calendar — Select this item to add a calendar to your book.

Custom Report — Select this item to add your most recent Custom Report to your book.

2. Click **Add,** or from the **Books** menu, select **Add New Book Item**.

   Family Tree Maker adds the item you selected to the bottom of the **Outline for** list on the right (directly above the Index if you have one).

   Alternatively, you can add an item by dragging it from the "Available items" list on the left to the "Outline for" list on the right. Using this method, you can position the item anywhere in the "Outline for" list between the Title Page and the Index.

3. Repeat steps 1 and 2 to add other items for this individual to your book.

   Don't worry about the order of the items for now, you can rearrange them later as described in "Arranging Items in Your Book" in this chapter. If you decide to add the same item to different places in your book, you can rename one of the items so you can tell them apart (see "Changing Item Names and Other Properties" in this chapter).

   After you finish adding items for this individual, you can change the primary individual and add items for another individual.

4. From the **View** menu, select **Index of Individuals**.

   Family Tree Maker displays the Index of Individuals dialog box.

5. Select the name of the person you want as the new primary individual and then click **OK**.

   Family Tree Maker returns to the Books view and displays a list of trees and reports based on the new primary individual.

6. Repeat steps 1 through 3 to add items for this individual.

7. Repeat steps 4 through 6 to add items for all the individuals you want to include in your book.

Remember, you can stop working on your book at any time. Family Tree Maker automatically saves all of your changes. When you're ready to work on your book again, you can pick up right where you left off (see "Opening an Existing Book" in this chapter).

ADDING A TABLE OF CONTENTS
AND INDEX TO YOUR BOOK

Family Tree Maker helps you create a professional-looking book with a Table of Contents and an Index. If you choose to include these items in your book, Family Tree Maker will do all the work for you. It generates the lists for you, formats the layout, and maintains the page numbers and other information as you create your book.

To add a Table of Contents and Index to your book:

1. Select **Table of Contents** in the **Available items** list.

2. Click **Add,** or from the **Books** menu, select **Add New Book Item**.

    Family Tree Maker adds the Table of Contents to the bottom of the "Outline for" list and removes it from the "Available items" list — since you can have only one Table of Contents per book.

3. Select **Index** in the **Available items** list.

4. Click **Add,** or from the **Books** menu, select **Add New Book Item**.

    Family Tree Maker adds the Index to the bottom of the "Outline for" list and removes it from the "Available items" list — since you can have only one Index per book.

5. From the **Contents** menu, select **Options**.

    Family Tree Maker displays the "Options for Book Index" dialog box.

6. Select from the following options:

    Columns — Select either **One**, **Two**, or **Three** columns per page as the formatting for your index.

    Group first names under — Select this check box to group together the individuals who share a common surname. Deselect this check box to display each name as a separate "surname, first name" listing, as in previous versions.

    Display index letters — Select this check box to display the appropriate letter of the alphabet at the beginning of each alphabetical section.

7. After you've made your selections, click **OK**.

    Family Tree Maker displays the Index according to your preferences.

Changing the Number of Columns in an Index

Family Tree Maker allows you to choose whether to have one, two, or three columns per page in your index.

To choose the number of columns in your book index:

1. Select **Index** in the **Outline for** list.

2. Click **Edit**.

   Family Tree Maker displays the Index.

3. From the **Contents** menu, select **Options**.

4. Select the number of columns you want.

   One column — The book Index will be formatted using only one column per page.

   Two columns — The book Index will be formatted using two columns per page.

   Three columns — The book Index will be formatted using three columns per page.

5. Click **OK**.

CREATING TEXT ITEMS IN YOUR BOOK

The Text Item window is a mini-word processor that you can use to add text and pictures to your book. For example, you can include a family member's favorite recipes, jokes, or even a short biography. You can also insert images from your Family Tree Maker Scrapbook pages to make your book more informative and exciting to read (see "Adding Pictures to Your Book" in this chapter for details).

You will find many similarities between the word processing features in the Notes dialog box and the New Text Items window, including the ability to spell check your text. In addition, the New Text Items window has a convenient toolbar, more powerful formatting capabilities, and it can include Scrapbook pictures as well as text. If you're not familiar with word processors, you'll find it helpful to do "Part II: The More About Dialog Boxes," in Chapter 2, before you create text items. For help checking the spelling, see "Using Spell Check" in Chapter 6.

To create a text item in your book:

1. In the Books view, select **Text Item** in the **Available items** list.

2. Click **Add,** or from the **Books** menu, select **Add New Book Item**. Alternatively, you can add an item by dragging it from the list on the eft to the list on the right.

   Family Tree Maker displays the Add text item dialog box.

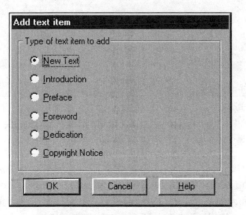

Figure 11-2. The Add text item dialog box

3. Select the option button that best describes the type of text item you want to create and click **OK**.

Family Tree Maker adds the text item you selected to the "Outline for" list on the right.

4. In the **Outline for** list, select the text item you just added and then click **Edit**. Alternatively, you can double-click the item.

Family Tree Maker displays a text item window. The name of the window is based on the type of text item you selected in step 3.

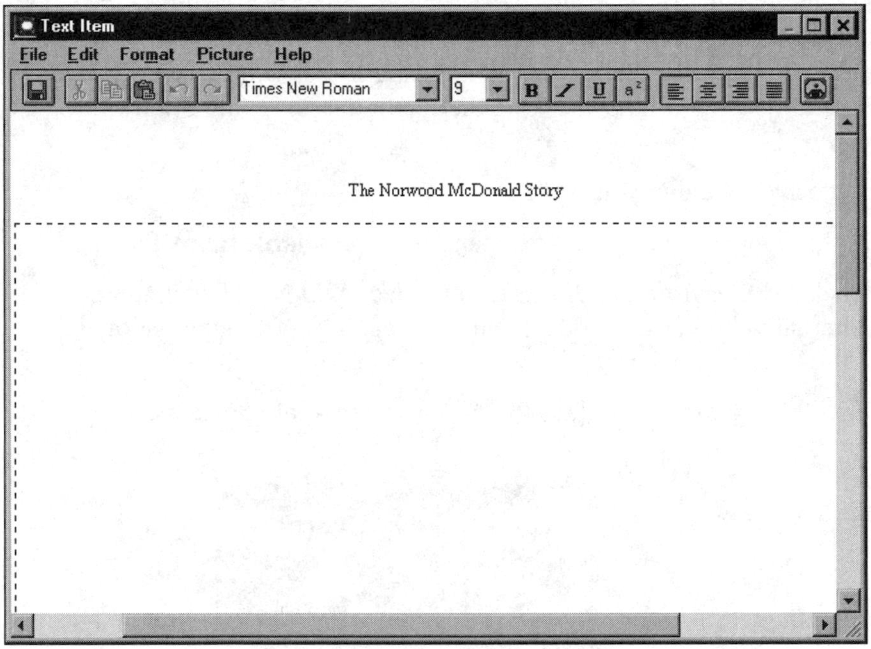

Figure 11-3. An example of a "regular" Text Item window

5. Type the text you want to include in your book. You can use the same keys you use to move around the Notes dialog box (see "Moving Around the Notes Dialog Box," in Chapter 5, for details).

Family Tree Maker displays your text in the Text Item window.

6. Use any of the following toolbar buttons and menu commands to enhance your text.

To do this...	Click this...	Or from the menu bar select...
Delete the selected text and place it on the Clipboard	✂	**Edit**, then **Cut**.
Copy the selected text to the Clipboard	📋	**Edit**, then **Copy**.
Insert text from the Clipboard at the cursor's location	📋	**Edit**, then **Paste**.
Undo the previous action	↰	**Edit**, then **Undo**.
Reverse the last Undo action	↱	**Edit**, then **Redo**.
Change the font selection	Times New Roman ▾	**Format**, then **Font**.
Change the font size	9 ▾	**Format**, then **Size**.
Make the selected text bold	**B**	**Format**, then **Style**, then **Bold**.
Make the selected text italic	*I*	**Format**, then **Style**, then **Italic**.
Underline the selected text	U̲	**Format**, then **Style**, then **Underline**.
Make the selected text superscript	a^2	**Format**, then **Style**, then **Superscript**.
Return formatted text to normal text		**Format**, then **Style**, then **Plain**.
Align the text on the left side of the page	≣	**Format**, then **Alignment**, then **Left Aligned**.
Center the text on the page	≣	**Format**, then **Alignment**, then **Centered**.
Align the text on the right side of the page	≣	**Format**, then **Alignment**, then **Right Aligned**.
Arrange the text into uniform blocks	≣	**Format**, then **Alignment**, then **Fully Justified**.
Insert a Scrapbook picture in your text	🖼	**Picture**, then **Insert from Scrapbook**.

Figure 11-4. A summary of Text Item window editing commands

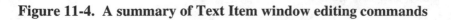

Moving or Copying Text from One Text Item to Another

As you create your book, you may find that you want to repeat the same text in more than one part of your book. For example, you may want to include a story about grandmother Smith delivering grandchild Jones in both the Smith and Jones chapters of your book. Or, you may decide that you want to move the story from the Smith chapter to the Jones chapter. Family Tree Maker lets you do just that.

Note: You cannot copy pictures from one text item to another. You can only copy text.

To move or copy sections of text from one text item to another.

1. In the **Outline for** list, select the text item that contains the text you want to move or copy, and then click **Edit**.

   Family Tree Maker displays the text item you selected.

2. Highlight the text you want to move or copy.

   To highlight text with a mouse, place the mouse pointer in front of the first character you want to select. Press and hold the primary mouse button while you drag the mouse until the last character you want to select is highlighted. Then, release the mouse button.

3. From the **Edit** menu, select **Cut** if you wish to move the text or select **Copy** if you wish to copy this text to another new text item.

   Family Tree Maker copies the highlighted text to the Clipboard.

4. From the **File** menu, select **Close**.

   Family Tree Maker closes the current text item.

5. In the **Outline for** list, select the text item where you want to insert the text, and then click **Edit**.

   Family Tree Maker displays the text item you selected.

6. Position your cursor where you want to insert the text. If you want the new text to *replace* existing text, highlight the existing text.

7. From the **Edit** menu, select **Paste**.

   Family Tree Maker pastes the text from the Clipboard into this text item and repositions any existing text, if necessary. Since the Clipboard is not erased until you use the Copy or Cut command again, you can paste the same text as many times as you like.

Copying Text from Another Windows Program into a Text Item

If you have family stories in another Windows program, you can copy them to the Clipboard and then paste them into a text item in your book.

Note: When you copy formatted text from another program, it appears as "Plain" unformatted text in Family Tree Maker (see Figure 11-4 to format the text).

To transfer text from another Windows program into Family Tree Maker:

1. In the other Windows program, copy the text to the Clipboard.

    If you need assistance with this, please consult the manual that came with the other program.

2. In Family Tree Maker, open the book where you want to add the text, and go to the text item where you want to place the information.

3. Position your cursor where you want to insert the text. If you want to use the new text to *replace* a section of existing text, highlight that section of text.

4. From the **Edit** menu, select **Paste**.

    Family Tree Maker inserts the text in your text item. If the text contained pictures in the other program, the pictures will not appear in the text item.

Since the Clipboard is not erased until you use the Copy or Cut command again, you can paste the same information as many times as you like.

Adding Page Breaks to Text Items

The **Text Item** editor shows each page exactly as it will print. The margins of each page appear as dashed, non-printing lines.

To **Add** a page break to a Text Item:

*   From the Text Item editor's **Edit** menu, select **Insert Page Break**

There are two ways to **Delete** a page break:

*   Position the cursor immediately *after* the page break (at the beginning of the following page) and press the **Backspace** key

*   Position the cursor immediately *before* the page break (at the end of the previous page) and press the **Delete** key

Saving a Text Item

As you add or change a text item, you should save it periodically. From the **File** menu, select **Save**. Family Tree Maker saves your text item as part of the current book. If you forget to save a text item, Family Tree Maker will prompt you to save it when you close the Text Item window.

Printing a Text Item

Just as you can control the printer settings for your trees, reports, and other views, you can control the printer setting for each of your text items. To change the printer settings for a text item, you must be in the Text Item window with that item displayed on the screen. For specific instructions, see "Setting Your Printer Options" in Chapter 10.

You can also print your text items independently from the rest of the book. This enables you to see if the text item looks the way you want it to look before you print the entire book. For specific instructions, see "Printing a Single Document" in Chapter 10.

Note: Although the book header and footer do not appear in the text item window, they will appear when you print a text item.

Closing a Text Item Window

After you finish creating or changing your text item, you will need to close the Text Item window to return to the Books view. From the **File** menu, select **Close**. If you haven't saved all of your changes, Family Tree Maker asks if you want to save them, and then returns to the Books view.

Sharing Book Text Items on the Internet

After you create a book, you may wish to use the Internet as a way to share your research with others via the World Family Tree. We encourage you to contribute, but you should be aware that Book Text Items, such as stories or recollections of family members or other personal matters are *not* made private with the "Privatize" feature (see "Protecting your Privacy" in Chapter 12). Please use caution and sensitivity when sharing books with others.

ADDING PICTURES TO YOUR BOOK

You can add pictures to your book by inserting pictures from your Family Tree Maker Scrapbooks into a text item. You must first add the picture to a Scrapbook in order to use it in a book. For information about adding pictures to a Scrapbook, see "Scrapbooks: Inserting Items" in Chapter 5.

To make it easier for you to place your picture where you want it, we recommend that you add your text before you add your picture.

Note: Although you can use the Copy and Paste commands to add pictures to your text items, we recommend that you avoid using this method because it stores an extra copy of the picture on your hard disk, and increases the size of your Family File. This requires additional disk space and may also affect Family Tree Maker's performance. To avoid this situation, follow the steps described in this section.

To add a Scrapbook picture to a text item:

1. In the **Books** view, go to the text item where you want to place the picture. See "Creating Text Items in Your Book" in this chapter.

2. In the Text Item window, position the cursor where you want to insert the picture.

3. From the **Picture** menu, select **Insert from Scrapbook**.

   Family Tree Maker displays the Individuals with Scrapbook Pictures dialog box.

   Note: The list of individuals with Scrapbook pictures also includes individuals with Marriage Scrapbook pictures.

4. In the **Name** field, type the name of the individual whose Scrapbook contains the picture you want to insert, or select the person's name from the list, and then click **OK**.

   Family Tree Maker displays the Insert Scrapbook Picture dialog box.

5. From the **Available pictures** list, select the picture you want to add.

   Note: If the picture you want isn't in the list, or if you selected the wrong Scrapbook, click **Select new individual** to select a different Scrapbook.

   Family Tree Maker displays the picture you select in the Preview area. If the picture does not display, select the **Preview Picture** check box.

6. If the picture has a caption and you want to display it in your Book, select the **Display Caption with Picture** check box.

    Note: The caption will not display in the Preview screen, but will appear in the text item.

7. Click **OK** to add the picture to the text item.

    Family Tree Maker displays the picture in the text item. At this point you have the following options:

    Move the picture — Select the picture and drag it to another location in the text item. If you don't like the new location, click the **Undo** toolbar button or from the **Edit** menu, select **Undo**.

    Size the picture — Select the picture, and then from the **Picture** menu, select **Size Picture**. In the Size Picture dialog box, type the new picture size in the **Picture width** field, and then click **OK**.

    Save the picture in the text item — Click the **Save** toolbar button, or from the **File** menu, select **Save**.

    Delete the picture from the text item — Select the picture, and then from the **Picture** menu, select **Delete Picture**.

    Add/edit a caption — Select the picture, and then from the **Picture** menu, select More About. In the More About Picture/Object dialog box, type or edit the caption in the caption field and then click **OK**.

    Close the text item window — Click the **Close** toolbar button or from the **File** menu, select **Close**.

Text Style Preferences for Captions

Text style preference settings for captions affect all captions in the current Book item, but not for other items in the Book. For example, you could have caption styles for pictures in one text item, which are different from the captions in other text items.

To edit the text style in a caption:

1. From the **Text Item** window, select the **Picture** menu.

2. From the **Picture** menu, select **Caption Text Style**.

    Family Tree Maker displays the "Text Font, Style, & Size" dialog box.

    Note: The caption is "linked" to the Scrapbook, so any changes you make to the caption in the Book view's "Text Item" window will also appear in the Scrapbook, and vice versa.

3. After you make your selections, click **OK**.

Family Tree Maker returns you to the Text Item window.

CREATING CUSTOM BOOK ITEMS

You may want to add reports to your book other than the standard book items listed in the Books view. You can do this by creating custom book items. For example, you may want to add a Map, Timeline, or Hourglass tree to your book, or perhaps you want to include a Custom Report with just your living relatives, specific items, a special font, and your favorite border. That's a lot of work! With the Create Custom Book Items command, you can save these settings to use again and again. You can even create other reports in the same view and return to the custom book item you saved earlier.

The usefulness of the Create Custom Book Items command doesn't end here. After you create a custom book item, you can add it to any book you create. You can also display your custom book items outside the Books view to create multiple versions of the same view.

To create a custom book item:

1. Select a view as described in "Displaying Your Family Information" in Chapter 8.

2. From the **Books** menu, select **Create Custom Book Item**.

Family Tree Maker displays the Create Custom Book Item dialog box.

3. In the **Please give a name to this new book item** field, accept the name Family Tree Maker suggests, or type a name for the item.

4. Click **OK** to save the item.

Family Tree Maker returns to the view you selected in step 1 and displays the name of the custom book item in the Title bar. The custom book item now appears on the list of "Available items" in all books.

At this point you have the following options:

Move to another view — From the **View** menu, select the view you want to display.

Exit "book item mode" and stay in the same view — From the **Books** menu, select **Leave Book Item**.

Copy, delete, or open a custom book item — See the next section, "Working with Custom Book Items."

Working with Custom Book Items

Once you've created a custom book item, you can return to it at any time. The steps below describe how to copy, delete, or modify a custom book item.

To copy, delete, or modify a custom book item:

1. From the **Books** menu, select **Custom Book Item**.

   Family Tree Maker displays the Custom Book Item dialog box.

2. In the drop-down list at the top of the dialog box, select **List of all Custom Book Items** to choose from a list of all your custom book items, or select a book to choose from a list of the items in a specific book.

3. Select the custom book item you want to copy, delete, or modify.

4. Click one of the following buttons:

   Copy — Displays the Copy Book Item dialog box. Type a name for the copy in the **Please give a name to this new book item** field, or accept the name that Family Tree Maker suggests. The item name must be unique. Family Tree Maker copies the selected item with the new name. Now, to quickly create a second item that is slightly different from the first, open the copy and change it.

   Delete — Removes the selected item from your Family File.

   Open — Displays the selected item. You can simply look at the view, or change it and Family Tree Maker will prompt you to save your changes.

5. If you selected **Copy** or **Delete** in the previous step, click **OK** to accept your changes and return to the previous view.

Adding a Bibliography to Your Book

You can use the Create Custom Book Item command to add a bibliography to your book. First, you customize a Bibliography report to include only the individuals in your book. Then, you can create a custom book item for this report and add it to your book.

To add a bibliography to your book:

1. From the **View** menu, select **Report**.

    Family Tree Maker displays the Report view.

2. From the **Format** menu, select **Report Format**.

    Family Tree Maker displays the Report Format dialog box.

3. Select **Bibliography** from the list and then click **OK**.

    Family Tree Maker displays the Bibliography report. This report includes source information for all the individuals in your Family File. If your book does not include information about all of the individuals in your Family File, you will need to customize the report to show only the individuals included in your book (see "Selecting Individuals to Include" in Chapter 9).

4. From the **Books** menu, select **Create Custom Book Item**.

    Family Tree Maker displays the Create Custom Book Item dialog box.

5. In the **Please give a name to this new book item** field, accept the name Family Tree Maker suggests, or type another name for the item.

6. Click **OK** to save the item.

    Family Tree Maker returns to the Report view.

7. Open the book to which you want to add the bibliography. See "Opening an Existing Book" in this chapter.

    Family Tree Maker opens the book you selected.

8. From the **Available items** list, select the bibliography report (it will have the name you entered in step 5), and then click **Add**.

    Family Tree Maker adds a copy of the bibliography to your book.

Adding Personal Items to Books

Family Tree Maker automatically keeps track of your Book's page numbers, but it can also reserve page numbers for external items — those special items you may want to add personally — after the book is printed. By using a Place Holder in your Book, Family Tree Maker will account for the necessary pages, leaving gaps in the number sequence exactly where you want them. After printing your Book, you can insert your external item's pages in the reserved Place Holder location.

To add an external item Place Holder to a Book:

1. From the **Book** view, select **Place Holder** in the Available items list, and then click **Add**.

   Family Tree Maker displays the "Place Holder Properties" dialog box.

2. You have your choice of the following options:

   Item name — Family Tree Maker displays the title "Place Holder" but you can enter any title you wish.

   # of pages — Use the up and down arrows (or type the number) to indicate the number of pages you wish to "reserve" for the item you will add later.

   This item begins a Chapter — Select this check box if you want the item to mark the beginning of a new chapter (and its title to appear in the Table of Contents as a chapter heading). If deselected, the item will appear as a section within a chapter.

   Start this item on odd numbered page — Select this check box if you want Family Tree Maker to place the selected item on a right hand page, preceded by a blank page. In most books, the first page of a chapter appears on a right-hand page with an odd page number.

3. Click **OK** to apply the settings and close the dialog box.

   Family Tree Maker adds the Place Holder item to the Table of Contents.

   Note: Click **Move Up** or **Move Down** to move the item up or down in the Outline list.

ADDING A HEADER AND FOOTER TO YOUR BOOK

Most printed books include a header and footer on each page. The header appears at the very top of the page and the footer appears at the very bottom of the page. For example, in this manual, the header is a double line and the footer is a single line with the chapter number or title and the page number. If you choose, you can include a header and footer in your book.

You can also choose to include or exclude the header or footer for a particular item in your book (see "Changing Item Names and Other Properties," in this chapter, for instructions).

To add a header and footer:

1. If you aren't in the Books view, open the book you want to change. See "Opening an Existing Book" in this chapter.

2. From the **Books** menu, select **Book Header, Footer**.

   Family Tree Maker displays the Book Header and Footer dialog box.

3. From the **Header** drop-down list, select a header format. If you do not want a header, select **None** from the list.

4. From the **Footer** drop-down list, select a footer format. If you do not want a footer, select **None** from the list.

5. To adjust the header and footer text style, click **Set Font**, select the text styles you want to use, and then click **OK**.

   For specific instructions on using this dialog box, see "Formatting Text" in Chapter 9.

6. After you make your selections, click **OK**.

   Family Tree Maker returns to the Books view.

CHANGING ITEM NAMES AND OTHER PROPERTIES

Family Tree Maker automatically assigns a title to each item in your book. If you like, you can change the name of an item as well as other item properties.

To change an item's name and other properties:

1. In the **Outline for** list, select the item you want to change.

2. Click **Properties**, or from the **Books** menu, select **Book Item Properties**.

   Family Tree Maker displays the Book Item Properties dialog box for the item you selected.

3. If desired, change any of the options listed below:

   Item Name — The name that appears at the top of the page associated with the selected item. To change the item's name, type the new name in this field.

   This item begins a Chapter — Indicates whether the selected item is a chapter heading or a section within a chapter. Select this check box to make this item a chapter heading. To make this item a section within a chapter, do not select this check box.

   Start this item on odd numbered page — In most books, the first page of a chapter appears on a right-hand page with an odd page number. If the selected item begins a chapter and you want Family Tree Maker to place it on a right-hand page, select this check box.

   Include the header in this item — In many books the header does not appear on certain pages, such as the Title Page or Dedication. To omit the header on the selected item's pages, leave this check box blank. If you want the header to appear on the selected item's pages, select this check box.

   Include the footer in this item — In many books the footer does not appear on certain pages, such as the Title Page or Dedication. To omit the footer on the selected item's pages, leave this check box blank. If you want the footer to appear on the selected item's pages, select this check box.

4. After you make your selections, click **OK**.

   Family Tree Maker returns to the Books view.

ARRANGING ITEMS IN YOUR BOOK

After you create your book outline, you can put the book items in any order you like. The only restrictions are that the Title Page must be the first item in your book, and the Index must be the last item (if you include one).

To arrange the items in your book:

1. In the **Outline for** list, select the item you want to move.

2. Click **Move up** or **Move down** to move the item up or down.

   Family Tree Maker moves the item up or down one row each time you click one of the Move buttons.

   Alternatively, you can use your mouse to drag an item to another position provided it is after the Title Page and before the Index.

3. Repeat steps 1 and 2 to move other items in your book.

CUSTOMIZING ITEMS IN YOUR BOOK

After you create your book outline, you can customize the book items to suit your taste. For example, you can change the information and formatting options in your trees and reports. Keep in mind that a well-designed book maintains a consistent look and feel throughout the book. For example, all the titles should use the same text styles and all the body text should use the same text styles (which may be different from the title styles).

Note: If you included a custom book item in your book and you customize it using the steps below, the changes you make will appear only in your book. The original custom book item remains unchanged. Likewise, if you edit the custom book item, as described in "Working with Custom Book Items" in this chapter, those changes will not appear in your book.

To customize the items in your book:

1. In the **Outline for** list, select the item you want to customize.

2. Click **Edit**, or from the **Book** menu, select **Edit Book Item**.

   Family Tree Maker displays the item you selected.

3. Customize the selected item as described below:

Trees and reports — Customize the content and format of your tree or report as described in Chapter 9, "Customizing Your Family Information."

Text Items — Add, change, or format text as described in "Creating Text Items in Your Book" in this chapter.

4. From the **View** menu, select **Books**.

Family Tree Maker returns to the Books view.

COPYING ITEMS TO ANOTHER BOOK

If you decide to create more than one book, you may want to include some items in another book. You can save time by copying items from one book to another book. When you copy an item, you create a custom book item based on an existing book item.

To copy an item to another book:

1. Open the book containing the item(s) you want to copy (see "Opening an Existing Book" in this chapter).

Family Tree Maker opens the book you selected.

2. In the **Outline for** list, select the item you want to copy.

Family Tree Maker highlights the item.

3. Drag the item to the **Available items** list.

Family Tree Maker copies the item to the custom book items portion of the Available items list. Repeat steps 2 and 3 to copy other items.

4. Open the book to which you want to add the item(s).

Family Tree Maker opens the book you selected and the copied item appears in the custom book items portion of the Available items list.

5. In the **Available items** list, select the custom book item you copied from the other book, and then click **Add**.

Family Tree Maker adds the item to the current book.

DELETING ITEMS FROM YOUR BOOK

If you decide you no longer want an item in your book, you can remove it.

To delete an item:

1. In the **Outline for** list, select the item you want to delete.

2. Click **Delete**.

   Family Tree Maker displays a dialog box asking you to confirm that you want to delete this item from your book.

3. To delete the item, click **Yes**. To keep the item, click **No**.

   Family Tree Maker returns to the Books view and the item you deleted no longer appears in the "Outline for" list.

CHANGING BOOK PROPERTIES

You can use the Book Properties dialog box to change the book title, author and page numbering.

To change the book properties:

1. From the **Books** menu, select **Book Properties**.

   Family Tree Maker displays the Book Properties dialog box.

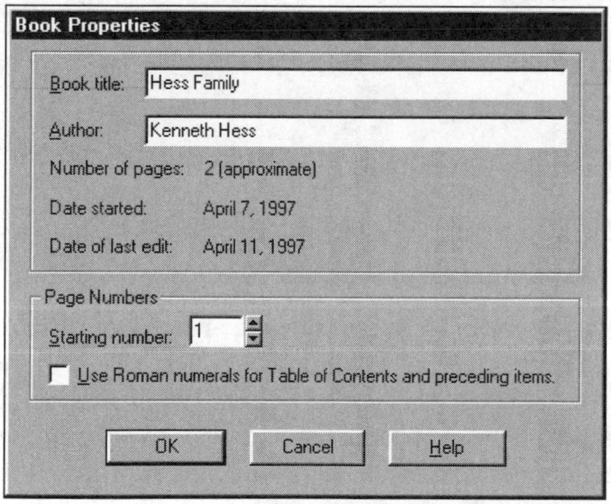

Figure 11-5. The Book Properties dialog box

2. Change any of the items described below.

Book title — The name of your book. To change the name, type the new name in this field.

Author — The name of the person who did most of the family research. In most cases, this will be your name.

Starting number — This determines the page number that will appear on the first page of your book. In most cases this number will be "1." To change this number, click the arrows in this field, or type a number.

Use Roman numerals for Table of Contents and preceding items — Many books use Roman numeral page numbers for pages that precede the Table of Contents. To use this format, select this check box.

3. Click **OK**.

Family Tree Maker returns to the Books view.

PRINTING YOUR BOOK

After you create your book outline, arrange the book items in the order you want them to appear, add a header and footer (optional), and adjust the item and book properties, you are ready to print your book.

When you print a book, Family Tree Maker uses the printer settings you chose for the individual items in your book. If you need to change the printer settings for a particular item in your book, follow the instructions in "Changing the Printer Settings for an Item in Your Book" in this chapter.

To print your book:

1. From the **File** menu, select **Print Book**.

Family Tree Maker displays the Print Book dialog box.

2. Select from the printing options described below:

Print range — Use this option to select the pages you want to print. To print all of the pages, select the **All** option button. To print just one book item, select the **Selected item** option button. To print a range of pages, type the page number of the first page that you want to print in the **From** field and type the page number of the last page you want to print in the **To** field. If you want to print only one page, type the number of that page in both the **From** and **To** fields.

Print color — If you have a color printer, select this check box to print in color. If you have a black-and-white printer, select this check box to print in grayscale. Deselect this check box if you want to print in black and white.

Print to File — If you want to print your book to a file and send it to your printer at a later time, select this check box. This option is especially useful if you want to print your book on a printer owned by someone who doesn't have Family Tree Maker. When you print, Family Tree Maker will ask for an "Output File Name." For instructions on copying the file to a printer, see "Printing an Extra Large Tree on a Large Piece of Paper" in Chapter 10.

Mirror Margins — Select this option button if you want the left and right margins you have set for each book item to "flip" on alternating pages. This allows you to have a larger margin on the "inside" edge if you want to copy the pages back to back. See "Changing the Printer Settings for an Item in Your Book," in this chapter, for information on how to set your margins properly for this feature.

Copies — Type the number of copies that you want to print.

3. Click **OK** when you are done making your selections.

Family Tree Maker prints your book.

Changing the Printer Settings for an Item in Your Book

To change the printer settings for an item in your book:

1. From the Books view, select the item you want to change in the "Outline for" list on the right.

2. Click **Edit**.

    Family Tree Maker displays the item you selected.

3. From the **File** menu, select **Print Setup**.

    Family Tree Maker displays the Print Setup dialog box.

4. Change the printer settings and then click **OK**. See "Setting Your Printer Options," in Chapter 10, for specific instructions.

    Note: If you'd like all of the odd-numbered pages of your book to have a larger left margin and all of the even-numbered pages to have a larger right margin, Family Tree Maker can do that for you automatically. Simply set the left margin for every book item larger than the right margin. Then when you print the book, select the **Mirror Margins** check box in the Print dialog box. This is especially useful if you plan to have the pages of your book photo copied back to back and bound.

OPENING AN EXISTING BOOK

After you create a book you can add to it or change it at any time.

To open an existing book:

1. From the **Books** menu, select **Open Book**.

    Family Tree Maker displays the Open Book dialog box.

2. Select the name of the book you want to open.

3. Click **OK**.

    Family Tree Maker displays the Books view for the book you selected.

DELETING A BOOK

In the event that you decide you no longer want a particular book, you can delete it from your Family File. When you delete a book you also remove everything in the outline for this book.

Note: If your book includes any custom book items, deleting a book will not remove these items from the rest of your Family File. When you delete a book, Family Tree Maker removes only the copy of the item you placed in that particular book outline.

To delete a book:

1. From the **Books** menu, select **Delete Book**.

    Family Tree Maker displays the Delete Book dialog box.

2. Select the name of the book you want to delete.

3. Click **Delete**.

    Family Tree Maker displays a dialog box asking you to confirm this action.

4. To delete the book, click **Yes**, to keep the book, click **No**.

    Family Tree Maker returns to the Books view and the book you deleted no longer appears in the list of Books available to open.

Chapter 12

SHARING YOUR FAMILY INFORMATION

Already in hot water at less than a year old, Bruce Storie enjoys a
reflective moment in his grandmother's basin/spa. Pictured here
in Valdese, North Carolina, he found his way westward and is now the
Technical Writer for Family Tree Maker.

SHARING YOUR FAMILY INFORMATION

Information sharing is an important aspect of the genealogy community. Just as Family Tree Maker helps you organize and research your family history, it also helps you share information with other family history enthusiasts.

This chapter shows you how to share information by participating in the World Family Tree Project, by exporting a branch of your family tree to share with family members using Family Tree Maker or another genealogy program, and by publishing information on the Internet.

THE WORLD FAMILY TREE PROJECT

Brøderbund is inviting all Family Tree Maker customers to participate in a remarkable genealogical opportunity — the World Family Tree™ Project. In 1995, the World Family Tree Project was started in response to our customers' many requests for a way to share their research with the ever-growing Family Tree Maker community. We invested in the equipment and know-how needed to compile all of those family trees. The result is a massive CD database, consisting of thousands of family trees and millions of individuals that is constantly growing!

Participating in the World Family Tree Project is important because it can help you, and others, advance your research. When you add your family tree to the World Family Tree Project, other family history enthusiasts can study it to see if there is a connection between your family tree and theirs. By making it easier than ever to discover these connections, the World Family Tree Project is contributing to many research breakthroughs and reunions between distant relatives.

You can use the multiple-volume World Family Tree CD collection to further your research, too! Imagine uncovering generations of new information about your family without even leaving your computer — you can do that when you find just one shared ancestor among the millions of records available. Now that the individuals in the World Family Tree Project are listed in the FamilyFinder Index, you can put the World Family Tree CDs to work for you right away.

Details of Participation

As you consider adding your family information to the World Family Tree Project, there are some important issues to think about. The following sections should answer some of your questions.

Benefits of Sharing Your Family File

The genealogy community is based on sharing — the more people share their family information with each other, the better the results for everyone. By participating in the World Family Tree Project you can do the following:

- Extend your family tree when others who share your ancestry locate your family tree.

- Help others who are searching for information that you have.

- Protect your family history data from loss or damage. Your family tree becomes part of a readily-accessible database, to be archived at the Library of Congress in Washington, D.C.

- Preserve your family history data so your descendants can access it. What a wonderful gift for future generations!

Protecting Your Privacy

If you have already imported or downloaded information from the World Family Tree, you have seen fields that display only the word "Private." While we encourage contribution to the World Family Tree — it's a great way to share information with family members and others around the world — it also raises the issue of how to protect the privacy of those family members who are still living.

Family Tree Maker allows you to automatically keep information about living individuals private, thus preventing this information from being accidentally printed, copied, or uploaded onto the Internet.

Note: A word of caution. Book Text Items, such as stories or recollections of family members or other personal matters are *not* made private with this feature. Please use caution and sensitivity when sharing Books with others.

When your tree becomes available on a World Family Tree CD, only the names, genders, and family links of living individuals will be published. We replace other information about living individuals with the word "Private."

When you send in your file, don't forget to include your name and address. If you wish, you can also include your email address and phone number. Although we do not publish this information with the CD, it will be made available to World Family Tree CD users who want to contact you through the Contributor Information Service on the Family Tree Maker Online Web site. We urge you to let us know if your address changes so that the Contributor Information Service is always up-to-date.

To use the Privatization feature:

1. From the **File** menu, select **Preferences,** then from the drop-down list, select **Privatize**.

   Family Tree Maker displays the "Privatize Information" dialog box.

2. Select the **Privatize** check box if you want Family Tree Maker to "hide" information on living individuals. The information made private includes Birth, Death, and Marriage facts, as well as additional items found in the "More About" dialog boxes, such as Facts, Medical, and Notes.

3. After you make your selections, click **OK**.

   Family Tree Maker returns you to your current view. As an added indication that you have selected to display text as Private, Family Tree Maker changes the background color of the family page to green.

   Note: Before uploading to the World Family Tree, Family Tree Maker must first process your complete, original file. However, the information on living individuals will be maintained as "Private."

Once selected, privatized text is active whenever you copy/export, upload or print within Family Tree Maker. When privatized, your file will become "read-only." However, you can deselect the Privatized mode at any time in the original Family File by returning to the Preferences dialog box.

Ensuring the Quality of the World Family Tree

We realize that much of the information in your family tree was probably collected by speaking with relatives. For this reason, we do not expect complete documentation of your family information. However, if you did get your information from sources outside of your family, we encourage you to record those sources in Family Tree Maker's source-citation fields (see "Recording Sources for Your Information" in Chapter 3). If you are not sure how to document your sources, see "Documenting Your Sources" in the Genealogy "How-To" Guide that comes with your Family Tree Maker program (see "The How-To Guide" in Chapter 1). You can also check the genealogy books at your local library, or ask a local genealogy society for more information.

We also understand that the potential for data errors exists, even in the most carefully researched family tree. Family Tree Maker can help you find possible errors (see "Checking Your File for Errors" in Chapter 6), but it's still up to you to correct the mistakes. Remember to research carefully and to avoid contributing confusing or misleading information.

By the same token, when you use the World Family Tree CDs, you should recognize that it is meant to be a research tool, not a source of completely error-free data. The genealogical information on World Family Tree CDs was contributed by genealogy enthusiasts like you, and has not been verified by Brøderbund. *Verify all information before adding it to your own collection of family information.*

Finally, we ask that you do not contribute information that infringes on copyrights, invades the privacy of others, or is defamatory or profane in any way. Again, please review the contents of your file carefully before you contribute it.

Your Participation is Important

Most genealogists feel that their work is never done, but we assure you that your family tree is valuable to other researchers, no matter how large or small, complete or incomplete. Whether you have just begun your family tree or you are looking to add more branches, contributing your family tree immediately is important to the creation of the World Family Tree Project.

We are sincerely excited about creating these opportunities for our customers. But don't forget, none of this can happen unless you contribute your file. Continue reading for contribution instructions. Become a part of the World Family Tree Project today!

How to Contribute Your File

You can contribute your Family File to the World Family Tree Project on a diskette or through Family Tree Maker Online. This section explains how to contribute your file using both of these methods.

Important: Before you contribute your files to the World Family Tree Project, please follow the procedures described in "Checking Your File for Errors" in Chapter 6. This will help maintain the quality of the information on the World Family Tree CDs.

Contributing Your File Online

After you check your Family File for errors, you can contribute it to the World Family Tree Project through the Family Tree Maker Online Web site.

To contribute a copy of your Family File online:

1. Start Family Tree Maker, and then open the Family File that you want to contribute.

2. From the **Internet** menu, select **Contribute to the World Family Tree**.

   Family Tree Maker starts your Web browser and connects you to the Internet. Next, it displays the Your Rights as a Contributor to the World Family Tree dialog box.

3. Read the information carefully and then click either **Yes** or **No**.

   By clicking "Yes," you indicate that you understand and accept your responsibilities as a contributor to the World Family Tree Project. In this case, Family Tree Maker copies your Family File to the Internet. If you click "No," Family Tree Maker cancels the contribution process.

4. Type the requested contributor information.

   Name, address — Brøderbund needs your name and address in case there is a problem with your Family File and we need to contact you. Family Tree Maker cannot finish the contribution process until you have filled in your first name, last name, street address (or P.O. Box), city, state, and zip. If your address is in a country other than the United States, Family Tree Maker does not require the state and zip fields. However, please fill out the entire address needed for mail delivery.

Phone (optional) — If you want Brøderbund to be able to contact you by phone, include your phone number. Don't forget your area or country code!

Date — Family Tree Maker uses the date from your computer's internal calendar. If the date is incorrect, please change it. It is vital to have the correct date on your Family File in case you later send us an updated version.

Email (optional) — If you have an email address and want Brøderbund or World Family Tree CD users to be able to contact you by email, include your email address.

5. Click **OK**.

    Family Tree Maker displays a progress indicator and uploads your Family File. This process may take several minutes depending on the size of your file, the speed of your modem, and Internet traffic.

6. When a message displays telling you that the transfer is done, click **OK**.

    Family Tree Maker contributes your file to the World Family Tree Project and closes your Web browser. Don't forget to end your Internet session to avoid unnecessary charges.

Thank you for contributing to a remarkable and unequaled source of linked genealogical data.

Contributing Your File on Diskette

After you check your file for errors, label an empty, formatted, 3.5" diskette with your name, address, and the present date. Use a standard diskette label sticker if you have one.

To contribute a copy of your Family File on diskette:

1. With the blank, formatted diskette in your diskette drive, start Family Tree Maker and open the Family File that you want to contribute.

2. From the **File** menu, select **Contribute to World Family Tree**.

    If you have the Family Tree Maker Online button set up, Family Tree Maker will ask if you want to contribute your file online or by diskette.

3. Click **Diskette**.

    Family Tree Maker displays the Your Rights as a Contributor to the World Family Tree dialog box.

4. Read the information carefully, and then click either **Yes** or **No**.

By clicking "Yes," you indicate that you understand and accept your responsibilities as a contributor to the World Family Tree Project. In this case, Family Tree Maker copies your Family File to the diskette. If you click "No," Family Tree Maker cancels the contribution process.

5. Select the **Destination Drives** option button corresponding to the diskette drive containing your blank diskette, or select **Working Directory** to store the file in the same folder (directory) and drive as your Family File. If you selected Working Directory, remember to copy this file to a diskette at a later time.

6. Type the requested contributor information.

Name, address — Brøderbund needs your name and address in case there is a problem with your Family File and we need to contact you. Family Tree Maker cannot finish the contribution process until you have filled in your first name, last name, street address (or P.O. Box), city, state, and zip. If your address is in a country other than the United States, Family Tree Maker does not require the state and zip fields. However, please fill out the entire address needed for mail delivery.

Phone (optional) — If you want Brøderbund to be able to contact you by phone, include your phone number. Don't forget your area or country code!

Date — Family Tree Maker uses the date from your computer's internal calendar. If the date is incorrect, please change it. It is vital to have the correct date on your Family File in case you later send us an updated version.

Email (optional) — If you have an email address and want Brøderbund or World Family Tree CD users to be able to contact you by email, include your email address.

7. Click **OK**.

8. **Important:** When Family Tree Maker finishes copying your Family File onto the diskette, write your name and address on a label and place it on the diskette (if you haven't already done so).

Please don't skip this important step. If your diskette is damaged in transit, the Family File will be unreadable, and the label is the only way we can identify it as yours.

9. Seal the diskette in a sturdy envelope and send it to:

> **Brøderbund Software, Inc.**
> Banner Blue Division
> World Family Tree Project
> P.O. Box 760
> Fremont, CA 94537-0760

Thank you for contributing to a remarkable and unequaled source of linked genealogical data.

Contacting a World Family Tree Project Contributor

You can request contact information for the individual who contributed a Family Tree in which you are interested. The Contributor Contact Information Service is easily accessible from within Family Tree Maker.

To request contact information:

1. From the **Internet** menu, select **Contact a WFT Contributor**.

    Family Tree Maker starts your Web browser and connects you to the Internet. Next, it displays the World Family Tree Contributor Contact Information Service screen.

2. Read the information carefully and then complete the request form.

    You will be notified by email with the contact information.

Your Rights as a Contributor to the World Family Tree Project

To ensure that you understand your rights as a contributor to the World Family Tree Project, please read the following information:

- By contributing your Family File to the World Family Tree Project, you give Brøderbund Software, Inc. (Banner Blue's parent company) the permission to reproduce, compile, and distribute all information in your contributed Family File along with other contributed Family Files.

- The World Family Tree products are copyrighted; however, our copyright does not limit you from publishing your own family information as you see fit, or from selling it or giving it to others.

- By contributing your Family File to the World Family Tree Project, you give Brøderbund Software, Inc. the permission to provide your name and mailing address to family history enthusiasts who are interested in contacting you.

- Do not contribute information that infringes on the copyrights of others, invades the privacy of others, or is defamatory or profane in any way.

- Brøderbund Software, Inc. retains the right to edit your Family File before its final publication on a World Family Tree CD. However, Brøderbund recognizes the importance of maintaining the integrity of the data in your file and of not changing important family information.

- Contributing your Family File to the World Family Tree Project does not entitle you to any compensation, monetary or other.

- By contributing your Family File, you are indicating that you have read and accepted these rights and responsibilities.

- Family Tree Maker and the World Family Tree Project are trademarks of Brøderbund Software, Inc.

EXPORTING A GROUP OF INDIVIDUALS

When you share Family Files with other family members, you can send them a copy of your entire Family File, or only a portion of your Family File. For example, you might want to send a particular branch of your family tree, or perhaps you want to send only your newly collected information. With the **Copy/Export Individuals** command, you can copy any portion of your Family File into a new Family File.

Note: You can also export information from specific Family Tree Maker reports in an ASCII or .RTF file format to share with individuals who don't own Family Tree Maker. See "Exporting Reports," in this chapter, more information.

To use the Copy/Export Individuals command, you must first create a document containing the group of individuals that you want to export. This also helps you see if the correct individuals are in the group before you export those individuals. Follow the steps below. For information about exporting your entire Family File, see "Copying and Exporting Files" in Chapter 13.

Exporting Individuals

1. Display an Ancestor tree, Descendant tree, Outline Descendant tree, Hourglass tree, Kinship Report, or Custom Report containing the group of individuals you want to export.

   See Chapter 8, "Displaying Your Family Information," and Chapter 9, "Customizing Your Family Information" for more information.

2. After you display your document, review it to make sure that it contains the correct set of individuals.

    Note: You don't have to worry about the other information in the document, because Family Tree Maker exports all information associated with the individuals you selected regardless of whether it appears in the tree or report.

3. From the **File** menu, select **Copy/Export Individuals**.

    Family Tree Maker displays the Copy/Export Individuals dialog box.

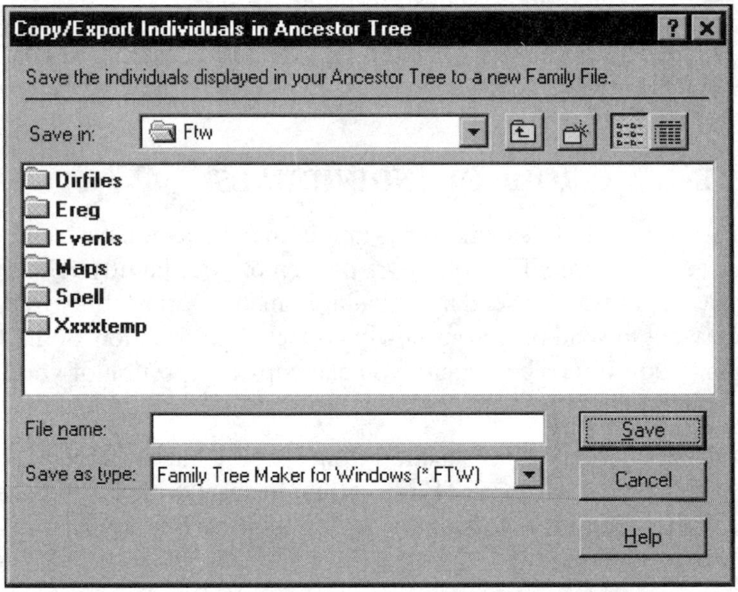

Figure 12-1. The Copy/Export Individuals dialog box

4. Click the **Save as type** drop-down list and select a file format for your new file.

    You can use any available file format. Be sure to choose a format that is compatible with the program that is going to read the file.

5. Type a name for your new file in the **File name** field.

6. Click the **Save in** drop-down list and select the drive where you want Family Tree Maker to create your new file.

    In the box below the "Save in" field, Family Tree Maker displays a list of all the files and folders for the selected location.

7. Double-click the folder where you want to store your new file.

8. After you make your selections, click **Save**.

   Family Tree Maker creates a new file containing a copy of the information for the individuals you selected in step 1. Your original Family File does not change in any way.

Exporting Reports

If you want to share information in a form that can easily be used by someone who does not own Family Tree Maker, you can export a Genealogy report, Bibliography report, or Documented Events report to an .RTF or ASCII file. The person receiving the file can then open it and print it in most Windows compatible word processing programs. Or, you may want to export the information in one of these reports to use in your own word processing or spreadsheet program.

To export a report to an .RTF or ASCII file:

1. Display a Genealogy, Bibliography, or Documented Events report.

   See "Displaying Reports" in Chapter 8 for details.

2. After you display your document, review it to make sure that it contains the correct set of individuals.

   See "Selecting Individuals to Include" in Chapter 9 for details.

3. From the **File** menu, select **Export Report** or **Export Genealogy Report,** depending on the type of report you displayed in Step 1.

   Family Tree Maker displays the Export Report dialog box.

4. Click the **Save as type** drop-down list and select a file format for your new file.

   You can use either .RTF (Rich Text Format) or ASCII (plain text). Be sure to choose a format that is compatible with the program that is going to read the file. RTF *preserves* document formatting, whereas ASCII strips it out. For example, ASCII would be more fitting for pasting text/data into an email message body.

5. Type a name for your new file in the **File name** field.

6. Click the **Save in** drop-down list and select the drive where you want Family Tree Maker to create your new file.

   In the box below the "Save in" field, Family Tree Maker displays a list of all the files and folders for the selected location.

7. Double-click the folder where you want to store your new file.

8. After you make your selections, click **Save**.

   Family Tree Maker creates a new file containing a copy of the report you selected in step 1. Your original Family File does not change in any way.

SHARING YOUR FAMILY INFORMATION ON THE INTERNET

When you visit the Family Tree Maker Online Web site, you can share your research with other Family Tree Maker users and look at family lines others are researching. You can do this by creating a home page and by looking at the home pages created by other Family Tree Maker customers. Home pages can include a variety of information, including trees and reports from customer's Family Files.

Creating Your Own Home Page

Creating your own home page with your family information is a great way to let other Family Tree Maker customers see which family lines you are researching. Since your home page will have a direct link from the Family Tree Maker Online Web site, other Family Tree Maker Online users can easily find it.

After you create your home page, you can add trees and reports from your Family File. See "Publishing a Family Tree on the Internet" and "Publishing a Report on the Internet," both in this chapter.

Note: You must enter at least one individual's name on the Family Page before you create your own home page. See "A Quick Overview" in Chapter 3.

To create your own home page on Family Tree Maker Online:

1. From the **Internet** menu, select **Go Online**.

   Your Web browser opens and displays the Family Tree Maker Online home page. If this is the first time you're using Family Tree Maker Online, complete the online registration form.

   Note: If you see the screen shown in Figure 12-2, refer to the "Troubleshooting" section (Appendix B) at the end of this guide.

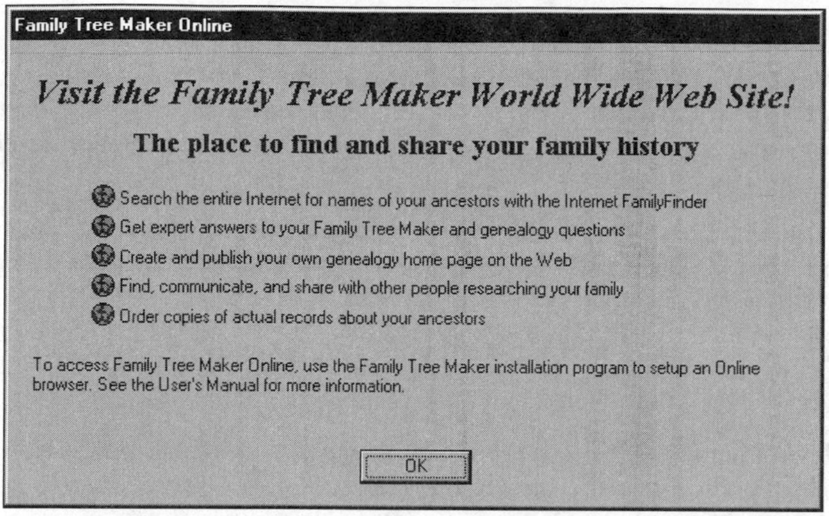

Figure 12-2. The Family Tree Maker Online invitation dialog box

2. Click the **Home Pages** option that appears under the *Genealogy Community* header in the blue bar along the left side of the page.

   Family Tree Maker Online displays the User Home Page Web page.

3. Click the **Create a new home page or edit an existing home page** link.

4. Click the **Create a new home page** link.

   Family Tree Maker Online displays the Create Your Own Home Page Web page. This page contains a form for you to fill in. Family Tree Maker Online uses this information to create your home page.

5. In the **Title** field, type the title you want to appear at the top of your home page.

6. In the **Contact Information** fields, type the information you want to provide for people to contact you.

   Notice that Family Tree Maker Online supplies the information you entered when you registered the first time you used Family Tree Maker Online.

   Note: Please keep in mind that the Internet is a public forum. Anyone who has access to the Internet can access this information.

7. If you already have a personal home page, type the address and title of this page in the **URL Information** and **Description** fields, or you may link to the home page of a friend or relative.

8. In the **Text** field, type the text you want to appear on your home page.

    For example, you might want to enter information about the family lines you're researching, or you can post an announcement about an upcoming family reunion, or perhaps you want to share news about recent births and deaths in your family.

9. In the **Style** list, select the option button for the layout format you want to use. You can view a sample of each Style by clicking the **Sample** link next to an option.

10. After you complete the form, click the **Create Home Page Now** button.

    Family Tree Maker Online displays a sample of your home page.

11. Review the information on the sample page. If you want to make any changes, click your Web browser's **Back** button. If you are satisfied with the sample page, click the **Create Home Page Now** button again.

    Family Tree Maker Online displays a message indicating that your page is complete. It may take several hours for the page to appear in Family Tree Maker Online.

    Don't forget to close your Internet connection when you're done exploring the Internet. Depending on your setup, you may need to close both your browser and the connection to your Internet Service Provider.

Visiting User Home Pages

If you would like to see which family lines other Family Tree Maker customers are researching, visit their home pages to find out. And, don't forget to visit your own home page while you're there.

To visit a home page:

1. From the **Internet** menu, select **Go Online**.

    Your Web browser opens and displays the Family Tree Maker Online home page. If this is the first time you're using Family Tree Maker Online, complete the Online registration form.

2. Click the **Home Pages** option at the top of the window — just below the Family Tree Maker Online title.

    Family Tree Maker Online displays the User Home Pages Web page.

3. In the **Look at Other Home Pages** section, click the first letter of the last name of the person whose home page you want to view.

Family Tree Maker Online displays either a list of additional letter choices or a list of the people with home pages that begin with the letter you selected. If you see a list of letters, continue clicking the appropriate letters until you see a list of names. Alternatively, you can click the **Search** option at the top of the window, and type the name you want to find.

4. Click a person's name.

   Family Tree Maker Online displays the home page of the person you selected. Click your Web browser's **Back** button to select another name.

Don't forget to close your Internet connection when you're done exploring the Internet. Depending on your setup, you may need to close both your browser and the connection to your Internet Service Provider.

Publishing a Family Tree on the Internet

After you create your home page, you can add a family tree or report from your Family File. For information about adding a report, see "Publishing a Report on the Internet" in Chapter 12. Your family tree will include the following information for each of the individuals you choose to include:

- Birth date and location
- Marriage date and location
- Death date and location

To publish a family tree on the Internet:

1. From the Family Page, click the **Internet** menu, then select **Publish Family Tree to the Internet**.

   Family Tree Maker displays a dialog box asking if you want to publish your tree online.

2. Family Tree Maker displays the Individuals to Include dialog box.

3. Select the individuals you want to include and then click **OK**. For specific instructions, see "Selecting Individuals to Include" in Chapter 9.

   Family Tree Maker displays a progress meter while the tree is being copied to your home page. As the transfer is beginning, Family Tree Maker also displays a dialog box asking whether you want to contribute your Family File to the World Family Tree Project.

4. If you have already checked your Family File for errors and want to contribute it to the World Family Tree Project, click **Yes**. Otherwise, click **No**.

Family Tree Maker continues transferring your family tree to your home page and displays a confirmation dialog box when the transfer is complete.

5. After you finish reading the confirmation message, click **OK**.

Don't forget to close your Internet connection when you're done exploring the Internet. Depending on your setup, you may need to close both your browser and the connection to your Internet Service Provider.

For instructions on how to view your tree on the Internet, see "Visiting User Home Pages" in this chapter. The title of your tree now appears as a link on your home page.

Note: When you first publish your tree, it may take several hours for it to appear on your home page.

Publishing a Report on the Internet

After you create your home page you can add a report from your Family File. You can choose to display any amount of information and it can be in one of three formats: **Outline Descendant tree**, **Columnar report** (choose from any of the report formats available in the Report view), or **Genealogy report** (choose from any of the formats available in the Genealogy Report view). For example, you can choose to display a simple Outline Descendant tree showing only your immediate family or you can choose to display something as elaborate as a multiple-column custom report showing information about all of the individuals in your Family File.

To publish a report from your Family File on the Internet:

1. From the **View** menu in Family Tree Maker, select the view that you want to use to create your report (either a Report, Genealogy Report, Kinship Report, or Outline Descendant Tree). For more information see Chapter 8, "Displaying Your Family Information."

2. Using any of the features available on the **Contents** or **Format** menus, select individuals and make formatting choices (see Chapter 9, "Customizing Your Family Information").

    We recommend that you focus on the content of your report more than the formatting. The format of your report may look very different on the Internet than it does within Family Tree Maker. This is because the HTML language used to display information on the Internet has limited formatting capabilities. Some Family Tree Maker formatting options, like colors and borders, may not transfer to the Internet at all.

Note: Please keep in mind that the Internet is a public forum. Anyone who has access to the Internet can access the information you include in your report.

3. From the **Internet** menu, select **Go Online**. Skip this step if you already have an open connection to the Internet.

   Family Tree Maker opens your Web browser, connects you to your Internet service provider, and takes you to the Family Tree Maker Online Web site.

4. Click Family Tree Maker on the Windows 95 taskbar or press ⌨ + ⌨ (Tab) to switch back to Family Tree Maker.

   Family Tree Maker returns to the report or tree view that you prepared for your home page.

5. From the **Internet** menu, select **Publish Report to the Internet**.

   Family Tree Maker displays the Publish Report on the Internet dialog box.

6. Click **OK** to continue.

   Family Tree Maker displays a progress meter while the report is being copied to your home page. As the transfer is beginning, Family Tree Maker also displays a dialog box asking whether you want to contribute your Family File to the World Family Tree Project.

7. If you have already checked your Family File for errors and want to contribute it to the World Family Tree Project, click **Yes**. Otherwise, click **No**.

   Family Tree Maker continues transferring your report to your home page and displays a confirmation dialog box when the transfer is complete.

8. After you finish reading the confirmation message, click **OK**.

Don't forget to close your Internet connection when you're done exploring the Internet. Depending on your setup, you may need to close both your browser and the connection to your Internet Service Provider.

For instructions on how to view your report on the Internet, see "Visiting User Home Pages" in this chapter. The title of your report now appears as a link on your home page.

Note: When you first publish your report, it may take 15 minutes for it to appear on your home page.

Publishing a Family Book on the Internet

In addition to trees and reports, you can publish a family book to your home page and share a more complete representation of your family history. Here are a few things to keep in mind when you publish your family book on the Internet:

- You must create a home page on Family Tree Maker Online before you can publish a family book on the Internet. See "Creating Your Own Home Page" in this chapter for instructions.

- Your book must include a Table of Contents and an Index. If you don't have these items in your book, Family Tree Maker prompts you to add them when you publish the book.

- Some of the text styles in your book may not be available online. Family Tree Maker Online maintains your text styles whenever possible.

- Any images you inserted do not appear in the online version of your book.

- Fan trees appear as box style trees in the online version of your book.

- Each tree in your book can contain up to 2,000 individuals, and you can have a combined total of up to 60,000 individuals in all the trees in your book.

- If your book contains more than 10,000 pages, you must create a shorter version of the book before you publish it on the Internet.

To publish a book on the Internet:

1. Display the book you want to publish on the Internet.

2. From the **Internet** menu, select **Publish Book to the Internet**.

   Family Tree Maker displays a dialog box informing you that it is preparing your book for publication.

3. Click **OK** to continue.

   Family Tree Maker paginates the book and looks for a Table of Contents and an Index. If it does not find these items, it prompts you to add them.

   Next, Family Tree Maker asks if you want to contribute your Family File to the World Family Tree project (see "The World Family Tree Project" in this chapter for details).

4. Click **Yes** to contribute your Family File, or **No** to continue without contributing your Family File.

   Family Tree Maker begins copying your book to our Web server and displays a progress meter during the process.

5. Wait for the book to finish uploading.

   Family Tree Maker displays a message indicating that the upload is complete and that you can view your book on your home page in about 30 minutes. The title of your book will appear as a link on your home page. Simply click the link to view your book.

Chapter 13

MANAGING YOUR FILES

Marylou, David Jr. and Sr., and Michele Geoffrion are pictured
enjoying the Russian River in California in the summer of 1957.
Gigi Geoffrion, Quality Assurance Lead for Family Tree Maker and
future younger sister, has a predisposition to strong opinions
like her older sister Michele, pictured here.

MANAGING YOUR FILES

This chapter describes things that you can do with Family Files, such as opening them, backing them up, copying them, compacting them, and combining them.

CREATING NEW FAMILY FILES

To create a new Family File:

1. From the **File** menu, select **New Family File**.

    Family Tree Maker displays the New Family File dialog box.

2. Type a name for your file in the **File name** field.

    Your file name can be as long as you want. Family Tree Maker will automatically add the ".FTW" extension to the name you type.

3. After you enter a name for your new Family File, click **Save**.

    Family Tree Maker creates the new Family File for you and then displays the Family Page. This is where you'll begin entering information about your family.

    Note: You must create a file and enter at least one individual before all options are enabled on the menu and button bar.

OPENING EXISTING FILES

Using these instructions, you can open any type of Family Tree Maker file including: Family Tree Maker for Windows, Family Tree Maker for DOS, Family Tree Maker for Macintosh, Backup and Compressed Family Tree Maker files, as well as PAF and GEDCOM files.

Note: If you're importing a file from the Macintosh version of PAF, you must first save the PAF file in PAF's DOS format before attempting to open it in Family Tree Maker. See your PAF User's Guide for more information.

Opening Family Tree Maker Files

1. From the **File** menu, select **Open Family File**.

    Family Tree Maker displays the Open Family File dialog box.

2. Click the **Look in** drop-down list and select the drive where the file you want to open is located.

    In the box below the "Look in" field, Family Tree Maker displays a list of all the files and folders on the selected drive.

3. Double-click the folder that contains your file.

    If you are unsure where your file is, click **Find file** and follow the instructions in "Finding Files" in this chapter.

    Note: You cannot use a Family Tree Maker file while it is on a diskette (or other removable media). Before opening it, Family Tree Maker displays the Copy/Export dialog box so you can to transfer the file to your hard drive (see "Copying and Exporting Files" in this chapter for instructions on this dialog box).

4. Click the **Files of type** drop-down list, and select the format you want (see Figure 13-1).

    Family Tree Maker displays a list of the files of the type you selected. Note that the list includes only the files that are located in the folder you selected in step 3.

5. Select the name of your file in the box below the "Look in" field, and then click **Open**.

    If you are opening a Family Tree Maker for Windows file on your hard drive, skip the remaining steps.

    If your file is not a Family Tree Maker for Windows file, or your file is on a diskette, Family Tree Maker displays a dialog box. You must rename your file so that Family Tree Maker can copy your original file and then convert the copy to a Family Tree Maker for Windows file.

6. To change the location of the copy, click the **Save in** drop-down list and select the drive and folder where you want to store the copy.

7. In the **File name** field, accept the name Family Tree Maker suggests or type a new name, and then click **Save**.

Family Tree Maker recreates your file as a Family Tree Maker for Windows file and then displays a Family Page containing one or more individuals from your file.

Note: If you're importing a GEDCOM file and Family Tree Maker encounters any difficulties, it offers you the choice to view a list of warnings and errors. After viewing the error list (if necessary), you can begin working with your Family File.

To open a...	Select...
Family Tree Maker for Windows file	Family Tree Maker for Windows (*.FTW)
Family Tree Maker for Macintosh file	Family Tree Maker for Macintosh (*.FTW)
Family Tree Maker for DOS file	Family Tree Maker for DOS (*.FTM)
Backup Family Tree Maker file	Family Tree Maker Backup (*.FBK)
Compressed Family Tree Maker file	Family Tree Maker Compressed (*.FBC)
File from another genealogy software program that supports GEDCOM	GEDCOM (*.GED) After you finish step 6, continue with "GEDCOM Import and Export" in this chapter.
PAF files from PAF version 2.1 or later	Personal Ancestral File To add the information in your PAF file to your current Family File, see "Combining Files" in this chapter.
Any type of file that Family Tree Maker can read	Family Tree Maker (*.FTW,*.FTM,*.FBK,*.FBC,*.GED)

Figure 13-1. File Type Options

FINDING FILES

There may be times when you need to find an existing file to use with Family Tree Maker. You can begin a search from two different locations:

- From the **File** menu, select **Open Family File**. Family Tree Maker displays the Open Family File dialog box.

- From the **Picture/Object** menu, select **Insert Picture from File** (available only from the Scrapbook view). Family Tree Maker displays the Insert Picture dialog box.

From either of those dialog boxes, follow these steps to find your file:

1. Click **Find file**.

   Family Tree Maker displays the Find File dialog box. Now you can tell Family Tree Maker where to look for your file, following steps 2 through 4 below. Your search will take less time if you enter the most exact locations you know.

2. Click the **File format** drop-down list, and then select a file type.

   The selection of file types depends on which dialog box you were in when you opened the Find File dialog box. If you were in the Import Picture dialog box, Family Tree Maker lists graphics file formats. If you were in the Open File dialog box, you see the valid file format options. If you don't know which file format your file is saved with, select the last format in the list: **All Files (*.*)**. This will display all the files in the search area — not just Family Files.

3. Click the **File name** field, and type a file name if you already know part or all of it.

   You can type any valid file name, using the asterisk symbol (*) to indicate "any," or a question mark (?) to hold the place of characters if you're unsure of the exact spelling but know the length of the file name. For example, you could type **sm?th.*** if you didn't recall whether the Smith Family File used the spelling "Smith" or "Smyth" and you didn't know the file type. If you know that the file you're looking for has a name that is six letters long, you can type **??????.*** to retrieve a list that excludes all shorter and longer titles.

4. Click the **Search** drop-down list and then select a set of drives for Family Tree Maker to search.

   The list will give you the choice of selecting a single drive or a combination of drives. Your search will take more time if Family Tree Maker has to search in many different locations, so don't include a drive in your search if it's unlikely that your file is stored there.

5. After you make your selections, click **Search**.

   Family Tree Maker searches in the designated areas and lists the matching file paths in the Found files box.

6. If several file names appear in the box, use the scroll bar to scan the list for the file name you're trying to find. To open a file in the list, you can either select the file name then click **Open**, or double-click the name in the list.

   Once you open a file, you can begin working with it.

BACKING UP YOUR FAMILY FILE

Family Tree Maker does not have a Save command, but a Backup command instead. This is because Family Tree Maker is a database program that saves your information regularly while you use the program, as well as when you quit. Family Tree Maker saves your information both in your regular .FTW Family File and also in a special **backup** file that is in the same directory and has the same name as your Family File, but with the extension **.FBK**. The .FBK backup file is what Family Tree Maker will try to open if your original Family File is ever damaged.

Note: Since Family Tree Maker automatically saves the information that you enter, you cannot get rid of your latest changes by quitting the program without saving. To get rid of any changes, you must fix them manually. Or, following the directions below, make your own backup files regularly so you can revert to an old file.

You can also make your own compressed backup files to store on diskettes, on removable tape or disk cartridges, or in other directories. These compressed backup copies will have the extension **.FBC**. Making regular backup copies of your Family File can help ensure that you won't lose all of your genealogical information if something ever happens to your Family File. If you are entering a lot of information, we also strongly recommend that you keep a current set of compressed backup files. It's a good idea to backup as often as once every hour or once per session — you never know when you will have a power failure! If you are planning to backup to a diskette drive, be sure to have blank, formatted diskettes handy.

Note: To ensure that your hard work and time are not wasted, we suggest using new disks, make at least two copies of your backup files, and be sure to store them in a safe place.

If you want to make a copy of your Family File to share with someone who uses Family Tree Maker, follow the steps below. If you want to share your Family File with someone who uses a different software program, see "Copying and Exporting Files" in this chapter.

To make your own compressed backup file:

1. From the **File** menu, select **Backup Family File**.

   Family Tree Maker displays the Backup Family File dialog box.

Backup Family File

Select the destination where you would like your backup Family File stored, then click OK.

Currently selected backup destination:

C:\FTW\McDonald-Storie.FBC

Backup Destination Choices

○ Floppy Drive (A:)

○ Floppy Drive (D:)

● Working directory (C:\FTW\)

○ Custom directory (C:\FTW\)

Change filename or directory...

OK   Cancel   Help

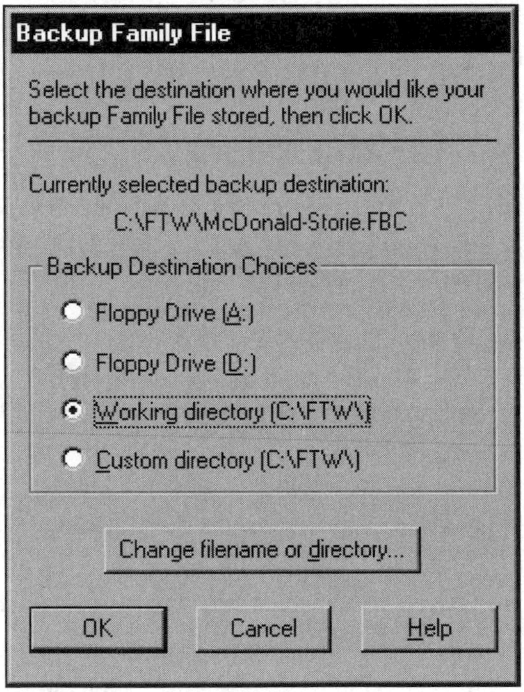

Figure 13-2. The Backup Family File dialog box

2. The "Currently selected backup destination" field lists your default backup location. To accept this location, click **OK**. To change the location of your backup, select one of the **Backup Destination Choices** option buttons described on the next page:

3 ½" Floppy Drive [A:] — Places your backup files on a 3 ½" diskette in Drive A:.

ZIP drive — If you have a **ZIP drive**, or some other backup media installed, the dialog box will display that drive location as one of your options.

Working directory — Places your file in the directory where Family Tree Maker is installed.

Custom directory — Places your file in the directory you choose on your hard drive. If you select **Custom directory**, click **Change filename or directory** to choose a new backup destination in the Change Filename or Directory dialog box. Use the **Look in** list to select a location, and then type a name in the **File name** field. Family Tree Maker will automatically add the .FBC file extension to the name you type.

3. After you make your selections, click **OK**.

    If the backup file that you want to create already exists, Family Tree Maker will warn you and may not let you create the file, depending on whether you have chosen to allow files to be overwritten (see "Selecting Startup Preferences" in Chapter 1). Otherwise, Family Tree Maker copies your Family File to the file name and destination that you selected.

    If you are backing up a large file to a diskette drive, Family Tree Maker will ask you to insert new diskettes as needed. When the backup requires multiple diskettes, be sure to label them in the order in which they are used. At the end of the backup process, Family Tree Maker will advise you that your Family File was successfully backed up.

Opening Backup Files

If your original Family File is damaged or you want to revert to a previous copy, you need to restore it from a backup. Backup files are stored as either .FBK or .FBC type files. (See "Backing Up Your Family File" in this chapter for a description of these two types of files.)

To open a backup file:

1. From the **File** menu, select **Restore From Backup**.

   Family Tree Maker displays the Open Backup Family File dialog box.

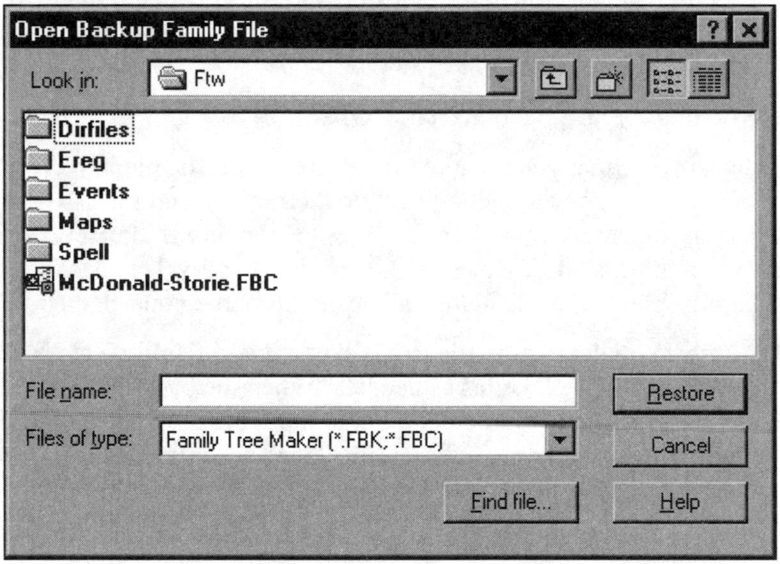

Figure 13-3. The Open Backup Family File dialog box

2. Click the **Look in** drop-down list and select the drive where the backup file you want to open is located.

   In the box below the "Look in" field, Family Tree Maker displays a list of all the backup (.FBC and .FBK) files and folders on the selected drive.

3. Double-click the folder that contains your backup file.

   If you are unsure where your backup file is, click **Find file** and follow the instructions in "Finding Files" on page 462.

   Note: You cannot use a Family Tree Maker file while it is on a diskette (or other removable media). Before opening it, Family Tree Maker displays the Copy/Export dialog box so you can transfer the file to your hard drive. See "Copying and Exporting Files" in this chapter for instructions on this dialog box.

4. Select the name of your backup file in the box below the "Look in" field, and then click **Open**.

   Family Tree Maker displays the Save as dialog box. You must supply a file name that is different than any of your existing Family Files.

5. To change the location of the restored file, click the **Save in** drop-down list and select the drive and folder where you want to put the restored file.

6. In the **File name** field, accept the name Family Tree Maker suggests or type a new name, and then click **Save**.

   Family Tree Maker restores your backup file as a Family Tree Maker for Windows file and then displays a Family Page containing one or more individuals from your file.

COPYING AND EXPORTING FILES

You can make a copy of your Family File or export it to a different file format. If you want to export your file to the GEDCOM file format, see "Exporting GEDCOM Files from Family Tree Maker" in this chapter.

Note: If you want to copy your Family File onto a diskette, make sure that the file is small enough to fit on a single diskette. If your file is too large to fit on a single diskette, follow the instructions for "Backing Up Your Family File" in this chapter.

How to Copy and Export Files

1. From the **File** menu, select **Copy/Export Family File**.

    Family Tree Maker displays the New Family File dialog box.

2. Click the **Save as type** drop-down list and select the format that you want for the copied file.

3. In the **File name** field, type a new file name.

4. Click the **Save in** drop-down list and select the drive and folder to which you want to copy your file.

5. After you make your selections, click **Save**.

    If you chose "Family Tree Maker 3.0 for Win/Mac" or "Family Tree Maker 4.0 for Win" in step 2 above, Family Tree Maker displays the Facts to Export dialog box. In this case, continue with the next step. If you chose any of the other file types in step 2, Family Tree Maker copies or exports your file to the location and file name that you chose.

6. Now you must select which information to export to your file. Family Tree Maker automatically exports most of the information. If you have sources for this information, they are also exported.

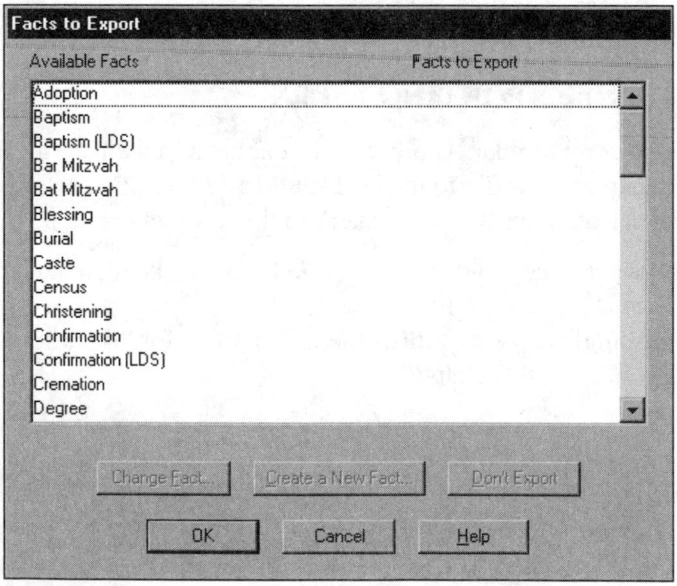

Figure 13-4. The Facts to Export dialog box

There are two lists in this dialog box. The list on the left, **Available Facts**, contains all of the Family Tree Maker fact names for the fields that you can export to the file. The list on the right, **Facts to Export**, contains the list of fact names actually being exported.

7. To export a fact field, select the fact name from the Available Facts list. If you don't want to include the fact, select it and then click **Don't Export**. The "move right" symbol (=>) disappears and the fact will not be exported.

8. Click **Export fact**.

   If you can use more than one fact name to export the information, Family Tree Maker displays the Change Fields dialog box shown in Figure 13-5. In this case, continue with step 9. If you can use only one fact name for that information, Family Tree Maker automatically inserts the fact name in the list on the right, opposite the name of the current Family Tree Maker fact. In this case, skip to step 11.

9. In the Change Fields dialog box, select the fact name that you want to use to describe the information you want to import..

10. Click **OK** to return to the Facts to Export dialog box.

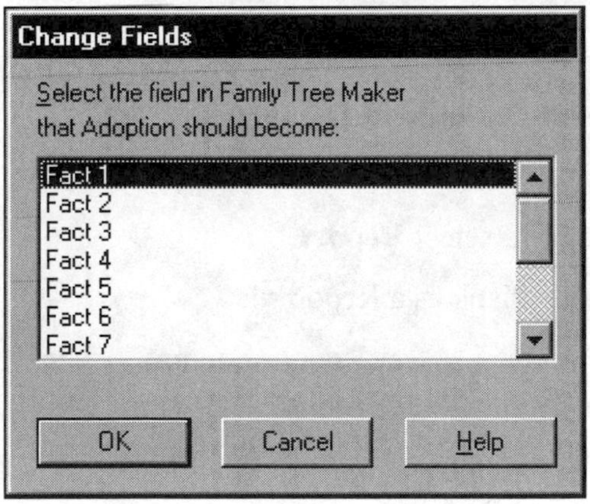

Figure 13-5. The Change Fields dialog box

11. Repeat steps 7 through 10 until all Family Tree Maker fields that you want to export have the appropriate fact names opposite them in the "Facts to Export" list.

12. If you want to change the mapping of a field after you've selected it, select the fact name in the "Facts to Export" list and then click **Change fact**. If this button stays grayed out, the mapping for that field is preset and cannot be changed.

13. After you make your selections, click **OK**.

Family Tree Maker returns to the Facts to Export dialog box.

14. Click **OK** again.

Family Tree Maker creates the Family Tree Maker version 3.0 or 4.0 file.

SPLITTING FILES IN WINDOWS 95

There are occasions where it may be helpful to "split" your family file, creating a smaller subsection to export. For instance, you may be working with someone related to you on one branch of your family and don't want to overwhelm them with your spouse's family as well. Or, perhaps you have two Family Files and only want to copy a couple individuals from one to the other.

Family Tree Maker lets you accomplish these kinds of tasks by splitting your Family File. We will discuss one method, based on a Custom Report view, but there are two other views from which you can accomplish this task. For more information, from the **Internet** menu, select **Technical Support** and follow the links to **Exporting selected individuals to a new file**.

To Export selected individuals from a Custom Report:

1. From the **View** menu, select **Report**.

Family Tree Maker displays a Report view.

2. From the **Format** menu, select **Report Format**. Then, from the list of available items, select **Custom Report** and click **OK**.

Family Tree Maker displays a Custom Report.

3. From the **Contents** menu, select **Individuals to Include in Report**.

Family Tree Maker displays the Include dialog box.

4. Select **Selected Individuals**, then click **Individuals to Include**.

At this point, you tell Family Tree Maker which individuals, or branch, you want to export.

5. First, click (remove all) to clear any individuals out of the right-hand window who may have been included in previous reports.

6. Choose the individuals you want to include in the new file to export.

Individuals may be selected one at a time from the left window, then moved to the right window by clicking the **Include** (right arrow) button.

To include the ancestors or descendants of a specific individual, select that person in the left window and then click **Ancestors** or **Descendants**.

To search for individuals who meet specific criteria, click **Find**.

7. From the **File** menu, select **Copy/Export Individuals in Report**.

    Note: There are two Copy/Export commands in the File menu. Be sure to select the *second* one in the list. Selecting Copy/Export *Family File* by mistake copies your entire Family File, not the selected individuals.

8. Click **Save in**, and then from the drop-down list, select the drive to which you want to save the new file.

    A list of the files and folders on your selected drive appears in the box below the Save in field. Double-click the folder into which you want to save your new file.

9. In the **File name** field, enter the name for your new file, then click **Save**.

    The resulting file now contains your selected individuals and is ready to export.

DELETING FILES

If you need to delete files, you can use the Windows file management utilities "My Computer" and "Windows Explorer."

To delete files:

1. Follow the steps in "Finding Files" in this chapter to locate the file you want to delete.

2. Write down the drive, folder, and file name.

3. From the **File** menu, select **Exit** to leave Family Tree Maker.

4. Go to either **My Computer** or **Windows Explorer**, and navigate to the drive and directory that contains the file you want to delete.

5. Highlight the file you want to delete.

6. From the **File** menu, select **Delete**.

    Windows deletes the file you selected in step 5.

See your Microsoft Windows User's Guide or on-screen Help for more information about finding files and using the Delete command.

Compacting Family Files

If you have recently deleted Picture/Objects from your Family File you may have noticed that the size of your Family File did not change. That's because Family Tree Maker reserves the space previously occupied by the deleted Picture/Object for future use. If you aren't planning to replace the Pictures/Objects you deleted, you can have Family Tree Maker eliminate that reserved space from your file.

To eliminate the reserved Picture/Object space from your file:

1. Start Family Tree Maker and open the Family File that you want to compact.

2. Use the short-cut key combination: **Ctrl + Alt + C**.

   Family Tree Maker begins compacting your file and displays a progress meter during the process. When Family Tree Maker is done compacting your file it displays a message.

3. Click **OK**.

GEDCOM IMPORT AND EXPORT

GEDCOM is a standard file format for exchanging information between genealogy programs. The acronym GEDCOM stands for GEnealogical Data COMmunications. The Family History Department of the Church of Jesus Christ of Latter-day Saints (LDS Church) developed the GEDCOM standard.

You can use GEDCOM to transfer information into Family Tree Maker from another genealogy program that supports GEDCOM and vice versa. By importing or exporting GEDCOM files, you avoid retyping information.

Importing GEDCOM Files into Family Tree Maker

To import a GEDCOM file in Family Tree Maker for Windows:

1. Complete steps 1 through 7 in "Opening Family Tree Maker Files" in this chapter.

   Family Tree Maker reloads your file as a Family Tree Maker for Windows file and then displays the Import from GEDCOM dialog box.

2. Some programs format information differently than Family Tree Maker. Using the options listed below, you can reformat your information.

   Location — Some programs, like Personal Ancestral File (PAF), have longer location fields than Family Tree Maker does. For example, PAF can hold the location "Warren, Trumbull County, Ohio, United States of America." Select the **Keep first part if location fields are too long** option button to keep the first part of the location. The example above would become "Warren, Trumbull County, Ohio." Select the **Keep last part if location fields are too long** option button to keep the last part of the location. The example above would become "Ohio, United States of America."

   Delete underscore from names — Some programs (like PAF) add an underscore between compound names (for example, St._Germaine). Select this check box to replace the underscore with a space.

   Add spacing in location fields — Some programs don't put spaces between the city, county, and state in location fields. Select this check box to add the normal space between these words, if necessary.

3. Click **OK**.

   Family Tree Maker automatically imports the fields (including sources) in the GEDCOM file and maps the GEDCOM tags to the appropriate Family Tree Maker fact names. See figures 13-6, 13-7, and 13-8 over the next pages for a list of the GEDCOM tags.

   Once the import is complete, you can verify that the fact names Family Tree Maker selected are the ones you want. Simply view the More About Facts dialog box for any individual in the file. For more information about changing the fact names, see "Entering Facts" in Chapter 5.

Note: If you're importing a file from the Macintosh version of PAF, you must first save the PAF file in PAF's DOS format before attempting to open it in Family Tree Maker. See your PAF User's Guide for more information.

This tag	Stands for this	This tag	Stands for this
Abbr	Abbreviation	City	City
Addr	Address	Co	County
Adr1	Address1	CutoffYr	Cutoff year
Adr2	Address2	Colo	Color
Adop	Adoption	Comm	Comment
Afn	Ancestral file number	Conc	Concatenation
Age	Age	Conf	Confirmation
Agnc	Agency	Conl	Confirmation LDS
Alia	Alias	Cont	Continued
Ance	Ancestors	Copr	Copyright
Anci	Ancestor interest	Corp	Corporation
Anul	Annulment	Crem	Cremation
Arvl	Arrival	Ctry	Country
Asso	Associates	Data	Data
Attr	Attribute	Date	Date
Auth	Author	Dau	Daughter
Bapl	Baptism LDS	Deat	Death
Bapm	Baptism	Desc	Descendants
Barm	Bar Mitzvah	Desi	Descendant interest
Basm	Bas Mitzvah	Dest	Destination
Birt	Birth	Div	Divorce
Bles	Blessing	Divf	Divorce filed
Blob	Binary object	Dprt	Departure
Blsl	Blessing LDS	Dscr	Physical description
Buri	Burial	Dwel	Dwelling
Caln	Call number	Educ	Education
Cast	Caste	Emig	Emigration
Caus	Cause	Endl	Endowment LDS
Ceme	Cemetery	Enga	Engagement
Cens	Census	Even	Event
Chan	Change	Fam	Family
Char	Character	Famc	Family child
Chil	Child	Famf	Family file
Chr	Christening	Fams	Family spouse
Chra	Adult christening	Fath	Father

Figure 13-6. GEDCOM tags

This tag	Stands for this	This tag	Stands for this
Fcom	First communion	Natu	Naturalization
Fema	Female	Nchi	Number of children
File	File	Nick	Nickname
Fmt	Date format	Nmar	Number of marriages
Form	Format	Nmr	Number of marriages
Fost	Foster	Note	Note
Gedc	GEDCOM	Npfx	Name prefix
Givn	Given name	Nsfx	Name suffix
Grad	Graduation	Numb	Number
Head	Header	Obje	Object
Hist ID	History ID#	Occu	Occupation
Husb	Husband	Ordi	Ordinance
Idno	Identification number	Ordl	Ordination LDS
Ille	Illegitimate	Ordn	Ordination
Immi	Immigration	Page	Page
Indi	Individual	Pedi	Pedigree
Info	Information	Phon	Phone number
Isa	Is a kind of	Plac	Place
Labl	Label	Post	Postal code
Lang	Language	Priv	Private
Lega	Legatee	Prob	Probate
Lds	LDS	Prop	Property
Lvg	Living	Publ	Publication
Male	Male	Quay	Quality of data
Marb	Marriage bann	Race	Race
Marc	Marriage contract	Refn	Reference number
Marl	Marriage License	Rela	Relationship
Marr	Marriage	Reli	Religion
Mars	Marriage settlement	Rema	Remarks
Medi	Media	Repo	Repository
Misc	Miscellaneous	Resi	Residence
Moth	Mother	Resn	Restriction
Name	Name	Reti	Retirement
Namr	Name religious	Rfn	Record file number
Nati	Nationality	Rin	Record ID number

Figure 13-7. GEDCOM tags, continued

This tag	Stands for this	This tag	Stands for this
Role	Role	Titl	Title
Schema	Schema	Town	Town
Sex	Sex	Trlr	Trailer
Sibl	Sibling	Type	Type
Slgc	Sealing child	Unit	Unit
Slgp	Sealing parent	Vers	Version
Slgs	Sealing spouse	Wife	Wife
Son	Son	Will	Will
Sour	Source	Event1	_fa1
Spfx	Surname prefix	Event2	_fa2
Ssn	Social Security Number	Event3	_fa3
Stae	State	Event4	_fa4
Stake	Stake	Event5	_fa5
Stal	Stake LDS	Event6	_fa6
Stat	Status	Event7	_fa7
Stil	Stillborn	Event8	_fa8
Subm	Submitter	Event9	_fa9
Subn	Submission	Event10	_fa10
Surn	Surname	Event11	_fa11
Temp	Temple	Event12	_fa12
Text	Text	Event13	_fa13
Time	Time		

Figure 13-8. GEDCOM tags, continued

Note: Please note that the tags listed in Figures 13-6, 13-7, and 13-8 show an accumulation of GEDCOM tags through version 5.5. Therefore, this list is not specific to a particular GEDCOM version.

Exporting GEDCOM Files from Family Tree Maker

You can export your Family File(s) to a GEDCOM file format. To do this, you need to name the file in the Copy/Export Family File dialog box and then select your export options in the Export to GEDCOM dialog box.

Naming the GEDCOM file

To open the Export GEDCOM dialog box:

1. From the **File** menu, select **Copy/Export Family File**.

    Family Tree Maker displays the Copy/Export Family File dialog box.

2. Click the **Save in** drop-down list and select the drive where you want to place the file.

    In the box below the "Save in" field, Family Tree Maker displays a list of all the files and folders on the selected drive.

3. Double-click the folder where you want to place your file.

4. Click the **Save as type** drop-down list and select **GEDCOM (*.GED)**.

5. In the **File name** field, type a name for the file or keep the name that Family Tree Maker suggests.

6. Click **Save**.

    Family Tree Maker displays the Export to GEDCOM dialog box.

Selecting the Export to GEDCOM Options

To select the Export to GEDCOM options:

1. Make your selections. Each of the options is described below.

    File Type — The "Destination" field allows Family Tree Maker to check for requirements of the program that will read the GEDCOM file. Use the table below to make a selection. The **FTW** file type offers the most complete export; select it if you plan to later reimport the file into Family Tree Maker for Windows. If the program you are exporting to is not listed, choose **PAF**.

    Note: You can import Family Tree Maker for Windows files into Family Tree Maker for Macintosh using the "Family Tree Maker 3.0 for Win/Mac" format. For more information, see "Copying and Exporting Files" in this chapter.

Select this...	To create this type of file...
ANSTFILE	Ancestral File of LDS Church
NPS	Temple submission to LDS Church
PAF	Personal Ancestral File, 2.1 or later
ROOTS	Roots II, Roots III, Roots IV, Roots V, or Visual Roots
FTM	Family Tree Maker for DOS
FTW	Family Tree Maker for Windows

Figure 13-9. Destination file types

When you make a selection in the "Destination" field, Family Tree Maker makes suggestions for the "GEDCOM" and "Character set" fields. However, if Family Tree Maker's suggestions are incorrect for your purposes, make your own selections. Whenever possible, select **Version 5.5** in the "GEDCOM" field; it offers the best export. When you don't know which file type to use, or when you're exporting to PAF version 2.31 or earlier, select **Version 4**.

Indent records — You can select this check box to make the file more readable in a word processor. However, some programs cannot read indented records, so it is best *not* to select this check box.

Abbreviate tags — Most programs use abbreviated tags instead of long tags, so it is best to select this check box. ("Tags" are labels for the fields of information in the GEDCOM file. For example, the tag for occupation is "OCCU". For a list of tags, see Figures 13-6, 13-7, and 13-8.

2. Click **OK**.

Family Tree Maker automatically exports all the fields (including sources) in your Family File and maps the field names to the appropriate GEDCOM tags.

COMBINING FILES

If you have several GEDCOM, PAF, or Family Tree Maker files, you can join
them together to create one large Family Tree Maker for Windows file. If your
files contain overlapping information, Family Tree Maker automatically
combines exact duplicates and then lets you compare possible duplicates so you
can decide whether to combine them or not.

Important: Be cautious when you join files. If you don't work carefully, you
may accidentally combine two unique individuals. We suggest that you first
make backup copies of the files you want to combine (see "Backing Up Your
Family File" in this chapter) so you can return to a previous version if your
combined file doesn't turn out as you expected. Also, after you finish combining
files, print some trees and reports so that it's easy to see whether you've made
any mistakes.

When you combine files, the first step is to open the files that you want to
combine. The **destination** file is the file to which you want to add information,
and the **source** file is where you get that information. The destination file
becomes larger, and the source file remains the same size.

Opening the Files

1. Make sure that the correct Family Tree Maker *destination* file is open. See
   "Opening Family Tree Maker Files" in this chapter for details.

2. From the **File** menu, select **Append/Merge Family File**.

   Family Tree Maker displays the Open Family File dialog box.

3. In the **Look in** list, select the location of the *source* file. If you are unsure
   where your file is, click **Find file** and follow the instructions in "Finding
   Files" in this chapter.

4. Click the **File of type** drop-down list and select the source file format.

5. Select the name of your file in the box below the "Look in" field.

6. Click **Append file**.

   Family Tree Maker displays a warning message.

7. Read the warning and then click **OK**.

   Family Tree Maker displays the Individuals to Include dialog box. Continue with the next section.

Selecting Individuals to Include

The next step in combining files is to select individuals from the source file to merge into the destination file. To do this, you use the Individuals to Include dialog box displayed at the end of the previous step.

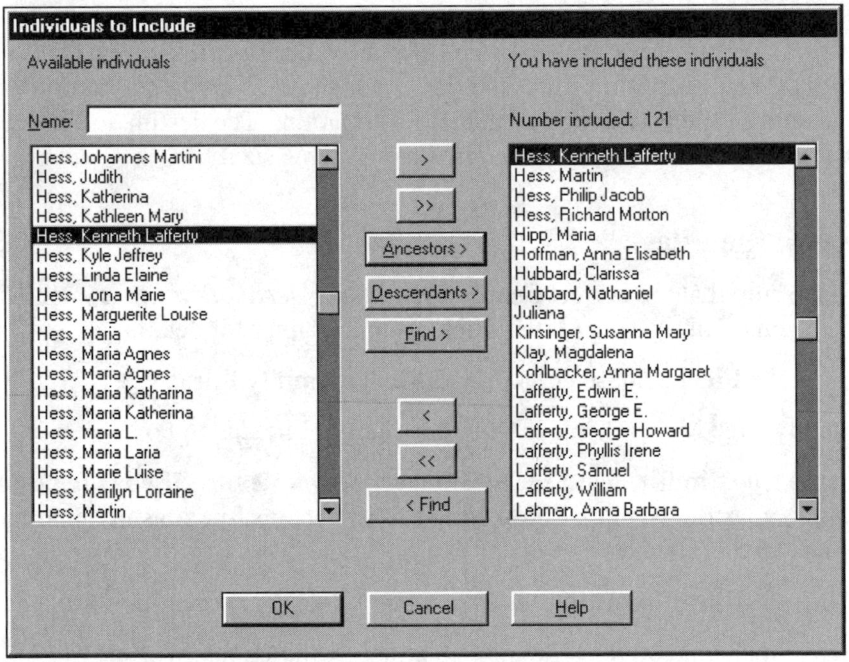

Figure 13-10. The Individuals to Include dialog box

1. Select a group of individuals to merge by adding them to or removing them from the list on the right.

   If you need help selecting a group of individuals, see step 4 in "Selecting Individuals to Include" in Chapter 9.

2. After you create a group of individuals to merge, click **OK**.

   Family Tree Maker displays the Append File dialog box. Continue with "Appending and Merging Information" below.

Appending and Merging Information

The last step in the process of combining files is to append or merge the information. The Append File dialog box gives you information about both the source file and the destination file. At this point, you have two choices. You can merge the information in the two files together, carefully eliminating possible duplicate information with Family Tree Maker's help. Alternatively, you can append all of the information from the source file to the destination file without checking for or eliminating any duplicates. You can then later go through your file and eliminate duplicate information using the instructions in "Merging Individuals" in Chapter 6. If you want to completely quit this operation at this time, click **Cancel**. Otherwise, continue reading below.

You can do three different things from the Append File dialog box:

Display Merge Report — Displays a list showing whether each of the individuals in the source file is an exact match, possible match, or not a match for someone in the destination file. We strongly suggest that you read this report carefully before you begin merging operations. This will help you avoid making mistakes. See "Displaying a Merge Report," below.

Merge matching individuals — Review the exact matches and possible matches one-by-one and decide which to merge.

Append only (no merge) — Adds all the information in the source file to the destination file, without merging anyone. See "Appending All Information," in this chapter.

Displaying a Merge Report

A merge report is informational only; you cannot use it to change the contents of either your source or destination file. Read the report carefully so that you know in advance how Family Tree Maker will handle each individual if you proceed with a merge. You may append only at this time, then consult the report and merge at a later time.

To see a merge report:

1. Click **Display Merge Report**.

   Family Tree Maker displays the Merge Report dialog box.

2. Carefully read the information displayed to the right of each name.

   The "Birth date" column helps you identify each individual in the list. The "Data differences" column tells you if an individual from the source file is a new individual, a possible match, or an exact match for someone already in the destination file.

   The words "New individual" indicate a new individual and the words "No differences" indicate an exact match. If someone is a possible match, the report lists which fields in the source and destination files contain differing information.

3. To see how the information in a field differs, highlight the field name and look at the **Individual #1** and **Individual #2** fields at the bottom of the dialog box.

   "Individual #1" is the individual being merged. "Individual #2" is the existing individual.

4. To print the report, turn on your printer and click **Print**.

   Family Tree Maker displays the Print dialog box.

5. After you finish reviewing the Merge Report, click **Done**.

   Family Tree Maker returns to the Append File dialog box.

Merging Matches with Confirmation

To merge matching individuals one by one:

1. Click **Merge matching individuals**.

   If you have not already looked at the Merge Report, described above, Family Tree Maker will ask if you want to view it. Click **Yes** to see it, or click **No** to move on.

   When you click "No," or if you already looked at the Merge Report, Family Tree Maker displays one of two things: Merge source (only if one exists), or the Merge Individuals dialog box. In this dialog box, you can compare the information associated with the "possible match" individuals — those who appear to be the same person in both files, but whose information differs slightly.

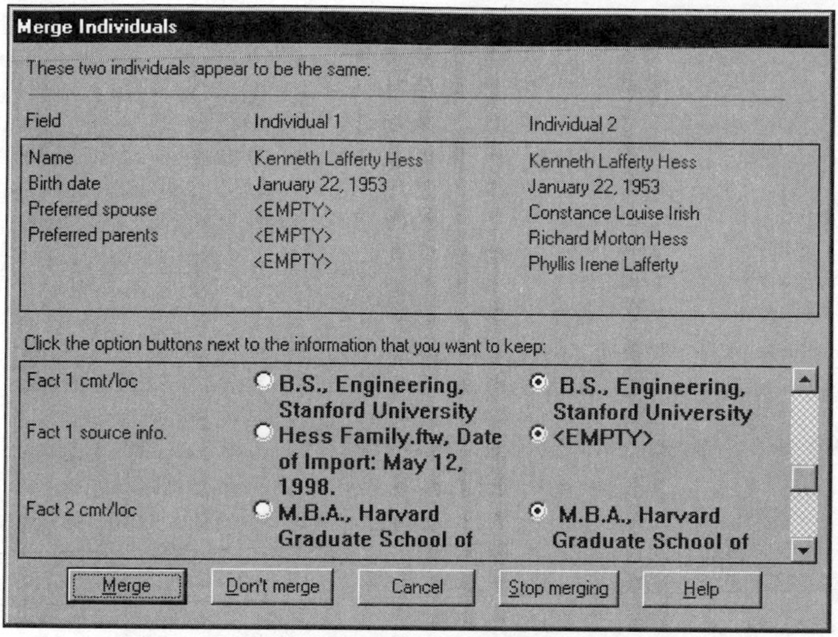

Figure 13-11. The Merge Individuals dialog box

2. Look through the information in the second and third columns. The lines at the top of the dialog box contain names of parents and spouses to help you identify the individual. This information is for reference only, and Family Tree Maker will not merge or discard it.

   Some information may be displayed with option buttons. Scroll through the list, clicking the option button next to the information you want to deep. Any information shown without option buttons will automatically be added to the More About Facts page as Alternate Facts.

   If you think that the information in the two columns belongs to the same individual, click **Merge**. If you think that it belongs to two separate individuals, click **Don't Merge**.

When you click "Merge," Family Tree Maker combines the information from the two records. If there are two sets of data for a given fact, Family Tree Maker creates an "alternate" fact for it. See "Adding Alternate Facts" on page 141. Family Tree Maker joins together differing Notes and Scrapbooks. If there isn't enough room for both sets of Notes or Scrapbook pages, Family Tree Maker will include all of the first individual's information and as much of the second individual's as it can fit. In addition, if two mothers or two fathers are listed as having a "Natural" relationship with the individual, one of the relationships is changed to "Unknown."

When you click "Don't Merge," Family Tree Maker does not merge the two individuals. Instead, both individuals will appear in your Family File.

Repeat step 2 with the next set of information.

Note: If at any time you want to discontinue merging information without saving your merges or combining your files, click **Cancel**. Family Tree Maker displays a Family Page in the destination file.

If there is no more information to compare, Family Tree Maker displays a Merge Report.

3. Click **OK** when you are done viewing or printing the reports.

   Family Tree Maker displays a Family Page.

4. After you finish merging, print some trees and reports *before* you quit Family Tree Maker. Check the documents to make sure that you didn't make any mistakes when merging the files. If you did make mistakes, you can reverse the merge by going to the **Edit** menu and selecting **Undo Merge** *before* you quit Family Tree Maker. You cannot reverse a merge after quitting and restarting Family Tree Maker.

   You can also use the Find command to see the results of your merge. From the **Edit** menu, select **Find individuals** to display the Find Individuals dialog box. Then, in the Find Individual dialog box, select **Merged or appended individuals** in the **Search** field. For more complete instructions, see "Locating Individuals in Your Family File" in Chapter 4.

   Additionally, if after the merge you need to link some of the merged individuals to existing individuals in your file, see "Changing Relationships in Your Family File" in Chapter 6 for more information.

Appending All Information

To add all of the individuals from the source file to the destination file without merging any information:

1. Click **Append only (no merge)**.

    Family Tree Maker adds *all* individuals, facts, Scrapbook items, etc., from the source file to the destination file.

2. Unless all of the individuals from the source file are new individuals, you will later need to remove the duplicate individuals from your Family File. See "Merging Individuals" in Chapter 6 for instructions.

FAMILY FILE STATUS

To get information about your Family File, such as the number of individuals it contains and its size in kilobytes:

1. From the **Help** menu, select **Family File Status**.

    Family Tree Maker displays the Family File Status dialog box.

2. After you finish reading the information in the dialog box, click **OK**.

    Family Tree Maker closes the Family File Status dialog box.

GETTING INFORMATION ABOUT YOUR SYSTEM

System Information gives you important information, such as the amount of memory available to your computer and the display type. If you call our technical support lines, a technical support representative may ask for this information.

To display the System Information dialog box:

1. From the **Help** menu, select **System Information**.

    Family Tree Maker displays the System Information dialog box.

2. If you would like to access standard Windows utilities, such as the Control Panel, system editor, or Windows Explorer, click the **Run** drop-down list and select it from the list.

3. After you finish using this dialog box, click **OK**.

    Family Tree Maker returns you to the previous view.

APPENDICES

John Henry Helwig, shown here in his Knights Templar of Nevada City uniform, is the great-grandfather of Family Tree Maker's Technical Services Supervisor, Ken Schott. John Helwig helped drive the oxen across the plains to California to find fortune during the Gold Rush.

OTHER PRODUCTS

For more information about any of our other products, or to request a catalog of products, call The Learning Co./Parsons Customer Service at (319) 395-0115, or Fax at (319) 395-7449. If you prefer, you can mail the order card in the back of this manual or write to:

The Learning Company
1700 Progress Drive
P.O. Box 100
Hiawatha, IA 52233-0100.

If you would like us to notify you about any new programs, services, or accessories, be sure that we have your current address. Send in your registration card or the change of address card located in the back of this manual.

In addition to the items listed below, we also direct the World Family Tree™ Project. For information about the World Family Tree Project, and to learn how to contribute your Family File, see Chapter 12, "Sharing your Family Information.

FAMILY ARCHIVES

The creators of Family Tree Maker also produce over 100 Family Archive CDs. Designed to help you find your ancestors faster and easier than ever before, Family Archive CDs contain indexes to millions of records that you can view directly through Family Tree Maker. Once you find information about your ancestors, you can copy it directly to your Family File. This collection includes information about more than 220 *million* people!

Convenient and economical, each CD includes references to hundreds of thousands—sometimes millions—of names, with information derived from marriage records, census records, Social Security records, pedigree collections, military records, church and cemetery records, and more. Some of our most popular Family Archive CDs are the twenty volumes of World Family Tree CDs. These CDs contain family trees submitted by Family Tree Maker customers and other family history enthusiasts dedicated to helping others find their families. Each World Family Tree CD contains up to 6,000 trees and up to 3 million names.

Family Archive CDs are available separately and as value-priced bundles. Call The Learning Company at (800) 548-1806 for further information. Don't miss this opportunity to see what Family Archives are all about!

PARCHMENT PAPER

We offer antique-finish parchment paper that you can use to print your trees. The paper is for use with tractor-feed printers or laser printers. See the order card in the back of this manual for details.

ORG PLUS

Org Plus automatically draws organization charts and tree diagrams. You can also use it to generate reports such as phone lists or salary summaries directly from your charts. Available for DOS, Windows, and Mac, it's an indispensable tool for managers in all types of businesses. In fact, over 400 of the Fortune 500 companies use *Org Plus*!

TROUBLESHOOTING

Although we hope you never have any problems while using Family Tree Maker, sometimes things just go wrong. If you do have a problem, first try to locate the solution in this chapter. Figure B-1 below will help you.

For this type of problem...	See page...
Installation problems	495
Family Tree Maker Online problems	515
Printing problems	501
Error messages	504
Display problems	506
Computer problems	507
CD-ROM problems	512
Print setup problems	514
What if I can't find my ancestor's name?	515

Figure B-1. Troubleshooting sections

Another place to look for information is in Family Tree Maker's "README" file. This file contains last-minute information that is not in the manual. To see the "README," click **Start**, select **Programs**, select **Family Tree Maker**, and then select **FTW Read Me**.

If the suggestions in this chapter don't solve the problem, remember that the most up-to-date information is always available to you online at:

www.FamilyTree Maker.com/support.html

You can also contact The Learning Company's Banner Blue Division Technical Support for assistance. See "Contacting Technical Support" at the end of this chapter.

SYSTEM REQUIREMENTS

Family Tree Maker requires an IBM PC or compatible that meets the requirements listed below. Please realize that these are the minimum requirements. As with all programs, a faster processor, more RAM, and more free disk space will enhance performance.

Also keep in mind that the more family information you enter, the more free hard disk space and available RAM you will need. If you plan to include many pictures, sounds, or videos in your Family Tree Maker Scrapbooks, you will need a substantial amount of hard disk space.

If your system does not meet these minimum requirements, *we cannot guarantee the program will function correctly*. You will need to upgrade your system to meet these requirements if you wish to use Family Tree Maker.

Component	Minimum Requirement
CPU	P90 or faster (P120 recommended)
Operating System	Microsoft® Windows® 95 or higher
RAM	16MB RAM (32MB recommended) **Note:** As with all Windows programs, more RAM and a faste CPU will improve performance.
Free Disk Space	50MB (after installation) recommended
CD-ROM Drive	This drive must be part of your system — as opposed to a drive that you access via a network
Monitor	640x480 display, 256 colors or higher
Printer	Most popular Windows printers are supported
Mouse	Microsoft compatible

Figure B-2. System Requirements

You can take advantage of Family Tree Maker's optional features with the following optional devices: Printer or plotter, Modem, Scanner, Kodak Photo CD-compatible CD-ROM drive, Sound card, and Video capture card.

WINDOWS BASICS

This section describes some of the tasks you can perform on Family Tree Maker files using the features that are available in Windows.

Renaming a Family Tree Maker File

To rename a Family Tree Maker file:

1. Close Family Tree Maker.

2. From the Windows 95/98 **Start** menu, select **Programs**, then **Windows Explorer**.

   Explorer displays the folders on your hard drive (usually drive C).

3. Click the **FTW** folder in the left side of the Explorer window.

Note: If you installed Family Tree Maker in a different folder, be sure to click on this folder instead.

   Explorer displays the sub-folders and files in the FTW folder.

4. In the right side of the Explorer window, click the Family File you'd like to rename.

5. From the **File** menu, select **Rename**.

6. Type the new file name.

   Be sure to include the same file extension as the original file (.FTW, .FBK, etc.).

7. From the **File** menu, select **Close**.

Moving a Family Tree Maker File

To move a Family Tree Maker file:

1. Close Family Tree Maker.

2. From the Windows 95 **Start** menu, select **Programs**, then **Windows Explorer**.

   Explorer displays the folders on your hard drive (usually drive C).

3. Click the folder or drive in the left side of the Explorer window that contains the file you'd like to move.

    Explorer displays the sub-folders and files located in that folder or drive.

4. In the right side of the Explorer window, click the file you'd like to move.

5. From the **Edit** menu, select **Cut**.

6. In the left side of the Explorer window, click the drive and folder into which you'd like to move the file.

7. From the **Edit** menu, select **Paste**.

    Explorer pastes the file into the selected folder. Your file should appear in the bottom of the list of files on the right side of the Explorer window.

8. From the **File** menu, select **Close**.

Displaying File Extensions

The default in Windows is to display file names without their extensions. Sometimes it is useful to be able see the file extension to further identify the file. For example, in Family Tree Maker your Family File will have the same name as your backup file - the only difference is the file extension. See the next section for a description of the file extensions Family Tree Maker uses.

To have Windows display file extensions:

1. From the Windows 95 **Start** menu, select **Programs**, then **Windows Explorer**.

    Explorer displays the folders on your hard drive (usually drive C).

2. From the **View** menu, select **Options**.

    Explorer displays the View tab of the Options dialog box.

    Note: In Windows 98, select Folder Options, then click the View tab. Deselect "Hide file extensions."

3. Click the **Show all files** option to select it.

4. Click the **Hide MS-DOS file extensions for file types that are registered** check box to *remove* the existing check mark.

5. Click **OK** to save your changes and close the dialog box.

Family Tree Maker File Extensions

Family Tree Maker uses the following file extensions:

- .FTW – This is the "regular" Family File extension. All Family Files you create will have this extension.

- .FBK – This is the file extension for automatically created backup files. Each time you close the program, Family Tree Maker automatically makes a backup copy of your Family File using this file extension.

- .FBC – This is the file extension used when you create a compressed backup file using the Family Tree Maker Backup command.

- .GED – This is the file extension for a GEDCOM file.

INSTALLATION PROBLEMS

Read through the items in bold print below to find your particular problem. The possible solutions are listed below each problem.

Your system locks up during installation (you may get the message: "This program has performed an illegal operation and will be shut down").

- Close any programs you're using including shortcut toolbars that remain on your desktop, such as Microsoft Office.

- Follow the instructions in "Closing Other Applications" in this Appendix.

- CD-ROM Read Ahead may be interfering with proper installation. See "CD-ROM Problems" in this Appendix for instructions on turning off the Read Ahead feature.

- Click on the "Details" button when the error appears and record the module in which the error occurred. You may recognize it as a video or printer driver, in which case you should install the latest video or printer driver from the device's manufacturer.

- See "Checking Your Hard Disk for Problems" in this Appendix for instructions on performing a "Scan Disk" on your hard disk.

Your system locks up after completing about 34% of the installation.

The date on your system clock is probably incorrect. To change the system clock:

1. Click the Windows 95 **Start** button.

2. Select **Settings**. From the sub-menu, select **Control Panel**.

3. Double-click the **Date/Time** icon.

   Verify that the year is set to the current year.

4. Click **OK** once you've made your changes.

5. Start the Family Tree Maker installation again.

A message appears saying "Cannot find d:setup" (or one of its components). Check to be sure the path and filename are correct and that all required libraries are available."

- Make sure you type the correct letter for your CD-ROM drive. Often, d: represents the CD-ROM drive, in which case you would type `d:setup`

- You may have entered something other than `d:setup` in the "Open" field of the Windows **Run** dialog box. Check what was entered.

- The CD-ROM may be damaged. Contact Banner Blue Technical Support for assistance.

A message appears saying "Trouble reading file. File may be damaged or have read-only status."

- See "CD-ROM Problems" in this chapter for instructions on cleaning the CD-ROM and try the installation again.

- CD-ROM Read Ahead may be interfering with proper installation. See "CD-ROM Problems" in this chapter for instructions on turning off the Read Ahead feature.

- Virus protection software may be interfering with proper installation. Follow your virus protection's instructions on disabling virus protection and try the installation again.

I put the installation CD in and nothing happens.

The Windows 95 Autorun feature may be turned off.

1. Click the Windows 95 **Start** button, then select **Run**.

2. In the **Open** field, type `d:setup`

Note: The "d" in "d:setup" stands for drive d. If you are installing from a CD-ROM drive other than drive d, type that letter instead. For example, to install from drive e, type `e:setup`

3. Click **OK**.

The Family Tree Maker installation program doesn't ask for the second or third CD-ROM when installing.

- The entire program is on the first CD-ROM. The second and third CD-ROMs only contain data for the FamilyFinder Index and do not need to be installed.

A message appears saying that you don't have enough disk space to install the program.

- You may be out of space on the drive where Windows is installed, the drive where you're attempting to save, or the drive where your temporary folder is located. See "Disk Space" in this Appendix.

FAMILY TREE MAKER ONLINE PROBLEMS

Read through the items in bold print below to find your particular problem. The possible solutions are listed below each problem.

The Online button doesn't work. Nothing happens when I click the Online button.

1. From the **Internet** menu, select **Browser setup**.

2. Follow the online instructions to complete setup.

   Family Tree maker displays a confirmation message saying that the browser has been successfully set up.

Additional Considerations

If your browser still won't launch when you click the Online button, go to the Technical Support link at **http://www.familytreemaker.com**, and look for information about Online issues. Print the instructions for the appropriate browser and follow them step-by-step.

Additional notes for America Online users

We recommend upgrading to the AOL version designed specifically for Windows 95 or 98. Otherwise, you may have problems with Online FamilyFinder reports and related features.

Verify that your Windows configuration file (WIN.INI) contains the appropriate references to America Online. Go to the Technical Support link at **http://www.familytreemaker.com**, and look for information about Online issues. Print the instructions for your version of America Online and follow them step-by-step.

You can access Family Tree Maker Online using the Online command, but you can't access the features available only to Family Tree Maker customers.

First, verify that you have an online account.

- The first time you click the Online button and log into Family Tree Maker Online, you'll come to a Welcome screen. You can either verify an old account or register as a new user. You must be registered *Online* to get access to the special features reserved for Family Tree Maker users. This *Online* registration is different than regular software registration. Regular software registration makes you eligible for special upgrade pricing and periodic information about new products, releases, and pricing. *Online* registration is the method we use to set up an account which identifies you as someone who is eligible to use all of the special features reserved for Family Tree Maker users while you are logged on to the Family Tree Maker Online Web site.

If you're sure you have established an online account with our Web site and are still having problems, there are a few things to try:

- Click the **Online** button in Family Tree Maker. This should take you directly to Family Tree Maker Online after you log into your Internet Service Provider. Just starting your web browser (such as Netscape Navigator or Internet Explorer) and typing the address for our Web site won't always work.

- Make sure you're using the same web browser and computer you used when you first registered with us online.

- Make sure you're accepting cookies. Both Netscape Navigator 4.x (including Communicator) and Microsoft Internet Explorer 4.x let you disable cookies. Also, there are programs and browser plug-ins that will block cookies for security reasons. To use Family Tree Maker Online features, you will need to disable or uninstall these types of programs. Family Tree Maker stores a cookie on your hard drive when you submit your online registration. It then uses this cookie to verify your account.

- Empty the web browser's cache and history (these are called Temporary Internet Files in Internet Explorer).

Note: If you've done all of these things, and you still are not recognized as an existing user, it is likely that you have duplicate accounts. You can't access the members-only portions of our site until one or more of these accounts is deleted. Contact Technical Support for assistance.

Why do the paragraphs on my Home Page run together?

There is a problem that causes the paragraphs on your home page to run together when using Microsoft Internet Explorer 3.x. Upgrade to Microsoft Internet Explorer 4.0 or use Netscape Navigator 3.x or 4.x and you will not experience this problem.

I subscribed to the online World Family Tree volumes and other archives, but I can't access them.

OR

I received a message saying that the Family Finder Agent has found information for me. When I go to your Web site and click Agents, there is no information there.

- Make sure you're only trying to access the archive you subscribed to. Carefully follow the instructions on our Web site for accessing and transferring the trees to your computer.

- Make sure you're using the same browser and computer you used when you first created the request(s).

- If you are a Family Tree Maker user, you must access the Web site via the same method that you used when creating the Agent request or subscribing to the online volume. If you clicked the Online button when you created these items, you must click the Online button to access them. If you went directly through your web browser and did not use Family Tree Maker's Online button, you must use this same method again.

- Make sure you're accepting cookies. Both Netscape Navigator 4.x (including Communicator) and Microsoft Internet Explorer 4.x let you disable cookies, and for both programs this option is set in the preferences. Also, there are programs and browser plug-ins that will block cookies for security reasons. To use Family Tree Maker Online features, you will need to disable or uninstall these types of programs. Family Tree Maker stores a cookie on your hard drive when you submit your online registration. It then uses this cookie to verify your account.

- Empty the web browser's cache and history (these are called Temporary Internet Files in Internet Explorer).

I'm having problems publishing reports and InterneTrees, or submitting files to the World Family Tree Project.

- Verify that you set up your browser correctly. See "The Online button doesn't work" in this chapter for directions.

- Verify that you have an online account. See "You can access Family Tree Maker Online using the Online command, but you can't access the features available only to Family Tree Maker customers" in this chapter for directions.

- Are you behind a firewall? This can be an issue if you're using a cable modem or accessing our Web site from work. You cannot submit files online, nor publish reports or trees to our Web site when behind a firewall.

- Your issues may be due to Internet traffic. If you're confident everything's set up correctly, clear the cache on your browser and try again later.

PRINTING PROBLEMS

Read through the items in bold print below to find your particular problem. The possible solutions are listed below each problem.

Family Tree Maker is printing slowly.

- Printing from Windows, especially when printing graphics, can be slow. If you want it to print faster, you can try printing at lower quality, but the output won't look as nice.

- The Windows Spool Settings may be slowing it down. To disable these features, see your Microsoft Windows User's Guide. You may also need to consult the documentation that came with your printer.

- Your computer may be running low on memory or resources. You must have at least 50% free resources while printing. See "Memory and Resources" in this chapter.

- The Windows Temp folder may be full.

The letters are replaced with symbols or garbage characters are printing.

- You may be using a symbol font, such as Dingbats or Wingdings. Try switching to a TrueType font such as Arial.

- You may have the wrong printer driver. See "Print Setup" in this chapter.

- Your printer's memory may have been corrupted during the last print job. Reset the printer by turning it off, waiting a few seconds, and then turning it back on again.

- If you are printing to a serial printer, you may have an incorrect port, baud rate, or parity setting in Print Setup. See "Print Setup" in this chapter.

- You may have a bad printer cable. Try using a new one.

    Note: Many new inkjet printers require an IEEE 1284 bi-directional printer cable and will not work with a standard parallel cable.

- Your computer may be running low on memory or resources. You must have at least 50% free resources while printing. See "Memory and Resources" in this chapter.

- Your printer may not be able to handle all the information being sent to it. Check for error messages on the printer and consult your printer manual for possible solutions.

The boxes are printing without text or the text is printing without boxes.

- Check the Items to Include dialog box (on the **Contents** menu) to make sure that you have chosen to include items in your boxes.

- Family Tree Maker has an option to print trees without boxes. Check the Box, Line, & Border Styles dialog box (on the **Format** menu).

- Your printer's memory may have been corrupted during the last print job. Reset your printer by turning it off, waiting a few seconds, and then turning it back on again.

- Make sure you haven't selected the "Print empty" option in the Print dialog box (on the **File** menu).

- You may have the wrong printer driver. See "Print Setup" in this chapter.

- The Windows Spool Settings may be interfering. To disable this feature, see your Microsoft Windows User's Guide.

- Your computer may be running low on memory or resources. You must have at least 50% free resources while printing. See "Memory and Resources" in this chapter.

The pictures are not printing clearly.

- The brightness setting may be too dark. In the view you're printing, open the Print Setup dialog box (on the **File** menu), click **Brightness**, and choose a lighter setting. See "Setting Your Printer Options" in Chapter 10.

- Image quality may have deteriorated during import. Try importing again using a lower compression setting. See "Controlling Picture Resolution and Compression" in Chapter 5.

- Try selecting a different file format when you import the graphic file. Family Tree Maker accepts a variety of common file formats.

- You may have the wrong printer driver. See "Print Setup" in this chapter.

- The Windows 95 Spool Settings may be interfering. To disable this feature, see your Microsoft Windows User's Guide.

- Open the FTW.INI file. To do this, elect **System Information** from the **Help** menu. Click the **Run** drop down list and select **FTW.INI**. This will open the FTW.INI file in Notepad. In the [OPTIONS] section of the FTW.INI file, insert a new line and type `PrintColorImage=True` If there is not an [OPTIONS] section, you can create one at the bottom of the file by pressing **Enter** once and then typing `[OPTIONS]`

- The image may have been of poor quality to begin with. If possible, get a better quality image.

Absolutely nothing prints at all.

- Your printer may not be hooked up correctly. Check to see if it's turned on, online, and connected to the computer.

- You may have incorrect printer settings or the wrong printer driver. See "Print Setup" in this chapter.

- Your computer may be running low on memory or resources. You must have at least 50% free resources while printing. See "Memory and Resources" in this chapter.

- Your printer may not be able to handle all the information being sent to it. Check for error messages on the printer and consult your printer manual for possible solutions.

Text is printing outside boxes.

- You may have the wrong printer driver. See "Print Setup" in this chapter.

- Your printer may be using the wrong character spacing. Set up your printer so that the software is in control of what size character is printed, instead of having the printer set for one size character.

- You may be using a font that is not scaling correctly. Try using a TrueType font such as Arial.

- Your computer may be running low on memory or resources. You must have at least 50% free resources while printing. See "Memory and Resources" in this chapter.

You cannot get a printer file to print.

- Be sure that you are typing the correct command at the DOS prompt. For example, you could type `copy/b c:\ftw\mytree.prn LPT1` where "mytree.prn" is the file name, "c:\ftw" are the drive and folder where the file is located, and the printer is connected to LPT1.

- When you create the printer file, make sure that the printer listed at the top of the Print dialog box is the printer to which you will eventually print the file.

Family Tree Maker will not print on banner size paper.

- In the Windows Control Panel printer setup, set the paper size to **banner** and the paper source to **tray**.

- In Family Tree Maker printer setup, make sure the paper orientation is set to **landscape**.

I need to add or install a new printer in Windows

- To add a printer, click the **Start** button, then select **Settings**. From the sub-menu, select **Printers**. In the Printers window, double-click the **Add Printer** icon. This starts the Add Printers Wizard that will guide you through the process of installing the printer driver.

ERROR MESSAGES

Read through the items in bold print below to find your particular error message. The possible solutions are listed below each message.

A message appears saying "Family Tree Maker could not use the default printer."

- Install a printer driver even if you do not have a printer. Family Tree Maker needs a printer driver to format the items it displays on the screen.

- You need to reinstall your current printer driver. If the error persists, obtain the most updated driver for the printer.

A message appears saying "FTW caused a general protection fault in module OLE32.DLL or STORAGE.DLL."

Your file is damaged. Try opening the backup file first.

If you do not have a backup file, contact Technical Support.

I get an error message about the file OLENLS.DLL.

The Regional Setting for Windows needs to be set to English (United States).

1. Click the Windows 95 **Start** button, then select **Settings**. From the sub-menu, select **Control Panel**.

2. In the Control Panel window, double-click **Regional Settings** and select **English (United States)**.

    If it is already set to "English," set it to a different language, restart your computer, then set it back to "English (United States)."

An error occurs in KERNEL32.DLL, GDI.EXE, or USER.EXE.

*   Restart your computer and try again.

*   Follow the directions for "Booting Your Computer in Safe Mode" in this chapter.

*   Consult Microsoft's website about ways to increase resources within Windows.

A message appears saying that one of the library files needed to run Family Tree Maker needs to be reinstalled.

*   Reinstall Family Tree Maker. If the problem persists, contact Technical Support.

An item in the Scrapbook does not play as you expect, or gives a message that the server couldn't be found.

*   OLE Server applications must "register" themselves with Windows. Your OLE server may not be registered or installed properly. Try reinstalling the server application or consulting the server's manufacturer.

A message appears saying that Family Tree Maker has detected a possible problem with your file.

*   Click **Yes** to try to open your file. If the same or another error message appears after you click "Yes," try opening the backup file instead. See "Opening Backup Files" in Chapter 13.

A message appears saying that you don't have enough disk space to save or to run.

- You may be out of space on the drive where Windows is installed, the drive where you're attempting to save, or the drive where your temporary folder is located. See "Disk Space" in this chapter.

DISPLAY PROBLEMS

Read through the items in bold print below to find your particular problem. The possible solutions are listed below each problem.

The tabs along the right side of the Family Page have garbage characters on them or the text is not vertical.

- Your video driver may be incompatible with Family Tree Maker or you may need a new video driver. Try using Family Tree Maker with Windows in Safe Mode (see your Microsoft Windows User's guide). If the tabs display properly in Safe Mode you may need to lower the hardware acceleration for your graphics hardware. From the Windows 95 **Start** menu select **Settings**, then select **Control Panel**. From the sub-menu, select **System**. In the System window, select **Performance**, then select **Graphics**. Lower the Hardware Acceleration setting to **Basic Accelerator Functions**. Click **OK**, then click **Close.** Select **Yes** to restart Windows.

Images are not displayed clearly on the screen.

- Your system may not be using enough colors to display the image. Check the documentation that came with your computer for instructions on how to get more colors. (A video driver with 256 colors is the normal amount of colors required to display images clearly.)

- Try selecting a different file format when you import the graphic file. Family Tree Maker accepts a variety of common file formats.

- Image quality may have deteriorated during import. Try importing again using a lower compression setting. See "Controlling Picture Resolution and Compression" in Chapter 5.

- Try using the Insert Object command instead of the Insert Picture from File command.

- The image may have been of poor quality to begin with. If possible, get a better quality image.

Fonts are not displayed clearly on the screen.

- Make sure Family Tree Maker is maximized. Click the **Title Bar** with the right mouse button and select **Maximize**.

- Try changing the font used on the Family Page. Open Family Tree Maker. From the **Help** menu, select **System Information**. Click the **Run** drop down list. Select **FTW.INI**. This will open the FTW.INI file with the Windows Notepad program. Delete the semicolon in front of the line that reads: **FamPagFont=Arial Bold**. This will change the Family Page font to Arial Bold. From the **File** menu in Notepad, select **Save**. You need to restart Family Tree Maker for the settings to take affect.

  Note: The Family Page Font can be changed to other Windows fonts by replacing **Arial Bold** with the name of another Windows font installed on your system.

Not all information is viewable, or some is garbled when viewing a CD.

- See "CD-ROM Problems" in this chapter.

COMPUTER PROBLEMS

Sometimes you might experience a problem that does not fall into any of the categories mentioned above. The following section will give you some helpful hints on how to check some basic issues related to your computer.

Checking Your Hard Disk for Problems

There are only two kinds of hard disk drives: the ones that have failed and the ones that will fail. Every hard disk drive will eventually develop problems that can lead to erratic behavior and unexplained problems.

Windows 95 comes with a utility called ScanDisk that can detect and repair some of these errors. You should run this utility on a regular basis as preventative maintenance. This utility can detect and repair hard drive errors. Before running this utility, close all applications, including Family Tree Maker.

1. From the Windows 95 **Start** menu, select **Programs**, then select **Accessories**. From the sub-menu, select **System Tools**, and then select **ScanDisk**.

2. In the Scan Disk dialog box, select the **Automatically fix errors** check box and then click **Start**.

    If ScanDisk reports any errors, you should reinstall Family Tree Maker.

Disk Space

In Windows programs, many operations such as printing and saving require disk space. You might receive a warning message telling you that you don't have enough disk space, or you might encounter strange behavior of a program or function if disk space is insufficient.

To ensure that you have sufficient disk space, check the following:

- **Disk space available on the drive where Windows is installed**. With Windows 98 you need to have at least 110 MB free disk space available on the drive where Windows is installed. In addition, Windows needs at least 50MB of free disk space to run properly after Family Tree Maker has been installed. You may encounter problems if you have less.

- **Disk space available on the drive where Family Tree Maker is saving your Family File**. You generally need to have 3 times the size of your file available because of the way many Windows programs (including Family Tree Maker) save files. For example, if your file is 400,000 bytes, you actually need 1,200,000 bytes (1.2 MB) available to save it.

- **Temporary disk space**. Windows maintains a temporary folder, usually C:\Windows\Temp, for temporary storage space. This folder can get very full over the months and should be cleaned out on a regular basis. To do this, first close all programs, then start Windows Explorer. Go to the Windows\Temp folder and delete everything in it.

Memory and Resources

Family Tree Maker requires that you have at least 16megabytes of physical memory to run. We recommend, however, 32 megabytes or more for optimal performance. To check your available physical memory, from the Family Tree Maker **Help** menu, select **System Information**. Family Tree Maker displays the System Information dialog box, which displays your Physical Memory. If you can't start Family Tree Maker, then from the Windows 95 desktop, double-click **My Computer**. From the **Help** menu, select **About Windows 95**.

If your computer has only 16 megabytes of memory, Family Tree Maker might run slow at times and it might take a long time to perform certain tasks, especially if you have a large family file. You should try closing other programs to make more memory available.

If the performance is still sluggish, you might want to consider adding more memory to your system.

Booting Your Computer in Safe Mode

In Windows, you can start your computer in a special troubleshooting mode called **Safe Mode**. If you encounter problems or error messages when you run Family Tree Maker, try starting your computer in Safe Mode to see if you can bypass the error.

Note: When you start your computer in Safe Mode some of the hardware devices, such as the CD-ROM drive, may not work because Safe Mode does not load all of the hardware drivers.

To boot your computer in Safe Mode:

1. From the Windows 95 **Start** menu, select **Shutdown**.

    Windows 95 displays the Shut Down Windows dialog box.

2. Select **Restart the Computer?** and click **Yes**.

    Windows restarts your computer.

3. As soon as you hear the single beep as the system boots, press [F8].

    Windows displays the Boot menu.

4. From the Boot menu, select **Safe Mode**.

   Windows starts in Safe Mode. For more information about Safe Mode, refer to your Windows 95 manual.

5. Perform the action that caused the problem you experienced earlier.

   If you can bypass the error, this indicates that one or more programs on your computer are causing a conflict with Family Tree Maker. Programs that typically cause this type of conflict are hardware drivers and Terminate and Stay Resident (TSR) programs. You will need to determine which program or driver is causing the problem. If it is a hardware driver, contact the manufacturer to verify that you have the latest drivers. If it is a program, refer to that program's user manual for troubleshooting ideas, or consider disabling the program.

6. When you are ready to return to Normal mode, restart your computer as described in steps 1 and 2 and let your computer boot normally.

Closing Other Applications

On rare occasions, it can happen that other programs that are running in the background cause conflicts during installation or operation of Family Tree Maker. To make sure that only necessary programs are running before you install or run Family Tree Maker, follow these steps.

To check the tasklist:

1. Close any programs you are using.

2. From the desktop, press [Ctrl] + [alt] + [delete].

   Windows displays the Close Programs dialog box. It contains a list of all programs that are currently running.

3. If the list shows any programs other than Explorer and Systray, click the other program name and then click **End Task**.

Windows closes the program. Repeat these steps to close all programs other than Explorer and Systray.

"This program has performed an illegal operation" error messages

If you get an error message that begins with "This program has performed an illegal operation," - STOP! In this dialog box, click the **Details** button and write down the error description displayed in the lower half of the dialog. You do not have to write down all the numbers listed, just the sentence describing the error. An example would be:

"FTW caused an invalid page fault in module (name).drv" or

"FTW caused a general protection fault in module (name).exe"

Once you have recorded this information, click the **Close** button. Family Tree Maker will shut down.

Next, check "Error Messages" in this chapter for the error message you recorded. Follow the suggestions listed there. If you don't find the error message in that section, keep reading below.

- If the "module" listed in the error message contains the letters drv, it is a hardware driver, most likely your video or printer driver. You may be able to tell which, by the name of the driver. This type of message indicates that Family Tree Maker requested the driver to perform a certain task that the driver was not capable of handling. The most common resolution to these types of errors is to obtain the most current version of the driver from the manufacturer. For more information about these types of problems, see "Printing Problems" or "Display Problems" in this chapter.

- If the "module" listed in the error message contains a recognizable name of a program, it means there is another application running in the background that caused a conflict. See "Close Other Applications" and "Booting Your Computer in Safe Mode" in this chapter to resolve this conflict.

System Freezes or Locks Up

If your system stops responding completely, follow the steps below to troubleshoot the problem.

1. Press `Ctrl` + `alt` + `delete` on your keyboard.

   Windows displays the **Close Programs** dialog box.

   Note: If the system does not respond to pressing `Ctrl` + `alt` + `delete` within a few seconds, try it a second time. If this still yields no response, turn off the power to your system for about 10 seconds, then turn it back on to reboot.

2. In the list of applications, check for the wording "(not responding)." Highlight this application and click the **End Task** button.

 You might now see another window telling you again that this program is not responding.

3. Again, click the **End Task** button to close it.

 This should return you to the desktop from where you can perform a graceful reboot by performing the normal Windows shutdown process.

Once you system is running again, you should try to determine what caused this behavior. The most likely cause is a video driver conflict. See "Display Problems" in this chapter for further information.

It is also possible that this was caused by a conflicting application that is running in the background. See "Close Other Applications" and "Booting Your Computer in Safe Mode" in this chapter to resolve this conflict.

CD-ROM PROBLEMS

You're having trouble accessing a CD.

- There may be fingerprints or dust on your CD. Remove the CD from your CD-ROM drive and gently wipe the shiny side with a clean towel. Do not wipe in a circular motion around the CD. Instead, wipe from the inside edge to the outside edge.

- You may be using an old CD-ROM driver. Call your CD-ROM manufacturer and make sure that you have the latest version of the driver.

- Turn off the CD-ROM Read Ahead Feature. From the Windows 95 **Start** menu, select **Settings** and then **Control Panel**. Double-click the **System** icon. In the System Properties dialog, click the **Performance** tab and then click the **File System** button. Windows opens the File System Properties dialog box. Click the **CD-ROM** tab and in the **Optimize access pattern for** drop-down list, select **No read-ahead**. Note the original setting in case you want to revert to it at a later date. In the File System Properties dialog box, click **OK** to accept your change and then click **OK** again to close the System Properties dialog box.

- Family Tree Maker may be having trouble identifying your CD-ROM drive. In this case, you can list the drive in the FTW.INI file. To do this, select **System Information** from the **Help** menu. Click the **Run** drop down list and select **FTW.INI**. This will open the FTW.INI file in Notepad. Look for the line "**;FamFinderCD=X:**". Remove the semi-colon (**;**) from the beginning of the line and type the letter of the your CD-ROM drive in place of the "X". For example, if your CD-ROM drive is drive E, then change the line to FamFinderCD=E:\

- If you have specified the CD-ROM drive in the FTW.INI file, and you still experience problems, try the following. Select **System Information** from the **Help** menu. Click the **Run** drop down list and select **FTW.INI**. This will open the FTW.INI file in Notepad. Look for the line "**[Family Finder CD]**". Delete the lines *under* this section.

  Note: Make sure to only delete the lines directly under **[Family Finder CD]**. DO NOT delete any lines that are in a different section. Each section in the file starts with a word in brackets [ ].

- If you're trying to use a Family Archive CD in a multi-disc CD-ROM drive such as a CD-ROM changer or jukebox, you can only use the Family Archive CD in the first drive.

- Some display settings may effect your CD-ROM drive's ability to read information from the CD. To change your display settings, do the following. From the Windows 95 Start menu, select **Settings** and then **Control Panel**. Double-click the **Display** icon and then click the **Settings** tab. Try reducing some of the values in the "Desktop Area" and "Color Palette" areas. Then try accessing the CD again.

- If you are viewing a Family Archive CD and cannot see the entire window on your screen, you may need to increase the desktop area. From the Windows 95 **Start** menu, select **Settings** and then **Control Panel**. Double-click the **Display** icon and click the **Settings** tab. Increase your "Desktop Area" by moving the slider over one notch to the 800 x 600 pixel setting in the Desktop Area box.

PRINT SETUP

One of the nicest things about Windows is that it handles all printing. You don't have to install your printer over and over again in different programs — once your printer is installed in Windows, it should work with all Windows programs. If you're having trouble printing from Family Tree Maker, you may have an outdated printer driver or an incorrect setting in your print setup.

1. Make sure that your selection in print setup *exactly* matches the kind of printer you have. To check this, from the **File** menu in Family Tree Maker, select **Print Setup**. Using a driver other than the one specifically designed to work with your printer can cause unpredictable results. If you don't have the correct printer driver, contact your printer manufacturer or Microsoft for information on how to get the most current version.

2. Family Tree Maker allows you to have different settings in print setup for each view. For example, you could choose legal-size paper and one-inch margins for your Ancestor trees, but letter-size paper and half-inch margins for your Descendant trees. You could also select completely different printers for each tree! If you find that you can print correctly from one view, but not from another, compare the settings in Print Setup for each view to determine what is different between the two.

3. Try printing from another Windows program, such as Write or Notepad. If you experience the same problem, then the problem lies somewhere in either your printer or Windows setup. Contact Microsoft or your printer manufacturer for assistance.

4. Check your settings to verify that they match your system.

   From the Windows 95 **Start** menu, select **Settings** and then **Printers**. Right-click your printer icon, and select **Properties**.

   The Properties dialog box will tell you through which port Windows is printing. (A port is a place on your computer that the printer can plug into.) Check the documentation that came with your computer to find out which port your printer is connected to. This port should be the one shown in the Properties dialog box.

   In particular, if you are printing through a COM port (e.g. COM1), make sure that the settings for baud rate, parity, and stop bits match those set on your printer. If you aren't sure what the settings should be, consult your printer manual. You may also want to try decreasing the baud rate. Sometimes there's simply too much going on for Windows to talk to your printer at a high speed. Decreasing the speed will usually solve the problem. This is particularly true when printing to plotters.

5. Make sure you're using the most current driver available for your printer. You can check the version by going to the **File** menu in Family Tree Maker and selecting **Print Setup**. Click **Options** in the Print Setup dialog box. This will bring up a screen specific to your printer. There is usually an "About" button which gives information about the driver, including the version. If there isn't a button, then the version number may appear somewhere else in the dialog box. Check with your printer manufacturer to see if you have the latest version of the driver. (They can also tell you how to find out which version you have, if you aren't sure).

WHAT IF I CAN'T FIND MY ANCESTOR'S NAME?

When you're using the search features in FamilyFinder or on the Family Tree Maker Online Web site, it is possible that you won't always find the name you are looking for. If this occurs, don't despair! Here are a few things to consider before you give up:

First, it may be that the individual whose record you want to locate really is listed in the FamilyFinder Index, but the name has been disguised by errors or a name change. Because the FamilyFinder Index is compiled from many different sources, including hand-written census records more than a century old, there will be errors. Some of the errors are spelling errors, misinterpretations of names, transpositions of first and last names, first initials being used instead of first names, abbreviations being used instead of full or middle names (like Edw. Wm., instead of Edward William), and other errors. Even name changes may play a part in "hiding" a name. For example, if you are looking for the name of a female in the Social Security Death Index, look under her married name rather than her maiden name. For these reasons, as you look through the FamilyFinder Index, don't rule out entries that are similar, but not exact, matches of the names.

There are two places you can go for advice and more examples of common data errors. First, click the **Introduction** tab on the Family Archive in which you could not find your ancestor's name. You may find helpful information there. Second, see "Issues with using the FamilyFinder Index (and Family Archives)" in the Genealogy "How-To" Guide.

To read this topic:

1. From the **Help** menu, select **Genealogy "How-To" Guide**.

2. On the first screen of the Genealogy "How-To" Guide, select **FamilyFinder Index**.

    Family Tree Maker displays the topic "All About the FamilyFinder Index."

3. From that topic, select **Issues with using the FamilyFinder Index (and Family Archives)**.

Even if you still can't locate your ancestor's name in the FamilyFinder Index, a record with your ancestor's name may still exist. It might be that the record is in an index that is currently unavailable electronically, and therefore isn't included in the FamilyFinder Index.

CONTACTING TECHNICAL SUPPORT

You can call (510) 794-6850 to speak directly to a technical support representative Monday through Friday, 7:00 AM to 5:00 PM, (all times Pacific Standard Time).

Note: Please be in front of your computer with Windows running when calling Technical Support. The representative you speak with will need to ask you a variety of questions about your computer system and any error messages you may have encountered.

You can also call the Banner Blue Technical Support **Interactive Automated Help System** 24 hours a day, seven days a week, at (510) 794-6850. This number has pre-recorded voice instructions and can fax back written instructions.

Note: If you prefer, you can get help immediately on the Internet at: **www.familytreemaker.com/support.html**

If you are unable to call while at your computer, you can print your system information and have it with you when you call or send it when you write or fax.

Before you call, write, or fax, please do the following:

1. Start Family Tree Maker.

2. From the Help menu, select **System Information**.

   Family Tree Maker displays detailed information about your computer system.

3. Press `alt` + `print screen` (Print Screen).

   Windows makes a copy of the System Information dialog box and places it on the clipboard.

4. Click **OK** to close the dialog.

5. From the **File** menu, select **Exit** to leave Family Tree Maker.

6. Click the Windows 95 **Start** button and then select **Run**.

   Windows displays the Run dialog box.

7. Type **C:\WINDOWS\WRITE.EXE** and click **OK**.

   Windows opens WordPad.

   Note: You can use most other Windows word processing programs such as Microsoft Word if you prefer.

8. From the **Edit** menu, select **Paste**.

   Windows places a copy of the System Information dialog box in WordPad.

9. From the **File** menu, select **Print**.

   WordPad displays the Print dialog box. Be sure your printer is turned on and ready.

10. Click **OK** to print.

    WordPad prints the document.

11. From the **File** menu, select **Exit**.

    WordPad closes.

The Technical Support representative you speak to will ask you for the information contained on this print out, so be sure to have it with you when you call. If you write or fax instead, please be sure to include a copy of this print out with the information you send. Other information needed when writing or faxing is your name, address, phone number (including a good time to call) and E-mail address. Please remember to outline the steps, problem, or error message you are experiencing. This will allow us to provide the best possible response to you.

You can Fax your requests to (510) 795-4488 or **mail** it to: The Learning Company, Banner Blue Division, Attn: Technical Support, PO Box 7865, Fremont, CA 94537-7865.

INDEX

F

using (in Tutorial), 52–53
using keyboard in, 132
Index pages
    example of, 260
    in books, 411–12
    in Family Archives, 260
    in the Family Finder Index, 260
Individual label and card format, 375
Individual titles (Mr., Dr.). See Titles
Individuals
    copying groups to another file, 445–48
    deleting groups, 217
    deleting specific, 216–17
    excluding from calendars, 154
    excluding from trees, 155
    finding in your Family File, 130–33,
      137–41
    finding with the FamilyFinder Report,
      234–43
    merging, 222–27
    moving between, 119–41
    selecting for Descendant trees, 334–35
    selecting for Hourglass trees, 334–35
    selecting for Maps, 342
    selecting for Outline Descendant trees,
      334–35
    selecting for Timelines, 343
    selecting to include, 334–43
Information
    about your system, 485
    adding from Family Archives, 276–80
    checking for errors, 83, 86, 207–14
    copying from Family Archives to
      Family Files, 276–80
    displaying, 285–330
    editing, 88–90
    entering, 81–115, 161–62,
      163–65, 172–84
    entering sources for, 112–15
    finding, 137–41, 188
    merging, 479–85
    possible mistakes in, 86, 207–14
    saving, 77, 463–65
    viewing, 4
Information pages
    example of, 262
    in Family Archives, 262
    in the Family Finder Index, 262
    scrolling through, 263
    types of, 262
Inherited addresses, 150
Inserting

children in a Children list, 108
OLE objects, 179–84
Photo CD pictures, 173–76
pictures from files, 176–78
pictures from scanner/camera, 178
See also Pictures
text, 88–89
Installing
    Family Tree Maker, 15–18
    problems with, 495–97
    under Windows 95, 15–18
    Web browsers, 15–18
Intermarriages
    affect on Kinship reports, 110
    recording, 110
Introduction pages
    example of, 258
    in books, 413–15
    in Family Archives, 258
    in the FamilyFinder Index, 258
Items to Include
    in calendars, 366–68
    in Maps, 348–68
    in Scrapbooks, 378
    in trees, 348–51
    selecting, 348–68
    selecting (in Tutorial), 74–76

J

Jr., 92

K

Keyboard
    editing commands, 90
    using in fields, 42
    using in Index of Individuals, 132
    using in Insert Photo CD dialog box,
      175
    using in Notes dialog box, 158
    using on the Family Page, 83, 87
    using with Pictures/Objects, 190
Kinship reports
    defined, 307
    intermarriage's effect on, 110
    number of generations in, 346
Kodak Photo CD
    defined, 168
    inserting pictures into Scrapbooks,
      173–76
    picture compression/resolution, 200–
      201
    using with Family Tree Maker, 173–76

L

Label(s)
> changing, 84–85
> field, 83
> preferences for, 84–85

Labels and cards
> address inheritance, 150
> alphabetizing, 387–88
> border styles for, 381–82
> colors for, 381–82
> creating, 328
> default titles for individuals, 93–94
> entering addresses for, 150
> items to include in, 348–50
> name format, 355–57
> options for, 375
> printing for households or individuals, 375
> printing groups, 375
> selecting individuals, 336–41
> sorting, 387–88
> titles for individuals, 152
> viewing, 328

Large trees
> printing on plotters, 399
> reducing size of, 396–98

Last name(s)
> entering, 91–93
> missing, 93
> multiple word, 92
> with suffixes, 92

Layout
> of Ancestor trees, 288
> of Descendant trees, 293

LDS
> choosing format, 85
> using LDS date codes, 96

Letter Requests
> multiple language, 255

Lineage dialog box
> individual titles (Mr., Dr.), 152
> Reference number field, 154
> special relationships in, 152–55
> using, 152–55

Lines
> in boxes, 362
> page, 329
> styles for, 381–82

Location Check
> using in maps, 321

Location(s)
> entering, 99–101
> using Fastfields, 99

M

M.D., 92

Mac files, 459–61

Magnifying glass
> in Family Archives, 270
> in the FamilyFinder Index, 264

Maiden names
> *See also* Married name
> when to use, 91

Making backups of
> your Family File, 463–65

Maps
> adding date/time stamp, 368–70
> allow overlapping labels, 375
> ambiguous locations, 321
> creating, 313–24
> formatting, 314–20
> other display options, 375
> selecting individuals to include, 342
> selecting items to include, 348–68
> using Location Check, 321

Margins, 393

Marriage
> dialog boxes, 163–65
> ending status, 163
> entering details, 163–65
> fields, 103
> intermarriages, 110
> multiple, 124–26
> multiple (in Tutorial), 49–51
> Notes, 165
> preferred check box, 163
> private information, 103
> reference number, 163–65
> Scrapbook, 167

Married name
> format for females in trees, 353
> format for individuals, 154
> including in calendars, 367
> including in trees, 352–57
> instead of maiden name, 212
> *See also* Name(s).

Master Source, 113

Medical information
> Cause of death field, 152
> dialog box, 151–52
> field, 152

N

NOTES

NOTES

NOTES

NOTES

WARRANTY

IMPORTANT—READ CAREFULLY BEFORE USING THIS PRODUCT

LICENSE AGREEMENT AND LIMITED WARRANTY

BY INSTALLING OR USING THE SOFTWARE OR OTHER ELECTRONIC CONTENT INCLUDED WITH THIS AGREEMENT YOU ACCEPT THE TERMS OF THIS LICENSE WITH THE LEARNING COMPANY, INC., AND ITS AFFILIATES ("TLC"). IF YOU DO NOT AGREE TO THE TERMS OF THIS AGREEMENT AND YOU ARE ALSO THE ORIGINAL LICENSEE OF THIS PRODUCT ("ORIGINAL LICENSEE"), PROMPTLY RETURN THE PRODUCT TOGETHER WITH ALL ACCOMPANYING ITEMS TO YOUR DEALER FOR A FULL REFUND. THIS IS THE ENTIRE AGREEMENT BETWEEN THE PARTIES RELATING TO THIS PRODUCT AND SUPERSEDES ANY PURCHASE ORDER, COMMUNICATION, ADVERTISING OR REPRESENTATION CONCERNING THE PRODUCT. NO CHANGE OR MODIFICATION OF THIS LICENSE WILL BE VALID UNLESS IT IS IN WRITING AND IS SIGNED BY TLC.

LIMITED USE LICENSE. TLC and its suppliers grant you the right to use one copy of the accompanying product (the "Program") for your personal use only. This license, and the restrictions in this agreement, cover both the computer programs ("Software") and the other electronic content ("Content") of the accompanying product. All rights not expressly granted are reserved by TLC or its suppliers. This License does not constitute a sale and does not authorize a sale of the Program or anything created thereby. You must treat the Program and associated materials and any elements thereof like any other copyrighted material (e.g., a book or musical recording). This Agreement is governed by the internal substantive laws of the State of California (and not by the 1980 United Nations Convention on Contracts for the International Sale of Goods, as amended). In the event you fail to comply with any of the terms or conditions of this license, your rights to use the Program will end, you shall stop using the Program, remove the Program from your computer, and permanently erase all copies of the Program. You may be held legally responsible for any copyright infringement that is caused or encouraged by your failure to abide by the terms of this license.

YOU MAY NOT:

- Use the Program or permit use of the Program on more than one computer, computer terminal or workstation at the same time.

- Make copies of the materials accompanying the Program or make copies of the Program or any part thereof.

- Except as permitted by the Program, copy the Program onto a hard drive or other device and you must run the Program from the CD-ROM (although the Program itself may copy a portion of the Program onto your hard drive during installation in order to run more efficiently).

- Use the Program or permit use of the Program in a network or other multi-user arrangement or on an electronic bulletin board system or other remote access arrangement, or store it in a retrieval system or translate it into any other language.

- Rent, lease, license or otherwise transfer this Program without the express written consent of TLC, except that you may transfer the complete Program copy and accompanying materials on a permanent basis, provided that no copies are retained and the recipient agrees to the terms of this Agreement.

- Reverse engineer, decompile, disassemble or create derivative works of the Software. YOU MAY NOT MODIFY, TRANSLATE, DISASSEMBLE OR DECOMPILE THE SOFTWARE OR ANY COPY, IN WHOLE OR IN PART.

- Publicly perform or publicly display this Program.

- Use any of the content for any commercial purposes or any purpose other than for incorporation into projects produced with the Software for home entertainment, personal and educational purposes except as outlined herein.

LIMITED WARRANTY. TLC warrants to the Original Licensee only, that the Program shall be substantially free from defects in materials and workmanship for ninety (90) days from the date of purchase. If within 90 days of purchase the media proves to be defective in any way, you may return the media to The Learning Company, Attn: Returns, 190 Parkway West, Duncan, SC 29334. Please include a copy of your sales receipt, packaging slip or invoice, along with a brief note of explanation as to why you are returning the Program.

EXCLUSIVE REMEDY. The Original Licensee's exclusive remedy for the breach of this License shall be, at TLC's option, either (a) the repair or replacement of the Program that does not meet TLC's Limited Warranty and which is returned to TLC with a copy of your receipt; or (b) a refund of the price, if any, which you paid for the Program and associated materials. This Limited Warranty is void if the failure of the Program has resulted from accident, abuse, misapplication or use of the Program with incompatible hardware.

NO OTHER WARRANTIES. TLC, ITS AFFILIATES, AND ITS SUPPLIERS, IF ANY, DISCLAIM ALL WARRANTIES WITH RESPECT TO THE PROGRAM AND ACCOMPANYING MATERIALS, EITHER EXPRESS OR IMPLIED, INCLUDING BUT NOT LIMITED TO IMPLIED WARRANTIES OF MERCHANTABILITY, NON-INFRINGEMENT OF THIRD PARTY RIGHTS AND FITNESS FOR A PARTICULAR PURPOSE. TLC DOES NOT WARRANT THAT THE OPERATION OF THE PROGRAM WILL BE WITHOUT DEFECT OR ERROR OR WILL SATISFY THE REQUIREMENTS OF YOUR COMPUTER SYSTEM. THIS LIMITED WARRANTY GIVES YOU SPECIFIC LEGAL RIGHTS. DEPENDING UPON WHERE YOU LIVE, YOU MAY HAVE OTHER RIGHTS WHICH VARY FROM STATE/COUNTRY TO STATE/COUNTRY. TLC WARRANTS ONLY THAT THE PROGRAM WILL PERFORM AS DESCRIBED IN THE USER DOCUMENTATION. NO OTHER ADVERTISING, DESCRIPTION OR REPRESENTATION, WHETHER MADE BY A TLC DEALER, DISTRIBUTOR, AGENT OR EMPLOYEE, SHALL BE BINDING UPON TLC OR SHALL CHANGE THE TERMS OF THIS WARRANTY.

LIMITATIONS ON DAMAGES. This Program may contain significant or insignificant program errors, including errors which may cause an operational interruption of your computer system. The Program is provided "AS IS" and you assume responsibility for determining the suitability of the Program on your system and for results obtained. IN NO EVENT SHALL TLC, ITS AFFILIATES, OR ITS SUPPLIERS, IF ANY, BE LIABLE FOR ANY CONSEQUENTIAL OR INCIDENTAL DAMAGES WHATSOEVER ARISING OUT OF THE USE OF OR INABILITY TO USE THE PROGRAM OR PROGRAM PACKAGE, EVEN IF THEY HAVE BEEN ADVISED OF THE POSSIBILITY OF SUCH DAMAGES. THEY SHALL NOT BE RESPONSIBLE OR LIABLE FOR LOST PROFITS OR REVENUES, OR FOR DAMAGES OR COSTS INCURRED AS A RESULT OF LOSS OF TIME, DATA OR USE OF THE SOFTWARE, OR FROM ANY OTHER CAUSE. INCLUDING, WITHOUT LIMITATION, PRODUCTS LIABILITY, CONTRACT OR TORT DAMAGES. THEIR LIABILITY SHALL NOT EXCEED THE ACTUAL PRICE PAID FOR THE LICENSE TO USE THE PROGRAM. BECAUSE SOME STATES/COUNTRIES DO NOT ALLOW THE EXCLUSION OR LIMITATION OF LIABILITY FOR CONSEQUENTIAL OR INCIDENTAL DAMAGES, THE ABOVE LIMITATION MAY NOT APPLY TO YOU.

U.S. GOVERNMENT RESTRICTED RIGHTS. The Program and documentation are provided with restricted rights. Use, duplication or disclosure by the Government is subject to restrictions as set forth in subparagraph (c)(1)(ii) of The Rights in Technical Data and Computer Software clause at DFARS 252.227-7013 or subparagraphs (c)(1) and (2) of the Commercial Computer Software— Restricted Rights at 48 CFR 52.227-19, as applicable. The Contractor/Manufacturer is Brøderbund, 88 Rowland Way, Novato, CA 94945.

EXPORT RESTRICTIONS. You may not export or reexport the Software or any underlying information or technology except in full compliance with all United States and other applicable laws and regulations.

FURTHER ACKNOWLEDGEMENTS. You understand and acknowledge that (i) in order to utilize some features of the Program, you may need to purchase additional images, templates or other content; and (ii) TLC may, at its discretion or as required by its agreements with third parties, cease to support the Program. Support which TLC may cease to provide may include server access, web site support and the provision of enabling software. In the unlikely event this should happen, you agree that all monies paid shall be non-refundable.

MISCELLANEOUS PROVISIONS. If this Program was acquired outside the United States, then local law may apply. If you acquired this Software in Canada, you agree to the following: The parties to this License have expressly required that the License be drawn up in the English language/Les parties aux presentes ont expressement exige que la presente convention soient redigees en langue anglaise.

This License and your right to use the Program in any manner will terminate automatically if you violate or fail to comply with any part of this Agreement. Information in this Agreement is subject to change without notice and does not represent a commitment on the part of TLC.

SAVE THIS LICENSE FOR FUTURE REFERENCE

GUIDELINES FOR USING PRINT PRODUCTS

All characters, designs, logos, text, photos, clip art, fonts, graphics, templates, trademarks, and all other tools and projects contained in this product (the "Properties") are either owned by or used under license by The Learning Company, Inc. ("TLC") and protected under trademark, copyright, and other applicable laws. You may use the Properties to design your own creations, such as stationery, cards, signs, invitations and other items, as indicated on the product's box. This includes brochures, newsletters or other projects that promote your business, event, organization, etc.; provided, however, that although you may use the Properties to promote your business, you may **not** make commercial use of a Property as your business, nor may you use any of the Properties as a logo, trademark or similar designation of your business.

The Properties may be used for home entertainment, personal, and educational purposes only, and cannot be used for any product distributed commercially for sale. These designs are owned by TLC and its licensors, and it is a violation of your license and copyright law to use a Property in this way. All rights in any derivative works created by the use of a Property shall vest exclusively in TLC or its licensors. All rights in any derivative works created by the use of a Property shall vest exclusively in TLC or its licensors. These Properties may not be copied or downloaded in whole or in part except in the normal private use of the product. Any and all unauthorized use is strictly prohibited. Specifically, by way of example and not exclusion, except as otherwise listed in this paragraph:

YOU ARE NOT PERMITTED TO:

- Sell or redistribute the Properties.

- Use any of the Properties related to identifiable individuals or entities in any manner which suggests their endorsement or sponsorship of or association with any product, service or entity.

- Create immoral, obscene or scandalous works, as defined by the Federal Government at the time the work is created, using the Properties or any modification thereof.

- Use the Properties in electronic format, including on-line use, and multimedia applications, unless all of the following conditions are met:

  - The Properties are incorporated for viewing purposes only.

- The Properties do not comprise a significant portion of the content of the proposed use.

- A notice is included specifying that the Properties may not be saved or downloaded and are only to be used for viewing purposes.

- A credit to TLC's product is included in the proposed use.

- The Properties are embedded at no higher than a base resolution of 512x768.

- The Property is not used in a product which is similar to or competes with any of the features of any of TLC's or its suppliers' products.

Use of the Properties should include a TLC credit, which should read as follows:

"The images used herein were obtained from The Learning Company's Family Tree Maker product, © 1999 The Learning Company, Inc. and its subsidiaries, 88 Rowland Way, Novato, CA 94945 USA. All rights reserved."

THE FOLLOWING GUIDELINES REFER TO PUBLICITY RIGHTS:

TLC makes no representation or warranty as to the right of users to utilize any individual's name, likeness, and/or image appearing in its print products. Users may not exploit any individual's name, likeness, and/or image WITHOUT first obtaining, directly from each such individual, the appropriate rights of publicity license.

Year 2000 Compliance

A Learning Company product is "Year 2000 Compliant" when it compiles with the following four Rules:

Rule 1. No value for current date will cause any interruption in operation.

Rule 2. Date-based functionality must behave consistently for dates prior to, during, and after Year 2000.

Rule 3. In all interfaces and data storage, the century in any date must be specified either explicitly or by unambiguous algorithms or inferencing rules.

Rule 4. Year 2000 must be recognized as a leap year. However, if the Learning Company product is operating on equipment that is not Year 2000 compliant, or if the Learning Company product is operating in conjunction with other software that is not Year 2000 compliant, then the Learning company product will not necessarily perform on that equipment or with the other software after December 31, 1999.

The Learning Company is not responsible for any loss or damage that ma result from the Learning Company's products that are not Year 2000 compliant.